The Quest for the Kingdom of God:
Studies in Honor of George E. Mendenhall

The Quest For the Kingdom of God: Studies in Honor of George E. Mendenhall

Edited by

H. B. Huffmon, F. A. Spina, and A. R. W. Green

Eisenbrauns
Winona Lake, Indiana
1983

Library of Congress Cataloging in Publication Data

The Quest for the Kingdom of God.

"George Emery Mendenhall, a bibliography"; p. 293.
Includes bibliographical references and index.
1. Bible. O.T.—Criticism, interpretation, etc.—Addresses, essays, lectures. 2. Jews—History—To 586 B.C.—Addresses, essays, lectures. 3. Mendenhall, George E. I. Mendenhall, George E. II. Huffmon, H. B. (Herbert Bardwell) III. Spina, F. A. (Frank A.) IV. Green, Alberto Ravinell Whitney.
BS1192.Q47 1983 221.6 83-1648
ISBN 0-931464-15-3

CONTENTS

IV. Archaeology and History

V. Biblical Ideology

Indexes

George Emery Mendenhall: An Appreciation

GEORGE Mendenhall has been an unusually engaging scholar, teacher, and friend. It is not just a question of his marked creativity, but his sensitive humanity as well. Reared in village-farming communities of various Great Plains states, he has become an internationally active scholar concerned with the ancient Near East, and especially Biblical Israel. But whether his attention was given to cuneiform studies (Amarna and Mari), to the archaeology of Southeastern Turkey, Syria, Jordan, and Arabia, to the study and decipherment of ancient inscriptions, or to ancient Israel, his focus has remained on values and the means of social control.

In his inaugural address as a professor of Hamma Divinity School ("Christian Law" 1948), George Mendenhall emphasized that the early Christian community broke away from law, i.e., law that "has jurisdiction only over external acts" and is "enforced by a sovereign power." His attention has continued to focus on the ideology and dynamics of that community beginning in Israel of the Federation period and in the subsequent visions that developed from that. He found the emerging ideology to be that of the Mosaic Covenant:

> The Sinai covenant, therefore, marked the beginnings of a systematic recognition that the well-being of a community cannot be based merely upon socially organized force, nor can the political power structure be regarded, as in ancient pagan states, as the manifestation of the divine, transcendent order of the universe.

George Mendenhall has commented that his experience in the Pacific area during World War II as an interpreter of Japanese for the United States Navy, imprinted upon his mind the importance of the quest for the Kingdom of God. If one detects in him a kind of nostalgia for Federation Israel, it is really the dedication of a scholar to the concerns that such a community should represent.

This volume of essays is offered to George Mendenhall in appreciation of the light that he has found in the quest for that Kingdom of God, and shared in his classes, lectures and publications. The contributions come from his present and former colleagues and students from the University of Michigan, from the members over the years of the Biblical Colloquium, of which he was a founding member, and from some scholars especially concerned with areas of his work. The contributions do not reflect the great breadth of George Mendenhall's own work, for to be sure, his interests and research reach far more widely; but they do pay tribute to his own central concern.

Thy Kingdom Come!

The Editors

I

The Federation and the Early Monarchy

Two Models for the Origins of Ancient Israel: Social Revolution or Frontier Development

NORMAN K. GOTTWALD
NEW YORK THEOLOGICAL SEMINARY

WITH the publication of my recent book, *The Tribes of Yahweh*, there is now available a substantial body of argument for the hypothesis that ancient Israel originated in a social revolutionary movement composed largely of peasants. Building on the pioneer work of George E. Mendenhall,[1] I have developed the major contours of a social revolutionary model in running dialogue with what have been to date the dominant models of Israelite origins: nomadic, conquest, and amphictyonic models.[2]

The Social Revolutionary Model of Early Israel

My contention is that each of the prevailing models contains an element of truth but, standing alone and without the organizing perspective of social unrest and revolt, none is capable of doing justice to the emergence of premonarchic Israel. The *nomadic model* correctly refers to a component of pastoral nomads in early Israel and to a social organizational difference between Israel and its neighbors, but it vastly overstates the number of Israelite nomads, misconstrues the complex nature of ancient Near Eastern nomadism, and naively equates Israel's tribal social organization with a pastoral nomadic stage of development.[3] The *conquest model* correctly identifies a major military dimension in Israel's rise to power, but mistakenly posits that the attacks were launched

[1]G. E. Mendenhall, "The Hebrew Conquest of Palestine," *BA* 25 (1962) 66–87 = *BAR* 3 (1970) 100–120; idem, *The Tenth Generation: The Origins of the Biblical Tradition* (Baltimore: Johns Hopkins, 1973).

[2]N. K. Gottwald, *The Tribes of Yahweh: A Sociology of the Religion of Liberated Israel, 1250–1050 B.C.E.* (Maryknoll: Orbis, 1979).

[3]Ibid., 293–301, 435–63; C. H. J. de Geus, *The Tribes of Israel: An Investigation into Some of the Presuppositions of Martin Noth's Amphictyony Hypothesis* (Amsterdam: Van Gorcum, 1976) 124–87.

in a more or less unified way by outsiders invading from the desert.[4] In terms of their views of Israelites as "outsiders" to Canaan, the nomadic and conquest models tend to conjoin in support of one another. The *amphictyonic model* correctly observes that the several tribes of Israel were joined in a confederation, but it overlooks the sociopolitical matrix of the league arrangements and in its comparison between Israel and Greek sacral leagues misses the decisive social structural differences between Greek amphictyonic associations and the intertribal confederation of Israel.[5]

One of the features that nomadic, conquest, and amphictyonic models share in common is an exaggerated concentration on the religious "uniqueness" of Israel, an almost exclusive focus on religious factors to the neglect of the sociopolitical matrix and constitution of Israel.[6] In advancing a social revolutionary model of early Israel we are not only attending to the inadequacies in the other models but we are introducing a "demythologizing" or "secularizing" element that aims not to eliminate the religion, nor to reduce its importance, but to set the religion of ancient Israel in its necessary ancient social and cultural matrix, to give that religion a greater measure of social plausibility or credibility.[7]

The essence of the social revolutionary model is to see the emergence of ancient Israel as a combined sociopolitical and religious movement with its major base in the peasantry of Canaan. The movement aimed at creating an alternative society of independent farmers, pastoral nomads, artisans, and priestly "intellectuals" who were free from the political domination and interference of the hierarchic city-states that held the upper hand in Canaan. This movement was an intertribal alliance or

[4]Gottwald, *Tribes*, 191–205, 207–11, 217–18, 220–23; J. M. Miller, "The Israelite Occupation of Canaan," *Israelite and Judaean History* (ed. J. H. Hayes and J. M. Miller; Philadelphia: Westminster, 1977) 213–84.

[5]Gottwald, *Tribes*, 345–86.

[6]De Geus, *Tribes*, 1–68, beginning with B. Stade in 1887, traces a majority scholarly attraction to the virtually total autonomy of Israel's religion in the line of interpretation that culminated in Noth's amphictyonic hypothesis. Gottwald, *Tribes*, 591–607, shows that reflections on the social context of early Israel's religion—surprisingly even among advocates of the social revolutionary hypothesis—have characteristically been marred by assumptions about the autonomy of religion, with the result that religion is separated from Israel's society (as with J. Bright), or the society is viewed as a spontaneous creation of the religion (as with G. E. Mendenhall), or the social influences on religion are confined to "non-essentials" (as with G. Fohrer).

[7]The significance of G. E. Mendenhall's formulation of the peasant revolt model of Israelite origins lies precisely in the forcefulness with which it opened the way to a recovery of early Israel as a socially understandable historical agent (cf. Gottwald, *Tribes*, 220–27).

confederation, based not on pastoral nomadic cultural life but on the revitalization and extension of rural agricultural institutions with real and fictitious kinship ties, neighborhood and regional residence, and communal mutual assistance.[8] This counter-society had to provide for political self-rule, economic self-help, military self-defense, and cultural self-definition, which gave to its religion (so-called Yahwism) a very prominent role as an alternative ideology for understanding the legitimacy and efficacy of its revolution.[9]

The historical reality underlying the two polarized equations of "Canaanite = bad" vs. "Israelite = good" was not in the first instance an ethnic or religious polarization but a social structural polarization around the divisions between those who upheld the reigning hierarchic social order and those who struggled to bring a more egalitarian free peasant society into existence. Nevertheless, one ought not to oversimplify or standardize the reactions of people in Canaan to this growing social struggle, for these varied greatly according to the spatial framework and the temporal trajectory of the revolution. I have attempted an initial rough plotting of these cross-cutting and confused loyalties under the categories of Canaanites as enemies of Israel, Canaanites as converts to Israel, Canaanites as neutrals toward Israel, and Canaanites as allies of Israel,[10] a schematization that certainly calls for further nuancing and refinement.

The evidence for the social revolutionary model is drawn from biblical texts, extrabiblical texts, the material culture (especially the examination of rural agricultural complexes),[11] and comparative anthropological and sociological studies (ancient bureaucratic empires; retribalization and revitalization movements; peasant movements in unrest, rebellion, and revolution; social banditry).[12]

[8]Ibid., 293–341, 474–97, 584–87.

[9]Ibid., 65–66, 489–92, 594–97, 630–33, 636–37, 642–49, 692–709.

[10]Ibid., 498–583.

[11]J. E. Spencer and G. A. Hale, "The Origin, Nature, and Distribution of Agricultural Terracing," *Pacific Viewpoint* 2 (1961) 1–40; Z. Ron, "Agricultural Terraces in the Judean Mountains," *IEJ* 16 (1966) 33–49, 111–22; B. Golomb and Y. Kedar, "Ancient Agriculture in the Galilee Mountains," *IEJ* 21 (1971) 136–40; C. H. J. de Geus, "The Importance of Archaeological Research into the Palestinian Agricultural Terraces . . . ," *PEQ* 107 (1975) 65–74; L. Stager, "Agriculture," *IDBSup* 11–13; G. Edelstein and M. Kislev, "Mevasseret Yerushalayim: The Ancient Settlement and its Agricultural Terraces," *BA* 44 (1981) 53–56.

[12]Pertinent social scientific literature is extensively cited in the notes to Gottwald, *Tribes*, access to which is best gained through the Index of Subjects (N.B. the explanatory note on use of the Index, p. 842), and a brief list of social scientific titles for biblical studies appears in Gottwald, *IDBSup* 467. The Social

The intial responses to my articulation of the model have been a mixture of denial, skepticism, caution, fascination, curiosity, and varying measures of agreement. The agreements range from concurrence on limited points, through the recognition that the model is a respectable option—even if not clearly superior to the others—to the assertion that social revolution gives the most intelligible explanation of early Israel's origins and overall premonarchic form.[13] To show that the kind of modeling involved here is not a simple matter of "right/wrong," "yes/no" or "all/none," I want to share one particular response that stands in basic agreement with my notion that early Israel was a peasant movement in conflict with the surrounding society but suggests another way of looking at the same phenomena.

Early Israel as a Frontier Society

The sociologist Gerhard Lenski of the University of North Carolina prepared a critical review as a respondent to *The Tribes of Yahweh* at the 1979 Annual Meeting of AAR/SBL.[14] Lenski is a sociologist who stresses techno-environmental factors in human societies, has a broad understanding of peasant societies, and is also a neo-evolutionist in the sense that he believes archaeology, history, and sociology to demonstrate that social change worldwide is natural, directional, immanent, continuous, cumulative, necessary, and proceeds from uniform causes—although not evenly through time and space, as expressed by the important distinction between general and specific evolution.[15]

World of Ancient Israel Group of AAR/SBL is currently preparing "An Annotated Bibliography on the Social Scientific Study of the Old Testament," ed. F. S. Frick.

[13]Cf. the following reviews on *The Tribes of Yahweh*: B. W. Anderson in *TToday* 38 (1981) 107–8; W. Brueggemann in *JAAR* 48 (1980) 441–51; M. J. Buss in *RelSRev* 6 (1980) 271–74; M. L. Chaney in *Pac Theo Review* 14 (1981) 28–33; D. L. Christensen in *JSOT* 18 (1980) 113–20; R. W. Klein in *CurTM* 8 (Feb 1981) 53–54; B. J. Malina in *BTB* 12 (1981) 61; B. McCarthy in *The Ecumenist* 18 (1980) 17–22; C. Meyers in *CBQ* 43 (1981) 104–9; A. Myers in *The Reformed Journal* 31 (Mar 1981) 20–23; and F. Woo in *China Notes* 18 (1980) 142–43, which compares the religious factor in the ancient Israelite and modern Chinese peasant revolutions.

[14]Lenski's remarks were subsequently published in revised form as a review essay in *RelSRev* 6 (1980) 275–78, the text of which constitutes the basis for the present rejoinder.

[15]G. Lenski, *Power and Privilege: A Theory of Social Stratification* (New York: McGraw-Hill, 1966); G. and J. Lenski, *Human Societies: An Introduction to Macrosociology* (3d. ed.; New York: McGraw-Hill, 1978). For his succinct defense of neo-evolutionary social theory, cf. G. Lenski, "History and Social Change," *Amer Jour Sociology* 82 (1976) 548–64.

After summing up the gist of *The Tribes of Yahweh* sociologically, Lenski proposes

> to inquire as to the degree to which Gottwald's analysis squares with what social scientists have discovered to date about social and cultural dynamics during the agrarian era (i.e., from the invention of the plow to the beginnings of the Industrial Revolution).[16]

In terms of the data on peasant societies vis-à-vis social and political authorities, Lenski finds that my model of peasant unrest and revolt has ample precedent.

> Studies of agrarian societies of the past in both Europe and Asia have made it clear that large numbers of peasants in these societies were unhappy with their situation and blamed the upper classes and their agents. Moreover, this unhappiness often led to violence, ranging from isolated actions by individuals to widespread uprisings as in England in the fourteenth century or Germany in the sixteenth.[17]

Picking up on my observation that we do not have articulate firsthand evidence about other such social revolutionary breaks in the ancient Near East, Lenski goes on to focus on the *marginal territorial element* in ancient Israel which seems to show a continuity with many other societies where peasants have developed their own oppositional forms of life in *frontier conditions* that are sufficiently removed from the urban centers of power to allow a margin of freedom for independent maneuver. Sometimes technological conditions (I would add political conditions as well—NKG) transform such marginal territories into expanding frontiers that give birth to new societies. Of these he notes the United States, Australia, and Boer society in South Africa as examples. He then formulates the notion of a frontier model which, in his view, needs to be joined to the peasant revolt model in order to account for the peculiarities of Israelite beginnings.

> The interesting thing about these frontier societies is that they all share many of the social and cultural patterns Gottwald attributes to early Israel. All of them exhibit an antagonism toward the traditional centers of power and toward the institutional arrangements that supported those centers. Populist and democratic ideologies developed and often acquired a quasi-religious status. Small farms tended to be the rule, especially in the early stages of frontier expansion. And, perhaps to complete the story, frontier societies have had a relatively short half-life. In other words, as they grew and prospered, they tended to revert to the more traditional ways of life, although never entirely.

[16]Lenski, *RelSRev* 6 (1980) 275, cols. 1–2.
[17]Ibid., 275, col. 2.

> This is not to suggest that any of these societies has duplicated the experience of early Israel. That would obviously be impossible. I believe, however, that we may be able to get a better understanding of the dynamics of Israel's early development if we conceptualize the process in frontier-society terms as well as in the peasant-revolt-model terms Gottwald advocates. In other words, a combined frontier-society peasant-revolt model may explain more than a pure revolt model.[18]

The "more" that the frontier model explains better than the peasant revolt model is, for Lenski, composed of three facets:

(1) For one thing, he believes that a frontier model better accounts for Israel's origin in the thirteenth century rather than centuries earlier or later. He appears to mean by this that into the centuries-long hostility and friction between rulers and subject peasants in Canaan, the thirteenth century introduced new technological factors (such as iron for agricultural tools, intensive terracing, improved water supply) that opened up the Canaanite highlands as a viable frontier for Israelite occupation.

(2) Lenski further suggests that the frontier model has a slight edge in accounting for the dramatic new character of Yahwism as a religion set off sharply from the Baal cult inasmuch as an Israelite movement based in the heart of the old Canaanite plains society would not so easily have broken with the ancient fertility cults as an Israelite society spawned in the hilly frontier region.

(3) Lastly, Lenski contends that the frontier factor better explains the eventual reversion of Israel to the statist system and its abandonment of the tribal system. Frontier situations, being transitory phenomena, tend to fade back into greater likeness to the dominant society once material conditions improve and the circumstances of life are not so different between heartland and frontier. Even so, the distinctive history of the frontier lives on with sufficient force to make a cultural difference between the two regions.

By introducing the frontier model into a discussion of Israelite origins, Lenski taps a significant vein of historiographic and social scientific theory devoted to the explanation of major sociohistoric change since the beginning of the Age of Discovery about 1500 A.D. A major problem in evaluating Lenski's proposal is that, although he articulates "a *combined* frontier-society peasant-revolt model" (italics mine), he does not specify *how* they are combined. In my view, the way in which "frontier" and "social revolution" are articulated—whether the one subsumes the other or both are subsumed under some third schema—is critical for determining the precise relevance of the frontier analogy to early Israel. After reflecting on his observations and doing some modest study in the voluminous literature on the frontier hypothesis, especially

[18]Ibid., 276, col. 1.

in American historical studies, my basic conclusion is that in the case of early Israel a frontier conception helpfully *nuances* a social revolutionary model but is *subsumed* under it as a description of the special circumstances in which the social revolution was generated and in which it prospered.

To begin with, I would want to give a lot of thought to the extent to which particular frontier societies represented major social change or actual social revolution. The United States may be viewed as exhibiting an internal frontier that moved westward from the original Atlantic seaboard settlements.[19] Or the United States may be viewed in its entirety as a frontier extension of its British, and more widely European, home base.[20] It seems to me that on either way of viewing matters, frontier America did not produce a major structural social revolution. As against England, there were certainly social changes. The aristocratic feudal institutions in the strict sense did not transplant successfully from England to the United States. It may be argued that in some respects the internal American frontier contributed toward more populist political measures and toward vigorous voluntarism in social forms, acknowledged as a "frontier process" by many who do not accept major aspects of the total frontier thesis. Nonetheless, the basic system of property relations did transplant and in fact the capitalist beginnings in England were developed more freely and exquisitely in this country than in the homeland. It is also patent that the U.S. frontier was an imperial frontier that shattered the native Indian cultures. It brought the outright conquest and plunder of one people by another people who held the advantage in military technology and political organization.

In 1893, the American historian Frederick Jackson Turner launched the frontier thesis with the programmatic statement: "The existence of an area of free land, its continuous recession, and the advance of American settlement westward, explain American development."[21] Turner and others elaborated the frontier thesis at length in an effort to explain such diverse phenomena as American individualism, practicality, regionalism, nationalism, isolationism, and democratic institutions and values. The frontier thesis has been subjected to extensive criticism, as much for

[19]This is the overwhelmingly prevalent view of American historians influenced by the frontier thesis of F. J. Turner.

[20]The whole of North America, as one part of the vast overseas colonies, was viewed as the enriching economic frontier of metropolitan Europe by W. P. Webb, *The Great Frontier* (Cambridge: Harvard University, 1952). The U.S. as a political and cultural frontier of Europe was stressed by C. J. H. Hayes, "The American Frontier—Frontier of What?," *Amer His Review* 51 (Jan 1946) 199–210.

[21]F. J. Turner, "The Significance of the Frontier in American History," *The Frontier in American History* (New York: Henry Holt, 1921) 1.

what it ignored as for what it claimed, and it is probable that some aspects of the thesis are far more cogent than others.[22] Among the criticisms has been the contention that the frontier thesis neglects the high importance of urban industrial development and especially the role of conflict between labor and capital.[23] It has been argued that the main population movements were from farm to farm and from farm to city, and not from city to farm, thus muting the claim that the frontier served as a "safety-valve" for urban social unrest.[24] It has been observed that the thesis misses the rapidity with which the frontier was monopolized and controlled by capitalist interests, as displayed in the activities of land speculators and railroads.[25] The frontier thesis is said consistently to overlook the salient feature of rapid development of agriculture on the frontier in order to accumulate exports for the fueling of major industrial capital development.[26] All in all, it appears that the notion of upward

[22]For pro and con treatments of the frontier thesis, cf. G. M. Gressley, "The Turner Thesis—A Problem in Historiography," *American Themes: Essays in Historiography* (New York: Oxford, 1968) 261–90; G. R. Taylor, ed., *The Turner Thesis Concerning the Role of the Frontier in American History*, (3d. ed., Lexington, MA: D. C. Heath, 1972).

[23]C. A. Beard, "The Frontier in American History," *New Republic* 25 (Feb 16, 1921) 349–50; idem, "Culture and Agriculture," *Sat Rev Lit* 5 (Oct 20, 1928) 272–73; idem, "The Frontier in American History," *New Republic* 97 (Feb 1939) 359–62; J. C. Almack, "The Shibboleth of the Frontier," *Historical Outlook* 16 (May 1925) 197–201; A. M. Schlesinger, Jr., *The Age of Jackson* (Boston: Little, Brown, 1946).

[24]C. Goodrich and Sol Davison, "The Wage-Earner in the Westward Movement," *Pol Science Quar* 50 (June 1935) 161–85; 51 (Mar 1936) 61–116; idem, "The Frontier as a Safety-Valve: A Rejoinder," *Pol Science Quar* 53 (June 1938) 268–71; M. Kane, "Some Considerations on the Safety-Valve Doctrine," *Mississippi Valley His Review* 23 (Sept 1936) 169–88; F. A. Shannon, "The Homestead Act and the Labor Surplus," *Amer His Review* 41 (July 1936) 637–51; idem, "A Post Mortem on the Labor-Safety-Valve Theory," *Agricultural History* 19 (Jan 1945) 31–38.

[25]L. M. Hacker, "Sections or Classes?," *The Nation* 137 (July 1933) 108–10; T. P. Abernethy, *Frontier to Plantation* (Chapel Hill: University of North Carolina, 1932); idem, *Western Land and the American Revolution* (New York: Macmillan, 1937); idem, "Democracy and the Southern Frontier," *Jour of Southern History* 4 (Feb 1938) 3–13; idem, *Three Virginia Frontiers* (Baton Rouge: University of Louisiana, 1940); R. Hofstadter, "Turner and the Frontier Myth," *Amer Scholar* 18 (Aut 1949) 433–43; idem, *The Age of Reform* (New York: Alfred Knopf, 1955).

[26]W. A. Williams, *The Roots of the Modern American Empire: A Study of the Growth and Shaping of Social Consciousness in a Marketplace Society* (New York: Random House, 1969) traces the links between farmer pressure for expanded foreign markets and the growth of American imperialism abroad after 1898. In

social mobility has been vastly overstated as a factor in American history—and with it the role of the frontier as the spatial symbol of that presumed mobility.

In summary, the U.S. frontier was very much a frontier of capitalist and imperialist expansion and domination. The value of the frontier hypothesis when the detailed patterns of settlement and development are studied is chiefly to show how American economic and political world power was amassed by drawing on vast continental resources in the context of intensive capital accumulation. If the frontier attenuated or delayed social conflict, it did nothing to change the fundamental structure of American property relations and the abiding political clout of capitalist wealth. Thus, the pertinence of the U.S. frontier at least for understanding the ancient Israelite "frontier" is limited. If Lenski's qualification of the social revolutionary model is to have more weight it will be necessary to uncover analogies from frontiers that actually produced social revolutions.[27] Early Israel was not a frontier in which expanding Canaanite city-state organization populated and mastered the highlands. On the contrary, it was a frontier in which elements of the indigenous population organized a sovereign society that broke with city-state organization in favor of re-tribalization. In brief, the frontier context in Canaan produced a sharper social break in the case of Israel than did the frontier context in North America. I suspect that the same would be true of the two other examples cited by Lenski: Australian and South African Boer societies.

With this preliminary evaluation of the frontier thesis in mind, I wish to comment on Lenski's application of the frontier-society model to the above mentioned three aspects of early Israelite experience.

---

particular, he shows that Turner gave scholarly crystallization to a wide feeling in the American agricultural hinterland and that Turner's expansionist frontier notion was carefully studied by imperialist statesmen such as Theodore Roosevelt and Woodrow Wilson (see esp. pp. xii–xviii).

[27]The drastically limited appropriateness of the ancient Israelite religion-society nexus as an analogy for the United States is treated in N. K. Gottwald, *"Church and State" in Ancient Israel: Example or Caution in Our Age?* (The Department of Religion Lecture Series; Gainesville: University of Florida, 1981 [pamphlet]), and the same analogy is critically evaluated from the viewpoints of American history and theological concepts in N. K. Gottwald, "Are Biblical and U.S. Societies Comparable?," *Radical Religion* 3/1 (1976) 17–24. On the application of the Turner thesis to world frontiers, see W. D. Wyman and C. Kroeber, eds., *The Frontier in Perspective* (Madison: University of Wisconsin, 1957). E. R. Wolf, *Peasant Wars of the Twentieth Century* (New York: Harper & Row, 1969) 293, remarks on frontier areas, peripheral to state control, that enhance the tactical mobility of dissident and rebellious peasants, as in China and Mexico.

(1) I have difficulty seeing that the thirteenth century origin of Israel can be satisfactorily accounted for by stressing either frontier or peasant revolt factors as separable or "pure" models. In fact, we seem to be in theoretical trouble when we divorce social movements from their material basis, including the topography and material conditions which frame the forces of production. As I understand Lenski, I judge that he would agree with me on this point. If we begin with a model of social revolution, we already have an interwoven skein of factors forming a combined technological, economic, social, political, cultural, and religious revolution. Within the combined revolution, we can readily identify a cluster of topographical, ecological, technological, communication and control factors which organize nicely around the model of the frontier or marginal territory, more exactly elucidated by Lenski as a *technologically expanded frontier*. Indeed, more than fifty years ago, Albrecht Alt contributed much to our understanding of how the Canaanite highlands formed just such a special, somewhat privileged zone, for the entrenchment of early Israel.[28]

Unless we are careful, however, there is some danger of converting this insight into bare "technologism," so that the frontier becomes an independent spontaneous source of social restiveness. The frontier must be coupled with the broad-based grievances and restiveness in the direction of an alternative political economy and society that had deep roots in the Canaanite heartland, reflected inchoately in the Amarna age but at that time lacking organizational and ideological coordination. What is important about the frontier in the highlands is that it provided a suitable zone for giving expression to the discontent as well as opportunity for the embodiment of an alternative society. Frontier conditions, freshly expanding, facilitated the socioeconomic and political impulses fanning out from the broader Canaanite political economy and provided a milieu in which they could be realized in large measure.[29] As I expressed it in *The Tribes of Yahweh*:

[28]A. Alt, "The Settlement of the Israelites in Palestine," *Essays in Old Testament History and Religion* (Garden City: Doubleday, 1968; German original, 1925) 179–204. Gottwald, "A Program of Historical Cultural-Material Research into Early Israel," *Tribes*, 650–63, incorporates comments on Alt's contribution. E. R. Wolf, *Peasant Wars*, 293, observes that "the tactical effectiveness of such [peripheral] areas is strengthened still further if they contain defensible mountainous redoubts," as was the case in Mexico, Algeria, and Cuba. M. L. Chaney, "Ancient Palestinian Peasant Movements and the Formation of Premonarchic Israel" (forthcoming in *BA*) welds the historico-territorial conditions of the Canaanite highlands pioneered by Alt with the factors conducive to peasant revolutions elucidated by Wolf.

[29]A rather similar point is made about the initiating role of religious dissenting traditions in shaping frontier life in the U.S.: "Dissenting democracy,

We can readily project a high rate of failure in efforts to erect a bronze-based agricultural tribal society in the highlands. In order to succeed, the renegades needed to gather enough people, well enough fed and housed, skilled enough in the new methods required by upland agriculture (including the construction of terraces and water systems), to be able to extend mutual aid to one another, to absorb and encourage newcomers, and finally to defend themselves collectively against the constant efforts of the politically declining Canaanite city-states to reassert their control over the upstarts and over that portion of the means of production which the rebels had "stolen" from them. It was a long, "uphill" struggle, and Elohistic Israel, which preceded Yahwistic Israel in the central highlands, represented the most successful effort prior to the breakthrough of biblical Israel.[30]

(2) Lenski raises the intriguing question as to how correspondent Yahwism was to specifically frontier conditions as against conditions prevailing in the coastal plains. It is difficult to know how to assemble evidence to test his argument. We do know that the established El and Baal cults were not restricted to the plains but appeared also in the hill country, and also that El theology and imagery were taken over by Yahwism. We also know that Yahweh's imagery and imputed acts were flavored frequently with "hill country" symbolism and addressed to the vital interests of marginal agriculture. At this point we must observe a pronounced caution in drawing a sharp line between the supposed overwhelming concern of Israelite religion with "history" and of Canaanite religion with "nature." As the incidence of divine warrior theology in Canaan and Israel clarifies, Canaanite religion was definitely committed to legitimating the "history" of hierarchic city-states, on the one hand, while on the other Israel fully appropriated "nature" as the proper domain of free peasants awarded by their fully accredited and empowered new deity.[31]

It seems to me that here too, social revolt and frontier conditions cannot properly be split apart. The cults of the high gods centered in the plains regularly appear to have penetrated the marginal hilly areas,

---

equalitarianism, system of calling, and organization did not spring from the wilderness. Instead, they moved in the opposite direction: Pioneer Dissenters carried these qualities into the forests and propagated them among their neighbors. . . . The frontier provided the physical setting and the limits but did not determine the pioneer social organization and culture" (T. S. Miyakawa, *Protestants and Pioneers. Individualism and Conformity on the American Frontier* [Chicago/London: University of Chicago, 1964] 239).

[30]Gottwald, *Tribes*, 661–62.

[31]Ibid., 903–13, on the implications of the social revolution model for an understanding of divine warrior theology and the sociopolitical and cultural import of covenantal theology.

possibly in diluted or mixed forms. And of course we must bear in mind that we know amazingly little about the popular forms in which Canaanite religion was entertained and practiced, say by peasants around Megiddo or Gezer in the plains or by peasants around Shechem or Hebron in the highlands.

All in all, however, it is evident that the specific thrust and intensity of Yahwism required more than frontier distance to come into play, since the new religion presupposes a powerful social impulse and effective organizational mechanisms. At this point the role of the Levites, or Yahwistic intellectuals, is probably of great importance, constituting one of the undeveloped aspects of my hypothesis that invites enlargement. My guess is that the Levites were not frontier provincials for the most part, or at least their key leaders were not. The tradition of their coming out of Egypt and their habit of moving about Israel and being distributed throughout the tribes suggest cosmopolitanism and a critical pan-tribal function. I am inclined to view them in the category of "'rootless' intellectuals of the new order" who, in many documented situations, have made common cause with peasant uprisings.[32] If this be so, then the religious counterculture of Israel had an impetus and a frame of reference from beyond the frontier, while its particulars and modes of expression satisfied and were shaped by the interests peculiar to the highland frontier peoples. The result was that the Yahwistic intellectuals merged their social and political fortunes with the Israelite peasants which in turn fertilized and energized the distinctive Israelite political economy and subculture within Canaan.

(3) With respect to Lenski's point about the reversion of early Israel to monarchy and social stratification, here too the relevant conceptualization is not the frontier as an alternative to social revolution but the frontier as an area of lapsed social revolution, reinvaded by hierarchic institutions from within Israelite society. The structural changes constitutive of early Israel were eroded once the domain of political Israel was extended far beyond the hills to include the plains conquered by David and to absorb the venerable structures of sociopolitical domination

[32]Wolf, *Peasant Wars*, 287–88, describes these intellectually and culturally advanced petty officials, professionals, and teachers as "purveyors of skills . . . based on literacy." For the Levites, the competency may not have been so much literacy per se as their command of an articulate tradition that framed oppression and the possiblities of deliverance as code symbols of the society. Also worth close scrutiny is Wolf's specification of factors that make peasants hesitant to fuse with intellectuals and that are overcome only by sharply favorable objective circumstances (ibid., 289–90, drawing on D. Hindley, "Political Conflict Potential, Politicization, and the Peasants in Underdeveloped Countries," *Asian Studies* 3 [1965] 470–89, and R. N. Adams, "Power and Power Domains," *América Latina* 9 [1966] 3–21).

which were then extensively reimposed on the hill country by Solomon. In this regard, I would point not only to the importation of hierarchic political institutions into Israel but also to the incorporation of a large Canaanite population into the territorial state of Israel and the attendant introduction of non-Israelite personnel into the state apparatus and the military forces.[33] When I speak of "Canaanite" in this context I do not refer to ethnic foreigners in the customary ill-defined sense but rather to people who did not have the social revolutionary history that the highland Israelites experienced, people who were not in a position to comprehend the meaning of joining the social body of Israel as an intertribal movement toward social equality.[34] They were people who would require "re-education" to become Israelites in the full socio-cultural sense, and it is by no means clear that David and his monarchic successors were interested in acculturating these newcomers to old Israelite consciousness since their main agenda was to strengthen the centralized power of the new Israelite state.

Social Equality in Early Israel

While for the most part Lenski absolves *The Tribes of Yahweh* of the charge of imposing modern categories to the distortion of Israelite social reality, he does suspect that I have overstated the degree of social equality among early Israelites. I concede that some statements in the book, particularly if taken in isolation from the total argument, may appear overdrawn or idealistic.[35] Since completing the book, I have also come to put more stress on the resistance to social equality within Israel itself that resulted from the mixtures of peoples from many different sociohistorical experiences who joined in the Israelite movement and from the tendencies toward social privilege within powerful families and affluent regions.[36] It is well known that within peasant societies there are

[33]A. Alt, "The Formation of the Israelite State in Palestine," *Essays in Old Testament History and Religion* (Garden City: Doubleday, 1968, German original, 1930) 288–93.

[34]On the incorporation of Canaanites into David's kingdom, cf. Gottwald, *Tribes*, 159, 175, 182, 204, 364, 368–69, 418–19, 576–77, and on various shifting biblical meanings of "Canaan/Canaanites", cf. ibid., 55–56, 498–503, 586.

[35]In retrospect I now see that, given the range of meanings attachable to the term "egalitarian," it was unfortunate that my most exact clarification of Israelite "social equality" (the organizational principle of equal access to basic resources for all adult members of the society) was reserved for a note near the end of the study (ibid., 697, 798–99 n. 635) where M. Fried's conceptualization of the principle is cited.

[36]A considerable number of references concerning the incomplete social revolution of ancient Israel appear in the text, but none is developed at length

frequent divisions among the more impoverished and the more affluent peasants.[37] The battle for social equality was not simply between Israel and its neighbors; it was a battle internal to Israelite society, which should occasion no great surprise, for just such internal struggle has characterized every social revolution that we know anything about.

It remains clear, however, that the catalytic social factor which precipitated the formation of large-scale Israel as an association of tribes was an intentional "opening toward equality" that deliberately set up institutional structures and pressures toward equality, understood as approximately equal access through extended families to the basic resources or means of production, and that was concomitantly expressed in the shaping of community decisions. An axial shift toward social equality shows up across an extensive field of institutional arrangements, socioeconomic practices, and literary and cultural features: in land tenure, in prohibition of interest on loans, in *gō*ʾ*ēl* mutual aid customs, in limitations on the priestly establishment, in attitudes toward sex and death, in historiographic content and style, in ethical norms and legal motivations, in poetic imagery, in genealogical constructs, and probably also in so-called "holy war" practices, to name only some of the more striking instances.

At one point in the text I state that "Israel *thought* it was different because it *was* different; it constituted an egalitarian society in the midst of stratified societies."[38] Lenski observes that he would feel more comfortable had I written that "Israel constituted a much less stratified society than its neighbors."[39] Now it is certainly true that I could have written the sentence that Lenski prefers because I agree with it as far as it goes. Had I done so, however, I would find such a statement far too weak and much too incomplete to do justice to the decisive intentional break between Canaan and Israel, particularly in the context of tracing the internal relations between social organization and theological assertions such as Yahweh's exclusivity and abnormal jealousy and the special election of Israel by Yahweh.

What I might more exactly have said is something like this: "Israel *thought* it was different because it *was* different: it constituted an *intentional* egalitarian society in the midst of *traditional* stratified societies." The term "intentional" as I use it means more than strong subjective motives, preferences, or orientations of will (so-called "good intentions" in spite of predominantly contradictory behavior); it means

(cf. Gottwald, *Tribes*, 43, 59, 318, 323, 325–26, 389, 409, 416–17, 429–33, 462–63, 485, 489–92, 495, 617, 619, 641–49.

[37]Wolf, *Peasant Wars*, 290–92.

[38]Gottwald, *Tribes*, 693.

[39]Lenski, *RelSRev* 6 (1980) 276, col. 2.

objective action to make deliberate structural alterations in society which created sustained pressures and mechanisms to level unequal access to resources even though not all inequalities were removed or prevented from arising. In short, Israel was egalitarian in its conscious deployment of societal power.

Ethical Judgment and Historical Hindsight

In some ways the most challenging aspect of Lenski's critique of *The Tribes of Yahweh* is his uneasiness with what he detects as an inappropriately simplistic moral judgment of Canaan and Israel. It is best to hear his precise words:

> In reading *The Tribes of Yahweh*, especially the second half of the book, I could not escape the feeling that there was, beyond the scholarly analysis, an unfortunate judgmental element which cast Israel in the role of hero and the Canaanites in the role of villain. There is, of course, historical precedent for this. Virtually all biblical scholars, fundamentalist and radical alike, have done the same.
>
> One wonders, however, whether a somewhat stronger case cannot be made for the Canaanite social system. No less a scholar and moralist than Karl Marx was able to call the bourgeoisie a progressive force in human history when viewed in proper historical context. This does not mean that the same was necessarily true of the princes of the city-states of Canaan, but it should, at least, cause us to consider the issue.
>
> When we do this, we cannot fail to note that Israel herself quickly came to adopt much of the Canaanite social system once she won control over the cities of the plain. Was this merely a failure of will or a lack of proper leadership, or was this a reflection of an altered social situation which made the old tribal system unworkable? Or, to put the matter another way, how much latitude did the Canaanite elite really have?[40]

Lenski's demurrers and questions definitely deserve response since they go to the heart of what present day discoverers of the social revolutionary origins of ancient Israel are to make of this strikingly novel reinterpretation of biblical origins. Lenski's difficulties are in fact related to my own objections to Mendenhall's tendencies to "moralize" and "idealize" Israel's social revolution.[41]

At one level in my study I am reporting on the ethical evaluations made by the early Israelites. Most of the time I am not so much making a case for or against Israel or Canaan as I am trying to see the case Israel presented for itself and what relation that argument bore to Israel's

[40]Ibid.

[41]Gottwald, *Tribes*, 222, 226, 232–33, 591, 599–602, 606, 608; idem, "The Hypothesis of the Revolutionary Origins of Ancient Israel: A Response to Hauser and Thompson," *JSOT* 7 (1978) 39–40, 43, 45.

social organization in process. At one point I remark on the spectrum of ethical evaluations that Canaanites were likely to have made concerning Israel.[42] A close reading of those remarks will show that I understand just how strong a case Canaanites could make for their hierarchic social order and how really plausible and commanding it was, mustering as it did centuries of political and cultural hegemony brilliantly justified by its official interpreters. To be an Israelite was indeed a risky business in every way imaginable, including struggle with the ethical stigmas of folly and perverse evil.

I am also appreciative of Lenski's reminder that Marx regarded capitalist social relations as a progressive force vis-à-vis feudalism. I am still striving to assess how progressive the economic formation of the ancient bureaucratic state was when viewed at various points in its history. Much of the difficulty has to do with how the ancient Near Eastern political economic formations should be conceptualized, whether loosely as feudalism, or a combination of patrimonial, prebendal, and mercantile domains, or an Asiatic mode of production involving a strong centralized state imposed on traditional villages through the nexus of a "tax/rent couple."[43] If we adopt the argument that the strongly centralized state was necessary to develop large-scale irrigation agriculture, we can opt for a progressive thrust within it. Since, however, there is still so much uncertainty and debate over this "hydraulic hypothesis" of the origin of the state in the ancient Near East, I am hesitant in drawing conclusions. In any case, Marx saw capitalist social relations as progressive only up to a certain point, namely, the point where the improvement of the forces of production was fettered by the relations of production so that the boons of the new productivity in goods, services, and ideas were restricted arbitrarily to a minority and

[42]Gottwald, *Tribes*, 595–96.

[43]On the evidence for Canaanite and ancient Near Eastern societies as broadly feudal in character, see ibid., 391–94, 737–38 n. 149; 755–58 nn. 293, 295, 303; 767–68 nn. 407–8, 410. Concerning patrimonial, prebendal, and mercantile domains, see E. R. Wolf, *Peasants* (Foundations of Modern Anthropology; Englewood Cliffs: Prentice-Hall, 1966), esp 50–59, 73–77. Concerning the Asiatic mode of production, see B. S. Turner, *Marx and the End of Orientalism* (Controversies in Sociology, 7; London: Allen & Unwin, 1978) and, for the formulation of "tax/rent couple," see B. Hindess and P. Q. Hirst, *Pre-Capitalist Modes of Production* (London: Routledge & Kegan Paul, 1975), esp. 192; idem, *Mode of Production and Social Formation: An Autocritique of "Pre-Capitalist Modes of Production,"* (London: Macmillan, 1977). For a discussion of these theories of the mode of production in relation to Canaan and Israel, together with bibliographic citations, see N. K. Gottwald, "Early Israel and 'the Asiatic Mode of Production' in Canaan," *SBLSP* 10 (1976) 145–54 (forthcoming in revised form in *BA*).

denied or rationed to a majority, precisely when the means for their wider appropriation were technically available. If the earliest Near Eastern states had once been progressive, at some point they may have reached the limits of the "goods" (goods both as things and as social and cultural possibilities) that they could deliver and thus ceased to advance the over-all good or general welfare of society.

In such terms, Israel's attempted break with the ancient Near Eastern state structure could be evaluated as a progressive undertaking, although perhaps totally premature and in any case ultimately unsuccessful for any number of reasons. At any rate, Israel's social revolution flowered objectively for a period of two centuries and left strong imprints on later Israel and on the whole history of the West. Just what we are to make of that early revolutionary upthrust and of its surviving imprints is a very large question. I find it possible and even necessary to respond positively to this Israelite undertaking without denying the social integrity and good faith of Canaanites and without prejudging how possible it actually was for such a retribalizing break with the ancient Near Eastern state to endure and spread. As far as I can see, the social revolution of Israel would have had to spread much farther than it did in order to have created a "balance of power" favorable to the continued success of its form of retribalized social organization. For instance, had Israel's social revolution spread to the Philistines, the immediate external threat that prompted the rise of monarchy in Israel would have been avoided. But as long as any strong centralized state existed in the ancient Near East or vicinity there would have been the threat of foreign conquest of the retribalized societies. Furthermore, social revolutions often lead to further internal conflict and sometimes to the recrudescence of hierarchy by means of counterrevolution.

As for the ethical judgments that interpreters will make of ancient Canaanite and Israelite social organization, they will depend greatly on the social location, assumptions, and commitments of the interpreter. Perhaps the example of a failed nonbiblical social revolution will help to illustrate my point. The Paris Commune of 1871 was a brief island in the capitalist seas of western Europe and it was engulfed within months of its onset.[44] Nonetheless, something was learned from the Commune to the benefit of later revolutions. I personally look with positive appreciation on the brief accomplishments of the Paris Commune, at the same time I see why it was incumbent on the wider French society to crush it. If I attempt to render my ethical assessment in terms of how I think I

[44]K. Marx, "The Civil War in France," *The Marx-Engels Reader,* ed. R. C. Tucker (New York: W. W. Norton, 1972; German original, 1891) 526–76; *Leon Trotsky on the Paris Commune* (New York: Pathfinder, 1970; original contents published 1905, 1917, 1920, and 1921 [pamphlet]); F. Jellinek, *The Paris Commune of 1871* (London: Gollancz, 1937).

might have responded as a participant in the social movements of late nineteenth century France—or of thirteenth century (B.C.) Canaan—I am reasonably sure that my response would have depended critically on my social locus, recognizing of course that some of the advantaged classes do characteristically opt for revolution and some of the disadvantaged classes fail to be aroused. In any case, it is an illusion that any of us can make uncontestable "neutral" class-transcending judgments about past or present historical conflicts.

Lenski is correct that the Canaanite elite did not have much latitude in its choices as long as it faithfully adhered to its role within the hierarchic system, but other Canaanites at the bottom of that society and in its middle ranges found their latitude for choice much wider. As for Israel's reversion to hierarchy, national defense within the international system of militarized states was unquestionably a major factor. Precisely here we can grasp the enmeshment of ethical assessment in the limits of social systems. As long as "Canaanite"-type social organization predominated in the ancient Near East, the ethical argument for it would appear superior to the ethical argument for "Israelite"-type retribalization. Many of the prophets, it seems, favored Israel taking great risks with national security. If I judge rightly what underlies their argument sociopolitically, they were implying something like this: if we decentralize, either by total retribalization or by sharply limiting the monarchic institutions, we will not have the imperial ambitions and the piles of surplus wealth that invite conquest and plunder. I am not at all convinced that Assyria would have desisted from attacking a retribalized Israel but the attacks might have been less severe and hardly more catastrophic than what transpired.[45] Of course all this is part of the unenviable position of a social venture that did not spread in a revolutionary way to other parts of the ancient Near East and so was isolated, contained, and destroyed, or at least thrown onto another plane in later Israelite-Jewish history.

Lenski properly highlights the ethical ambiguity of our historical hindsight and thereby he touches on the general problem of the relation of fact to value. It is evident that facts and values cannot be so neatly separated as disinterested scientific method proposes in its laudable endeavor to forestall premature conclusions based on tradition and "common sense." In *The Tribes of Yahweh*, I refer, for example, to "the

[45]On the internationally-focused "political realism" and "theopolitics" of the prophets, see N. K. Gottwald, *All the Kingdoms of the Earth: Israelite Prophecy and International Relations in the Ancient Near East* (New York: Harper & Row, 1964), esp. 350–87, concerning theories about the prophetic political orientation and a sketch of various prophetic models for international relations.

critical intersection between lawful social process and human freedom," an intersection that continually recurs "amid the supersession of social forms through time."[46] It seems to me that ethical judgments about history are estimations of how exercisable freedom has been used within the available factual options at the time. Thus the facts entail value judgments, are always valued in certain ways, but never incontestably because the facts are multitudinous and are always clusters or patterns of interconnected facts variously joined and weighted.[47]

The Israelites could give excellent moral reasons for their choices, and so could the Canaanites. The Israelites had "facts," openings for exercisable freedom, to sustain them, and so did the Canaanites. Different values were opposed in different arrays of social forces operating in the same broad field of facts. An ethical justification could be given for both and definitely was given. In the course of working through the data I find myself valuing the Israelite break with Canaan positively as a needful thing and, at the same time, valuing the Canaanites for their resistance as the complementary needful resistance in order to clarify that this was not an abstract contest of ideas but a social struggle with high stakes and without any absolute arbiter, other than Baal and Yahweh, whose credentials were clearly acceptable only to those already committed to pursuing their vital interests as they saw them. Of course this is not the whole of our interest in the Canaanite-Israelite social conflict. Israel's social revolutionary origins happen to lie at the base of the entire biblical tradition and thus at the foundation of Judaism and Christianity. Consequently there is an immediate religious interest and stake in Israel's social revolution that the Paris Comune, for example, does not possess. What we are to make of those revolutionary origins of our religious traditions constitutes a central issue in contemporary theology, an issue that cannot possibly be separated from the social stance of centemporary religious bodies and theologians any more than Israel's social revolution and religious faith were divisible.

The Internal Relations of the Social Revolutionary Process

It is apparent that this initial encounter between frontier and social revolutionary models calls for much more careful inquiry, not only into early Israel but also into the range of comparative sociological data relevant to the application of the models to Israel. It is worth stressing in

[46]Gottwald, *Tribes*, 708.

[47]For a perceptive discussion of the relation between facts and values in a historical material "ethical" outlook, interpreted according to a philosophy of the internal relations connecting and conditioning all social phenomena, see B. Ollman, *Alienation. Marx's Conception of Man in Capitalist Society*, (2d. ed.; Cambridge: University Press, 1978), chap. 4, esp. 45–47.

conclusion that both models appear to share a common apprehension of the interconnectedness of material and non-material factors as facets of a social whole in process. Both models try to take into account the material factors more fully and integrally than the previous nomadic, conquest, and amphictyonic models. Consequently, it appears that we are involved here not merely with one or another model comparable to all the others in what it covers, but we are considering a new order of modeling: one that does not simply put material and non-material factors side by side in order to draw external connections between them, stressing now one or the other factor and one or another external connection between factors, but a model in which the vital internal relations among all the factors are sought after and brought to expression as an interacting totality.

It may be that my dissatisfactions with Mendenhall and with Lenski have to do with my perception that each in his own way is in danger of magnifying one element as an independent variable in the social revolution in such a fashion that the intertwined factors, once dissected, are not easily recoverable as an operative whole. In my judgment, Mendenhall's independent variable of Yahwism as the Kingdom of God leads toward a too-narrow "religious idealism," while Lenski's independent variable of the expanding frontier leads toward a too-narrow "technologism." I reaffirm my previous formulation of the internal relations of Israel's social revolutionary process in gaining a foothold in the Canaanite highlands and in defining its social structure and cultural style,[48] together with my estimate of the theoretical explanatory yield of such a cultural material hypothesis.[49]

In a sense crucial to methodology, everything about ancient Israel proves to be *both* material and religious. Thus, clarifications of the circumstances and processes of Israel's early formation, such as Lenski has sought to sharpen by means of frontier categories, are not esoteric technicalities but simultaneous and integral clarifications of the full range of Israel's life and thought.

> In short, the basic tenet for future research and theory is clear and commanding: only as the full *materiality* of ancient Israel is more securely grasped will be able to make proper sense of its *spirituality*.[50]

[48]Gottwald, *Tribes*, 662.
[49]Ibid., 662–63.
[50]Ibid., xxv.

The Sack of Israel

JOHN L. MCKENZIE
CLAREMONT, CALIFORNIA

ONE does not know whether to call pre-monarchic Israel a planned society or not. The structures of that society are different enough from other societies in its contemporary world to call for question and comment. One may say with Amos that two men do not walk together by chance. On the other hand, one sees the danger of reading contemporary ideas into ancient societies. The one to whom this tribute is paid has alerted the present generation of scholars to the singular qualities of pre-monarchic Israel without falling into the trap of modernizing it.[1] It is impossible to discuss the general topic of value systems and social controls in pre-monarchic Israel, opened by George Mendenhall, without attending to the large reconstruction Norman Gottwald has thrown into the ring.[2] This essay will point out a few areas where the social values of ancient Israel were substantially altered, and point out a few reasons for the change to which Gottwald did not sufficiently attend.

The features of pre-monarchic Israel which made it a radical departure from the city-states of Canaan and Mesopotamia of the Late Bronze Age are clearly seen in the sources and are not disputed among scholars; they have been set forth by Mendenhall and by Gottwald, and I do no more than recall them here.[3] There was no monarchy and no visible central government which could be seen in the sources. "Israel" as a political unit simply did not exist; there were no agents or channels of political activity for "Israel." There is one and only one episode where "all Israel" takes concerted military action, the war of Deborah and Barak, and the sources tell us that not even then did all Israelites join the united action. More important, they neither describe nor imply

[1]G. E. Mendenhall, "Ancient Oriental and Biblical Law"; "Covenant Forms in Israelite Tradition"; and "The Hebrew Conquest of Palestine," *The Biblical Archaeologist Reader 3* (ed. E. F. Campbell, Jr., and D. N. Freedman; Garden City: Doubleday, 1970) 3–24, 25–53, 100–20; *The Tenth Generation: The Origins of the Biblical Tradition* (Baltimore: Johns Hopkins, 1973).

[2]N. Gottwald, *The Tribes of Yahweh* (Maryknoll: Orbis, 1979).

[3]Mendenhall, *Tenth Generation*, xi–xii, 1–31; Gottwald, *Tribes of Yahweh.*

any political machinery through which united action could occur. There is no visible system of taxation enforced by any central body, and no "services" rendered by a central government. The correct word for pre-monarchic Israel seems to be anarchy.

Without a monarchy other things also did not appear. Late Bronze Age kingdoms and city-states often exhibit a professional military aristocracy of chariot warriors.[4] Early Israel went to war by assembling the men of the villages when the alarm was sounded. Mendenhall has pointed out that the social organization of the villages was on a small scale, without a military aristocracy.[5] Nor was there an aristocracy of landowners. Although it does not appear in the laws, scholars are satisfied from allusions such as that in the story of Naboth (1 Kings 21) that the earliest system of land tenure in Israel kept land within the family and thus made the acquisition of large estates difficult.[6] The law of jubilee was an ideal rather than a practical expression of the traditional prejudice against land monopoly.[7] It can be legitimately conjectured that the two roots of aristocracy, professional soldiery and land ownership, were not unrelated. The conjecture is legitimate because they have so often in history been closely related. The gift of land has often been the only reward a sovereign could offer for military service, and it was usually a gift of someone else's land.

Without a monarchy and an aristocracy early Israel appears to have been a classless society. J. van der Ploeg about thirty years ago noticed the strange absence of any words in biblical Hebrew which clearly designate a nobility.[8] There was indeed the sharp class division between slave and free; we do not want to idealize pre-monarchic Israel. But within the community of Israel a certain social equality was achieved which was not found elsewhere in the Late Bronze and Early Iron Ages. Likewise there seems to have been no wealthy class. Early Israel was a community without merchants and without the wealth which accumulates through trade. I do not know whether the antiquity of the use of the word *Canaanite* to designate merchant has been traced.[9] It is at least

[4]J. Bright, *A History of Israel* (Philadelphia: Westminster, 1959) 49–59; Mendenhall, *Tenth Generation*, 123–41, 142–73.

[5]Mendenhall, "Government, Israelite," *IDBSup*, 372–74.

[6]Gottwald, *Tribes of Yahweh*, 266–67, 798.

[7]Even Robert North accepts this (*Sociology of the Biblical Jubilee* [AnBib 4; Rome: Pontifical Biblical Institute, 1954]), although I am sure he would no longer wish to stand by all the views expressed in this work.

[8]Van der Ploeg, "Les chefs d'Israël et leurs titres," *RB* 57 (1950) 40–61; "Les 'nobles' Israélites," *OTS* 9 (1951) 49–64.

[9]A look, perhaps too hasty, at recent studies of this word discloses that no progress has been made in its understanding in twenty years. Perhaps the word is telling us something so obvious that we cannot see it.

as old as Hosea (12:8). Perhaps it is no more and no less significant than the use of *foreign woman* to designate a prostitute. There was a time when both merchandising and prostitution were gainful occupations in which no decent Israelite would engage.

It has, to my satisfaction, finally been established that early Israel was monotheistic. Whenever there was an Israel there was a Yahweh. Israel remembered that there had been other gods, but the other gods were always "foreign." Furthermore, Yahweh was a liberator of the oppressed, as Gottwald has shown at great length.[10] It is only fair to recall that Hammurabi wrote that the gods had commissioned him to liberate the oppressed.[11] But the gods of Hammurabi had no such legend of salvation as the Israelites told about Yahweh. What historical roots this legend may have need not concern us. It affirms the unique character of Yahweh as the god of the oppressed. The gods of Mesopotamia and Canaan furnished theological support for a landowning and mercantile oligarchy which monopolized wealth. The visible symbol of this theology was the temple or temples in ancient cities, where the god dwelt like a king or a noble. Early Israel rejected the symbol without perhaps seeing all the implications of the symbol they rejected. When Solomon built a temple, the implications became clear and explicit. I doubt that early Israel had any professional priestly class, just as it had no professional merchants or soldiers. The need for professional priests arose with the need of ministers to the temple establishment by which the monarchy and the oligarchy legitimated themselves.

We have, then, the simplest society and the simplest culture: non-political, non-military, non-commercial. It seems that the essential social values of early Israel lay in not being something and not having something which they knew very well in their contemporary world. The early Israelite ideal of well-being seems to have been very well described as the peasant sitting under his vine and under his fig tree with none to terrify. When we first meet the phrase in literature it had almost certainly become archaic and expressed a nostalgia for a long lost past rather than a realistic hope for any near future.[12] Under the monarchy, "none to terrify" would include the tax-collector, the landlord and the money-lender. The threat of foreign invasion was rare until the years of the final collapse of both Israel and Judah. When Elisha asks the woman of Shunem whether he could do her a favor by mentioning her to the king or to the military commander, she answers, "I live among my own

[10]Gottwald, *Tribes of Yahweh*, 63–125.

[11]*ANET*, 3rd ed., 164, 178.

[12]If I read Walter Brueggemann correctly (and it is not that hard) we certainly agree that Solomon and his successors were chief among those who terrified the Israelite peasant ('Vine and Fig Tree': A Case Study in Imagination and Criticism," *CBQ* 43 [1981] 188–204).

ᶜ*am*" (2 Kgs 4:12–13). In this security not even the king or his chief commander could do anything for the Israelite peasant.

One is tempted to call the culture of early Israel a pastoral idyl. One hesitates because pastoral idyls have never existed except in the imaginations of sophisticated poets of decadent ages. The romance of the pastoral idyl, like the romance of the American West, is found only in literature; the hard reality of pastoral and agricultural life in ancient Palestine was made up of endless grinding toil from dawn to dusk, the ever present threat of disaster from drought, bandits, crop failure and insects, disease, starvation and early death. Yet there was also a reality of "the good old days" in Israel, just as there was a reality behind the good old days of the American West. The reality was a time no longer remembered, when the Israelite peasant was normally free of those who terrified, those mentioned above: the tax-collector, the landlord and the money-lender. The harsh realities of the past are dimmed in the collective memory when they are compared with the harsh realities of the present, and when it is known that these present harsh realites were not always there. The American West was harsh and cruel, but it was not an industrial slum. The early Israelite at times felt that Yahweh had withheld his bounty, but he was assured that Yahweh was on his side. The creditors and tax-collectors whose rapacity afflicted him, as well as those whom they represented, he recognized as his enemies.

One does not know with how much reflection early Israel made it impossible for individuals to amass great wealth. Certainly the law or custom—not recorded in our sources, as we have noticed—by which land was retained within the family was a deliberate move against the growth of large estates. Whether the absence of a merchant class was a deliberate rejection of a part in a well established system of international commerce or simply the unplanned result of Israel's lack of resources and skills as well as of its geographical isolation from existing routes and centers of trade may be left an open question.[13] Even after Solomon Israel never became a commercial center. Archaeology has revealed a quite active international Near Eastern trade in luxury goods during the second and first millennia B.C.; this trade was, as it has always been, limited to a very thin upper crust social and economic level. In this trade early Israel played no part. From "the good life," as it was lived in the Bronze Age, Israel was excluded. Geography and natural resources may have had more to do with this exclusion than the free choice of Israelite society; but it seems that the exclusion was accepted. Early Israel lived content with the simple life.[14]

[13]H. Schmökel, *Geschichte des Alten Vorderasien* (Handbuch der Orientalistik 2/3; Leiden: Brill, 1957) 239–41.

[14]But see the militant anti-luxury passages in Amos 6:3–7; Isa 3:16–26; 5:11–14.

But not all Israelites. Here we encounter the blind alley which so often lies at the end of historical investigation into the ancient world. Ancient historical sources do not relate what we call social and economic history. At best they sometimes preserve materials from which we can draw conclusions about social and economic history. They tell us that the elders of Israel desired a king "like all the nations" (1 Sam 8:5). The phrase itself is a value judgment written by a later scribe; it does not quote the language of the Israelites, and probably does not express their explicit desires. We know that Israel experienced late a social and economic development which other Near Eastern kingdoms had experienced much earlier. This development can be summed up in one phrase as the enrichment of an oligarchy. One does not believe that this happened by chance. We read in the sources that it was the elders of Judah and of Israel who invited David to be king (2 Sam 2:4; 5:1–3). One may set aside quite legitimate questions about the spontaneity of these invitations. But it is fairly safe to conclude that the elders did this because they thought it was good for them.

When one reads the description of the wealth of Solomon (1 Kgs 10:14–26), it becomes clear that the monarch was certainly the beneficiary of the social and economic revolution, even when one discounts the exaggerations of legend in the account. Such wealth had not been known in Israel before; and there is no reason to think that David reigned in rustic simplicity in contrast to his successor. It may be futile to ask whether David was driven by the lust for power or the lust for wealth; one does not exclude the other. Power certainly acquires and secures wealth. But in forging the instrument of wealth which the monarchies of Israel and Judah became, David had and needed the help of others who were admitted to the oligarchy and a share in wealth and power. Who were they?

The presence of a foreign conquering military aristocracy is attested for more than one Bronze Age kingdom and city-state.[15] It is not attested for Israel. But a few elements of the situation should be recalled. We know that the power base of David was a group of several hundred professional warriors who owed no allegiance except to their chieftain (1 Sam 22:2). His rise from bandit chieftain to warlord to king may be illustrated by many examples, which include men as far scattered in space and time as William the Conqueror and Chiang-kai-shek (who, to be strictly accurate, became not a king but a head of state). David's warriors had no country of their own any more than the buccaneers of Henry Morgan. There were certainly foreign officers among them; it is doubtful that Uriah the Hittite, who assumed a good Yahwist name, was

[15]The Hyksos, the Hurrians, the Philistines; Bright, *History*, 55–58, 151–54; Schmökel, *Geschichte*, 154–70, 231–37.

the only "foreigner" in a group to whom the rest of the world were "foreigners."

Was David himself of foreign origin? Neither his name nor the name of his father is clearly Hebrew. One might say that the name Obregon is clearly Spanish; there is always a shade of doubt about personal names when their bearers pass from one language to another. Jesse and David are not clearly anything. There is also the strange relationship between David and the Philistines—who were certainly a foreign conquering aristocracy if any one ever was. One may say that David met them as fellow professionals—at times allies, at other times competitors, but never really enemies. David took service with the Philistines. He could not have established himself as king of Judah except as a vassal of the Philistines. One concludes that he rebelled successfully against his overlords. Once he established himself as the independent king of Israel, we hear no more of the Philistines. There is no record of any treatment of the conquered Philistines like the treatment of the Moabites, the Aramaeans, the Edomites (2 Sam 8:2–14) and the Ammonites (2 Sam 11:30–31). The Philistines remained peaceful neighbors of Israel and Judah throughout the period of the monarchy; they were not conquered by David nor incorporated into his territory. One cannot show that David was of foreign origin, still less can one say precisely of Philistine origin; one can only say that nothing told us about David excludes the possibility except the Judahite genealogy with which he has been furnished.

It is indeed one of the ironies of history that the city which has become the world symbol of Judaism entered history as an enclave within the land of Israel populated almost entirely by non-Israelites.[16] Jerusalem was captured by David's forces as his personal plunder. It became the seat of his palace and his administration and the residence of his officers and his retainers. It is called the city of David almost as if that were its name; the entire city was the royal palace, in the large sense of the term. David did not at once establish it as the religious center of Israel; there was probably deep opposition to this idea which is vestigially preserved in the oracle of Nathan (2 Sam 7:5–7). But the temple was built by Solomon and the last visible symbol of faith of ancient Israel was incorporated into the oligarchy.

We have, then, all the elements of a foreign conquering aristocracy. But we can find others who had a part in the development. We have already observed that the merchants were called Canaanites. It seems that

[16]I base this remark on A. Alt's article, "Jerusalems Aufstieg" (*Kleine Schriften zur Geschichte des Volkes Israel* 3 [München: Beck, 1959] 241–57), but even more on extending his treatment of Samaria in "Der Stadtstaat Samaria" (*Kleine Schriften*, 3, 254–302) to Jerusalem.

they were called Canaanites because they were Canaanites. Solomon is described as a merchant prince like his friend the king of Tyre (1 Kgs 10:14–29). Again we may discount the exaggerations of legend. Again also we need not assume that this was created entirely by Solomon. In ancient Near Eastern kingdoms trade was a royal monopoly. The risks were great, but they were matched by the huge profits of successful enterprise. The king had resources beyond those of any single merchant; the merchants who acted as his agents reached profits beyond the hopes of the isolated entrepreneur. In order to create this trading monopoly David and Solomon were forced to introduce foreign merchants, which does not imply that they were reluctant to do so; Israelites were totally without the experience and the skills required for successful trading. It is now known that the Assyrian Empire was a trading empire, and that their conquests grew vaster and vaster as the network of trade, which they had to control, expanded.[17] This throws light on the motivation of David's conquests. The innocent scribe of the books of Samuel once refers to the rest Yahweh gave to David from his enemies roundabout (2 Sam 7:1). Or was he so innocent? He would more accurately have referred to the rest which Yahweh gave to the peoples roundabout from David.

The development of large landholdings may with good probability be associated with the military aristocracy of David. This process has happened so often in so many and such diverse places and periods that we may risk assuming that it hapened in Israel too. As mentioned above J. van der Ploeg noticed thirty years ago the absence of any titles of nobility in ancient Israel. It is now commonplace that early Israel was a social democracy. The roots of nobility go back to the ownership of land, and land was usually the reward which a conqueror gave to his associates. Land came to the king in other ways, of which the story of Naboth is an illustration (1 Kings 21). The narrator no doubt reports correctly that the perversion of justice in the case of Naboth was a scandal; but the story also reports a way in which land could be forfeited to the crown. One notices that in the story of Absalom both Absalom and Joab appear as landlords (2 Sam 14:30). No one seems to have asked how they acquired their property, nor whether all royal sons and royal officers were landlords. Land could also be forfeited by indebtedness. The lender is a figure who appears with the merchant and the landlord. The peasant could secure credit only by pledging a harvest which he had not yet reaped. The records we have of ancient interest rates are appalling;

[17]This is briefly stated by Bright, *History*, 252. It is worthy of note that the forty years which lay between the *Cambridge Ancient History* and the *Handbuch der Orientalistik* added nothing to the economic and social history of the Assyrian Empire.

in a marginal agriculture like that of ancient Palestine it was easy for indebtedness to lead to loss of land and to slavery. The king was the largest landlord and the largest lender.

In addition he disposed of the revenues of taxation. The new economy of the oligarchy could not function with the simple anarchy of pre-monarchic Israel. The monarchy demanded an army of civil administrators, which is described in simple populist language in 1 Sam 8:11–18. Like most populist speeches the passage employs exaggerated rhetoric; even with the rhetoric discounted the reality which appears is frightening enough. It is abundantly clear that taxation in ancient kingdoms was not for essential services, but that it was a form of extortion by which the ruling oligarchy enriched itself.[18] The scribe of 1 Samuel tells us that taxation under the monarchy was no different from taxation under other monarchies. George Mendenhall once remarked that the functions of the ancient king were war and law. I wonder whether he would accept a revision which would read "war and taxes."

It was a universal ancient practice that a form of taxation imposed upon the impecunious was a period of forced labor exacted from the subjects during the year. For some unknown reason the Israelites simply refused to accept this. Yahweh was in Israelite legend the god who had delivered their fathers from slavery in Egypt. Actually he delivered them from forced labor if from anything, the forced labor which was a traditional and accepted part of the life of the Egyptian peasant. The idealized picture of Solomon tells us that he imposed forced labor on the foreign population but not on the Israelites (1 Kgs 9:21–22). We know very well that that is not true. The rebellion of ten tribes against Rehoboam, according to 1 Kings 12, arose over the issue of forced labor; and the dialogue between Rehoboam and the tribal representatives presupposes that forced labor was imposed by Solomon. The tribal representatives ask that it be lightened, not removed. The villain of the Exodus narratives is not some unknown Egyptian king but Solomon.

The monarchy also demanded an army composed of skilled professionals such as could not be supplied by the tribal levies which early Israel had rallied to its defense. The hard core of such a professional force was David's original gang of bandits, constantly sustained by volunteers drawn from Israelites and others who were attracted by the rewards of soldiering. When they were not at war, they lived off the land; the writer of 1 Samuel says as much. During much of David's reign it seems they were at war. David's wars were purely and simply wars of

[18]It was my intention to add a learned remark on the jars inscribed *lmlk*. My inability to find anything pertinent led me once again to reflect on our strange practice of keeping archaeological evidence inaccessible to all save the excavators.

conquest, except for those wars which he had to wage to manage his unruly subjects of Israel and Judah. Two such wars are mentioned even in the sanitized sources of 2 Samuel. The names of Solomon's chariot cities are not mentioned, but historians have often been struck by the fact that indications of their location do not suggest that they were well located to defend the frontier.[19] Solomon's frontiers were not threatened. The chariot cities were the headquarters of flying squadrons of police who imposed the yoke and the whips with which Solomon, in the words attributed to Rehoboam, afflicted his subjects. Among other blessings of civilization which David and Solomon anticipated was the police state.

One may ask what had happened to the ancient Yahwist traditions of Israel. One may ask, but we really do not know what form the ancient Yahwist traditions had in early Israel; the literary sources come from the monarchy, and proper attention has never been given to the political manipulations of the scribes of David and Solomon. Certainly one who is convinced of this manipulation will read the sources with a bias; perhaps such a bias is a corrective against being misled by a whitewashing job which has endured for centuries. We do not know how much Israelite law is pre-monarchic. Early Israel was a pre-legal society, and only under the monarchy did what was remembered of its mores and folkways get put in writing. There was no firm legal tradition to oppose to the decrees of the king. We can be sure, even though we cannot trace the literary development, that the Yahwism of early Israel was not a belief in the divine election of David as king and of his dynasty as perpetually chosen; that early Israelite faith did not represent David as a savior figure through whom Yahweh would realize his good will towards Israel and through whom he would establish a world reign of peace and justice over all nations. As Solomon enthralled Yahweh as a patron of the dynasty, so David had initiated the process by which Yahweh ceased to be the god of Israel and became the god of the king. The liberator god had become the symbol and the patron of an oppressive oligarchy.

The canonization of David in Jewish and Christian belief has long rendered it impossible to view him critically. I suggest that only by following such leads as I outline here can we reach a historical and theological understanding of the phenomenon of the Israelite monarchy.[20]

[19]The recent commentary of J. Gray (*I & II Kings* [Philadelphia: Westminster, rev ed. 1970] 249) does not really touch the problem. Speculations such as those cited on pp. 246–48 make the suggestion I propose quite modest.

[20]Probably by sheer coincidence, the *JBL* issue current at the time of this writing (99/4 [1980]), contains three articles which approach the David legend quite critically: P. K. McCarter, "The Apology of David" (489–504); J. Levenson and B. Halpern, "The Political Import of David's Marriages (507–18); and J. C. Vanderkam, "Davidic Complicity in the Deaths of Abner and Eshbaal: A Historical and Redactional Study" (521–39).

I believe that ultimately the monarchy makes sense only as the imposition of a foreign aristocracy upon Israel. I conclude with a personal literary critical note. Some years ago I published a theology of the Old Testament in which I refused to include the theme of messianism as proper to the theology of the Old Testament.[21]

An earlier essay written for a collection was expanded by the editors by the addition of a section on messianism because of the same refusal. The editors of the collection added this section without my knowledge or consent.[22] I wish to take this opportunity to disavow it publicly. This essay has set forth reasons for that position which at the time I wrote these previous efforts were not clear in my mind. They are clearer now, and so this has been written. I agree that the question needs further discussion. But I now feel much more certain that Jesus never accepted the title of Messiah.

[21]J. McKenzie, *A Theology of the Old Testament* (Garden City: Doubleday, 1974) 267–317.

[22]J. McKenzie, "Aspects of Old Testament Thought," in *The Jerome Biblical Commentary* (ed. R. E. Brown, J. A. Fitzmyer, and R. E. Murphy; Englewood Cliffs: Prentice-Hall, 1968) Article 77, Sections 152–63.

Succession and Genealogy in the Davidic Dynasty

JAMES W. FLANAGAN
UNIVERSITY OF MONTANA

W. ROBERTSON SMITH'S 1888–89 "Lectures on the Religion of the Semites" represented the first attempt to relate systematically the study of the Bible to evidence gathered from other cultures by the social sciences. Although his effort was followed in Europe during the first half of the twentieth century by scholars such as Max Weber, Antonin Causse, and others,[1] social scientific studies were largely ignored by biblical scholars until the 1950s and 60s when George Mendenhall revived an interest in them with his examination of covenant form in the Old Testament (1954) and his peasant revolt hypothesis, proposed as an explanation for the settlement in Israel (1962).[2] With two articles, Mendenhall succeeded in awakening biblicists to the fact that social scientific methodologies could supplement, if not supplant, the traditional literary and historical criticisms that had become the standard tools of their trade.[3]

The renewed interest in comparative biblical studies broadly conceived has developed along several fronts simultaneously. Both structuralists and historians have applied comparative materials to biblical evidence in order to escape nineteenth century presuppositions about Israel's religious faith and to pose questions that would otherwise be inconceivable. Although the structural and historical approaches have often been applied independently, a few studies such as David Jobling's

[1]See R. E. Clements, *A Century of Old Testament Study* (London: Lutterworth, 1976); S. T. Kimbrough, *Israelite Religion in Sociological Perspective* (Wiesbaden: Otto Harrassowitz, 1978) 99–106; J. W. Rogerson, *Anthropology and the Old Testament* (Oxford: Blackwell, 1978).

[2]"Covenant Forms in Israelite Tradition," *BA* 17 (1954) 50–76; "The Hebrew Conquest of Palestine," *BA* 25 (1962) 66–87.

[3]See N. K. Gottwald and F. S. Frick, "The Social World of Ancient Israel," *SBLSP* (Missoula, Montana; Scholars, 1975) 1. 165–78; E. Leach, "Anthropological Approaches to the Study of the Bible During the Twentieth Century," presented at National Meeting of Society of Biblical Literature, Dallas, Texas, 1980.

examination of Jonathan's role in the Samuel narratives have used structuralist techniques borrowed from linguistics in order to ask historical questions. Taking a fresh look at old material, he asked how the divinely chosen house of Saul could have been legitimately replaced by the Davidic dynasty and concluded that the Jonathan narratives were composed to answer this question and to make the shift theologically acceptable to the believing community of the compiler's day.[4]

Jobling's explanation is helpful not only because it brings us to the topic of this article, but also because, I believe, a similar interpretation can be proposed for the rest of the books of Samuel as well. Drawing upon studies on tribal leadership and urbanization, I have described the books as explanations for shifts in power that accompanied the emergence of the Jerusalemite monarchy. Kings replaced tribal leaders; Jerusalem replaced Shiloh and Hebron; and the house of David replaced the house of Saul. Each change required explanation and legitimation such as that provided by the compilers of Samuel.[5]

Here I propose to pursue the same investigations a step further by using the genealogical records pertaining to Saul and David in order to trace the geographical, political, and personal shifts that occurred during their reigns. I am interested in the transfer of royal office and power in the period between Saul's accession (1 Samuel 9–11) and Solomon's succession (1 Kings 1–2) rather than in the long-term historical consequences of the transfers. Therefore, the study will be descriptive and not analytical for it will not take up the problems which later theologians and historians, biblical or otherwise, have raised by interpreting the dynasty in messianic categories and by rooting messianic hopes in the person of David.

Mendenhall has been joined by Gottwald in depicting the pressures which nudged the Yahwistic tribes along the road toward centralized organization as being internal as well as external.[6] The tumult which they have identified in internal tribal affairs during that period did not abate in the post-tribal and monarchic eras.[7] Instead the perplexing and rapid social, political, and religious changes afforded aggressive and combative individuals exceptional opportunities for disrupting relationships and seizing unpredicted advantages. Samuel's vacillation as he anguished over whether to lend his legitimacy to centralized government surely reflected the turmoil and quandary that was felt within the

[4]D. Jobling, *The Sense of Biblical Narrative* (Sheffield: JSOT, 1978) 6.

[5]See J. W. Flanagan, "The Relocation of the Davidic Capital," *JAAR* 47 (1979) 223–44; "Chiefs in Israel," *JSOT* 20 (1981) 47–73.

[6]N. K. Gottwald, *The Tribes of Yahweh: A Sociology of the Religion of Liberated Israel, 1250-1050 B. C. E.* (Maryknoll, NY: Orbis, 1979).

[7]Flanagan, "Chiefs," 55–58.

population as it struggled with the developments that were being thrust upon the country from all sides.

Saul's leadership failed to bring an end to the trauma. Even if we allow for intentional discrediting by unsympathetic biblical writers as some have suggested,[8] his term in office must be labelled a failure. He enjoyed several military successes before finally being killed on the battlefield, but all in all he failed to stabilize the country or to rise above his own suspicions. Saul's paranoia appears in the Bible as the cause of many of his problems because it crippled his ability to act decisively and put him at odds with members of his own household. When his eldest son Jonathan established a strong bond of loyalty and affection with David,[9] Saul interpreted the act as an affront to his dynasty and as a reason to place David under house arrest (1 Sam 18:1–4). In spite of this, Jonathan stood by David and saved him from one of Saul's assassination plots (1 Samuel 20). As a result, David spared Mephibosheth, Jonathan's son, from the slaughter of the Gibeonites (2 Sam 21:7) and took him and his son, Mica, into the custody of his court, although such hospitality also served as house arrest (2 Samuel 9).

The role of Saul's daughter, Michal, was similar to that of her brother, although her life eventually manifested some of the same ambivalences as her father's. She was bound in marriage to David (1 Samuel 18) and devised a plan to save him from her father's wrath (1 Samuel 19). But she was taken from David and given to Palti as wife (1 Sam 25:45), perhaps as Saul's ploy for weakening David's claim within the northern ruling house.[10] Her return was set down as a condition before David began negotiations with Abner for Ishbosheth's crown (2 Sam 3:12–16), but after her return, she fell into disfavor with David and was confined childless to the Jerusalem palace (2 Samuel 6). The biblical narrative, therefore, portrays her as moving from trust to distrust of David while David's position was transformed from one of weakness to strength.

Although Saul's suspicions had been incapacitating, they eventually proved correct, and his and Michal's view came to be shared by others. It was during the time that David was driven into exile by his son, Absalom, that the silenced voices of dissent began to be raised. Mephibosheth rejoiced at David's misfortune and voiced his hope that the throne had been returned to the house of Saul (2 Sam 16:3). Shimei, son of

[8]See J. Blenkinsopp, "The Quest for the Historical Saul," in *No Famine in the Land: Studies in Honor of John L. McKenzie* (ed. J. W. Flanagan and A. W. Robinson; Missoula, Montana: Scholars, 1975) 79–99; and David Gunn, *The Fate of King Saul* (Sheffield: JSOT, 1980).

[9]P. K. McCarter, Jr., *1 Samuel* (AB 8; Garden City: Doubleday, 1980) 306, 399.

[10]Ibid., 400.

Gera, hurled accusations at David for his treatment of the northern house (2 Sam 16:5–8), and Sheba, son of Bichri, expressed his displeasure with David by leading a revolt (2 Samuel 20). In a sense it seemed as though the instability David had caused within the house of Saul had come to haunt his own.

The intrigues within Saul's family did spill over into the Davidic house where they caused shifting alliances, oppression, assassination, and murder. Saul massacred the priests at Nob for giving protection to David (1 Sam 22:1–19); Abner was murdered as a result of his treason against Ishbosheth on behalf of David (2 Sam 3:27; 4:7); Asahel, son of David's sister Zeruiah, was killed (2 Sam 2:23); Ishbosheth and Amasa, son of David's sister Abigail, were killed; and Joab, Amnon, Absalom, Adonijah, and Shimei all eventually met tragic deaths (2 Samuel 13–1 Kings 2). In sum, of the individuals who played prominent roles in the affairs of the Davidic court, only Abiathar, David's priest who had supported Adonijah's succession, and Abishai, a son of Zeruiah who had witnessed Absalom's murder, seem to have been spared. Abiathar was stripped of his office (1 Kgs 2:35), and Abishai simply dropped from sight. We can assume that their deaths were either not remembered or were of no interest to the biblical writers.

I have not stressed the sequence of agents of these deaths which would illustrate how one tragedy begot the next because we cannot be certain of the chronology in every instance. Still, the chain of events created by the assassins and counter-assassins is clear enough to reveal the intense, interconnected series of power struggles that characterized the period. As is typical in tribal societies, successful leadership in Israel was leadership that survived. The capable leader was one who outwitted and dominated his opponents even though he may have suffered temporary setbacks.[11] The symbiosis of loyalty and largess that bound followers to leaders was much more fluid than is often presumed by Westerners who are conditioned by experiences of relatively stable democratic governments. Allegiances, and consequently power, could shift almost instantly when a new leader was thought to offer more advantages than the old. Thus, a winner, or one who was expected to be victorious, in these struggles wielded enormous influence and enjoyed a distinct advantage. Personal charm, agility with the sword, a keen sense of timing, patience in defeat, and magnanimity in victory were among the talents the successful tribal leader had to have in order to win and hold the coalitions that would assure his survival.[12]

[11]See A. F. Robertson, "Ousting the Chief: Deposition Charges in Ashanti," *Man* 11 (1976) 410-27.

[12]See D. Howarth, *The Desert King* (London: Quartet Books, 1980) 25–29; M. Almana, *Arabia Unified* (London: Hutchinson & Benham, 1980) 30.

When the treachery visible in the narratives of Samuel is compared with the genealogical materials, David's rise from amid the ruins of Saul's house can be easily seen. By the time David was firmly established in Jerusalem, every male in direct line of descent from Saul except two or three ineligible successors was dead. Only his grandson, Mephibosheth, and his great-grandson, Mica, seem to have survived. In any case, their physical handicap, minority, and secondary status probably prevented them from succeeding.

Genealogical charts of Saul's and David's families help us visualize the wake of destruction that followed David's rise to power:[13]

1 Sam 14:49–51

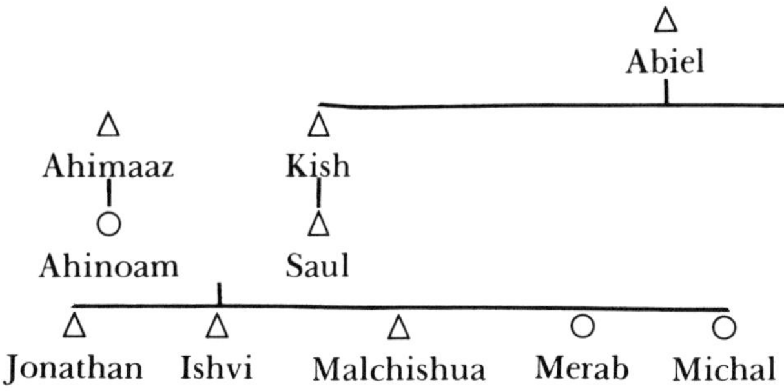

1 Sam 31:2 = 1 Chr 10:2

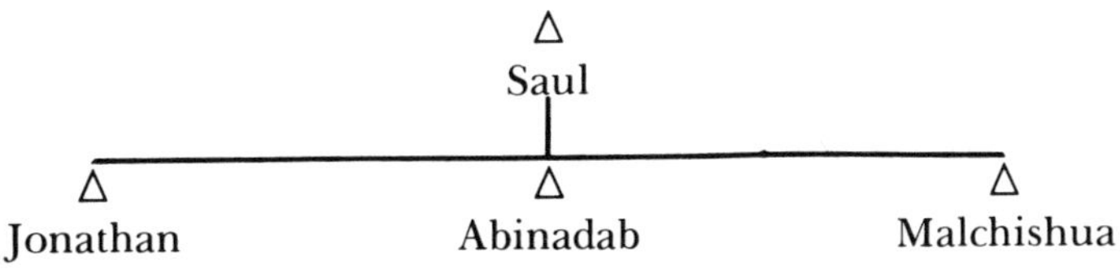

2 Sam 21:7–8

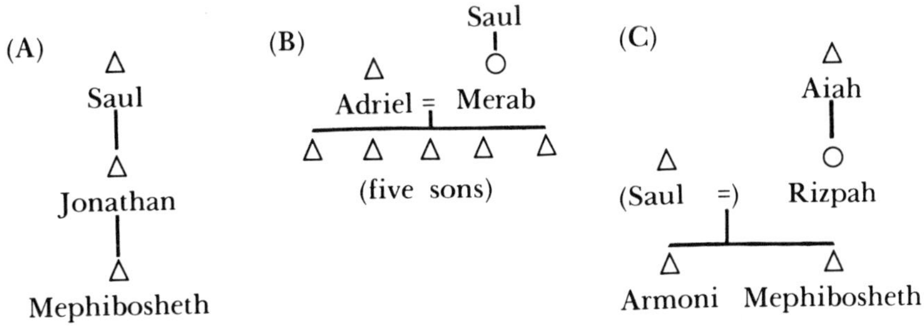

[13]Symbols used in the charts are: Δ signifies males; O signifies females; = signifies marriage or concubinage.

I Chr 8:33–40

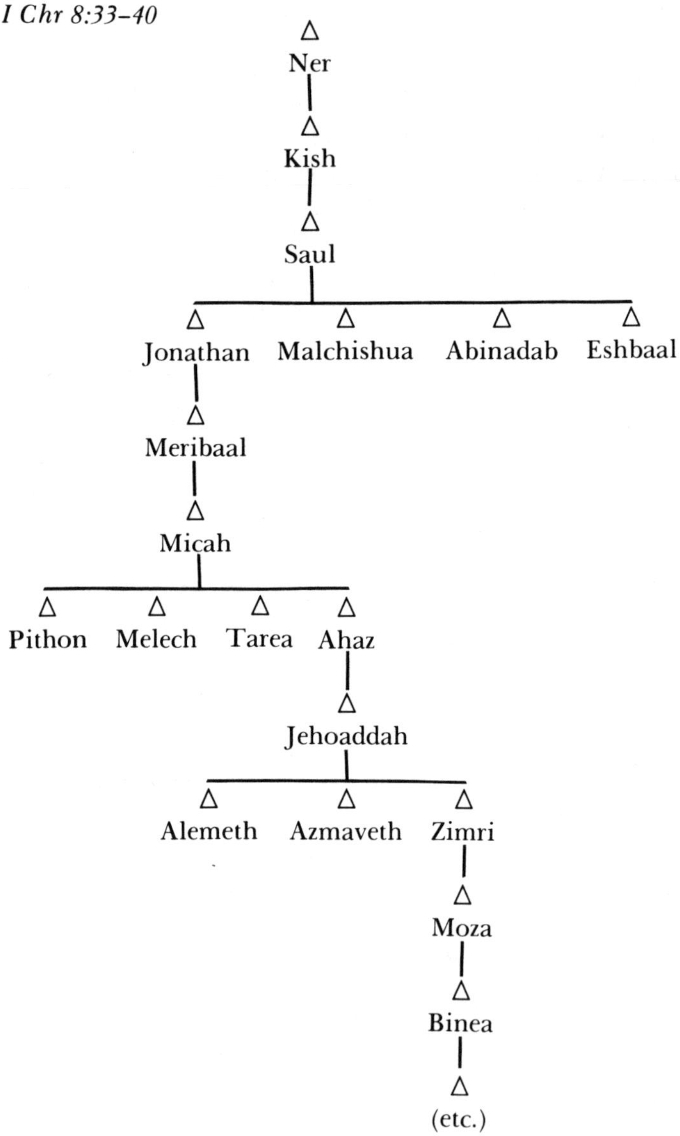
Ner
Kish
Saul
Jonathan
Malchishua
Abinadab
Eshbaal
Meribaal
Micah
Pithon
Melech
Tarea
Ahaz
Jehoaddah
Alemeth
Azmaveth
Zimri
Moza
Binea
(etc.)

I Chr 9:39–43

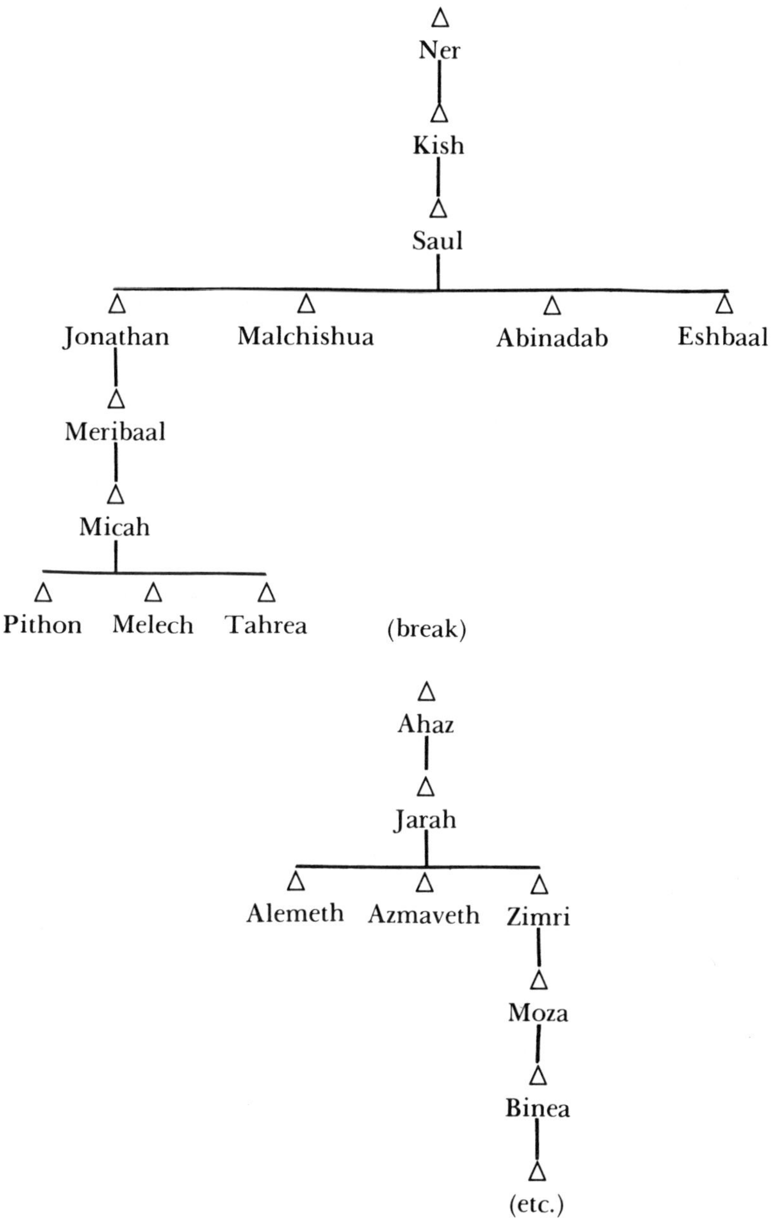
Ner
Kish
Saul
Jonathan
Malchishua
Abinadab
Eshbaal
Meribaal
Micah
Pithon
Melech
Tahrea
(break)
Ahaz
Jarah
Alemeth
Azmaveth
Zimri
Moza
Binea
(etc.)

Ruth 4:18–22

2 Sam 17:24

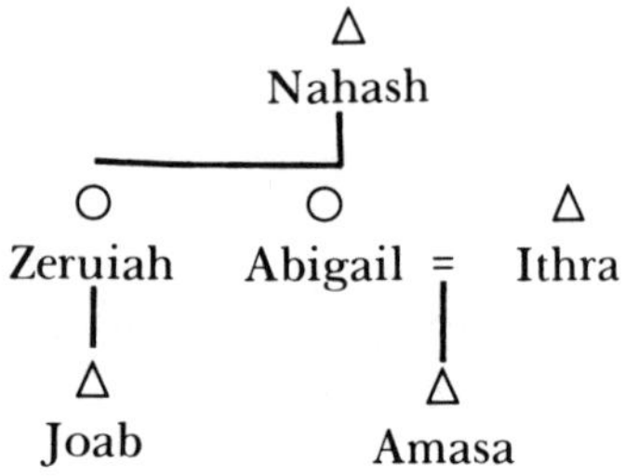

2 Samuel 11; 12:24–25

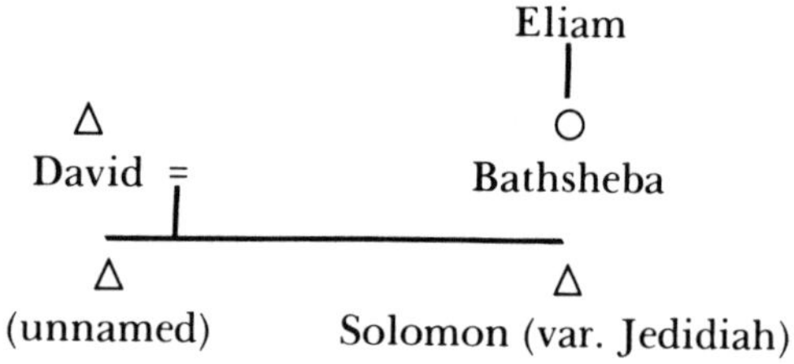

I Chr 2:9–17

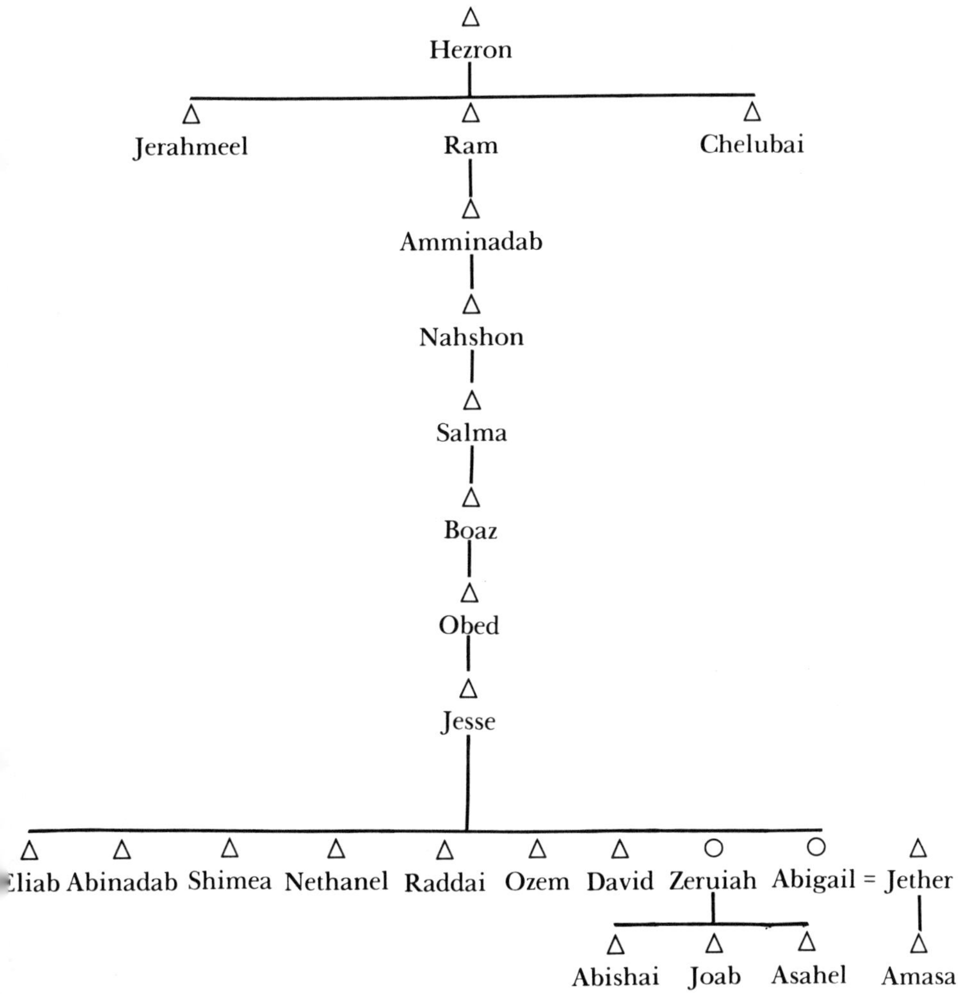
Hezron
Jerahmeel
Ram
Chelubai
Amminadab
Nahshon
Salma
Boaz
Obed
Jesse
liab
Abinadab
Shimea
Nethanel
Raddai
Ozem
David
Zeruiah
Abigail = Jether
Abishai
Joab
Asahel
Amasa

(Lists of sons with mothers' names born to David at Hebron and Jerusalem)

2 Sam 3:2–5	*1 Chr 3:1–9*	*1 Chr 14:3–7*
(Hebron)	(Hebron)	
Amnon (Ahinoam)	Amnon (Ahinoam)	
Chileab (Abigail)	Daniel (Abigail)	
Absalom (Maacah)	Absalom (Maacah)	
Adonijah (Haggith)	Adonijah (Haggith)	
Shephatiah (Abital)	Shephatiah (Abital)	
Ithream (Eglah)	Ithream (Eglah)	
2 Sam 5:13–16		
(Jerusalem)	(Jerusalem)	(Jerusalem)
Shammua	Shimea	Shammua
Shobab	Shobab	Shobab
Nathan	Nathan	Nathan
Solomon	Solomon ("four by Bathshua")	Solomon
Ibhar	Ibhar	Ibhar
Elishua	Elishama	Elishua
	Eliphelet	Elpelet
	Nogah	Nogah
Nepheg	Nepheg	Nepheg
Japhia	Japhia	Japhia
Elishama	Elishama	Elishama
Eliada	Eliada	Beelida
Eliphelet	Eliphelet	Eliphelet

Although anthropologists have used kinship and genealogies in order to analyze societies and determine their economic bases,[14] few studies by either anthropologists or biblical scholars have related their discoveries to the biblical literature. Johnson, Finkelstein, Malamat and Wilson are the exceptions.[15] Of these, Wilson's work has been the most extensive and provides the best basis for further investigations. He compared genealogies from primitive societies with lists and genealogies from Mesopotamia and the Bible, almost entirely Genesis material, in order to illustrate how the similarities in form and function transcend geographic, cultural, and temporal boundaries. Some general conclusions

[14]See J. Goody, *Production and Reproduction* (Cambridge: Cambridge University, 1976).

[15]See M. D. Johnson, *The Purpose of Biblical Genealogies* (Cambridge: Cambridge University, 1969); J. J. Finkelstein, "The Genealogy of the Hammurapi Dynasty," *JCS* 20 (1966) 95–118; A. Malamat, "King Lists of the Old Babylonian Period and Biblical Genealogies," *JAOS* 88 (1968) 163–73; "Tribal Societies: Biblical Genealogies and African Lineage Systems," *Archives européenes de sociologie* 14 (1973) 126–36; R. R. Wilson, "The Old Testament Genealogies in Recent Research," *JBL* 94 (1975): 169–89; *Genealogy and History in the Biblical World* (New Haven: Yale University, 1977).

reached in these studies will facilitate our examination of the Saulide and Davidic materials.

In the first place, genealogies strictly speaking are distinguished formally from lists of ancestral names by the statements of relationship the former contain. Thus, in a genealogy the relationship between the individuals named is stated, but in a list it is not.

Genealogies may be classified as segmented, i.e., those containing segments or "branches" (usually not more than three generations in depth), and linear, i.e., those expressing only a single line of descent and therefore lacking segmentation. Linear genealogies are usually limited to ten or twelve generations, but some such as those in Chronicles are exceptions to this norm.[16]

Genealogies can be oral or written, a difference which depends upon the manner of composition and not upon whether the material is now found in writing. When oral genealogies such as those in the Bible are preserved only in written form, it becomes difficult to determine their original mode of composition although segmentation may be an indication of a former oral mode, even though not all segmented genealogies are oral.

Fluidity, the movement of names onto, within, and off genealogies, is an important common trait. Because of this phenomenon, when lineages are altered or relationships changed, often within a very short time, the fluctuations are recorded by changes in the genealogies. The modifications allow the genealogy to remain functional and "true," otherwise it would become useless and would be forgotten. The feature is especially prominent in oral genealogies because they serve as mnemonics, but it is also found less frequently in written genealogies and lists which have "frozen" their oral predecessors. This characteristic may seem peculiar to students of the Bible who are accustomed to submitting genealogies to endless emendations in order to remove the apparent contradictions that are thought to have crept in through copyist error, textual corruption, or faulty redaction. From the social scientific perspective, many of the would-be discrepancies are instead signs of the life of the genealogy.

Genealogies function in the domestic, politico-jural, and religious or cultic spheres of a society's life and may serve different functions in several spheres simultaneously. As a result, several differing genealogies can be used at the same time in order to represent the relationships that are peculiar to different spheres of life. Since an individual's or group's relative position may vary from sphere to sphere, names may stand in different positions in order to reflect the real situations. In any case, genealogies fluctuate as the relationships within a particular sphere

[16]Wilson, *Genealogy and History*, 9.

change. For example, if a group migrates, its names will probably be dropped from the genealogy of its former region and may be added to one in the new area of residence. Or if the group retains some rights in the original region while gaining others in the new area, its names might appear in genealogies and lists from both areas. Whatever the situation, the genealogies must be kept current or they will no longer serve their intended function and will be lost.

Finally, even though genealogies are not intended to be historiographic sources, once names have been established and recognized by a community as true, a genealogy is presumed to be historically accurate because it reflects the real life situation of rights and statuses in its time. This is especially so if the individual who holds the genealogical knowledge enjoys status and influence within the community for then his recollection will be the one which will be presumed to reflect the existing state of affairs.[17]

The genealogies cited above have been selected for their usefulness in ascertaining the domestic, political, social, and religious relationships of the period under review. They do not include, for the most part, the many references to names where these are merely part of an individual's name (e.g., x, son of y) nor the citation of the exact relationship between individuals (e.g., x *son* of y *daughter* of z) since these are clear in most instances. I have not constructed genealogies where the form is lacking in the text except for the reference to Bathsheba in 2 Samuel 11 and the report of the massacre of Saul's family in 2 Sam 21:7–8, both found within passages that approximate genealogical narrative. The genealogies taken from Chronicles have been excised from longer genealogical sections, but no internal changes in the names or their order have been introduced.

A survey of the material reveals that the genealogies of Saul's house are segmented in the Samuel material and the later work of the Chronicler. This indicates that they were probably preserved orally at first and were used as mnemonics in the domestic and political spheres of the early monarchy. Their form contrasts with the linear genealogies that dominate the reports of the families of Jesse and David in Ruth and 1 Chronicles 2 and the lists in 2 Samuel 3 and 5 and 1 Chronicles 3 and 4. However, segmentation has been preserved in the Davidic records where these portray David as the youngest son of Jesse (1 Chronicles 2) and link him to the house of Nahash, king of the Ammonites, through his "sisters" Zeruiah and Abigail (2 Samuel 17 and 1 Chronicles 2). The association suggests some political connections between the two sides of the Jordan and explains the prominence enjoyed by Abishai, Joab, and Amasa, sons of David's sisters.

[17]See L. Bohannan, "A Genealogical Charter," *Africa* 22 (1952) 307.

The differences between the Saulide and Davidide records reflects Saul's proximity to the tribal period and the absence of centralized bureaucracy during his time as well as the changing situation under David when segmented genealogies were losing their significance as menemonics. The situation is analogous to that revealed in Mesopotamian lists.[18]

Variants are found at nearly every level in the genealogies. In some cases these may be due to intentional copyist adjustments in the post-biblical era, such as the substitution of Michal for Merab in the Codex Vaticanus of 2 Samuel 21, while others no doubt owe to confusion in earlier scribal periods. The shifts that concern us, however, are those that reflect fluidity in the ancient society, a type that is not easily explained by copyist error. Ner appears in 1 Samuel 14 as brother of Kish and father of Abner, but is elevated in 1 Chronicles 8 and 9 to Saul's direct line of descent as father of Kish, while Abner is dropped completely. The segmented genealogy in the first case is from a period before Abner's death and indicates that he, or more probably his father, played an important role in the descent line of Abiel. Had Saul's line been completely truncated, Abner might have been eligible for succession, but once he had been killed for his involvement with Ishbosheth, he was discredited, his memory served no mnemonic function, and his name was forgotten. His father's status, however, had already been assured for reasons not recorded, and so he was promoted to status among Saul's ancestors.

The classic problems surrounding the names of Mephibosheth = Meribbaal and Ishvi = Eshbaal = Ishbosheth (2 Sam 2:8) are evident in the genealogies. The fluctuation in names and positions are both examples of fluidity. Ishvi = Eshbaal moves between second- and fourth-born, perhaps because he was overshadowed by his brothers, while other sons of Saul vacillate between second- and third-born. Mephibosheth also shifts from being son of Jonathan to son of Saul by the concubine Rizpah, but it is impossible to determine in this case whether one or two individuals were involved. If Saul had a son Mephibosheth, then he was probably considered ineligible as a successor because he was born of a concubine. If the individual was actually Jonathan's son, then the rise in status might reflect a time when all other sons had been killed and he was the only surviving link between Saul and the rest of the descendants who were to keep the house alive.

Jonathan's descendants appear to have been more important for these lists than for the narrative material of the Bible. Mephibosheth = Meribbaal was remembered long after his death as were his descendants, some of whom were cited in segmented genealogies which probably

[18]Wilson, *Genealogy and History*, 135.

reflect oral usage. Such recollections suggest that the lineage retained importance within the society and continued to play an influential role even after the rise of David. This information helps us understand David's relationship to Meribbaal and his son Mica(h) recorded in 2 Samuel 9.

The break in the genealogy in 1 Chronicles 9 before Ahaz's name and the change in the name of his son compared with 1 Chronicles 8 are evidence of the manner in which the Chronicler linked originally separate genealogies. The mixing of segmented and linear forms there and in 1 Chronicles 2 are additional indications of the technique of combining materials. A similar process can be seen in the joining of 2 Sam 3:2–5 with 2 Sam 5:14 in order to form 1 Chr 3:1–9.

Jesse's and David's lineages reflect fewer changes and therefore seem to have been more stable although the lists do contain some fluctuations. Eliab son of Jesse (1 Chronicles 2) may have been changed to Elihu, David's brother mentioned in 1 Chr 27:18 as the head of the tribe of Judah. The name of Abigail's son fluctuates between Chileab and Daniel, and she appears as both wife and sister of David, although again Abigail may have been a common name and these may have been two individuals. Shammua's name becomes Shimei in 1 Chronicles 3, and the names of several other sons of David move onto and within the lists of his family. Shimea appears to have been particularly problematic especially when the genealogical lists are compared with narratives containing the names of Shammua (1 Sam 16:6–9), Shimeah father of Jonadab (2 Sam 13:3), and Shimei father of Jonathan (2 Sam 21:21). Elishua, Elishama, Eliphelet, and Elpelet suffer the same confusion, and Jether and Ithra, husband of Abigail, seem to have been the same person. No doubt all these individuals played peripheral roles in the community, so their names were easily confused.

In view of the role she eventually played in the history of the monarchy, the uncertainty surrounding Bathsheba = Bathshua is particularly striking. Only two sources remember her place in the genealogy (2 Samuel 11 and 1 Chronicles 3) although she does appear elsewhere in narrative materials (1 Kings 1–2). Several reasons may be suggested for the apparent slight. First, the names of the wives/mothers were important during David's Hebron years, but they lost significance when the capital was transferred to Jerusalem. The former capital had been governed by family and tribal customs in which position within the group was remembered and administered by genealogies. In polygamous societies where order of birth is difficult to determine or remember, wives of chiefs may be ranked so that only the children of the highest or favorite wife are eligible for succession. Should there be no male heirs from the first wife, her daughters may take precedence over sons of lower ranking wives,[19] or the rights may pass to the second wife and so on. Rights are determined by local rules and customs, and the possibilities are numerous. For example, in some societies only children born after the parent has assumed office are eligible, in others children of non-succeeding males are shed from the eligibility list, and so on.[20] In any case, the wives'/mothers' names were important in Hebron while in Jerusalem the development of the bureaucracy, the increased use of writing which offered others means for recording eligibility, and the sheer multiplication of wives, concubines, and children led to the mothers' names being omitted. The genealogists remembered only that Bathsheba or Bathshua had been the mother of four sons, Solomon being one of them.

A second reason for Bathsheba receiving so little attention was the fact that she was linked with Solomon's success rather than David's. It has been suggested that the Bathsheba episodes are secondary additions to the Court History in 2 Samuel 9–20 and that they were added after Solomon's accession, in spite of the embarrassing implications for David, when it became necessary to justify his inheritance and succession rights as son of David.[21] The fluidity of her name in the genealogies supports such an interpretation.

What other information can be gleaned from a comparison of the genealogies and narratives from this period that will assist in understanding the life of the early dynasty? The predatory and ravishing character of kinship relations in ancient Israel is certainly apparent. But there is also information to be gained that can be used to disentangle the complicated processes of social development that have been compressed, telescoped, and twisted as selected themes have been woven together by the biblical writers.

Societies evolving from segmented tribal egalitarianism (acephalous organization in the jargon of the social scientists) toward monarchic statehood pass through definite, predictable stages. Elman Service identified them as tribes, bands, chiefdoms, and states.[22] Although he has reduced the list by combining tribes and bands,[23] his model has been

[19]T. Earle, *Economic and Social Organization of a Complex Chiefdom* (Ann Arbor: Museum of Anthropology, University of Michigan, 1978) 176.

[20]See J. Goody, "Introduction," in *Succession to High Office* (ed. J. Goody; Cambridge University, 1966) 33–39.

[21]See J. Flanagan, "Court History or Succession Document? A Study of 2 Samuel 9–20 and 1 Kings 1–2," *JBL* 91 (1972) 172–81.

[22]E. R. Service, *Primitive Social Organization* (2nd ed.; New York: Random House, 1962).

[23]See E. R. Service, *Origins of the State and Civilization* (New York: Norton, 1975) 71–103.

widely accepted by anthropologists[24] and has been used effectively as an interpretive aid in several related disciplines such as archaeology and sociobiology.[25]

Even though the stages in social development can be divided for descriptive and analytical purposes, in the course of human affairs the boundaries separating one from the other are less discrete, and characteristics of one phase tend to overlap into the next. Since my purpose is not to determine the chiefly versus kingly traits of Saul or David or Solomon, a topic I have addressed elsewhere,[26] I shall limit the discussion to those factors that help us understand the transitions that are evident within the genealogies.

Internal pressures toward centralized rule move a society in that direction even in the absence of external enemies. The leadership abilities of the "big man" in an egalitarian society evoke positive responses and feelings of dependence from the people until the leadership is stabilized in the role of chiefs. The chief's popular role as redistributor of goods results in a cyclic increase in his power: the more favor he wins by redistributing from his storehouse, the more people depend upon him and are willing to join him in battle, to pay him allegiance in goods and services, and to support his continuation as chief. The more the people depend upon him, the more he can distribute, and so on.[27] The *majlis* of the chief becomes increasingly important as a force for political stability.[28]

David's rise depended upon such acts of largess. Magnanimous gestures are reported throughout his rise: gestures toward his men at the expense of the priests of Nob (1 Samuel 21), toward the distressed, discontented, and debtors at the caves of Adullam (1 Sam 22:1–2), and toward both the Philistines (1 Sam 27:8–12) and his friends and neighbors including the elders of Judah (1 Sam 30:26–31) where the generosity aided individuals and groups whom David would eventually lead. It is especially interesting to note the case of Nabal (1 Samuel 25) for there David took from a sheikhly type after threatening a raid, and once his dominance had been proclaimed through Abigail's gifts, he sealed the relationship by his marriage to Nabal's widow. This illustrates how

[24]E.g., M. Harris, *Cultural Materialism* (New York: Random House, 1979); R. Cohen and E. R. Service, eds., *Origins of the State* (Philadelphia: Institute for the Study of Human Issues, 1978).

[25]E.g., K. V. Flannery, "The Cultural Evolution of Civilizations," *Annual Review of Ecology and Systematics* 3 (1972) 399–426; H. J. M. Claessen and P. Skalnik, eds., *The Early State* (The Hague: Mouton, 1978); E. O. Wilson, *On Human Nature* (Cambridge: Harvard University, 1978).

[26]Flanagan, "Chiefs in Israel."

[27]See Service, *Origins*, 94; Earle, *Economic and Social Organization*, 172, 195.

[28]See Almana, *Arabia Unified*, 176–80.

David's rise was affected by the relationships that appear in the genealogies.

The rise of a leader often includes marriage into another tribe, even into that of an incumbent chief. The community which is satisfied with the generosity of their leader expects that his benevolence will be passed on to his sons. In the absence of male heirs, rights are sometimes passed on through daughters, or more precisely to husbands of daughters (Num 27:1–11; 36:1–2).[29] In David's case, optative affiliation seems to have been employed using Michal as the contact with Saul's family. This phenomenon, first described by Firth[30] and now recognized as a factor in succession and inheritance in a number of societies[31] is the practice which allows newly married couples to choose to affiliate with either parental group usually including a choice of residence.[32] The couple generally elects the family that will bestow the higher status upon them. The practice is a form of adoption that allows the husband to stand in his wife's stead and to inherit from and succeed her father.

David's covenant with Jonathan associated him with the house of Saul as Jobling has indicated and as has been noted above. What has not been emphasized is the fact that David's marriage to Michal, while in residence with her father, placed him in the descent line of Saul. At the time of succession, however, for David to assume office all the eligible males ahead of Michal, including perhaps Abner in the collateral line, had to be rendered ineligible. Optative affiliation creates enormous tension in patrilineal groups because of the competition it encourages among males when an in-law is perceived as intruding into the family domain. In this case, David is portrayed as having played a mostly passive role, but there is reason to suspect that his involvement was more forthright than stated by the biblical writers.

With the help of Abner, Ishbosheth's accession in the North had gone unchallenged, although the Philistine threat forced the new leader to govern from exile (2 Sam 2:8). The situation appeared tranquil on the surface: a weak direct-line descendant held office in exile, a strong independent chiefly leader with estranged ties to the predecessor's house was in power in the neighboring territory, the estranged relation was on good terms with the enemies of the North. The balance was delicate in spite of the apparent tranquility, and it could not last. The obstacles in the way of a "final solution" that would win David the leadership of the North were easily identified. David saw them and set about removing them.

[29]See Gottwald, *Tribes*, 266.

[30]R. Firth, "A Note on Descent Groups of Polynesia," *Man* 57 (1957) 4.

[31]See Service, *Primitive Social Organization*, 162; Earle, *Economic and Social Organization*, 175.

[32]Service, *Primitive Social Organization*, 153.

He had to reclaim Michal as his wife since she held his rights to succession; Abner had to be eliminated so that Ishbosheth's regime would collapse. If these things happened, David could let the Israelites choose him as their leader and then control or remove second-level contenders like Mephibosheth, sons of concubines, grandsons, and others who might prosper to his detriment in the more stable environment he would create. The plan was not complex, and it was easily executed with patience and a willingness to launch a new beginning.

In tribal societies the rise to leadership can be a highly competitive and violent process with contenders continually vying for paramountcy leaving a trail of assassinations, frustrated pretenders, and exiled losers in their wake.[33] The encroachment and usurpation can be so extreme that nomadic groups often relocate in order to find a strong chief. As a result there is an ever-changing balance of power among groups whose unity depends almost completely upon their allegiance to a particular chief.[34] David's competition with Saul, Ishbosheth, and his own sons falls into this category. Supporters followed him, but he was also willing to move to wherever he could find a base of support.

Migration is a convenient means of escaping problems by withdrawing to a remote area far away from the incumbent's authority where a potential leader can demonstrate and develop his skills while creating a power base of his own. Outlying areas also offer an unsuccessful candidate recently defeated in a struggle for paramountcy a way of breaking away from the incumbent's group and of forming an independent chiefdom in a peripheral area. In many instances, the move may bring only a temporary lull in the competition before the exiled individual makes his next attempt at the high office.

Such maneuvers have an effect upon descent lineages and genealogies which are adjusted and changed to reflect the actual social relationships. Structurally, the new leadership gives rise to newly developed genealogical patterns such as conical clans and, related but separate phenomena, *ramage* descent groups.[35]

In societies where the first-born son is expected to succeed his father through primogeniture, second and subsequent sons splinter off from their father's line while still retaining rights within the ancestral house. They begin their own lineage with themselves at the head of the *ramage*.[36] In effect, they form conical clans so that while the father's inheritance and office may pass from him to his first-born, then to the

[33]See Robertson, "Ousting the Chief," and F. Barth, *Nomads of South Persia* (Boston: Little Brown, 1961) 84.

[34]Barth, *Nomads*, 85.

[35]Service, *Primitive Social Organization*, 155.

[36]Ibid., 158.

first-born of the son, and so on, the inheritance and office of the second son are passed down to his offspring rather than reverting to the original line. An individual's relative position in the descent group is ranked and regulated by genealogy.[37] A diagram illustrates the pattern:[38]

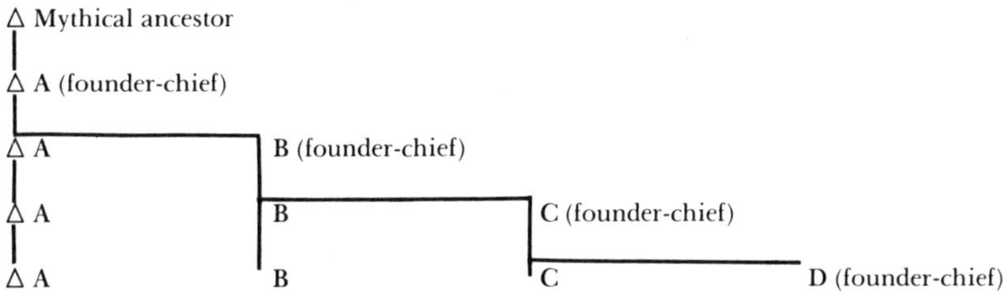

Should a line be truncated by the death of all heirs, a childless marriage, or other causes, the descent moves collaterally. For example, if the grandson of founder-chief A were to die along with the great-grandson, founder-chief B would become eligible to succeed the son of founder-chief A. The matter is usually not so easily resolved, however, because of polygamous marriages, power struggles, and optative affiliation which make the succession lines indistinct.

In David's case, many of the factors found separately in other societies were combined in a way that turned the indeterminacy of succession to his advantage. He had perceived Saul's hostility toward him and had guessed that he would lose in competition with Jonathan for succession to Saul. Grasping the realities of the situation, David withdrew to a remote area outside Saul's immediate domain where he affiliated himself with the enemies of Israel and cultivated a following among other outcasts and the people of Judah. This disparate lot finally elevated him to the leadership of Judah. The records that have been preserved for his family from Hebron indicate that genealogies were being kept orally for his ramage with him at its head and his sons listed in order according to their mothers' position. No attempt was made to link David's Hebron authority to the house of Saul or to his association with the northern court.

When Ishbosheth's incompetence was made obvious by Abner's treasonous negotiations, David insisted that Michal be returned to him, thus reestablishing his kinship ties with the northern house. Once reunited to Michal, it was only a matter of time before Abner and Ishbosheth would fall victims to treachery and the people of Israel would turn to David for leadership.

[37]Earle, *Economic and Social Organization*, 168.
[38]Service, *Origins of the State*, 80.

But the competition did not end with David's accession as ruler of Israel nor with his relocation of the capital in central, neutral Jerusalem. Instead, as in other societies, he became the victim of schemes similar to those that had befallen the house of Saul. Because he reigned in part as a stand-in for his wife and because the leadership requirements were becoming more complex with the expansion of the empire, kinship alone could no longer be the determinant of succession. Optative affiliation usually means that the patrilineal descent from father to grandson is interrupted only in the generation of the daughter whose husband rules in her place, for normally the offspring of that marriage would continue the line of the daughter's father. But because Michal was barren (2 Samuel 6), it was not clear whether the rights should revert to the mother's line, perhaps via the crippled Mephibosheth's son Mica, or to the sons of David by other wives. In the midst of the indeterminacy, struggles that were interfamilial and intergenerational ensued. Mephibosheth assumed that the overthrow of David meant the throne would return to the house of Saul. Absalom assumed that as son of David he was eligible, and Adonijah made the same assumption. Collateral males, Joab and Amasa, and allies, Shimei and Sheba, took sides in the struggles that pitted the house of Saul against the house of David and the generation of David against that of his sons and Saul's grandson. Because Adonijah's pre-mortem succession was supported by individuals who bore Yahwistic names while Solomon's support came from non-Yahwists,[39] we must be cautious when dividing the competitors into established camps. Instead, the internal strife suggests that the selection process continued to be indeterminate as the tribal values were breaking down under the pressure of an emerging bureaucracy.

The review of the events reported in the narratives and of the form and function of the genealogies pertaining to Saul and David supports several conclusions about the founding of the Davidic dynasty. First, the trauma Israel experienced in establishing the dynasty was common for societies undergoing similar rapid development. If this group was unique, it was not because of the problems it faced. Instead, the Yahwists suffered the same treacheries and deceits as have plagued other nations.

Second, in the eyes of his contemporaries, David inherited Saul's office by his marriage, but he held a second office as leader of Judah by a separate claim that did not depend upon his association with Saul or his marriage to his daughter. David won the Judahite office by organizing and maintaining a power base composed of individuals and groups who felt a strong personal allegiance to him. He had been their "big man" and protector; he had been their provider; he had become their redistributor of booty and bounty. As Barth discovered with other peoples

[39]See G. E. Mendenhall, "The Monarchy," *Int* 29 (1975) 168–70.

who search until they find a suitable unifying leader,[40] the Judahites found unity in David who formed them into a cohesive group and led them to nationhood.

Centralized office developed earlier in the North than in the South where David formed his own conical clan and descent group. When he assumed office in the North, he continued his former tasks and did not make any effort to unite the two groups. There is no evidence in the genealogies that suggests David had tried to link his family with Saul's descent line. Instead the two groups continued to harbor contrasting feelings and aspirations, and David continued to play these effectively as checks and balances which helped him to retain his tenuous hold on the North (cf. 2 Sam 19:44; 20).

Third, a single, clear plan for succession had not been determined by the end of David's reign. In the past David had profited from uncertainty, and an indeterminate succession offered him opportunities again. Because of the demands of the leadership role by that time, the office required someone who could maintain the delicate balance between the two groups David headed and someone who, if not acceptable to both groups, could at least retain control by force. The people had gotten one leader who arose as a war lord to unify his followers in battle (Saul). Three had risen by primogeniture, pre-emptive or otherwise (Ishbosheth, Absalom, and Adonijah). One had emerged because of his military prowess, his generosity, and his kinship ties (David). Now they would be led by one who succeeded because his mother convinced his father that he could keep the united kingdoms together (Solomon). The genealogies reflect these struggles, and they enable us to understand the succession patterns in the Davidic dynasty.[41]

[40]See n. 34.

[41]I am indebted to the National Endowment for the Humanities and the American Center of Oriental Research in Amman, Jordan, for awarding me a Fellowship during the Spring semester 1981 in order to pursue research on the monarchy in the Early Iron Age. I appreciate the comments and encouragement of Dr. James Sauer, Director of ACOR at that time. I am also grateful to Professor Jack Goody and his colleagues in the Department of Social Anthropology at Cambridge University for their gracious hospitality and assistance during the Michaelmas Term 1980.

II

Covenant and Law

Enforcing the Covenant: The Mechanisms of Judicial Authority in Early Israel

ROBERT R. WILSON
Yale University

IN 1954 George Mendenhall published two seminal articles that have had a lasting impact on the study of early Israelite law and society.[1] On the basis of a careful analysis of ancient Near Eastern treaties, Mendenhall suggested that the disparate groups composing premonarchical Israel were bound together by a covenant with Yahweh, a covenant having a form resembling that of the Hittite suzerainty treaty. According to Mendenhall, the covenant pattern is most clearly visible in Joshua 24 and in the Decalogue, both of which impose specific obligations on the Israelite vassals of Yahweh. Thus on the basis of Hittite analogies Mendenhall indissolubly linked law and covenant in early Israel. Although the Decalogue cannot itself be considered law in a strict sense because it lacks prescriptions for communal action against offenders, it nevertheless served as a statement of Israelite legal policy and influenced all judicial proceedings.[2] Early Israelite legal processes and specific collections of laws, such as the Covenant code (Exodus 21–23), conformed to the stipulations of the Decalogue for the simple reason that ignoring the stipulations would have been regarded as a breach of the covenant and would have provoked the wrath of Yahweh against the covenant community. Such a threat to communal well-being could not be tolerated, and as a result the community was quick to punish covenant breakers.[3] All laws thus at least indirectly can be considered to have divine sanction by virtue of their covenantal context.

Since the publication of Mendenhall's important articles he has worked out his views in greater detail, and many other scholars have thoroughly explored and debated the concept of covenant.[4] However,

[1]G. E. Mendenhall, "Ancient Oriental and Biblical Law," *BA* 17 (1954) 26–46; "Covenant Forms in Israelite Tradition," *BA* 17 (1954) 50–76.

[2]Mendenhall, "Ancient Oriental and Biblical Law," 28–29.

[3]Mendenhall, "Ancient Oriental and Biblical Law," 31–32.

[4]For a statement of Mendenhall's most recent views, see *The Tenth Generation* (Baltimore: Johns Hopkins University, 1973); and "Social Organization in Early Israel," *Magnalia Dei: The Mighty Acts of God* (ed. F. M. Cross *et*

this scholarly debate has paid little attention to the specific procedures by means of which covenant law might have been applied and enforced in early Israelite society. Mendenhall himself sheds some light on the problem in his discussion of the legal curbs which Israel imposed on the free exercise of blood-vengeance.[5] Yet the basic question of how the covenant was enforced remains to be explored. It therefore seems appropriate in a volume honoring Mendenhall's work to consider in greater detail the mechanism of judicial authority in premonarchical Israel.

I

In every society notions of judicial authority are strongly linked with the society's social structure. For this reason the question of the sources of judicial authority in Israel is an easy one to answer for most of the nation's history. Once the Israelite monarchy became firmly established, the entire social structure gradually conformed to the hierarchically organized political system. Concepts of law and authority in such monarchical systems are reasonably comprehensible and have received a fair amount of study by biblical scholars.[6] In any monarchy politico-jural authority is centralized in the hands of the king, who usually delegates power to those below him in the hierarchy. In governments of this type power flows vertically. Members of the often elaborate bureaucracy perform their tasks with authority derived from the king. In turn the king receives from those below him the political and economic support necessary to sustain the royal court. The judicial system thus operates under the authority of the king, who is typically seen as the guarantor of justice and perhaps even as chief judge. The king establishes and maintains the legal system and enforces judicial decisions through the actual or threatened use of physical force.[7]

Although it is not clear that a royal judiciary of this sort was fully operational during the early monarchical period, there is little doubt

---

al.; Garden City, NY: Doubleday, 1976) 132–51. Recent discussions of the concept of covenant may be found in L. Perlitt, *Bundestheologie im Alten Testament* (Neukirchen-Vluyn: Neukirchener, 1969); and D. J. McCarthy, *Treaty and Covenant* (2d ed.; Rome: Biblical Institute, 1978).

[5]Mendenhall, *Tenth Generation,* 69–104.

[6]See e.g., the treatments of Mendenhall, "Ancient Oriental and Biblical Law," 40–44; G. C. Macholz, "Die Stellung des Königs in der israelitischen Gerichtsverfassung," *ZAW* 84 (1972) 157–82; and K. W. Whitelam, *The Just King: Monarchical Judicial Authority in Ancient Israel* (Sheffield: JSOT, 1979).

[7]For a more extensive discussion, see R. R. Wilson, *Genealogy and History in the Biblical World* (New Haven: Yale University, 1977) 40–44 and the literature cited there.

that after the judicial reform of Jehoshaphat the legal system in Judah was firmly under royal control.[8] According to 2 Chr 19:4–11, Jehoshaphat set up a hierarchical judiciary, the first tier of which consisted of royally appointed judges in all of the fortified cities (2 Chr 19:5). It is not clear whether these justices were supposed to hear all local cases or whether they heard only cases referred from the village courts. However, there is no doubt that these officials derived their authority from the king, who personally commanded them to act justly (2 Chr 19:6–7). The second tier of the judicial system consisted of a high court in Jerusalem, where the king appointed Levites, priests, and family heads to hear religious cases and legal controversies (2 Chr 19:8).[9] Within this high court the chief priest presided over religious matters, while the "prince" (*nāgîd*) of the house of Judah presided over civil cases. The Levites served as court officers (*šōṭĕrîm*) (2 Chr 19:11). The Jerusalem tribunal apparently considered cases referred by the judges in the fortified cities and was not an appeals court for ordinary individuals. The central court was to instruct the local judges so that they would not render a verdict that would incur the wrath of Yahweh (2 Chr 19:10). Like the lower courts, the Jerusalem court clearly operated under the aegis of the king. He appointed the judges and officials, and the head of his own tribe, Judah, was preeminent in matters of civil law. By virtue of the court's location in the capital, the king may also have been in a position to influence judicial decisions and thus to shape the rulings of the lower courts that were advised by the central judiciary. If the covenant played any role at all in the Judean legal system during this period, covenant stipulations were clearly enforced by royal authority, and breaches of covenant were tried and punished by means of a tightly controlled royal judiciary.

Although it is fairly easy to sketch the rough outlines of the royal judicial system, it is much more difficult to uncover the mechanisms of judicial authority during the premonarchical period. Relatively few biblical sources shed any light on the issue, and much of the information that can be recovered comes from a single source: the work of the Deuteronomistic Historian. Furthermore, there are continuing scholarly debates about the precise structure of the social system within which

[8]Whitelam, *Just King*, 185–206; G. C. Macholz, "Zur Geschichte der Justizorganisation in Juda," *ZAW* 84 (1972) 321–40; A. Phillips, *Ancient Israel's Criminal Law* (Oxford: Basil Blackwell, 1970) 18–19; W. F. Albright, "The Judicial Reform of Jehoshaphat," *Alexander Marx Jubilee Volume* (ed. S. Lieberman; New York: Jewish Theological Seminary of America, 1950) 61–82; R. Knierim, "Exodus 18 und die Neuordnung der mosaischen Gerichtsbarkeit," *ZAW* 73 (1961) 146–71.

[9]For a discussion of the textual problem in 2 Chr 19:8, see Whitelam, *Just King*, 199–200.

covenant law functioned. Yet, in spite of all these difficulties scholars have reached a broad consensus on the shape of early Israelite society and on the nature of its judicial system.

It is generally agreed that the basic social unit of premonarchical Israel was the extended family (*bêt-ʾāb*).[10] This group was usually based on genuine blood relationships and was composed of three or four generations of kin who traced their genealogies to a common ancestor four or five generations removed from the youngest member of the family. However, the social functions of the extended family are still a matter for debate. The most comprehensive treatment of this question can be found in the work of Norman Gottwald, who argues that the typical extended family consisted of two or more nuclear families and might easily encompass between fifty and one hundred people. Members of small extended families presumably shared the same house, while members of large extended families were housed in a cluster of individual dwellings. In either case the extended family was a self-sufficient economic unit which was capable of sustaining itself with a minimum of outside help.[11]

Although Gottwald's description of the *bêt-ʾāb* is one that most scholars would accept, recent archaeological research suggests that some modifications may be necessary. Excavations at Tel Masos have uncovered some of the earliest examples of the Israelite "four-room house." These houses, which are to be dated to the middle of the twelfth century B.C.E., are between seventy-two and ninety-six square meters in area and are not connected with each other in any way. By applying standard formulas for calculating the number of people that can be housed in a given floor area, it can be determined that each of these houses sheltered only six or seven people. Excavations at other sites seem to point in the same direction and suggest in addition that each household was virtually self-sustaining.[12]

This archeological evidence is suggestive, but more research must be done before the data can be interpreted properly. However, at this point two possible interpretations suggest themselves. First, each house may represent a *bêt-ʾāb*. If this turns out to be the case, then the "extended

[10]Whitelam, *Just King*, 39; Mendenhall, "Social Organization," 143–44; C. H. J. de Geus, *The Tribes of Israel* (Assen: Van Gorcum, 1976) 134–35; N. K. Gottwald, *The Tribes of Yahweh* (Maryknoll, NY: Orbis, 1979) 285–87.

[11]Gottwald, *Tribes of Yahweh*, 285–92.

[12]For a discussion of the archaeological evidence, see Y. Shiloh, "The Four-Room House—Its Situation and Function in the Israelite City," *IEJ* 20 (1970) 180–90; and F. S. Frick, "Religion and Sociopolitical Structure in Early Israel: An Ethno-archaeological Approach," *SBLASP* 1979, 2.243–44 and the literature cited there. For a discussion of the use of similar techniques in the study of modern villages, see P. J. Watson, *Archaeological Ethnography in Western Iran* (Tucson: University of Arizona, 1979).

family" was considerably smaller than Gottwald and others have previously thought. Second, the houses may be those of nuclear families. If this proves to be true, then it would mean that the nuclear family was a more important part of the social structure than current theories suggest. In addition, the status and social functions of the extended family would remain unclear. If each nuclear family was self-sufficient, then what role did the extended family play in the economy? If the extended family was an important part of the social system, then why has it left no archeological traces? Clearly there is no way to answer these questions without further evidence, but it may be that the lower levels of the Israelite social structure were more complex than scholars have previously thought.

Just as most scholars agree that the *bêt-ʾāb* was the basic Israelite social unit, so they also agree that several *bêt-ʾābôt* could join together to form a *mišpāḥāh,* often translated "clan." However, the precise nature and functions of the *mišpāḥāh* are still unclear. The traditional view, still maintained by some scholars, is that the *mišpāḥāh* was a genuine kinship group composed of *bêt-ʾābôt* tracing their lineages to a common ancestor.[13] Recently, however, this view has been challenged. Because the *mišpāḥāh* and its dwelling place often coincided, Mendenhall has suggested that the next larger social unit after the *bêt-ʾāb* was simply the village, in which unity was based on geographical and cultural proximity rather than on actual kinship.[14] In a similar vein, Gottwald has carefully sifted all of the evidence on the *mišpāḥāh* and concluded that it was a protective association of extended families. Such associations were designed to insure the survival and well-being of their constituent *bêt-ʾābôt* and played an important role in protecting them from military threats.[15] Although both Mendenhall and Gottwald make strong cases against understanding the *mišpāḥāh* as a genuine kinship group, the fact remains that the unity of the *mišpāḥāh,* whatever its basis, is expressed in kinship terms, and the significance of this fact remains to be determined.

Finally, most scholars agree that several *mišpāḥôt* could band together to form a tribe (*šēbeṭ/maṭṭeh*). Although the biblical text describes the tribe as a kinship group, few modern scholars accept this notion. Rather tribal unity seems to have been based on a number of factors, including geographical proximity, common religious and cultural experience, and the need for more military protection than could be provided by an individual *mišpāḥāh.*[16]

[13]De Geus, *Tribes of Israel,* 136–38; Whitelam, *Just King,* 42–44.

[14]Mendenhall, "Social Organization," 143–44.

[15]Gottwald, *Tribes of Yahweh,* 257–84.

[16]Mendenhall, "Social Organization," 144–46; Gottwald, *Tribes of Yahweh,* 245–56.

According to the scholarly consensus, then, premonarchical Israel possessed a four-level social structure. The largest social unit, the nation of Israel itself, was subdivided into tribes, which in turn were composed of protective associations and extended families.[17] By carefully collecting all of the meager evidence on the judiciary in this period, scholars have also agreed that judicial activity took place at all four levels.

At the lowest levels of the social structure, judicial authority resided in the *paterfamilias*, who, at least at one time in Israel's history, apparently held virtually absolute power to control those in his household (see Genesis 31 and 38). Presumably this was true both at the level of the nuclear family and at the level of the extended family, although the two levels are not usually distinguished in the narratives. The right of the *paterfamilias* to enforce family and community customs and laws and to punish legal and covenantal breaches seems to have persisted well into the monarchical period. To be sure, there are laws restricting the power of the *paterfamilias* (Num 5:11–31; Deut 21:18–21; 22:13–21), but these laws are difficult to date, and there is no way of knowing whether or not they were in effect during the premonarchical period.[18]

In the case of disputes between extended families, judicial proceedings took place at the level of the *mišpāḥāh*. Evidence on the nature of such proceedings is difficult to recover, and most scholars therefore draw their information from the reconstruction made by Ludwig Köhler in his classic essay "Justice in the Gate."[19] Although Köhler obtains most of his evidence from the monarchical period, it is usually assumed that his reconstructed picture is also accurate for the pre-monarchical period. According to Köhler, judicial proceedings between members of different extended families took place in the town gate, where the "elders" (presumably the heads of extended families) gathered to hear the arguments between the two individuals involved. Accusations were made, defenses offered, and witnesses heard, and the elders then rendered a verdict.[20]

Evidence for judicial proceedings at the tribal level is almost nonexistent. Gottwald has suggested that perhaps assemblies of "tribal

[17]In the light of the above discussion about the possible importance of the nuclear family, we should perhaps speak of a five-level system: nation, tribe, protective association, extended family, and nuclear family.

[18]Whitelam, *Just King*, 39–42; J. M. Salmon, "Judicial Authority in Early Israel," Th. D. dissertation, Princeton Theological Seminary, 1968, 24–41; J. R. Porter, *The Extended Family in the Old Testament* (London: Edutext, 1967).

[19]L. Köhler, *Hebrew Man* (London: SCM, 1956) 149–75. See also the more recent reconstruction of D. A. McKenzie, "Judicial Procedure at the Town Gate," *VT* 14 (1964) 100–104.

[20]Whitelam, *Just King*, 42–44; Salmon, "Judicial Authority," 41–46; J. L. McKenzie, "The Elders in the Old Testament," *Bib* 40 (1959) 522–40.

elders" were sometimes convened to hear cases referred from local courts, but there is no good evidence for such procedures, and it is therefore likely that the tribe played little role in the Israelite judiciary.[21]

Finally, it has often been alleged that some sort of central judicial authority existed in premonarchical Israel. In recent scholarship this position has been argued most forcefully by Martin Noth, who invokes the list of the so-called minor judges (Judg 10:1–5; 12:7–15) in order to claim that the Israelite amphictyony included the central office of "the Judge of Israel." This official may have been responsible for hearing appeals from lower courts, but it is more likely that he was responsible for interpreting and enforcing the covenant stipulations that bound together the amphictyony.[22] A number of scholars have accepted Noth's thesis that a single national judge had the responsibility of administering Israel's divine law.[23] However, in recent years both the amphictyonic hypothesis and the concept of "the Judge of Israel" have been sharply challenged.[24] Reexamination of the biblical data suggests that there is simply no evidence to support Noth's claim that a central judicial official existed in Israel before the rise of the monarchy. On the basis of the Samuel narratives it might be argued that in some cases individual judges operated within a restricted geographical area, perhaps at the level of the *mišpāḥāh*, but such figures would have had no national judicial functions.[25] If, as some scholars have recently contended, chiefs occasionally functioned in premonarchical Israel at the national level rather than simply at the level of the *mišpāḥāh*, then it might be that such central political leaders also had the same sort of judicial authority exercised by later Israelite kings.[26] However, even if this view should prove to be accurate, these political figures seem to have existed in Israel only for brief periods of time, and their appearance does not argue for the existence of a central judicial office.

On the basis of this outline of the early Israelite judicial system it is possible to draw a fairly clear picture of the loci of judicial authority, but that picture is far from complete. There can be no doubt about the

[21]Gottwald, *Tribes of Yahweh*, 340.

[22]M. Noth, *The History of Israel* (New York: Harper, 1958) 101–103; "Das Amt des 'Richters Israels,'" *Festschrift Alfred Bertholet* (ed. W. Baumgartner *et al.*; Tübingen: Mohr, 1950) 404–17.

[23]Phillips, *Israel's Criminal Law*, 21; D. A. McKenzie, "The Judge of Israel," *VT* 17 (1967) 118–21; Salmon, "Judicial Authority," 221–304.

[24]See, for example, the thorough treatments of De Geus, *Tribes of Israel*; and A. D. H. Mayes, *Israel in the Period of the Judges* (London: SCM, 1974).

[25]Mayes, *Israel in the Period of the Judges*, 55–67; Whitelam, *Just King*, 47–69; De Geus, *Tribes of Israel*, 204–206.

[26]Frick, "Religion and Sociopolitical Structure," 233–53; J. W. Flanagan, "Chiefs in Israel," *JSOT* 20 (1981) 47–73.

source of judicial authority in the lower levels of the social structure. In the family the *paterfamilias* exercised such authority and was presumably responsible for enforcing the covenant stipulations in his own household. At the level of the *mišpāḥāh*, judicial authority resided in the elders or heads of extended families, but the extent of their authority is unclear, for it is difficult to determine how they reached and enforced their decisions. Some scholars seem to envision the process as a kind of representative democracy in which the members of the *mišpāḥāh* granted authority to their representative elders and then agreed to abide by the decisions that they reached.[27] Other scholars have suggested that the *mišpāḥāh* may have had a single political leader capable of enforcing the decisions of the elders. However, if such a figure existed, his power apparently rested on the authority granted to him by the elders.[28] In either case it is not clear how far the elders were able to go in enforcing the covenant law. At the highest levels of the social structure the locus of judicial authority appears to be obscure almost to the point of being non-existent. If one accepts Noth's amphictyonic model, then it might be possible to argue that at the national level individual tribes routinely banded together to punish covenant offences committed by one of the member tribes. However, if one rejects the amphictyonic hypothesis and the national officials that go along with it, then the most one can say is that the tribes' allegiance to the covenant might have prompted them to unite to enforce the covenant stipulations. One might also simply say that at the national level the covenant laws were enforced by divine authority. However, in either case the actual mechanisms of enforcement remain unclear.[29]

II.

It is unlikely that a much more sophisticated picture of Israel's early judiciary will emerge unless new evidence is uncovered. However, it is possible to elaborate the existing picture by bringing some contemporary anthropological evidence to bear on the problem. Although such evidence can only be suggestive and can throw no light on the unique features of the early Israelite judicial system, the comparative material can provide a clearer understanding of how judicial authority is exercised in analogous social systems.[30]

[27]Köhler, *Hebrew Man*, 149–75; McKenzie, "Judicial Procedure," 100–104.

[28]De Geus, *Tribes of Israel*, 206.

[29]Gottwald (*Tribes of Yahweh*, 695–96) holds that Levites had teaching functions throughout Israel and might have also helped to enforce the covenantal laws. However, a more thorough study of the history of the Levites must be made before further conclusions can be reached.

[30]For a discussion of the problems involved in using anthropological material in the study of biblical texts, see Wilson, *Genealogy and History*, 11–18.

The relevance of anthropological evidence is suggested by the fact that the lower levels of early Israelite society were composed of groups based on actual kinship. Furthermore, the kinship metaphor was extended to the upper levels of the social structure, even though the cohesion of these large social units was not based on kinship but on factors such as geographical proximity, common cultural experience, and shared religious allegiances. Social systems of this type which use the language of kinship to describe the interrelation of various social groups are called lineage systems and have been extensively studied by anthropologists. Although discussions of lineages tend to generalize about their structure and functions and to ignore the specific characteristics of individual lineages, such comparative material can still be used safely by biblical scholars as long as their generalizing tendency is recognized.

Because lineage systems use as their structural model the nuclear family (two or more children of the same parent), lineages are formally characterized by segmentation. At the lowest structural level, the minimal lineage, only two generations are involved: parents and their children. However, two or more minimal lineages can be related to each other by claiming descent from a common ancestor in the third generation. The slightly larger lineage thus created can in turn be seen as part of a still larger lineage, and this process could, at least theoretically, be carried on indefinitely. Ever larger lineage groups could be formed, and as a result the whole society would resemble a hierarchy of nesting lineages.[31]

Segmentary lineage systems are marked by a stress on social unity and can often be viewed as corporate entities. Although large lineages are composed of distinct individuals and groups, these individuals and groups perceive themselves to be locked together in a complex web of social relationships. Interpersonal and intergroup linkages may be based on a number of factors, including actual kinship, geographical contiguity, cultural similarity, shared history or religious beliefs, and political or economic dependence. However, group unity is usually expressed in kinship terms and concretized in the form of a genealogy. Lineage members see themselves as a unit over against other lineages and frequently celebrate that unity by joining together in common ritual activities. In turn, outsiders recognize the lineage as a single unit and thus validate the lineage members' own perception of themselves.

Yet, even though lineages emphasize social unity, they also embody tendencies toward disunity and segmentation. Large lineages are composed of individuals and groups related in a hierarchical structure that

[31]For a more thorough analysis of the structural features of lineages, see Wilson, *Genealogy and History*, 18–37 and the literature cited there.

has both horizontal and vertical dimensions. On the horizontal plane, each segment of the lineage is composed of two or more people or groups that regard themselves as individuals who are equal but who are nevertheless linked together in certain social contexts. The normal way of expressing this relationship genealogically is to portray the individuals or groups as children of the same parent. They are separate and theoretically equal social entities but still related through their common ancestor. Horizontal relationships of this sort are likely to be highly fluid as individuals and groups shift their alliances to fit different social contexts. Thus, for example, while two minimal lineages might see themselves as an economic unit distinct from and opposed to other economic units, on ritual occasions the same two lineages might feel themselves to be linked with their economic rivals. On the vertical plane, the "nesting" characteristic of lineages means that some individuals and groups are superior to others in the same lineage. Differences in social status, political and economic power, and religious authority are expressed in genealogical terms by placing people and groups on different levels in the hierarchical system. Seen in this light, lineages embody a principle of inequality that is regularized and controlled within the overall unity of the social system.

Social pressures thus exist in lineages both on the horizontal and on the vertical planes. On the horizontal plane individuals and groups who see themselves united in certain contexts also see themselves as opposed to other individuals and groups, and social friction may develop between the antagonists. On the vertical plane, individuals and groups on the top of the social hierarchy will try to exert their influence on those below them, while individuals and groups at the bottom of the hierarchy will actively resist pressure from their superiors. Normally, strong feelings of overall group unity on the part of lineage members are sufficient to keep both types of social friction in check. However, if pressures become too great, fission will take place, and dissident lineage segments will break away to join other lineages or to establish an independent life.[32]

[32]For general discussions of the operation of lineage systems, see M. Gluckman, "Introduction" to J. C. Mitchell and J. A. Barnes, *The Lamba Village* (Cape Town: University of Cape Town, 1950) 1–19; J. Middleton and D. Tait, "Introduction," *Tribes Without Rulers* (ed. J. Middleton and D. Tait; London: Routledge & Kegan Paul, 1958) 1–31; M. Fortes and E. E. Evans-Pritchard, "Introduction," *African Political Systems* (ed. M. Fortes and E. E. Evans-Pritchard; London: Oxford University, 1940) 1–23; M. Fortes, "The Structure of Unilineal Descent Groups," *American Anthropologist* 55 (1953) 17–41; M. G. Smith, "On Segmentary Lineage Systems," *The Journal of the Royal Anthropological Institute* 86/2 (1956) 39–80; M. Fortes, *Kinship and the Social Order* (Chicago: Aldine, 1969); and M. H. Fried, "The Classification of Corporate

The peculiar structural characteristics of segmentary lineages have a direct impact on their judicial systems. In a large lineage uninfluenced by outside political forces, the mode of judicial procedure normally depends on the level at which the proceedings take place. In the lower levels of the lineage, where social linkages are based on actual kinship, the heads of lineage segments have sufficient authority to enforce the society's laws and customs within their own segments. However, in the case of legal conflict between lineage segments which are related to each other by claiming descent from a fictitious or a dead ancestor rather than from a living one, the judicial process is more complex. Because of the level at which the conflict takes place, no living person is in a position to exercise authority over the disputants. A resolution to the conflict must therefore be sought voluntarily by the people involved, or other members of the society must mediate the dispute in such a way as to preserve lineage unity.

In typical cases of disputes between individuals or lineage segments, the task of mediation is normally performed by the heads of other segments on the same genealogical level. The task of these lineage elders is a delicate one. The disputants usually come to the hearings with the support of their respective lineage segments, so the individuals' quarrel has already polarized the whole lineage to a certain extent. If the mediators attempt to impose a solution that is not acceptable to one of the disputants, then his supporters may not accept the solution, and the result may be a split in the lineage. Similarly, if the mediators impose a solution that is not acceptable to the majority of the society, the society will not bring to bear the social pressure necessary to enforce the decision. The mediators must therefore seek to reach a solution which is perceived as just by all of the parties involved and by the society as a whole.

The task of mediation begins at the very beginning of the judicial process. Most proceedings begin when one individual lodges a formal complaint against another. The complainant asks the lineage heads to hear his case, and they must then decide whether or not the difficulty is serious enough to warrant a trial. If they decide that the tensions between the disputants are not serious enough to threaten the unity of the society or if the elders feel that no wrong has actually been done, they are likely to dismiss the request for a hearing rather than risk

Unilineal Descent Groups," *The Journal of the Royal Anthropological Institute* 87 (1957) 1–29. For detailed analyses of individual societies organized by means of lineage systems, see E. E. Evans-Pritchard, *The Nuer* (Oxford: Clarendon, 1940); M. Fortes, *The Dynamics of Clanship among the Tallensi* (London: Oxford University, 1945); and M. Fortes, *The Web of Kinship among the Tallensi* (London: Oxford University, 1949).

polarizing the society by holding a trial. If, however, they decide that the conflict is potentially damaging to the social structure or that an actual crime has been committed, then they will hold a formal hearing at which both disputants will be present. The hearing is often begun by a ritual stressing the justness of the hearing process and the fairness of the elders. References to justice appear throughout the hearing and are designed to convince the onlookers to accept the final solution to the dispute. Even though the members of the society know that elders are sometimes corrupt, the ideal of justice is still maintained.[33]

During the hearing process itself both disputants are allowed to speak, and both may be questioned at length by the elders, who are usually already familiar with the facts of the case. Witnesses may be called and questioned, and in some instances onlookers may volunteer information. In the case of interpersonal disputes, the elders then attempt to suggest a compromise that will be acceptable to both parties. If the elders are successful, then the dispute ends, and the unity of the lineage is preserved. In criminal cases, the process is more difficult, for the elders must actually determine guilt. If they find a defendant guilty, they must still be sure that their verdict has adequate public support, for it would be difficult to impose penalties if the majority of the society thought the verdict unjust. A standard way of soliciting communal support for a guilty verdict is to invite the defendant to confess his guilt. If he does so, then there is little danger of his lineage segment or the society in general refusing to accept the decision.[34] If the elders feel confident that their verdict will be accepted, then they will impose a penalty. Where there is no prescribed penalty, the elders must again negotiate one which is acceptable to all of the parties involved and to the society as a whole. Once this is done, the judicial process ends, sometimes with a communal ritual expressing the unity which has been restored to the lineage.[35]

It should be noted that lineage elders usually try to avoid involving either the spirits of the dead or the gods directly in the judicial process. Although mediums or diviners are sometimes consulted to determine whether or not a crime or injury to the social structure has taken place,

[33]On this point see J. L. Messenger, "The Role of Proverbs in a Nigerian Judicial System," *Southwestern Journal of Anthropology* 15 (1959) 64–73.

[34]J. C. Vergouwen, *The Social Organization and Customary Law of the Toba-Batak of Northern Sumatra* (The Hague: Martinus Nijhoff, 1964) 350–52.

[35]For extensive discussions of lineage judicial procedures, together with numerous examples of individual cases, see P. Bohannan, *Justice and Judgment among the Tiv* (London: Oxford University, 1957); M. Gluckman, *The Judicial Process among the Barotse of Northern Rhodesia* (Manchester: Manchester University, 1955); *The Ideas in Barotse Jurisprudence* (New Haven: Yale University, 1965); and P. H. Gulliver, *Social Control in an African Society* (London: Routledge & Kegan Paul, 1963).

such procedures are normally kept out of the trial itself.[36] This is so because once responsibility for the verdict is removed from the elders and given to supernatural agents, the possibility of negotiation disappears. The defendant will be judged either guilty or not guilty, and there is no way to appeal a divine decision. Removing the mediating elders from the judicial process increases the likelihood of communal dissatisfaction with the verdict, particularly if the people are not convinced of the ability of the medium or diviner.[37]

However, in some instances judicial appeals to the spirits cannot be avoided. In cases of witchcraft accusation, for example, the spirits must be consulted because by definition humans cannot observe the activities of a witch. Only the spirits can determine the guilt or innocence of the accused.[38] Similarly, certain types of ritual crimes which are committed against the spirits themselves can only be brought to light by consulting the spirits directly. In these cases the elders are likely to try even harder to obtain additional proof of guilt in order to forestall possible communal dissent. They will seek a confession after guilt has been determined, or they will try to devise some other technique to support the accuracy of the verdict.[39]

Because of the large role which communal consensus plays in lineage judicial proceedings, it is easier to reach an acceptable solution when small lineages are involved than it is to obtain a consensus in large lineages. Legal processes therefore become less effective as the size of the lineage increases, and the likelihood of dissension over legal decisions becomes correspondingly greater.[40]

III

If the anthropological data surveyed above is applied to the biblical evidence summarized earlier, then it would suggest the hypothesis that Israelite lineages functioned most effectively at the level of the *bêt-ʾāb*, where the *paterfamilias* could exercise judicial authority directly. In the case of larger lineages, such as the *mišpāḥāh*, where lineage unity was

[36]For a rare exception, see J. Middleton, *Lugbara Religion* (London: Oxford University, 1960).

[37]For a discussion of the interaction between diviners and their societies, see R. R. Wilson, *Prophecy and Society in Ancient Israel* (Philadelphia: Fortress, 1980) 51–62 and the literature cited there.

[38]Wilson, *Prophecy and Society*, 73–76.

[39]Note, for example, the various techniques described in E. E. Evans-Pritchard, *Witchcraft, Oracles and Magic among the Azande* (Oxford: Clarendon, 1937) 21–386.

[40]Gulliver, *Social Control*, 135; M. Gluckman, *Politics, Law and Ritual in Tribal Society* (Chicago: Aldine, 1965) 193.

based on geographical proximity rather than on actual kinship, there was no single individual who could exercise judicial authority. For this reason judicial processes presumably involved the sort of mediation and concern for lineage unity that is apparent in the anthropological data. When lineage unity was achieved, the lineage itself became the source of judicial authority that enforced the covenant law and punished its transgressors. At the next level, the tribe, lineage unity was much weaker, and if similar sorts of judicial proceedings took place at this level at all, they were probably less effective and conclusive than they were in smaller lineages. The same would be true at the national level, where one would expect it to be even more difficult to obtain the necessary communal consensus.

This hypothesis can be tested, at least in a preliminary way, by examining briefly two accounts of judicial proceedings in the premonarchical period: the story of the rape of the Levite's concubine (Judges 19–21) and the story of the sin of Achan (Joshua 7). Both stories are presumably developed forms of earlier accounts, and both clearly betray the hand of the Deuteronomistic Historian, but it would be wrong to conclude that the judicial proceedings recounted in them are simply a reflection of a Deuteronomic judicial system created long after the events being described.

The first story seems to be composed of two elements, each of which may have had an independent life before being combined in the present narrative. The first element, the account of the Levite's experiences, closely resembles the similar story recorded in Genesis 19 and may have been influenced by it. The second element, an account of an Israelite war against Benjamin, may reflect an actual historical event. However, both elements are now highly developed, and Judges 20 in particular has been reworked by the Deuteronomistic Historian.[41] Still, elements of normal judicial procedures are observable in the final shape of the text.

In its present form the story tells of some Benjamites living in Gibeah who rape and kill a Judahite woman from Bethlehem. The woman is the concubine of a Levite, who, at least according to the Deuteronomist's view, had no inheritance in Israel but was under the direct protection of Yahweh (Judg 19:1–26; Deut 18:1–2). Because the crime involves individuals from two different cities (*mišpāḥôt*?) in two different tribes, it could theoretically have been handled in two ways.

[41]For discussions of the literary and tradition history of the passage, see J. A. Soggin, *Judges* (Philadelphia: Westminster, 1981) 278–83; R. G. Boling, *Judges* (Garden City, NY: Doubleday, 1975) 277–79; M. Noth, *Das System der zwölf Stämme Israels* (Stuttgart: W. Kohlhammer, 1930) 162–70; and O. Eissfeldt, "Der geschichtliche Hintergrund der Erzählung von Gibeas Schandtat," *Kleine Schriften* (Tübingen: J. C. B. Mohr, 1963) 2.64–80.

First, the tribe of Benjamin could simply have convened its lineage heads in order to try and punish the men belonging to one of its lineages. Second, the matter could have been handled at the tribal level. The latter course of action is chosen, and the tribes convene at Mizpah to decide how to respond. They hear the testimony of the Levite and decide to punish the malefactors from Gibeah (Judg 20:1–11). However, when the tribes request that the Benjamites hand over the men from Gibeah, the Benjamites refuse, perhaps because the severity of the proposed unified tribal action seems out of proportion to the crime. In any case, the Benjamites' refusal destroys Israel's national unity and escalates into a full-scale war between Benjamin and the rest of Israel. At the same time, the unanimity of the remaining tribes has apparently been shaken by Benjamin's actions, and they seek oracular advice from Yahweh before proceeding with the battle (Judg 20:12–18). When they are soundly defeated, they become even less sure of their course of action; they weep all night and again inquire of Yahweh for instructions (Judg 20:23). The process is repeated yet a third time before the Israelites finally obtain victory (Judg 20:24–28). Still, after the punishment had been carried out, the Israelites regretted the break in the social structure brought about by the ostracism of Benjamin. They therefore seek to repair the breach and restore national unity. This is accomplished first by punishing Jabesh-gilead for not participating in the original battle and then by providing the Benjamites with wives from the conquered city. In addition, the Israelites arrange for the Benjamites to steal wives from Shiloh, and the unity of Israel is restored (Judg 21:1–24).

To be sure this narrative is not concerned with the judicial process, and it certainly cannot be considered a historical account of how the national judiciary worked.[42] Yet the narrative contains traces of two features that are characteristic of judicial proceedings in large lineages. First, because of the large size of the group, consensus on a verdict and on the appropriate punishment is difficult to achieve. Benjamin does not cooperate with the rest of the tribes and actually splits the lineage structure. The men of Jabesh-gilead also do not participate and are finally driven out of the lineage and destroyed. Furthermore, the majority of the Israelites frequently seem unsure of their course of action and repeatedly ask for divine instructions. Yahweh is thus involved in specifying the punishment but not in determining the verdict. Second, the Israelites throughout the story are concerned with maintaining national unity. They lament the ostracism of Benjamin and finally devise a way to reunify the nation.

[42]On this point, see Salmon, "Judicial Authority," 191–221.

In the story of the sin of Achan at least two older narratives have been woven together. Although the main thread of the narrative concerns the conquest of Ai, into this account has been woven the Achan story. The Achan story itself may have been adapted for etiological purposes, but it is doubtful that the story was created simply to provide an etiology.[43] In its present unified form, the whole text now clearly reflects the Deuteronomist's theology of the conquest and his interest in the institution of holy war. Yet, at the same time, the account contains features of lineage judicial proceedings. In this case the crime is cultic. Achan violates the holy war legislation and takes objects devoted to Yahweh. There were apparently no witnesses to the theft, so the people do not know that a crime has been committed until they meet an unexpected defeat in battle. Clearly, the only way to uncover the problem is to inquire of Yahweh directly, and the inquiry reveals the nature of the crime that has been committed (Josh 7:1–12). However, the inquiry also specifies the way in which the guilty party will be identified. The people are to gather before Yahweh and a series of lots cast to locate the thief, who is then to be burned (Josh 7:13–15). This method of determining guilt by oracle is a dangerous one to use in any lineage trial because there can be no doubt that *somebody* will be identified as guilty. There is no possibility of appeal, and the death penalty is specified, so there can be no negotiation about the punishment. In such situations communal dissension over the verdict is likely to occur, and for this reason the elders conducting the trial are careful to do everything possible to obtain popular support for the outcome. Joshua follows these standard procedures in the narrative that follows. The lots are cast as Yahweh had directed, and Achan is duly chosen. Joshua then invites Achan to confess his guilt, and in fact he does so, thus assuring the onlookers that the oracles had been accurate (Josh 7:19–21). Furthermore, he furnishes additional proof of his guilt by describing the hiding place of the stolen goods, something that only the real thief would know (Josh 7:21). The goods are recovered and shown to the people to demonstrate the veracity of Achan's confession (Josh 7:22–23). Now convinced of Achan's guilt and the justice of both the trial and the punishment, they join with Joshua in carrying out the sentence (Josh 7:24). The people stone Achan, and by participating in this communal ritual reaffirm the unity of the lineage (Josh 7:25–26).

[43]For a discussion of the literary and tradition history of the passage, see J. A. Soggin, *Joshua* (Philadelphia: Westminster, 1972) 96–104; M. Noth, *Das Buch Josua* (2d ed.; Tübingen: J. C. B. Mohr, 1953) 43–51; J. Gray, *Joshua, Judges and Ruth* (London: Thomas Nelson, 1967) 80–83; and B. J. Alfrink, "Die Achan-Erzählung," *Miscellanea Biblica et Orientalia* (ed. A. Metzinger; Rome: Pontificium Institutum S. Anselmi, 1951) 114–29.

Again it is difficult to argue that this story is an accurate historical record of typical judicial procedures in early Israel, although it diverges enough from standard Deuteronomic judicial procedures to rule out the possibility that it is the creation of the Deuteronomists (cf. Deut 17:2–13). However, the similarities between the biblical account and the anthropological descriptions of lineage judicial procedures do suggest that at least some of the biblical writers were familiar with such procedures. If so, then in early Israel judicial authority above the level of the family may well have lain in the complex interactions of the Israelite segmented lineages.

Covenant in Narratives from Late OT Times

DENNIS J. MCCARTHY, S.J.
PONTIFICAL BIBLICAL INSTITUTE

DISCUSSION of covenant as an element in Hebrew religious and social structures has concentrated on the pre-exilic period.[1] This was indeed the more creative period in which distinctive features of Yahwist religion and society received their direction. However, it is not the whole story. The post-exilic transition to a new world did not merely pass *en bloc* forms solidified earlier. New events and new ideas modified the forms in transition, and a relatively complete view of covenant before our era must take into account these modifications or present an unreal unity.

One may admit this in theory but protest that in practice our material is too narrow to answer the essential questions, for this study confines itself practically to Ruth, Jonah, Esther, Daniel 1–6 and, from the apocryphal (deutero-canonical) books, Tobit, Judith, Greek Esther and 1–2 Maccabees. I exclude the Greek addition to Chronicles–Nehemiah, 1 Esdr 3:1–5:6, as a wisdom debate and 4 Maccabees as a diatribe. Neither is narrative. 3 Maccabees, indeed, is narrative but it is so derivative (compare the Heliodorus episode in 2 Maccabees) as to offer us nothing of value. Of course, the largest block of post-exilic narrative, Chronicles–Nehemiah, cannot be ignored, but I have treated it fully

[1]So Mendenhall *Law and Covenant in Israel and the Ancient Near East* (Pittsburgh: The Biblical Colloquium, 1955 = *BA* 17 [1954] 26–46, 49–76), a classic indispensable for understanding the relation of covenant to law, and W. Beyerlin *Herkunft und Geschichte der ältesten Sinaitraditionen* (Tübingen: J.C.B. Mohr, 1961) look especially to Exodus; K. Baltzer, *The Covenant Formulary* (Oxford: Blackwell, 1971) covers even Qumran but always with a view to a single form whose origins go back to early times; D.J. McCarthy, *Treaty and Covenant* (AnBib 21A; 2d ed.; Rome: Pontifical Biblical Institute, 1978) treats Exodus through 1 Samuel; and E. Kutsch, *Verheissung und Gesetz* (BZAW 131; Berlin: De Gruyter, 1973) and L. Perlitt, *Bundestheologie im Alten Testament* (WMANT 36; Neukirchen-Vluyn: Neukirchener Verlag, 1969) treat covenant as a *religious* concept as a phenomenon of the later but still pre-exilic Deuteronomic movement.

elsewhere.[2] Here I shall depend on this and merely call on my earlier conclusions to develop the argument. At the outset I merely note that this last collection of books shows a vital feeling for covenant based on a tradition of covenant renewals. They kept a tradition alive, but even in Ezra–Nehemiah it is becoming confused and weakened.

The restriction to narrative material for the largest part is methodological. Our information about pre-exilic covenant comes from elements contained in narratives. Since the language, age and genre of a piece have such influence on its content, it is proper to investigate in the first instance the same content in different periods through the same genres insofar as this is possible.[3] Indeed, the problems with the chronology of other sources, Psalms and the like, are so great that they are hardly available as evidence for historical development, which must depend on firm dates. As it is, we can work with a block of Semitic material firmly fixed in the 4th–3rd centuries and another, mostly Greek, from the middle of the second century B.C.E. We know where we are in time. Interestingly, all the sources share many pertinent features, even that part which is closer to Chronicles–Nehemiah in time and so might be expected to differ. With regard to the non-narrative materials, what turns out to be important is that they confirm and even explain the conclusions indicated by our narratives.

However, we must return to the question of genre for a moment. I insist on comparing narrative with narrative, but what sense does this make? While Genesis, Exodus, Deuteronomy, Joshua, and Samuel, our principal older sources, are narratives, they are very different from our material. They are very large narratives—would that the word saga had not been cut off for us by its misuse for German *Sage*!—with some claim to be historical, to tell of things with an origin or at least a connection with real events. Our material is mostly short and tightly organized narrative. It is also fictional. Ruth, Jonah, Tobit, Judith and Esther are frankly novelle of various kinds, and Daniel 1–6 is a collection of folktales. Even 1–2 Maccabees are a kind of history new in Hebrew writing, as edifying and pathetic as possible on the Hellenistic pattern.[4] Ruth as a novella sets out to show God's support for loyalty, a wisdom motif,[5]

[2]"Covenant and Law in Chronicles–Nehemiah," *CBQ* 44 (1982) 25–44.

[3]See T. Hawkes, *Metaphor* (The Critical Idiom; London: Methuen, 1972) 80–92, on the close relationship between manner of speech and the thing spoken of. He gives abundent references. However, his nominalist *identification* of word and reality is obviously to be rejected.

[4]See M. Hadas, *Hellenistic Culture* (New York: Columbia University, 1959) 126; D. S. Russell, *The Jews from Alexander to Herod* (The New Clarendon Bible, OT, vol 5; Oxford: Oxford University, 1967) 185–86.

[5]O. Kaiser, *Introduction to the Old Testament* (Oxford: Blackwell, 1975) 192; O. Eissfeldt, *The Old Testament: An Introduction* (Oxford: Blackwell, 1966)

but with deep roots in covenant tradition. Jonah is a legend using *Märchen* motifs to illustrate the conflict between human desires of prophets and demands of divine office.[6] Daniel 1–6 are exemplary tales showing the mastery of God and the fundamental importance of fidelity to him. Tobit, Judith, and Greek Esther (Hebrew Esther combines nationalism with an etiology for Purim) are also novelle marked by motifs from the court history and especially the Greek romance with its use of famous names, pathos, sudden providential interventions, "documents" where possible (contrast Hebrew with Greek Esther), and love interest. In its small way even Susannah meets the definition.[7] There is plentiful use of folklore motifs: for example, prowess from the seemingly weak (Judith, Esther), the splendors of court (Esther), the "grateful dead" (Tobit), the traduced wife and the young but wise judge (Susannah).[8] Tobit, obviously, and even Hebrew as well as Greek Esther show wisdom influence. Of course all these different elements are used to produce polemic against the enemies of the true God.[9] And so all these novelle are exempla showing that God's will will be done and that the virtuous life is the good life.[10]

Indeed, the choice of the basic form, the novella, is significant here. It means concentration on particular, unconnected episodes with no real attempt to give an historical overview within which the particular has meaning. The contrast with the sprawling accounts of the Pentateuch and the Former Prophets is striking—and an example of the way form of expression affects content. The tightly-plotted novella cannot be all-inclusive as the story cycle can. The contrast is more than literary too: the older literature was engaged in showing Yahweh guiding all history and community so that long narratives and legal collections came together easily enough. For the post-exilic writers the theological point was already a given, not something that needed illustration in an ongoing account of divine guidance of history. So also God's guidance is already manifest in the given law, to be read and interpreted, not to be

---

481. The legal action described in Ruth 4:1–12 is important not just because it is unique in the OT but also because it is an early example of developing interest in legal details.

[6]Kaiser, *Introduction*, 195; Eissfeldt, *Introduction*, 405.

[7]See Hadas, *Hellenistic Culture*, 128, 181; R. H. Pfeiffer, *History of New Testament Times with an Introduction to the Apocrypha* (New York: Harper, 1949) 199. The tale also has some characteristics of the "court history": M. Hengel, *Judaism and Hellenism: Studies in their Encounter in Palestine in the Early Hellenistic Period* (2 vols.; Philadelphia: Fortress, 1974) 30, 101.

[8]Pfeiffer notes the folklore elements in his discussions of each of the novelle.

[9]So, for example, Greek Esther, Judith: Hengel, *Judaism*, 112.

[10]For the exemplary tale see Pfeiffer, *History*, 197, 199; Russell, *The Jews*, 191; J. Bright, *A History of Israel* (2d ed.; London: SCM, 1972) 426.

discovered as history was experienced and reflected upon. The world view was a given, and one told gripping or moving tales to illustrate this for the life of the individual.

This, of course, raises problems for our method. We concentrate on narrative to have comparable sources of evidence. Yet the narrative modes are so different. Can we compare them profitably? I believe we can and we must. Narrative is an over-arching genre, historically one of the three categories which together with lyric and drama embrace all literature. This historical fact shows a real intuition, but it is not the basis of argument here. Rather, we must realize that empirically narrative is a continuum moving from the all-embracing unity of mythic epic which expresses a whole culture toward ever-greater differentiation as fiction (romance) is distinguished from fact, particular truth (account of an event) from general (didactic inculcation of principle through tales) and so on, but narrative always remains narrative.[11] This is more easily seen by a look at contrasts. Narrative retails an event, not, directly, an idea. In the OT a law would be a contrast: it is about a possible event, to be sure, but it is not concerned with recounting the actual event but with telling what is right to think and do in case of such an event. Again, narrative is ostensibly about events and not feelings or reactions. Contrast the love of the law expressed in so many ways in Psalm 119 and the account of the progress of a case in Ruth 4.

Narrative, then, tends to recount events and their interconnections, not expound ideas or express emotion directly. But it has many different modes—some more, some less objective, some factual, some simulated factual, some frankly unrealistic—but still the parts are not irrevocably separated. Older, all-inclusive narrative could include a brilliantly plotted novella like the Joseph story, along with dull lists of ancestors and descendants. It uses traditional folklore motifs even when dealing with historical events. All this sounds like our literature, plotting, use of traditional motifs, constructed lists. Ours is not on so vast a scale, but shares much with the older writings. In sum, narrative literature uses indirection (event) instead of exposition or emotional expression to make its point and so as a genre forms a unity whose members are comparable. Further, when it is didactic as ours is, it must have realistic elements. No one learns from what is totally foreign to the realities of experience. Thus even this fictional mode must reflect the real. Hence its validity as a source of information about covenant, among other things.

But what information? Even the word covenant is rare. After being quite frequent in Chronicles-Nehemiah, ברית disappears from our

[11]See R. Scholes and R. Kellogg, *The Nature of Narrative* (New York: Oxford University, 1966) chaps. 1–3; Northrop Frye, *Anatomy of Criticism* (Princeton: Princeton University, 1957)—stimulating but with less empirical backing than Scholes and Kellogg.

Hebrew sources, Jonah, Ruth and the Hebrew in Daniel 1–6 (it does make a modest reappearance in Hebrew Daniel after chap. 6). It would appear that the simple word usage is conforming to what Chronicles-Nehemiah shows: a growing confusion about ברית and an inexactness in its application. The development seems to have gone on until the word almost disappeared; words and realities are correlative. διαθήκη is in little better case. It appears in Jdt 9:13, Wis 18:22, 23 times in Sirach, 10 times in 1 Maccabees and 3 times in 2 Maccabees. Not a high yield at all.

Moreover, in our literature διαθήκη is very hard to distinguish from law, a totally fixed code of conduct. Conventionally one translates it "covenant," but often "rules" would come closer to the feel of the word. It is the law, "commandment," as it is commonly expressed, which, for example, guides Tobit's life (1:12; 5:14), though he is devoted to his people as the people of God. The law is what he wants others to follow (4:5; 6:13; 14:9), for it is the guide to goodness which means justice and prosperity (Pr Azar 29; Tob 3:4–5; 6:13; Jdt 5:18). Instead of destroying Daniel, fidelity to "the law of his God" (דת אלהה 6:6) confounds his enemies who tried to use it against him. Guarding the law is a major object of the Maccabean revolt.[12] The law has many excellencies: it comes from the prophets (2 Macc 2:2), it offers malediction or benediction like the Deuteronomic covenant (2 Macc 3:1; 5:19–20; 10:38), it is promise and salvation (2 Macc 2:17–18) and it is fixed, sure, a book (e.g., 1 Macc 1:56-57; 3:48) open to all.[13] Maccabees even hints at halakhic interpretation regarding the sabbath, sacrifices, fasting and suicide, the beginnings, in other words, of the procedure by which later Judaism adapted its fixed law to new circumstances.[14]

More telling for our argument, perhaps, than this direct adulation of law is the application to the keeping of the law of expressions strictly connected with covenant thought. They are not just names but evocative traditions which should call something of older covenant concepts to mind and only through them the law proper. Pr Azar 34 appeals to the covenant in parallel with the divine name so dear to *the* covenant book, Deuteronomy, and v 35 appeals for ἔλεος, probably חסד, which in such contexts meant convenantal associations. In Dan 9:4 every word is from Deuteronomy: שמר הברית והחסד לאהביו. Jdt 7:28 calls on heaven and earth

[12]For example, 1 Macc 2:19–27; 10:14. Discussion in B. Renaud, "La loi et les lois des livres des Maccabées," *RB* 68 (1961) 39–67.

[13]See J. Swetman, "Why Was Jeremiah's New Covenant New?" VTSup 26 (1974) 111–15.

[14]A. Oppenheimer, "Oral Law in the Books of Maccabees," *Immanuel* 6 (1976) 34–42; perhaps the process is already found in the rules of endogamy in Tobit: J. Gamberoni, "Das 'Gesetz des Mose' im Buch Tobias," *Studien zum Pentateuch: Kornfeld Festschrift* (ed. G. Braulich, O.S.B.; Vienna: Herder, 1977) 227–42.

as witnesses (μαρτυρόμεθα); elsewhere these are always witnesses to covenant. Judith keeping the law walked in the straight path of . . . God (13:20: ἐπ᾽ ἐθεῖαν πορευθεῖσα ἐνώπιον τοῦ θεοῦ ἡμῶν) just as the parenesis for the Deuteronomic covenant demanded. Finally, Tobit uses the Chronicler's formula for covenantal union with God: "If you turn (ἐπιστρέφητε) to him . . . then he will turn (ἐπιστρέφει) to you (13:6)," to encourage following the law.

Then there is the language which comes out of the Deuteronomistic History with its basis in covenant. Add Esth 10:9 (Rahlfs 10:3^{f}—the references which will be used for Greek Esther from now on): καὶ ἐρρύσατο κύριος ἡμᾶς ἐκ πάντων τῶν κακῶν τούτων, καὶ ἐποίησεν ὁ θεὸς τὰ σημεῖα καὶ τὰ τέρατα τὰ μεγάλα, ἃ οὐ γέγονεν ἐν τοῖς ἔθνεσιν might speak of the old covenant rather than a law-abiding people: see Hag 2:5, "The word which I covenanted with you when you came out of Egypt." ἡσύχασεν ἡ γῆ Ιουδα, 1 Macc 7:50, equates the proponent of the law, Judas Maccabeus, with a judge in an Israel faithful to the covenant, and 7:37, Σὺ ἐξελέξω τὸν οἶκον τοῦτον ἐπικληθῆναι τὸ ὀνομά σου ἐπ᾽ αὐτοῦ uses a favorite Deuteronomistic expression for Zion and the temple, here to be defended by obedience to the law (cf. 1 Macc 2:19–20). Indeed, even those who believe that the late Jewish Pentecost was a covenant feast must admit that in their own arguments the feast turned on a pledge to the law, not on a personal and community pledge of relationship to the Law-Giver.[15] The language is all very covenantal, but the stress is not on a personal union with God and community but rather on the rules, which in the old days were merely the means to define the union.

Scholars commonly explain that the concentration of the cult in Jerusalem was a major, if not the major force compelling this emphasis on law. The Diaspora groups, unable to join in the official worship and so proclaim their religious identity, could display their convictions by studying and living a special set of rules.[16] So their lives centered on the law inscribed in the sacred books.

There is surely considerable truth in this, but in itself it is over-simplistic. It ignores the strong feeling of identity which a central feature, a person, or a place felt somehow especially close to divinity can give a religious group, though most of its members never come near the central feature. St. Peter's with its services is a real center for people who never see it and cannot really imagine it. An unusual unity of religio-national feeling centered on the divine emperor of Japan among a people who never saw or heard him. Even so odd a figure as the Agha

[15]See, for example, M. Weinfeld, "Pentecost as Festival of Giving the Law," *Immanuel* 8 (1978) 7–18.

[16]As Tobit did; see Gamberoni, "Buch Tobias," 234–37; J. Bright, *History*, 432; D. S. Russell, *Between the Testaments* (London: SCM, 1960) 47.

Khan, completely separated from his group in space, in culture, in feeling, is a focus of unity for a sect.

To underplay and even disallow the *possibility* of the temple cult's being an inspiriting, an identity-giving force, though it be known only in story and song, is to overlook a very real possibility which 2 Maccabees by itself shows to have been present in Judaism.[17] So, when John Bright notes that the post-exilic temple cult was paid for by alien rulers, he seems to conclude that this made the cult center less important, though it placed the immediate responsibility for the Yahwist cult on the Jewish community as such.[18] Possibly, but though less "official" in the sense of dominant because of political power, such immediate responsibility is usually more meaningful to a community than ceremonies supplied from above. The "community" temple should have invited a more vital, personal involvement than the old rites of the royal chapel of the Davidides, and this in the emotions of the whole community—all Jews and not just Judaeans.[19]

This is not to return to old-fashioned reconstructions of a "covenant feast" or the like, nor is it to deny that that concentration on Jerusalem had some of the effects ascribed to it. It is to warn against a simplistic view. A distant center is not necessarily an unreal center. In fact, what seems to have been effective was not a remote center of worship but a new attitude toward worship. It no longer demanded a real assent to covenant as a center of religion. Rather, in Bright's words: "Law no longer regulated affairs for an already constituted community . . . . Originally the definition of action on the basis of covenant, it itself became the basis for action, virtually a synonym for covenant and the sum and substance of religion."[20] Or, as Hengel puts it, ". . . the history of God with his people rested on a covenant . . . but the idea of the ontology of the law had taken hold among the majority." That is, the law is an eternal, uncreated absolute.[21] That is, instead of being first a person (community) to person pledge to a God whose wishes then

[17]See too Eissfeldt, *Introduction*, 598.

[18]Bright, *History*, 437.

[19]Bright, *History*, 447, points to the unity of this larger community; and see especially G. Widengren, "The Persian Period," *Israelite and Judaean History* (eds. J. Hayes and J. M. Miller; London: SCM, 1977) 489–538. For the feeling for the temple see, besides 2 Maccabees, Tob 1:3–8 (Diaspora) and Sir 7:29–31; 35:1–11 (Palestinian *and* Egyptian).

[20]*History*, 433.

[21]Hengel, *Judaism*, 305 with n. 293; Russell, *The Jews*, 117; on the law as a quasi-self-existent absolute see J. Bonsirvan, *Palestinian Judaism in the Time of Christ* (New York: McGraw-Hill, 1965) 80, and note biblical texts like Ps 119:89, 160; Sir 16:26–17:24.

became one's own, the first step in thought and action was a pledge to the law.

Some of this may be apparent in the "rubrics." The post-exilic codification in Leviticus is concerned with the proper carrying out of rites, especially sacrifices. Contrast Exod 24:3–8, where the mode of sacrifice is taken for granted and the meaning, covenanted union, is emphasized. Perhaps too the emphasis on expiation in *all* sacrifices after the exile had its influence. A community which so "paid its debt," restored its standing each day, could come to feel less and less a need for occasional massive covenant renewal. Finally, the stress on the splendor of worship, the singing, the magnificence of the priestly paraphernalia (cf. Sir 50:1–21), the sheer number of offerings, could be an authentic religious experience, but the present magnificence could obscure the salvific and covenantal events which were the original occasions of Israel's feasts.

Of course, this implies that in earlier times covenant in one form or another was central to worship, even if it was not the object of an annual feast or whatever. Still, it was kept before the worshipping community. Most striking evidence of this is the exchange of pledges between God and people in Deut 26:17–19:

> Today you are making this agreement with the LORD: he is to be your God and you are to walk in his ways and observe his statutes, commandments and decrees, and hearken to his voice. And today the LORD is making this agreement with you: you are to be a people peculiarly his own, as he promised you; and provided you keep his commandments, he will then raise you high in praise and renown and glory above all other nations he has made, and you will be a people sacred to the LORD your god . . . (NAB)

This is cultic: note the Deuteronomic liturgical "today," that is, present cultic experience and not mere memory. Then there is the "lyric" in Exod 19:3b–8 built on cultic language and so showing the familiar tie between covenant and cult. Bright is quite right to speak of covenant as an ongoing pledge,[22] though we may not know exactly how covenant was kept alive in the cult. Still, it is sure that times of crisis, when covenant was felt to be broken or when the covenant society was threatened, called for covenant renewal.[23]

The decline of covenant from this central position can be seen in tracing the trajectory whose beginning we see in Chronicles–Nehemiah.

[22]*History*, 443.

[23]On the connection of covenant renewal with crises, including changes of king, see D. J. McCarthy, "Compact and Royal Ideology: Stimuli for Covenant Thinking," *Studies in the Period of David and Solomon and Other Essays* (Tokyo: Yamakawa–Shuppansha/Winona Lake: Eisenbrauns, 1982); "Covenant and Law in Chronicles–Nehemiah," *CBQ* 44 (1982) 41–43.

In Chronicles the form for describing the rite of covenant renewal is clear and firm, and the result is a general renewal of the covenant pledge, the commitment to community and personal fidelity to the God of covenant. In Ezra–Nehemiah the post-exilic tradition is already enfeebled. The literary form describing covenant renewal becomes confused and repetitious. The object is not general renewal, but, assuming the general commitment without expressing and so reinforcing it, the concern is rather with particular stipulations and transitory problems. The rubrics for covenant renewal in Ezra–Nehemiah are not clear. They have been adapted to the peculiar situation of the times, not to deal with the relation between God and people as a whole. The rite is dying, and by the end of the second century it is quite dead, a matter for history and not religious practice. We shall return to demonstrate this, but right now our problem is still the relation between temple and the new emphasis on law.

It was the change in cultic practice as we have outlined it which was really significant here. It changed the feeling for covenant. Renewal kept alive the feeling of a personal commitment, a feeling which could have been shared from afar. Analogously, Deuteronomy expects the people to feel the force of the Sinai covenant experience over a six-century interval. But now there was no concrete action to keep the feeling alive.

Hence the need to find a replacement for the "cultic present" to keep the feeling and with it Judaism alive. However, the genius of the old covenant religion lay in the personal tie to the divine which created the larger atmosphere in which law could be lived in varying circumstances. If it were to be true to itself, Judaism needed to renew this tie, not merely find identifying signs like sabbath and circumcision enforced by law.

In part it solved this problem by internalizing law as wisdom. We have seen that for Tobit, Judith, and Azariah the law produces the results proper to wisdom—just treatment and prosperity. Law is actually tied to wisdom in Tob 4:5–19; 11:6–11; 13:8–11; Jdt 8:14–16, and fidelity to it is even identified with σοφία and σύνεσις in Jdt 8:29. 2 Macc 6:12 recognizes that law is for instruction, discipline, πρὸς παιδεῖαν, that is, law performs *the* basic office of wisdom. The "theoretician" Sirach makes it explicit in the paean to wisdom in 23:1–23.[24] This catches some of the personal character of covenant as a union expressed in life by following the Lord's guidance. However, it is not a union based on the pledge of a community united to God through covenant making or renewal as described in Deuteronomy, the Deuteronomistic History, and Chronicles–Nehemiah. It has rather the character of personal virtue, the result of the wise man's care and personal application. Still the move

[24]See the comments of Bright, *History*, 435–37, and Russell, *The Jews*, 116.

was shrewd. Even without the old emphasis on covenant the law was something internal, something one chose and grew in, not simply an impersonal decree. Further, this wisdom was still the law given by God who came to save a chosen people (Jdt 5; 7:28; Sirach extolling law *and* remembering God's acts: 44–50; 1 Macc 2:27; 2 Macc 2:17–18). The older idea of a law given personally by God, even if not formally covenantal and so a law "negotiable," changeable, was not irrevocably suppressed.

Another move reinforced this. Older religion had emphasized the saving deeds of Yahweh. These were not forgotten, but they were felt as realities more easily when they were made present again in liturgical action, the aspect of cult so strongly stressed in Deuteronomy but much older than that book. One re-enacted the "booths" of the wilderness, the Pasch, etc. When, for whatever reason—and we have suggested some above—they became largely stories while the cult became a magnificent spectacle, they might still be felt deeply, but the read word is distancing compared to the immediacy of action.[25] So one sought immediacy by emphasis on the omnipresent God (Psalm 139) and his attributes. Perhaps popular Greek philosophy was at work here too, but we are concerned with the religious effects, not causes. For whatever reason, one stressed that God was the Most High (עליא; Dan 4:31). He is παντοκράτωρ, "the Almighty."[26] He is eternal: ὁ ζῶν εἰς τοὺς αἰῶνας (Tob 13:2), ἀεί (Add Esth 8:12^{d}). He is of the heavens: אלהי השמים (Jonah 1:9), ὁ θεὸς τοῦ οὐρανοῦ (Jdt 5:8; 6:19). He is, then, entirely transcendent but not set apart, indifferent to the cosmos like Aristotle's prime mover, for example, for he is creator: אשר עשה את־הים את־היבשה (Jonah 1:9), κτίσης (Jdt 9:12; 2 Macc 7:23), and that by his mere word: εἶπας, καὶ ἐγενήθησαν (Jdt 16:14). He is also lord of all, δεσπότης (Tob 8:17; 2 Macc 5:20; 15:22), δεσπότης τῶν οὐρανῶν καὶ τῆς γῆς (Jdt 9:12), who sees all, τα πάντα κατόπτων (Add Esth 8:12^{d}). Even non-Jews recognize his sovereignty: in Dan 2:47 Nebuchadnezzar calls him אלה אלהין ומרא מלכין, "God of gods and lord of kings," in 6:27b Darius acknowledges his שלטנה, "dominion," and in Bel 5 he has lordship (ἔχοντα . . . κυριείαν) because he is the living God who according to Daniel created all things, a claim Cyrus implicity accepts when, after Yahweh's opponent, Bel, fails a typical folklore-type test, he turns the "god" over to Daniel's revenge. He has, then, all power, but he is not mere power. His power and greatness are principally shown in his mercy: Jonah 4:2 אל־חנון ורחום; Pr Azar 42—τὸ πλῆθος τοῦ ἐλέους σου (see also Tob 3:4; 8:17; Jdt 13:14; 1 Macc 4:24; 2 Macc 2:7). He consoles (2 Macc 7:6, παρακληθήσεται), intervenes, and saves (Jdt 8:17;

[25]On this see the remarks with references in Hawkes, *Metaphor*, 26–29.

[26]12 times in Maccabees, 5 in Judith; discussed in S. Fujita, "Temple Theology in the Second Book of Maccabees," *The Bible Today* 64 (1973) 1068.

9:11; Add Esth 10:3[f]; 1 Macc 4:30; 2 Macc 8:26; 12:6, σώζειν). Even when real evil arouses his proper anger (Jdt 8:8; 9:9; 2 Macc 5:17) he does not merely chastise. His punishment is discipline to teach his people and even Nebuchadnezzar (Daniel 4). His mercy thus knows discipline, that very positive element in the wisdom tradition, to be a good necessary for weak mankind.[27]

Such a God, all powerful but merciful and concerned, could easily be the object of a personal relation, a piety. He could be called "father" in ordinary prayer (as opposed to royal psalms and the like) in Tob 13:4, something unheard of in the older parts of the OT. Such piety, a very personal relationship to God *could* be a surrogate for the personalism of covenant and carry no trace of legalism. This God could be loved. The trouble is, we think of this as a highly individual emotion, as it probably was for the lonely Jew among strangers. Indeed, it is Tobit, a man apart from and misunderstood by his very Jewish neighbors, who is a model of this "new" piety which stood in for the personal relationship with God which covenant had given. Thus Tobit urges legal purity on all, but his urgings keep turning into exhortations to virtues like charity, chastity, and prayer, elements of piety beyond the merely legal.[28] Other texts stress a further element, trust: in Daniel the three young men exemplify it (התרחצו; 3:28), and without an encouraging word from anyone Judith faces trials with perfect trust in a loving God.[29] Indeed, her story is a link with the old tradition of "the God who acts," the God who initiated covenant, for it reflects the exodus story with an added emphasis on trust because as a woman she is a greater example of the virtue in a world where physical strength has been made to seem all-important.[30] Another element in this piety is humility. The humble (ταπεινός: Jdt 9:11; Add Esth 1:1[k]; 14:17[k]; 1 Macc 14:14), he who bends the knee (Jdt 6:18; Add Esth 4:17e) is protected by the Ruler of the World. This is a touch closer to a line of covenant thought. It represents something of the proper

[27]2 Macc 6:16, and see A. Jaubert, *La notion de l'alliance dans le judaisme aux abords de l'ère chrétienne* (Patristica sorbonensis, 6; Paris: Seuil, 1963) 80, and S. Virgulin, *Tobia* (Nuovissima versione della Bibbia, 13; Rome: Edizioni Paolini, 1978) 23–24. All these attributes mean an expanded vision of God but he remains the God who chose a people and preserves it (e.g., Add Esth 10:3[f]), not the impersonal Zeus of the piety of a Cleanthes.

[28]Gamberoni, "Buch Tobias," 233; Virgulin, *Tobia*, 26.

[29]A. Dubarle, *Judith. Formes et sens des diverses traditions* (AnBib, 25; Rome: Pontifical Biblical Institute, 1966) 1: 170–72; T. Craven, "Artistry and Faith in the Book of Judith," *Semeia* 8 (1977) 75–101.

[30]E. Zenger, "Der Judithroman als Traditionsmodell des Jahweglaubens," *Trierer Theologische Zeitschrift* 83 (1974) 65–80; P. Skehan, "The Hand of Judith," *CBQ* 25 (1963) 94–110.

attitude of the subject to his lord, and exactly that which the Chronicler demanded of the covenanted people.[31]

Sustaining such piety demanded prayer, and, in the eternal paradox of religious life, true prayer was the result of such piety. So prayer supported the actions of charity as in Tobit, hope and trust (Jdt 8:11–17; 14:10), fidelity (Add Esth 14:17^{u-y}) and humility. It is no surprise that our Greek books have as many as six verbs for prayer, "claim," ἀξιόω: 2 Macc 10:26; "cry out," βοάω: Tob 6:18; 12:6; Jdt 4:9–12; 6:18; "ask in need," δέομαι: Tob 3:11; Jdt 8:31; Add Esth 4:17^{b}; 4:17^{k}, 2 Macc 8:1; "appeal to," ἐπικαλέω: 2 Macc 3:15; 10:26, "say in one's heart," εἶπον ἐν καρδίᾳ: 1 Macc 9:46; and "pray" proper, προσεύχομαι: Tob 3:1; Jdt 11:17; 1 Macc 7:36. The nuances speak for themselves: one has confidence in need, one is open as with a father, one can even press a claim. The atmosphere is very personal indeed.

We noted the paradoxical interrelationship between prayer and penance. It is certainly present here. Prayer not only gave strength for humility; it was accompanied by expressions of them, fasting, sackcloth and ashes (Jonah 3:5–8; Esth 4:3; Add Esth 4:17^{k}; Jdt 4:14; 8:5–6; 10:26; 1 Macc 3:47; 11:71; 2 Macc 10:25). This is in the tradition of Chronicles–Nehemiah, where, however, these actions were parts of covenant renewal. Thus these late books carry on a tradition connected with covenant, just as the prayer forms follow the covenant formulation.[32] The role of penance obviously reinforced a late concept of prayer. Sacrifice was the supreme prayer (Tob 1:5–6; Jdt 4:14) but, since it was confined to Jerusalem, it was unavailable to someone who was not in that city but had an immediate need. Was there something one could do? The added element of penance surely increased the feeling that prayer was self-offering, the "sacrifice of a humble heart" (Ps 51:19; cf. 40:8).[33] Still, these actions and prayers, while personal like covenant, are individual.

[31]Note the Chronicler's emphasis on כנע, "bending the knee" before the Lord if covenant were to be kept: McCarthy, "Law in Chronicles–Nehemiah," *CBQ* 44 (1982) 31.

[32]The formulation consists of parenesis, often historical confession; has a transitional ועתה; and ends with a demand (cf. J. Muilenburg, "The Form and Structure of the Covenantal Formulations," *VT* 9 [1959] 347–65). See the great "hortatory prayers" in Ezra 9 and Nehemiah 9 and M. Gilbert, "La prière de Daniel. Dn 9, 4–19," *Revue théologique de Louvain* 3 (1972) 284–310 and "La prière d'Azarias (Dn 9, 26–45: Theodotion)," *NRT* 96 (1974) 561–82, and especially C. Giraudo, *La struttura letteraria della preghiera eucaristica: Saggio sulla genesi letteraria di una forma.* Tôdâ *veterotestamentaria*-B^{e}rākâ *giudaica-Anafora cristiana* (AnBib, 92; Rome: Pontifical Biblical Institute, 1981) for the form and individual-communitarian aspect of the prayers.

[33]Note too Pr Azar 15–16: discussion in Gilbert, "Azarias," 568, 570, 577; Jaubert, "Alliance," 85–86; Bonsirven, *Palestinian Judaism*, chaps. V-VI.

They do not usually represent the community, nor do they aim at renewing community but at helping the individual. Particularly they are not the community/hortatory prayers leading to covenant renewal in Ezra–Nehemiah.

Not that community is entirely forgotten. It is a hope of restoration in Daniel and Tobit. It is a close link with the pious family in Ruth, Tobit and Esther. That is, an element larger than the individual and strong in the old covenant has been retained in new forms, like hope for unity in the future or emphasis on a primary social structure, the family.

The temple too kept an important role, as we have claimed. It was the focus of efficacious prayer (Jonah 2:5, 8; Tob 13:10).[34] The Maccabees acted to preserve the center of the nation, its sanctuary, as well as the law (1 Macc 14:29; 2 Macc 13:10), for God was somehow especially present there. The law indeed had been attacked, but the Holy of Holies had been profaned (Dan 7:27; 1 Macc 1:37; 2:12; 2 Macc 5:16; 6:2).[35] This had to be undone to allow the Presence to be effective again. Hence a first object of the fighters for Judaism was to rededicate the temple even before they had won full freedom (1 Macc 4:36–58). 2 Macc 2:16–18 actually links Judas Maccabeus with Solomon and Nehemiah (cf. vv 8, 13). He is in the recognized line of temple builders and renewers. As for his power, he had achieved a renewal of national life undreamed of since the exile.

And all this puts the problem of covenant in a clear, even harsh, light. Why did the restorer of temple purity not renew covenant? Tradition called for it. Jehoiada had to renew covenant when he restored the national dynasty in the temple, and Josiah recalled an apostate people to their obligations in a temple covenant ceremony. In post-exilic tradition the temple had to be purified with a covenant renewal regularly. It was done under Asa, Hezekiah, Josiah and Nehemiah according to that tradition, while Solomon's original construction of the temple was the fulfilment of a covenant. This was the great tradition, and the Maccabees were certainly ready to use any means they could to accomplish their ends. Why did not Judas or Jonathan or Simon renew covenant, acting like the great leaders of old and so sharing in their prestige?

Apart from prestige there was also a very practical gain to be won. We know that a holy center can be powerful to unite even a group who may never be able to come near it. 2 Maccabees (and before it Jason of

[34]For the role of the temple in general, but especially in the Maccabean revolt, see J. Flussner, "Jerusalem in the Literature of the 2nd Temple Period," *Immanuel* 6 (1976) 42–50, and S. Fujita, "Temple Theology," 1068.

[35]In fact it was no longer especially Jewish or Yahwist since it was the common possession of the citizens of the *polis,* pagan as much as Jew: see P. Schaefer, "The Hellenistic and Maccabean Periods," *Israelite and Judaean History*, 580–82, 584.

Cyrene) shows how real the temple was in the life of the Diaspora of the time. It was a center of interest and devotion. How much more would this have been true for Palestinians who could hope to see and worship in it. These, the people it was most important for the Maccabees to win over, would surely have been impressed with a complete execution of the rites of purification and covenant renewal presented in a now canonical tradition. Still, covenant was not renewed.

One must ask why. One point leaps to the eye: the lack of prophetic guidance. Solomon had had such guidance through David, and he himself had spoken like a prophet, as had other kings.[36] Now prophecy had long been dead (Pr Azar 38; 1 Macc 9:27; cf. Zech 13:3–4), and there was no divine word to solve difficulties (1 Macc 4:46; 14:41). True, old forms of speech had survived. God works on the spirit of King Ahasuerus (Add Esth 5:1[e]), as he had on Cyrus in Ezra, but in Esther this is no more than an expression of the doctrine of providence, not a particular, personal intervention (Esth 4:14). God "roused the holy spirit of Daniel" (Sus 18: ἐξήγειρεν ὁ θεὸς τὸ πνεῦμα τὸ ἅγιον), but Daniel's spirit is the gift of wisdom (cf. 2:33) illustrated in his shrewd handling of Susannah's case, not the overwhelming force of the prophetic spirit as in Samuel, for instance. Again, reference to "the hand of God," a phrase with prophetic connections, is frequent. Nebuchadnezzar thinks universal power is in his hand, but Judith knows that her hand is the hand of God (Jdt 2:12; 8:33). So the author makes clear the real antagonists in the struggle, the proud king and God. In 16:5 Judith sings of her victory through the power God put in a woman's hand. According to 1 Macc 4:30 God overcame Goliath "by the hand . . . of David." In 5:62 Jews who were not of the family "through whose hands" Israel was to be saved lose a battle. The old language is there, but it no longer speaks of prophetic inspiration but of the power of providence and its instruments. As a result all Judas could do was rebuild the altar and offer sacrifices. Divine guidance was integral to the covenant renewal rite as expounded in Chronicles–Nehemiah. Without it a renewal was apparently impossible.

Lack of prophetic direction was not the only problem. This was merely negative, something missing. Some traditions surely worked positively against the Maccabees. Normally, priests like the Maccabees are not represented as renewing covenant. Usually it was Davidides like Solomon or Zerubbabel who built temples guaranteed by covenant or, like Asa, Hezekiah, and Josiah, renewed the covenant. In the case of Ezra it was an inspired leader (and one with the mandate of a king, even if not a Davidide) who conducted renewal ceremonies for the general community. (Nehemiah administers an oath to a particular group in

[36]See the evidence in McCarthy, "Law in Chronicles–Nehemiah," *CBQ* 44 (1982) 29–30.

5:8–13, but not to the community.) The priest Jehoiada did it only when renewal was desperately needed after Athaliah's abominations. Without there being an explicit statement of doctrine, it seems that covenant renewal belonged to the Davidides or, in their absence, to figures representing them or to inspired men. So the difficulty. There were no Davidides active and inspiration had all but officially been declared closed. With all their courage the Maccabees could not contravene so much tradition.

There is irony in the position of these anti-Hellenist zealots. They were limited by Greek influence which they might consciously reject but which was now part of the stuff of Jewish life. It is hardly possible to separate the devaluation of prophecy and the countervailing growth of the "intellectuals" and their wisdom from the prevailing atmosphere of rationalism which went back to Greece.[37] Even in the Maccabees' own special fields, war and ruling, unconscious classical influences seem to have had their effects.

For example, theirs is represented as a Holy War in which, of course, all glory goes to God. Yet at a crucial point Judas appeals to "manliness" (ἀνδρεία) and "honor" (δόξα, 1 Macc 9:10), which is heroic but has nothing to do with Holy War or trust like Gideon's (or Judith's). Then there is the ideal king described in 1 Macc 14:6–15: he is victorious over his enemies, keeps internal peace, his subjects prosper, he is called to world rule, he is just, helper of the oppressed and patron of the cult.[38] The picture is drawn from the ideal in the Psalms—except that the major element is missing: he is not first of all openly subject to God in a dependence which is the basis for all the rest of his powers and duties. The Hebrew king has become Hellenic. Thus, while theological reasons controlled much for the Maccabees, they were also victims of history. The old rites and their concomitant ideas were just that, old, and one could not simply return to them without further ado. To a new people they meant new things. A people willy-nilly under the influence of Greek wisdom and Roman politics had to find new ways to guarantee its identity, its central traditions.

The Maccabee regime's quick change from a revolt against Hellenism into an Hellenistic state is one sign of the pressures. Without a religious base no Jewish movement could retain its identity, and even so it could not remain entirely unaffected. Even ultra-conservative Qumran's asceticism was touched by Hellenism. Its hyper-exaltation of the Zadokites was uncanonical when it made priests the chief exponents of covenant

[37]This takes no position in the controversy about direct Greek philosophical influence on Jewish wisdom; it merely points out the unavoidable climate of the era.

[38]W. T. In der Smitten, "Zur judischen Königsideologie während des Hellenismus," *BO* 30 (1973) 12.

renewal, and this attitude was a reaction against the Hellenized Hasmonean priests. Even their organizational structure followed Hellenic models.[39] Still, members of the group did "enter into the covenant of God" and engage themselves by oath (1QS V, 7–9). I, 16–18 adds curses and blessing to the rite. There was an annual covenant renewal.[40] This seems to have all the features of the older covenant traditions, but it deviates. The members pledged themselves to the law of God,[41] not to God himself and so to his possible wishes as in the old way. Qumran reminds us that there may have been active covenant traditions in late pre-Christian times quite unknown to us. However, it is also an admonition to look more closely at our literature. Were these sectarians so apart after all? When we consider the achievements of the religion depicted in our books we find that they did keep alive a central element of the covenant in a new form. There may not have been the covenant pledge to God, but there was a very personal union with God based on a "law" which was not merely a set of external rules but conviction acquired through the studies encouraged by wisdom and the contemplations of piety. One can insist that this is individualistic while covenant emphasized the union of the community with God. But do our books forget community? Judith is heroic in defense of her religious community. So is Esther in the Greek religious legend. Tobit does stress family ties, but still the true Jew is the faithful one, not the relative who happens to share the same blood by accident of birth: note 4:7 which seems to exclude the unrighteous Jew from the community.

So our late narratives do emphasize factors central to covenant: personal commitment, community, fidelity. The problem is that these factors are not presented as elements resulting from a pledge to be God's people as in the classic covenant. One can understand to an extent. It was more reassuring after the condemnations of the prophets and the terrors of the exile to think less of covenant and its demands and more of promise, an unconditional commitment binding God to the people no matter what.[42] So appeal to the promissory covenant with the Fathers is favored (Pr Azar 34–35; 1 Macc 4:10; 2 Macc 2:1; Sir 44:19–21), or to the similar covenant with David (Sir 47:11; cf. 2 Chr 21:7). Or the psalmist

[39]Hengel, *Judaism*, 244.

[40]See Jaubert, *Alliance*, 214–19, on renewal; 117 on the Zadokites.

[41]Russell, *The Jews*, 167.

[42]Thus, in terms of the needs of the people, needs met by the OT writers, the development of the covenant idea was the reverse of that posited by J. Begrich, "Berit. Ein Beitrag zur Erfassung einer alttestamentlichen Denkform," *ZAW* 60 (1944) 1–11, and brilliantly defended by Kutsch, *Verheissung und Gesetz*, not a move from accent on pure grant to some kind of reciprocity, but from shared pledge to grant (promise).

turns the vocabulary of covenant and law into an assertion of God's sure promises:

He is the LORD our God;
In all the earth his decisions (משפטיו) prevail.
He called to mind his covenant from long ago,
the promise (דבר) he extended (צוה) to a thousand generations—
the covenant made with Abraham,
his oath given to Isaac,
the decree (חק) by which he bound himself to Jacob,
his everlasting covenant with Israel (Ps 105:7–10).[43]

Nevertheless, our literature keeps returning to the qualities demanded by the Deuteronomic covenant: commitment, community, fidelity. The elements of the old covenant are present even if not in perfect organic unity. They hardly could be. The charismatic makers of covenant like Moses or Joshua could not arise in a community which had all but officially declared prophecy dead. The institutional makers of covenant, the legitimate kings, were gone. Hence there was the turn to alternatives. Individual piety was prominent, a piety which used the attributes Greek thinkers ascribed to their gods and Prime Movers to stimulate devotion. However, this piety was always directed to a mighty, creative, merciful savior concerned for his people. Wisdom too was prominent. It did not abandon the old faith in experience and tradition, but it took a radical turn in making the law the highest wisdom. Wisdom was not abstract thinking but concentration on the revelation of a savior. Further, this savior was still worshipped in his temple where, according to tradition, covenant was renewed. All this was far from making covenant in the true sense the center of religion. What it did do was keep elements of covenant thought and feeling very much alive and so provide channels for revitalizing it.

Look at the temple, for example. It was the proper center of worship *for all.* It was a place of terrific awe (2 Macc 2:18; 3:12; Tob 14:5b). This last text is the telling one. It looks explicitly at the future, an attitude which the stress on covenant as promise had to foster. If the promise was sure and the present unsatisfactory, one could only look for something to come. The covenant of promise and the covenant of commitment—surely commitment is central to Tobit—can begin to come together.

There was, therefore, much hope but also the (probably vague) realization that the past cannot simply be restored whole, as the Maccabees and Qumran show. What to hope for in such circumstances? There was conversion and return for Jews (cf. Tobit 13), but not just for them. Jonah admits and praises outsiders. One grand effect of Judith's victory

[43]NEB version except for 7b.

is the conversion of the Ammonite, Achior (Jdt 14:10). The Diaspora, that enigma to Jew and Gentile alike, is to be the means to this: Tob 13:3–4. A covenant virtue will renew and enlarge the covenant people, for their fidelity will bring the errant peoples in.

We must go outside our material, though not the post-exilic era, to find this hope for the Gentiles put in covenant terms. The late text Isa 19:18–25 expresses Tobit's idea in those terms. Egyptian cities will "swear allegiance to the LORD." They will have a witness (עד) to their allegiance. They will return (שב) to him, a word with covenant reference in Deuteronomy.[44] And Egypt is just an example: the *extremes* of Israel's foes, Egypt and Assyria, the standard Hebrew figure for expressing a totality, will be brought in. So all will be like Israel, "my people," "my heritage," that is, members of the covenanted people. A passage like this reintegrates everything into the classic covenant. The peoples, not individuals, are to pledge themselves to personal fidelity to the LORD. The passage in Isaiah 19 simply puts into "legal" covenant language the poetic prayer of Tobit.

There was confidence, then, in a renewal, a renewal centered around a restored nation and temple. Note the quasi-messianic hymn to Simon in 1 Macc 14:4–14 and especially the awesome beauty of the temple of a city glowing with precious stones (Tob 13:16–17). Worship, the place where one met and pledged union with God in covenant, would be more telling than ever, restored and even open to all. It was not for nothing that this late literature and the society it sought to foster by example and exhortation preserved the elements of covenant, the old covenant ideals, in suspension, as it were. The ever-growing feeling of a need to revalue this older material created great pressure that must precipitate something covenantal and yet new. The eventual radical new departures produced two world religions. Covenant, even in an obscured state, remained a fruitful religious stimulus.

[44]Cf. H. W. Wolff, "The Kerygma of the Deuteronomic Historical Work," *The Vitality of OT Traditions* (by W. Brueggemann and H. W. Wolff; Atlanta: John Knox, 1975) 83–100.

In Praise of the Israelite *Mišpāḥâ*: Legal Themes in the Book of Ruth

BARUCH A. LEVINE
NEW YORK UNIVERSITY

FOR all its charm, the book of Ruth produces a certain *malaise.* Students of Israelite law and society have found it difficult if not imposssible to reconcile the many references to legal institutions contained in Ruth with the evidence of other sources, both biblical and comparative. There is an extensive literature dealing with these legalities, for their very elusiveness seems to have stimulated the scholarly imagination.[1]

Methodologically, the challenge is to establish, if we can, the attitude of the author of Ruth toward those laws and customs to which he refers directly, or alludes indirectly. How precise was he in utilizing legal themes?

This question has been addressed in recent years by D. R. G. Beattie, in a study entitled: "The Book of Ruth as Evidence for Israelite Legal Practice." Beattie postulates that the author of Ruth was committed to credibility, and that he would not "create a legal situation which his audience will know to be impossible." In another statement, Beattie speaks of the author's mandate to be "intelligible" to his readers.[2]

A comparison of Beattie's study with an earlier treatment of the same subject by Millar Burrows shows the difference between a legal and a literary approach to an ancient narrative. Burrows, an authority on Israelite marriage, keenly analyzed the legal problems hypothetically raised in the story of Ruth, and his determinations in this regard were predictably accurate. And yet, one senses the extent to which he forced

[1]In the past decade two new commentaries on the book of Ruth have appeared. We have Edward F. Campbell's volume (*Ruth* [AB; Garden City: Doubleday, 1975]), and that of Jack M. Sasson (*Ruth, A New Translation with a Philological Commentary and a Formalist-Folklorist Interpretation* [Baltimore: Johns Hopkins, 1979]). Campbell's discussion of the legal themes in Ruth is on pp. 27, 132–33, and Sasson's on pp. 228–29, respectively.

[2]Beattie, "The Book of Ruth as Evidence for Israelite Legal Practice," *VT* 24 (1974) 251–67.

this tale of devotion and virtue into a legal mold, alien to its essential character.[3]

Although I find Beattie's discussion to be an advance over most recent studies, which inevitably assume a high degree of legal precision in Ruth, I also find that it does not take into account some literary features and narrative devices characteristic of the book as a whole. Beattie argues that the author takes great care in presenting legal details; as, for instance, in describing the removal of the shoe as a symbolic act of conveyances (Ruth 4:7–8). But the mere presence of legal detail, expressed in technical language, does not prove the applicability of the actual legal instruments referred to in the story. The question that should concern us is whether the circumstances of the story, as the author himself fashioned it, call for those legal actions, or not. We shall have occasion to observe that the author of Ruth was capable of legal leaps, of glossing over the prerequisites for invoking certain Israelite laws, while at the same time exploiting the very dynamics of those laws to enhance the intricacy of his plot.

Beattie also attaches considerable importance to dating. In his view, Ruth is predominantly a pre-exilic creation, containing some few ingredients of late language appropriated in the course of transmission.[4] I must disagree with this assessment, and insist that greater emphasis be placed on late language. A composition should be dated on the basis of its latest linguistic components, if language is being used as the basis for dating, whether or not these ingredients are statistically extensive. One could, of course, discount elements blatantly identifiable as later interpolations, of which I doubt any occur in the main body of Ruth. There are also many clear indications of a literary-historical kind which bring us to the brink of the exile, and most probably take us into the early post-exilic period. I refer to biblical sources with which the author was decidedly familiar, and which are paraphrased and played-upon in Ruth.

The importance attached to dating has another implication, less apparent in Beattie's study than in most others. I refer to the notion of development. In the literature of the last century or so, scholars have interpreted the legalities in Ruth as variously representing very early or very late stages in the development of Israelite legal institutions. In this way, discrepancies between Ruth and other biblical sources are circumvented by positing that the author was privy to facts of law and life unknown to us, because he flourished in a period of biblical history otherwise undocumented.

This sounds good, in theory; but when we get down to cases, we encounter problems with tracing developments in biblical law. The

[3]Burrows, "The Marriage of Boaz and Ruth," *JBL* 59 (1940) 445–54.

[4]Beattie, "The Book of Ruth," 253–54.

levirate law provides a good example: there can be no doubt whatsoever that the author of Ruth was familiar with the Tamar episode in Genesis 38, for he evokes it in the marriage blessing (Ruth 4:12). Nor can there be any doubt that he knew the precise wording of the levirate law in Deut 25:5–10, for he ingeniously paraphrases its formulation in Ruth 4:5b, 10.

Now, if there is evidence of a trend in the performance of the levirate, it is definitely in the direction of mitigating this duty, not of expanding it, or broadening its application. This emerges from a comparison of the early Yahwistic narrative of Genesis 38 with the law of Deuteronomy 25. The Tamar episode makes the point that neglect of the levirate once endangered the continuity of Judah's line. To set matters right, all sorts of unusual, and normally reprehensible acts had to be undertaken. The Deuteronomic law, on the other hand, presents the levirate as an institution which still retained its traditional authority, but which had already begun to clash with the Israelite way of life and the organization of the family. The *levir* now has an option, and may refuse to unite with the childless widow of his deceased brother. A symbolic humiliation is imposed, which satisfies the tradition; but there is nothing illegal about releasing the widow to marry outside the family. One suspects in a majority of cases this was the option exercised, rather than levirate union, at least by the time that the Deuteronomic law was promulgated.

Now, if it was true that relatives other than a *levir* were obligated to marry the childless widows of their clan relatives, as is explicitly predicated in Ruth 4:5b, such would have been the case before the Deuteronomic law; and what is more, that practice would have antedated the Tamar episode as well. In neither one of these sources is it ever intimated that the *levir* could be replaced by anyone except another brother of the deceased, should the *levir* have been unable or unwilling to perform his duty, or have passed away. The Tamar episode can hardly be cited as evidence that at one time fathers-in-law united with their childless, widowed daughters-in-law![5]

It is my understanding that the author of Ruth entertained a meta legal attitude. His purpose was to extol the spirit, rather than the letter of Israelite law, as it functioned in the family and larger clan. He created

[5]This is virtually assumed by Robert Gordis ("Love, Marriage and Business in the Book of Ruth: A Chapter in Hebrew Customary Law," *A Light unto My Path: Studies in Honor of Jacob M. Myers* [ed. H. N. Bream *et al.*; Philadelphia: Temple University, 1974] 241–64, esp. 249). But, Gordis' logic is convoluted: since incest is forbidden by the law codes of the Torah, Judah's act would have been illegal, and would have rendered Perez illegitimate. Ergo, the levirate was not limited to the *levir*; otherwise, how could Perez' line have been accepted, even enobled? The heroic literature of the Bible was hardly bound by the laws of the Torah!

a story in which the ultimate purposes of several interlocking legal institutions, all expressive of collective, clan responsibility, were amazingly fulfilled; but their fulfillment came in a manner that exceeded the strict limits of legal applicability.

This assessment of the author's mentality requires some clarification prior to engaging the specific legalities projected in the book of Ruth, primarily the levirate and the system known as *gĕʾullâ* "redemption."

An important consideration in the study of Ruth is George Mendenhall's emphasis on "policy" as reflected in law. I agree with E. F. Campbell, who applies Mendenhall's analysis to the interpretation of Ruth, that our author was interested in law as a set of policies—the policy of assisting the widow and the poor, of accepting a stranger who sought refuge among the Israelites; the policy of rewarding devotion to the clan and family, and of recognizing loyalty on the part of wives to their husbands' families. The line of Judah, destined for royalty and for eschatology, survived because such "policies" were implemented all along the line. The term "policy" thus focuses our attention on norms and attitudes; on objectives, purposes and motivations, as they operated in biblical Israel, rather than depleting our attention by a static description of the requirements imposed by specific legislation.[6]

And yet, the author of Ruth recognized in the very detail of law a reflection of its lofty purposes. His statements are not of the prophetic variety, or even of the sort encountered in the Deuteronomic law codes, which often voice broad concepts endemic to the specific commandments. His interest is in the subtleties of law, and he is, in a sense, closer to the spirit of the priestly tradition and its detailed codes of practice. Our author was an artful manipulator of legalities! He transposed *laws* into *legal themes.* He utilized the formulas and technicalities of the legal *dicta* in a meta-legal way; and in so doing, successfully confounded generations of scholars!

The story of Ruth is cast against a social backdrop every bit as significant for the character of the story as its legalities. The social parameter of the story of Ruth is the *mišpāḥâ,* which I regularly translate "clan," for lack of a better term. By this I mean a patrilineal unit considerably larger than the immediate family, or even the "nuclear" family as defined by the incest code (Leviticus 18, 20, and Deut 27:20–21). Endogamous marriages often occurred within the same *mišpāḥâ,* usually between cousins. In fact, such marriages were encouraged, based on what we are told in certain biblical traditions. The system of *gĕʾullâ,* so basic to the literary framework of Ruth, was also a function of the Israelite *mišpāḥâ.*[7]

[6]See literature cited in n. 1.

[7]In Ruth, as in many other biblical sources, the term for the immediate family which shared a common domicile is *bayit,* "household." Thus, Naomi

With this background in mind, we can now proceed to examine the passage that has been central to most scholarly debates on the legalities in Ruth:

> He (Boaz) said to the redeemer (*gôʾēl*): The section of field which belonged to our kinsman, Elimelech, Noami *is offering for sale (mākĕrâ)*—she who just returned from the territory of Moab. I intend to serve notice on you as follows: Purchase [it] (*qĕnēh*) in the presence of those seated, and in the presence of the elders of my people. If you agree to redeem, then redeem (*gĕʾāl*)! But if you will not redeem—tell me, so that I may be so informed; for there is no other except you to redeem, and I succeed you.
>
> Thereupon he (the redeemer) responded: I will, indeed, redeem (*ʾegʾāl*)!
>
> Boaz then continued: *At the same time as you purchase* (*bĕyôm qĕnôtĕkā*) the field from Naomi—Ruth, as well (read *wĕʾet*), the Moabite woman, widow of the deceased, you must 'purchase' (*qānîtā*), so as to confirm the title of the deceased over his estate (Ruth 4:3–5).[8]

The above translation is intentionally stilted, so as to focus attention on the textual problems of this passage. A scribal error is assumed in the word *ûmēʾēt*, immediately following the Etnah, in v 5. Our translation takes the *mēm* in that word as a dittography, induced by the *mēm* in the name *nāʿŏmî*, the preceding word. On this basis read: *wĕʾet*. Less likely is the suggestion to follow the Vulgate reading, *quoque*, and read *gam ʾet*, which is what we find in v 10.

Most important, of course, is the question of Kethibh, *qnyty*, versus the Qere, *qānîtā*, in v 5b. In my opinion, the Qere is to be sustained on text-critical, as well as exegetical grounds. The Qere is an attempt to correct an error, induced by the occurrence of two 1st-person forms, *qānîtî* "I have purchased," in v 10, which rephrases the words of Boaz' charge. Recently, the Kethibh has gained new adherents, making it necessary to focus on the textual question.[9]

---

expresses the hope that her daughters-in-law will find security, each in "the household of her husband" (*bêt ʾîšāh*, Ruth 1:9; and cf. Num 30:11). Likewise, she urges each of them to return to "the household of her mother" (*bêt ʾimmāh*, Ruth 1:8; and cf. Cant 3:4; 8:2). In Ruth 4:11 the designation: *bêt yiśrāʾēl* probably means "the household (= family) of Israel (= Jacob)," and in 4:12 we find *bêt pereṣ*, "the household of Perez."

[8]The perfect form, *mākĕrâ* in v 3 need not refer to an action taken in the past, but may, as it does here, designate an action which merely began before the moment of speech. There is no need to point the word as a participial form, as once suggested by J. A. Bewer, "The Geʾullah in the Book of Ruth," *AJSL* 19 (1902–03) 143–48.

[9]See the extensive discussion by Sasson, *Ruth*, 121–22, and Beattie, "The Book of Ruth," 263–64.

In Ruth 4:3–5, and continuing through v 10 of that chapter, two significant verbs are employed: *gāʾal* "to redeem," and *qānâ* "to purchase, acquire," respectively. I begin with the latter because its occurrence in these passages of Ruth directly links them to the language in Jeremiah 32. That source preserves a unique account of an act of *gĕʾullâ* with respect to the field of a clan-relative. The prophet Jeremiah undertakes the legal process of *gĕʾullâ* for a symbolic purpose, which is stated in technical, legal language:

> Then Jeremiah said: The word of Yahweh came to me as follows: Hanamel, son of your uncle, Shallum, is about to come to you, and he will state: Purchase (*qĕnēh-lĕkā*) my field in Anathoth, for you have *jurisdiction over the redemption by purchase* (*mišpaṭ haggĕʾullâ liqnôt*).
>
> And, indeed, Hanamel, my cousin, came to me pursuant to the word of Yahweh . . . and said to me: Pray, purchase (*qĕnēh-nāʾ*) my field in Anathoth . . . for you have *jurisdiction over* [*preserving*] *the ancestral estate* (*mišpaṭ hayyĕruššâ*), and you bear *the* [*duty of*] *redemption* (*haggĕʾullâ*). . . .
>
> So, *I purchased* (*wāʾeqneh*) the field . . . . (Jer 32:6–9)[10]

In this passage the essential verb is *qānâ* "to purchase," and of *gāʾal,* "to redeem," only the nominal form *gĕʾullâ* is used. These two verbs, *gāʾal* and *qānâ,* are far from being synonymous. Hebrew *gāʾal* invariably connotes the retrieval of something lost, taken away; or about to be lost. This verb says nothing about the legal status of that which is redeemed, or about who then owns it. On the other hand, *qānâ* necessarily connotes possession, certainly so in legal contexts.[11]

Jeremiah 32 represents the classic act of redemption, in which purchase is material. The redeemer gains title to the field he has redeemed, a fact made explicit in Jer 32:7b: "For you have jurisdiction over the redemption by purchase." In Ruth 4:3–7, both nominal (*gĕʾullâ,* "redemption," vv 6, 7), and finite forms of the verb *gāʾal* occur alongside the verb *qānâ.* In Ruth, the verb *gāʾal* describes the overall process, whereas *qānâ* specifically refers to the element of purchase.

To indicate the significance of usage, I refer to Leviticus 25, a priestly code governing land tenure, in which forms of the verbs *gāʾal* and *qānâ* are prominent. In that code usage of the two verbs is, however,

[10]Hebrew *yĕruššâ* always connotes land or some other form of property, and never, in biblical usage, refers to a legal process. If *yĕruššat pĕlêṭâ* in Judg 21:17 is correct, the sense would be that some number of the persons belonging to the tribe of Benjamin remained alive.

[11]In late biblical Hebrew, the verb *qānâ* occasionally replaces *gāʾal,* as in Neh 5:8, "And I said to them: Did we not buy-back (*qānînû*) our Judean kinsmen who had been indentured to the gentiles." Cf. Lev 25:47 where the verb *gāʾal* is used in a similarly worded statement of law.

carefully differentiated. The verb *qānâ* is reserved exclusively for normal business transactions, but never for any act involved in redemption, *per se*. There is a reason for this: Leviticus 25 perceives of *gĕ᾿ullâ* in different terms. The redeemer from the clan *restores* what he redeems to his needy relative and does not gain title to the land for himself, so that one could say that he "purchased" it.[12]

This is the only interpretation that makes good sense out of the provisions of Lev 25:25–26. One who had been compelled to pledge or sell part of his holdings had the option of buying back his property, if he subsequently acquired the means to do so on his own. Or, he could await the advent of the Jubilee year, when his holding would revert to him automatically. A more fortunate solution would be for his *gô᾿ēl*, of the same clan, to restore his property to him. The interest upheld in the code of Leviticus 25 is that of the individual landowner, not of his whole clan. In this respect, the provisions of Leviticus 25 represent a basic departure from the classic pattern, reflected in Jeremiah 32. There we read that the prophet weighed out the price of the field in silver and had a deed of sale written registering Jeremiah as the new owner of Hanamel's field.

The author of Ruth, by using the verb *qānâ* as he does, clearly demonstrates that his reference is to the classic system of *gĕ᾿ullâ*, in which purchase was a central act. This explains why the unnamed redeemer reneged on his earlier willingness to "redeem" the field in question. He had been willing to purchase Elimelech's field, thereby alleviating Naomi's plight, but he was unwilling to agree to any arrangement that would require him to forfeit his title to what he had redeemed. To do so would "ruin" his own estate (Ruth 4:6).

Here, then, is a clear instance of our author's method in utilizing legal themes. He could be very precise, indeed, if by such precision he succeeded in making his plot revolve around a point of law.

Some scholars have been concerned about usage of the verb *qānâ* in Ruth 4:5b, 10, to designate acquisition of a wife, since that specialized meaning is not attested elsewhere in biblical Hebrew. The first point to be emphasized is that no deductions are warranted by the use of this verb, as far as the legal nature of marriage itself is concerned. No notion of marriage as purchase may be imputed to the author of Ruth. The fact is that usage of the verb *qānâ* in Ruth is restricted to two passages, where its function is stylistic, not technical. In 4:5a, the words: *bĕyôm qĕnôtĕkā*, "At the same time as you purchase" (the field), produce

[12]Contrast usage of the verb *qānâ* in Lev 25:14–15 as a term of reference for normal buying and selling, with usage of *gā᾿al* in vv 25–26, in the context of the redemption system, where *gā᾿al* functions as a reflex of *mākar* "to sell," just as *qānâ* does in general transactions.

the reflex: *qānîtā*, "You must purchase" (the woman) in v 5b. Similarly, *qānîtî*, "I have purchased" (the property) in v 9 produces the reflex: *qānîtî*, "I have purchased" (the woman) in v 10. In v 13, the verb which designates acquisition of a wife is the conventional one, *lāqaḥ*, "to take" a wife.[13]

Thus far in the discussion of our author's attitude toward the system of *gĕʾullâ* it has been my purpose to illustrate how Israelite law was utilized to enhance the plot of the story. I doubt very much, however, if the system of *gĕʾullâ*, in any of its known forms, was at all applicable to the circumstances of the story as the author himself fashioned it. After all, it is he who projected so many deaths into the life of a single family within a short span of time. In so doing, he created an ideal situation for applying the law of inheritance, not for invoking the duty of redemption!

These two legal systems, inheritance and redemption, shared the same social parameter, the *mišpāḥâ*, and had similar objectives. But in any given situation defined by law they were, nevertheless, mutually exclusive. If redemption applied, this meant that an owner of land needed assistance from a clan relative. If no such owner was alive, how could redemption take place?

Technically, Elimelech's field would have fallen to his sons, Mahlon and Kilyon, who apparently survived him. When they died, leaving no heirs, the provisions of Num 27:8–9 would have gone into effect. That priestly code, set forth in the context of "the daughters of Zelophehad," seems to embody widely held views on the succession of inheritance in biblical Israel. When one died without surviving heirs, his brothers became his heirs; but Mahlon and Kilyon had no brothers, or else the levirate would have applied to both Ruth and Orpah, theoretically. The next in line would have been the uncles of Mahlon and Kilyon, i.e., the brothers of Elimelech. But he had no brothers. Those who claim, quite transparently, that Boaz and the other redeemer were Elimelech's actual brothers, and who translate *ʾāḥînû* in Ruth 4:3 as "our brother," are deliberately forcing the text. One actual brother would hardly be described as more closely related than the other (Ruth 3:12–13; 4:4). Moreover, if Boaz and the other man were Elimelech's actual brothers, they would have inherited the field on this basis, so what need was there for redemption? Finally, as clan relatives, more likely cousins of Elimelech, Boaz and the unnamed redeemer would have inherited the field in due course.

[13]David Halivni-Weiss ("The Use of *qnh* in Connection with Marriage," *HTR* 57 [1964] 244–48) makes a good point about usage of the verb *qānâ* in early Rabbinic texts, such as the Mishnah. He finds that it is not used there to connote the acquisition of a wife per se, but only when marriage is associated with other legal actions involving purchase.

Some scholars have proposed that Naomi enjoyed special rights to the field of her late husband, such as might have been the case had the field in question been granted to Naomi by her father or brothers at the time of her marriage to Elimelech. Normally, such property was for the benefit of her children, but since these had died without surviving heirs, the land might have reverted to Naomi.

Such hypothetical constructions result from the effort to reconcile what is related in Ruth with Israelite law, and even with what is only presumed to be Israelite law! Had the author of Ruth truly intended to represent the legal situation faced by Naomi precisely and accurately against the background of the law codes, he would have told quite a different story.

When Naomi returned to Judea with Ruth and informed the good people of Bethlehem of all the tragedy that had befallen her family, it would have been determined that the abandoned field of Elimelech belonged to the relative who was next in the line of inheritance. That may have led directly to the unnamed redeemer, and to Boaz himself. After all, if they were the only redeemers around, they might well have been the only clan-relatives as well! I would go so far as to agree with those who suggest that the duty of *gĕʾullâ* extended to support of a childless widow like Naomi; but this would not imply any change of legal status as far as she was concerned. Widows did not inherit their husbands' wealth in biblical Israel.

The initial preconditions for invoking the duty of redemption are not present in our author's story. Our author merely utilized the precise legalities of the system of *gĕʾullâ* in order to epitomize the laudable motivations and purposes of that system. His meta-legal attitude is perhaps revealed most clearly in the fact that he proclaims the son born to Ruth and Boaz as the ultimate *gôʾēl* of Naomi:

> Blessed be Yahweh, who has not deprived you of a redeemer (*gôʾēl*) today, and may his name be perpetuated among the Israelites![14] He shall restore your vitality and maintain you in your dotage. For your daughter-in-law, who showed her love for you, bore him—she who has become more valuable to you than seven sons! (Ruth 4:14–15)

In Ruth, the system of *gĕʾullâ* functions as a structure, a framework for the story. What is remarkable about our author is that he fashioned a plot that virtually obviates the legal applicability of *gĕʾullâ*, as he

[14]H. Ch. Brichto ("Kin, Cult and Afterlife," *HUCA* 44 [1973] 1–54) proposed this translation for the formula *wĕyiqqārēʾ šĕmô bĕyiśrāʾēl*, in the context of a discussion of the continuity of the family and clan as a major concern in biblical Israel. This rendering in Ruth 4:14 was adopted in *The Five Megilloth and Jonah* (Philadelphia: Jewish Publication Society of America, 1969).

certainly understood the system, while at the same time utilizing its legal principles to stimulate magnanimous acts on the part of Boaz. He adroitly introduces the theme of redemption by having Naomi inform Ruth, relatively early in the story, that Boaz is *gō᾽ălēnû*, "our redeemer" (Ruth 2:20).[15] When he subsequently activates the legalities of that system, the reader is less likely to question his major premise, i.e., that *gĕ᾽ullâ* actually applies. Once this legal leap is accomplished, our author invests his story with legal detail which encourages credibility.

A similar approach should enable us to perceive how our author uses the theme of levirate marriage. He took his cue from Ruth's predicament as the childless widow of one of Elimelech's sons. Officially, there was nothing to tie Ruth to the family of her late husband, whose only brother had also died childless. A levirate union was out of the question. And yet, Ruth insists on sharing the fate of her mother-in-law, Naomi. As noted long ago by J. A. Bewer, there is a veiled allusion to the levirate in the taunting words of Naomi to her daughters-in-law near the beginning of the story.[16] Naomi bitterly laments her inability to bear additional sons whom her daughters-in-law might marry someday (Ruth 1:11–12). One is reminded of Tamar, patiently waiting for little Shelah to reach maturity (Gen 38:11).

A more obvious reference to the levirate is, of course, the mention of Tamar in the marriage blessing.

> May your household be as the household of Perez, whom Tamar bore to Judah (Ruth 4:12).

This suggests a parallel between Ruth and Tamar. Tamar was a woman who took bold initiatives on her own behalf, which resulted in preserving the family line of Judah when it was threatened with extinction. Her acts were a risk to her own life and compromised her father-in-law, but they achieved the effective goal of the levirate, through a substitution. Ruth also took initiatives that were bold, in their own way. Whether or not a sexual liason occurred between Ruth and Boaz at

[15]Naomi may have been following custom in referring to Boaz as a redeemer, because the term *gô᾽ēl* may have been part of the nomenclature of the clan. A relative would be so called because of his potential function, based on his clan relationship. I am thinking of the enigmatic term *mĕsārĕpô*, "his burner," in Amos 6:10, referring to a relative whose duty it would be to burn incense for the dead, if this interpretation is correct. The point is that this was the traditional duty of a certain relative. I wish there were some certainty as to the meaning of the rare term *môdāᶜ* (kethibh, *mydᶜ*) in Ruth 2:1. Intuitively, I prefer to see it also as a relational term, with a specific meaning in the nomeclature of the clan, rather than as merely a way of referring to a friend or acquaintance.

[16]See the literature cited in n. 8 above.

the threshing-floor, and the sexual allusions in the text certainly allow for this conclusion, Ruth's action in going to Boaz at night and placing herself at his feet while he slept was compromising and had to be kept secret.[17] She, too, achieved the purposes of the levirate with one who was not her *levir*, though her marriage to Boaz represented a highly laudable form of endogamy.

There is also a possible allusion to the levirate in the words Boaz spoke to Ruth at the threshing-floor:

> May you be blessed before Yahweh, my daughter. By your latter kindness (*ḥasdēk hāʾaḥărôn*) you have outdone your former one—by not attaching yourself to the young men, whether poor or rich (Ruth 3:10).

The "former" kindness refers to Ruth's initial commitment to her mother-in-law, with all this entailed. I take the reference to a "latter" kindness to mean that Ruth had kept herself available to Boaz and had not sought marriage with a man outside the clan. I find this interpretation preferable to the more romantic view that Boaz was praising Ruth for preferring him, personally, over a younger man. Throughout the story, Boaz' attentions toward Ruth are expressed in a subdued tone, and though they undoubtedly bespoke personal feelings they were not expressed as such, but rather as admiration for her virtue.[18]

If this interpretation is correct, we are reminded of the restriction stated in the levirate law, which prohibits the childless widow awaiting the *levir* from marrying outside the family (Deut 25:5). In a similar way, though the circle of relationships has been widened, Ruth awaited Boaz.

The clearest reference to the levirate occurs, of course, in Boaz' charge to the unnamed redeemer in Ruth 4:5b, and again in v 10, in a statement of Boaz. In both verses, the relevant words are: *lĕhāqîm šēm hammēt ʿal naḥălātô*, "to confirm the title of the deceased over his estate."

The sense of *hēqîm* in this formula differs from its meaning in the levirate law. Here, *hēqîm* means: "to fulfill, confirm," the opposite of *hēpēr* "to annul, void." This meaning is elsewhere attested in legal contexts, as well as occurring in covenant language.[19]

This is hardly the sense of *hēqîm* in the levirate law of Deut 25:5–10, where it is merely the reflex of *qûm*. Thus, in Deut 25:6 we read:

[17]See the extensive discussion in Sasson's commentary, 66–67, which provides valuable comparative material.

[18]This approximates the view of Ruth 3:10 conveyed in *The Five Megilloth and Jonah*, with p. 26, n. *b*.

[19]On legal usage of *hēqîm*, "to confirm, fulfill," see Num 30:14–15, relevant to the confirmation of vows already pronounced. On the synonymity of *hēqîm* and *ʿāśâ*, "to accomplish," see Jer 23:20; 30:24.

yāqûm ᶜal šēm ᵓāḥîw hammēt, "he shall 'stand' for the name of his deceased brother," and in v 7 we read: *lĕhāqîm lĕᵓāḥîw šēm,* "to 'raise up' a name for his brother," i.e., to produce an heir.

The author of Ruth evoked a clear association with the levirate law, while, at the same time, putting over on his readers a semantic transaction and a syntactic shift!

The system of *gĕᵓullâ* and the levirate law are the author's building-blocks. He assigns to his characters multiple roles. Most notably, Boaz functions both as *levir* and *gôᵓēl,* though neither role was mandated by the actual circumstances of the story. The laws of ancient Israel served to highlight the overriding concern of the author of Ruth—the history of the royal line of Judah. From the very start, women played an important part in preserving Judah's line. The tradition of self-help which operated within the Israelite *mišpāḥâ* provided the context for the efforts of these exceptional women, from Rachel and Leah, through Tamar, and reach to Ruth, whose adventure is cast into the generations just preceding the establishment of the Davidic dynasty. *Ḥesed* was the virtue of the Israelite *mišpāḥâ,* and human acts of kindness were fully rewarded by God's *ḥesed.* This was the experience of Ruth, the Moabite woman.

III

Prophecy and Poetry

The Social Role of Amos' Message

HERBERT B. HUFFMON
DREW UNIVERSITY

WHAT was the intended impact of Amos' message for the society of his time? What did Amos want to communicate to his audience? Part of the difficulty in answering this question is the necessity to sort out the redactional strata.[1] Another part of the difficulty is that most of our knowledge of the society of the kingdom of Israel in the time of Jeroboam II (786–746) comes by inference from the books of Amos and his younger contemporary, Hosea. A third issue is that Amos addresses people who understand themselves to be faithful to God. He does not address himself to the society of the kingdom of Israel generally, a society that surely included many who gave no particular allegiance—or at least no exclusive allegiance—to Israel's Yahwistic tradition and practice. In this respect Amos is unlike Hosea, who clearly points to a society that lacked religious unity, as do also the traditions associated with Elijah and Elisha about a century earlier, as well as the recent discoveries at Kuntillet Ajrud, dating to the ninth century. Amos basically ignores whatever religious differences there may have been. He addresses the faithful—faithful in their own eyes, that is.

2 Kgs 14:25 (cf. Amos 6:13, 14) notes that Jeroboam II "restored the border of Israel from the Entrance of Hamath as far as the Sea of the Arabah," reversing the fortune of Israel. Jeroboam II brought many changes to the northern kingdom. New territory, new population, and new prosperity must have meant an increasing disparity between the urban elite of the administrative and religious centers and the village population. Increasing development of socio-economic hierarchy is likely to produce tension within the traditional order. In any case, Amos' oracles clearly presuppose a sharp contrast between the urban elite and the village poor—a contrast not emphasized by Hosea. Furthermore, as Marlene Fendler has convincingly argued, neither the oppressed nor the

[1]For the purposes of this paper, I follow the carefully reasoned redactional analysis in H. W. Wolff, *Joel and Amos* (Hermeneia; Philadelphia: Fortress, 1977). Note, however, that passages deriving from the Amos school, in particular, commonly illustrate the direction of Amos' thought.

oppressors, as pictured in Amos, represent a homogeneous class.[2] Those who sell the innocent poor for money (2:6), e.g., presumably are middle-class merchants who are themselves pressed by creditors, rather than landowners, who would put the poor to work, or the wealthy, who could afford to purchase and keep debt slaves.

Throughout his oracles Amos addresses an audience that in its own sight is pious and faithful. He does not charge the people with running after other gods, as does Hosea.[3] Rather, Amos assumes that the hearers of the oracles understand themselves as God's chosen community ("you only have I known. . . ," 3:2), as connected with the Exodus, Wilderness and Settlement traditions (2:9–10, though Wolff assigns v 10 to the Amos school), as taking part in the Yahwistic cult at traditional religious centers such as Bethel and Gilgal (4:4–5; 5:5), and as confidently looking forward to the Day of the Lord (5:18). This assumption about the people's self-understanding also continues when Amos specifically addresses the exploitative, wealthy classes who can live in well-built houses and plant vineyards (5:11), especially those in the royal city of Samaria itself (4:1; 6:1). The oppressed and innocent poor have a prominent role in the oracles, but they are never specifically addressed. Even the modest hope indicated by "Seek me, and live" (5:4; cf. 5:14, from the Amos school) and—from the Amos school—"Perhaps the Lord . . . will be gracious to the remnant of Joseph" (5:15), does not single out those loyal to the old order, but concerns the "house of Israel" (5:1, 3, 4), i.e., the northern state generally.[4] The oppressed poor constitute only an indirect audience for the denunciation of the oppressors (2:6–7; 4:1; 5:11, 12; and 8:4, 6, from the Amos school), as are the neighboring peoples (1:3–2:5), some of whom, of course, are found within Jeroboam's realm, for denunciations spoken for the ears of Israel. Amos speaks to the people of the northern kingdom generally and to the privileged classes particularly.

[2]M. Fendler, "Zur Sozialkritik des Amos," *EvT* 33 (1973) 32–53, esp. 48–52. She opposes the more homogeneous picture of the groups in Amos as reconstructed by H. Donner, "Die soziale Botschaft der Propheten im Lichte der Gesellschaftordnung in Israel," *OrAnt* 2 (1963) 229–45, esp. 235–37, 243–45, and K. Koch, "Die Entstehung der sozialen Kritik bei den Profeten," *Probleme biblischer Theologie. G. von Rad zum 70. Geburtstag* (Munich: C. Kaiser, 1971) 236–57, esp. 243–46.

[3]5:26 is a secondary text; 8:14, from the Amos school, probably does not refer to other gods, as noted by E. Hammershaimb, *The Book of Amos, A Commentary* (Oxford: Blackwell, 1970) 128–30, and W. Rudolph, *Joel-Amos-Obadja-Jona* (KAT 13/2; Gütersloh: G. Mohn, 1971) 268–71.

[4]Wolff, *Joel and Amos*, 164, 236–38. Note the translation error on p. 237, where the last sentence of the first paragraph on v 4 should read, "However, there is no basis for denying derivation of vv 4–5 from Amos himself, as is done with v 6 and vv 14–15."

Amos' message is seemingly simple and straightforward: "The end is coming for my people Israel"; "I will pardon them no more" (7:8; 8:2). The end is coming because the traditional values have been abandoned by a society whose greed for wealth has led them to exploit the poor (2:6–7; 3:9–10; 4:1–3; cf. 8:4–6, from the Amos school), to overturn legal procedures (5:10–12), and to convert the cultus into a "foundation for . . . arrogance."[5] Moreover, the end is coming for all. No one—no group—is singled out as an exception. "Fallen, no more to rise, is the virgin Israel . . . there is no one to lift her up" (5:2). None can flee from the end; they cannot hide from God, whether in Sheol or captivity (9:1–4). Though Amos can announce the Lord's word as including "Seek me, and live" (5:4), the basic conclusion is that Israel has not sought the Lord, even in the face of severe prompting by famine, drought, infestation, and plague (4:6–11).[6] Not even the innocent poor, who are so often noted in the oracles, are marked for survival. The big house and the little house both are shattered (6:11), and God will put even the remnant (*ʾaḥărît*) to the sword (9:1), and he will see them hauled off with hooks (4:2; cf. 6:10; 8:10, from the Amos school). Amos is no peasant revolutionary, championing the poor without reservation. His prophetic, charismatic authority is not pitted against the bureaucratic authority of the urban elite as one of those "structurally powerless and inferior socially," as can so easily happen with such authority.[7] Positively construed, Amos' message is a plea for justice and righteousness, *mišpāṭ* and *ṣĕdāqâ* (5:24; cf. 5:7; 6:12), qualities of action that surely would benefit the poor and that might even be a source of life (5:4; cf. 5:14–15, from the Amos school—"perhaps the Lord will be gracious"). But what dominates is the word about the end. In the sequence of visions Amos does at first intercede for "Jacob" (7:1–6), but even this avails nothing. The concluding and decisive word is that God will pardon them no more, i.e., the end is coming (7:8; 8:2).

Given the dominance of the word about the end in Amos' message, the primary social role of his message is ideological, not practical. From Amos' perspective, he is announcing that the socio-economic life-style that has emerged in the northern kingdom, especially among the urban elite, is strongly opposed to the traditional values of Israel. He is announcing that socio-economic reorganization, or modernization, without compassion—power without love—is not the way for Israel. The

[5]Wolff, *Joel and Amos,* 104. Note Amos 5:21–24; 6:8; and 8:5–7, from the Amos school.

[6]The passage is of dubious authenticity. Wolff (*Joel and Amos,* 212–14, 217–18) assigns 4:6–11 to the Bethel redaction in the time of Josiah; however, Rudolph (*Joel-Amos-Obadja-Jona,* 172–75) argues strongly for authenticity.

[7]S. Walker, *Ceremonial Spirit Possession in Africa and Afro-America* (Leiden: Brill, 1972) 98.

resultant oppression of the poor cannot be tolerated. He is announcing also that Israel's enthusiastic participation in the cultus, even at the traditional sites of Bethel and Gilgal, leads only to a false sense of confidence. The cultus, including the festivals, cannot be taken for granted as effective, in the style of *ex opere operato*, but the precondition of an effective cultus is actual practice of justice and righteousness, which needs to flow "like a constant stream" (5:21–24).

Amos does not offer a program but a diagnostic judgment. The economic elite "are not troubled by the ruin of Joseph" (6:6), the sense apparently being that they are not troubled by "the sufferings of the oppressed and the wronged,"[8] or by such practices as might lead to the overthrow of Israel. These sufferings, though not detailed by Amos, are illustrated by reference to debt slavery (2:6; cf. 8:6, from the Amos school), a practice that is legally permissible but a situation in which the wealthy were supposed to assist the needy rather than exacting interest (Exod 22:24); to sexual abuse (2:7), perhaps exploiting a female servant, a *na*ᶜ*ărâ* (cf. Exod 21:7–9, in which the master may designate an ᵓ*āmâ*, a maidservant, for himself or for his son, but presumably not for both of them); to the misappropriation of pledges (2:8; cf. Exod 22:25–26); to unsuitable drinking (2:8); to abuse of judicial procedures (5:10, 12; cf. Exod 23:6–8); and perhaps to the use of fraudulent weights and measures (8:5, assigned to the Amos school; cf. Deut 25:13–16). By means of these references, as well as through many rather general comments, Amos points to the great contrast between the Yahwistic tradition, seemingly affirmed by Israel, and the socio-economic reality of the northern kingdom.

By announcing that the end is coming for Israel, Amos' message, taken at face value, does not really have a social role. There is only an understanding about the coming end. Amos, as has been pointed out, declines the option taken by naive primitivists; he is not like the Rechabites and does not call for a return to an idealized conception of the life forms of earlier Israel. Neither does his message offer the people "the bitter rebukes of a reformer"[9] and a summons to alter the socio-economic structures and thereby avoid God's punishment. Moreover, Amos makes no condemnation of wealth or new economic forms *per*

[8]So J. L. Mays (*Amos, A Commentary* [OTL; Philadelphia: Westminster, 1969] 117), most recently, over against many commentators (e.g. Wolff, 277) who interpret v 6b as a secondary reference to the political situation of the northern kingdom after the time of Jeroboam II.

[9]R. S. Cripps, *A Critical and Exegetical Commentary on the Book of Amos* (2d ed.; London: SPCK, 1955) 208; he sees Amos as offering a less than balanced analysis, especially since he "never once speaks of a fault in the *lower* stratum of society" (208).

se—the reference to building houses and planting vineyards (5:11) does not pit old wealth against new wealth. Most importantly, he does not exempt the poor and oppressed from the coming judgment. Whatever Amos' own social locus might have been—and the data are far from clear—he does not advocate "a right to revolution or self-help of the masses suppressed by the mighty."[10] Amos is God's messenger of the impending destruction and exile. From that perspective, the social role of his message would be ideological—it provides a way of understanding the real nature of Israel's present order and the meaning of the destruction that Israel is soon to experience because of that order. For his message to have a practical social role it would presuppose that there was a possibility of lessening or averting the end as proclaimed. Amos does not suggest that possibility, in spite of his admonition to the house of Israel, "Seek me, and live" (5:4), as even that brief shift is followed by the note that Gilgal and Bethel will surely experience disaster (5:5), a sequence similar to that already noted in the visions. Yet some of Amos' disciples held out hope for a "perhaps" (5:14–15), and that reminds us that Amos' audience might well have seen the social role of his message differently from Amos himself.

For those who took his message seriously but hoped for some alternative to the coming end, either due to the length of time intervening before the destruction or to confidence in God's mercy, Amos' message had a different role. His exhortations were not utopian. Weber's comment that "the king and political-military circles could make no use whatever"—i.e., no social role for them—"of the purely utopian exhortations and counsels of the prophets,"[11] does not apply to Amos. His having pointed to the ideological contrast between the present reality and the traditional values could promote a process of everyday adjustment in which the courts and the market practices could become responsive to the needs of the poor and protective of their interests. The affluent life of the urban elite need not be built on the exploitation of the poor nor express itself primarily in conspicuous consumption, and the cultus could become genuinely expressive and even joyful when related to justice and righteousness rather than indulgence.

As support for responding to the ideological contrast, Amos, in the one word of encouragement (5:4–5), connects "Seek me, and live," with "But do not seek Bethel . . ." The term *dāraš*, "seek," as pointed out by

[10]M. Weber, *Ancient Judaism* (Glencoe, Ill.: Free Press, 1952) 278, emphasizing that "no prophet was a champion of 'democratic' ideals." He states that Amos "pronounced the rule of the uneducated, undisciplined demos as the worst of all curses" (277).

[11]Weber, *Ancient Judaism*, 281.

Westermann,[12] is peculiarly associated with turning to God through a prophet. In this oracle Amos emphasizes that real turning to God comes not by way of the cultus, nor, surely, by way of the royal bureaucracy, of which Bethel, being a sanctuary of the king, is seen as a part (7:13), but by way of the prophet.[13] That is, the authority that can give impetus to a practical adjustment in life style is precisely God's charismatic empowerment of the prophet. Thereby the prophet's message can have a social role.

As a corollary of the affirmation that the power of the charismatic word can prompt a new direction, Amos emphasizes a related ideological point, viz., that Israel cannot continue to trust in the covenant-election tradition, for that may not be taken to mean that Israel has a privileged role as God's people. Rather, Israel is under greater obligation (3:2, "therefore I will punish you for all your iniquity"; cf. 9:7, from the Amos school).

An important aspect of the potential social role of Amos' message is that he does not condemn wealth in principle. Instead, the issues are how one acquires wealth and how one uses it.[14] Amos' message would be for the community to incorporate the compassion and concern of the old traditions with the new economic forms. (Note that many scholars now argue in favor of the rabbinic tradition that Amos himself was a moderately wealthy stockraiser and landowner, over against the conventional interpretation that he was a low-status worker, a peasant. Yet both these interpretations are without solid evidence.) Likewise, while opposing the conspicuous consumption and arrogance of the wealthy, Amos does not praise the poor as such or hold up ascetic practices as proper to Israel. The poor may be innocent and powerless over against the exploitative practices of the rich (note 2:6; 5:12), but Amos never suggests that they will escape the coming judgment. To be sure, the line of captives will be *headed* by the self-indulgent rich (6:7), but there will be others in the line. The poor, or at least some of them, may be left behind at the time of deportation (2 Kgs 24:14; 25:12; Jer 40:7; see also Jer 52:15, 16), but the poor do not escape the destruction of warfare and exile.

[12]C. Westermann, "Die Begriffe für Fragen und Suchen im AT," *KD* 6 (1960) 14–27. See also Wolff, *Joel-Amos,* 238; *Hosea* (Hermeneia; Philadelphia: Fortress, 1974) 186.

[13]Westermann, "Fragen und Suchen," 22.

[14]Mays (*Amos,* 11) says that "the affluence of the rich does not enter into Amos' portrait of evil because he was an ascetic by faith, a primitivist in cultural outlook. The wealth he denounces was specifically the result of oppression of the poor and corruption of the court."

Many of Amos' admonitions seem to be addressed to the people generally. "Those who desire the Day of the Lord" (5:18), whatever their precise expectations were, presumably included various strata of the society. Even the poor might happily anticipate a day of divine intervention. And as for false confidence in the cultus, there is no reason to suspect that that was a peculiarity of the rich or powerful. Indeed, a common feature of peasant religion is attention to traditional ritual forms rather than to higher-order interpretations of the meaning of the ritual.[15] All might go to Bethel or Gilgal (4:4–5, addressed to the *bĕnê yiśrāʾēl*, i.e., the people in general); all might enjoy the feasting and music (5:21–23), perhaps especially likely at harvest festivals; and all might well improve with regard to justice and righteousness (5:24), for even villages can have oppressors and economic stratification.

For those who took Amos' message seriously and responded, their sense of Amos' (or God's) intention may well have been anticipated by Amos.[16] Indeed, the harshness of Amos' word that the end was coming need not be taken to mean that Israel was *actually* without hope, and subsequent redactors, with the addition of words of hope and salvation, did not necessarily misunderstand Amos. Yet Amos certainly stresses how hard the people find it to respond and how late the hour is. Among other prophets we find oracles pointing to the great difficulty that the people have in really hearing what the prophet is saying, a point illustrated beautifully in Isa 6:9–13. Likewise, there are many passages in the Gospels that express the challenge to discipleship with sayings indicating how very hard it is to enter the Kingdom of God, for "No one who puts his hand to the plough and looks back is fit for the Kingdom of God" (Luke 9:62), and "It is easier for a camel to go through a needle's eye than for a rich man to enter the Kingdom of God" (Matt 10:25).[17]

Amos' message, if taken as a challenge, could serve as the ideological support for a reintegration of the old values with the new circumstances of the northern kingdom. It could serve to join the real meaning of the

[15]E. R. Wolf, *Peasants* (Englewood Cliffs, N.J.; Prentice-Hall, 1966) 100–106.

[16]J. M. Berridge ("Zur Intention der Botschaft des Amos. Exegetische Überlegungen zu Am. 5," *TZ* 32 [1976] 321–40; see esp. 324–25, n. 30) follows a number of commentators in arguing that the judgment speech, such as in Amos 5, may have been intended as a call to repentance. Yet "Seek me, and live" (5:4) is an uncommon leniency in Amos' message. The harshness of his oracles generally does not suggest that the listeners would immediately conclude that he was actually summoning them to repentance. Only those who really believed Amos about the end might take his words as such a summons.

[17]N. Perrin, *Rediscovering the Teaching of Jesus* (New York: Harper & Row, 1967) 142–45.

old traditions with the actions of the new socio-economic order. The modernization process need not exclude compassion and concern. Taken as a challenge, Amos' message is that the Kingdom of God could come—again.[18]

[18]On early Israel as the Kingdom of God, see G. E. Mendenhall, *The Tenth Generation. The Origins of the Biblical Tradition* (Baltimore: Johns Hopkins, 1973) 1–31.

Prophetic Eschatological Visions and the Kingdom of God

Walter Harrelson
Vanderbilt University

THE PROBLEM

This essay aims to show that the eschatological visions of certain pre-exilic prophets bear very close comparison with the eschatology of early Christianity. In particular I want to show that the category of "failure" as applied to the work of the prophets of Israel has often been used in unsatisfactory ways. My contention is that Israel's prophets failed in about the same sense that most prophets fail. They did not see the realization of their hopes. The kinds of success that follow in history usually fail to correspond with the success anticipated. This is as true of Christianity as of ancient Israel, of the Jewish heritage and of the Muslim.

Prophets want too much and often claim too much. But their failures have little to do with the value of their lives or the validity of their messages. Israel's prophets prior to the Exile kept threatening the people's destruction if they did not mend their ways. Eventually, Judah and Jerusalem, like North Israel and Samaria before them, did fall. The fulfillment of the prediction of destruction is no proof of the soundness of the prophecies of doom. A community of faith has every right to believe that the Babylonian exile was just punishment sent by its God. It is quite another matter if that theological judgment is misapplied by others in such a way as to estimate the actual moral qualities of ancient Israel in relation to the moral realities of its neighbor peoples. Non-Israelite readers, or indeed any later readers, of the prophetic corpus need to be careful not to misapply the theological judgments of the prophets of Israel.[1]

Similarly, the truth or falsity of the promises of the pre-Exilic prophets is not established on the basis of whether or not the promises came to pass historically. Though they do have their import for the period in which they are set, their long-term truth or falsity is not to be

[1]A brief treatment of this point is given in my review of *When Prophecy Failed*, by Robert P. Carroll, *Zygon* 16 (1981) 383–84.

established by non-Israelites. Ancient Israelites have every right to believe in a coming consummation of God's work on earth. Later communities of faith, tied to ancient Israel, have every right to see in their own traditions and experiences the coming-to-fulfillment of such promises. But later communities do not have a right to settle the truth or falsity of the ancient promises for ancient Israel on the basis of whether or not they came to pass. Just as the fall of Jerusalem in 587 did not, as historical occurrence, establish the truth of Jeremiah's prediction of imminent doom, so also the return from Babylonian exile did not establish the truth of his prediction that within seventy years God would restore the fortunes of the people. Promises are affirmations of a community's or an individual's faith; their validity is not impugned by non-realization, just as their validity is not established by realization.

It seems evident that Israel's great prophets had an extraordinary notion of the vocation of Israel under God. They saw the very future of the nations of earth bound up with the future of Israel. They saw Israel's failure, therefore, as affecting not only Israel but all God's people, and indeed the whole earth. When the covenant between God and people was breached, as of course it regularly was, people being people, devastation awaited not only the breakers of covenant but also others whose health in mysterious ways depended upon the health of the people of God. This is what gives to the prophetic messages such urgency and frequent shrillness. It is not just that the God of Israel will exact retribution upon the people for their apostasies; God will deal more severely with Israel than with any other people just because so much is at stake in the demand upon Israel that she fulfill the terms of covenant.[2]

Similarly, the promises God made to the people of Israel were understood by the prophets to have the same sweep and urgency. When Zion had come to be recognized as the center of the universe, the focal point for blessing on earth, Zion's future was recognized to be of importance for all peoples, not just for Israel. When the descendant from David's line had come to be viewed as the agent and representative of God on earth, the future of the dynasty was understood to be tied to that of the people Israel and of the nations of earth as well.

This universalizing of the vocation of the people Israel was not, of course, accepted by all of the leaders of Israel. It may have been accepted by only a few. It was not a "missionary" outlook in any sense of the term, for Israel had no summons to convert the nations. Its task was to fulfill the demands of covenant faith in such a way that God's purposes for Israel and for the neighboring peoples and for the world would find

[2]Amos 3:2 makes the point clearly. Gerhard von Rad's treatment of the eighth century prophets perhaps overstates this point in his portrayal of the prophets' picture of the absolute End that awaits. See von Rad, *Old Testament Theology* (2 vols.; New York: Harper & Row, 1962–65) 2. 99–125.

realization. And therein we have the dynamism of both judgment and promise. The judgment is so severe because so much depends upon public justice, the demonstration of what kind of existence under God is demanded. The maintenance of hope is equally urgent, for not to have confidence in the triumph of God's purposes for Israel and for the nations is to impugn God's power to save or God's desire to do so.

In this essay, I want to look at a familiar, if difficult, eschatological promise from the prophet Isaiah and see how its eschatological vision may illustrate this theological weight of the promises of Israel's prophets. The text selected is Isa 8:23–9:6 (English: 9:1–7). What I want to show is that this promise is at once tied to an immediate situation in Isaiah's lifetime, that it expresses a hope that he has for the near future, and that it also expresses a fundamental affirmation about God's utter reliability, about the prophet's assurance to the people that God's work on earth is finding and will find consummation. It is at one and the same time a historical text with a message for its own time, a promise for a time to come, and an existential affirmation of faith in God appropriate to all times, and demonstrable in no time at all. The truth of the passage does not depend upon the correspondence seen between it and the Christian revelation, as Christians will describe the matter. The truth of the passage is not exhausted either in its immediate import for the history of Judah and North Israel or in its power to affirm the fundamental commitment of God to the people of Israel. Its truth also includes the interior recognition by Isaiah, and probably by many others in his day, that God is already establishing righteousness and peace in our world, is claiming us to reflect that action of God to establish righteousness, and is inviting, urging, drawing us to be the harbingers of an era of peace that is not only coming but is already showing up in our world and within us.

No full treatment of the difficult text is possible here. We must be content to offer a translation, identify form and setting, and attempt to trace the import of the promise in the three senses just enumerated: as an oracle of salvation addressed to a given situation; as a prophetic promise for a period understood to be near at hand; and as an affirmation of faith that had and has existential weight in any and all times.

TRANSLATION

The following translation depends, as do the exegetical comments, upon the fine study by Hans Wildberger in his *Biblischer Kommentar Altes Testament* commentary:[3]

[3]Hans Wildberger, *Jesaja* (BKAT; Neukirchen-Vluyn: Neukirchener, 1965ff.) 362–89. Other recent treatments of value include Albrecht Alt, "Jesaja 8, 23–9, 6: Befreiungsnacht und Krönungstag," in *Kleine Schriften zur Geschichte des Volkes Israel* (2 vols.; Munich: Beck, 1953) 2. 206–25; Norman K. Gottwald, *All*

Introduction: 8:23

No gloom, then, for the one who was in straits![4]
In former times He made light of the lands of Zebulun and Naphtali,
But in latter days he is honoring[5] the Way of the Sea, Beyond Jordan, Galilee of the Nations.

Announcement of Salvation: 9:1

The people walking in darkness
have seen a great light.
Those dwelling in deep gloom—
on them light has shined.

Declaration to God: 9:2–3

You have magnified their joy,[6]
you have increased their rejoicing.
They rejoice before you
as with harvest joy,
As those rejoice
who divide booty.
For the yoke he bears,
the staff he shoulders,
and the rod of his oppressor
You have shattered
as on the Day of Midian.[7]

The Consequence: 9:4

For every boot trampling in the tumult,
and the garments rolled in blood,

---

the Kingdoms of the Earth (New York: Harper & Row, 1964) 148–62; A. S. Herbert, *The Book of the Prophet Isaiah, Chapters 1–39* (Cambridge Bible Commentary; Cambridge; Cambridge University, 1973) 71–76; R. E. Clements, *Isaiah 1–39* (NCB; Grand Rapids: Eerdmans, 1980) 103–9.

[4]The line may conclude the oracle of judgment in 8:19–22 and therefore not belong to our passage. See NEB and A. S. Herbert, *Isaiah 1–39*, 72–73.

[5]Opinions are divided on how to read *hikbîd*. Gottwald (*All the Kingdoms of the Earth*, 159) and Clements (*Isaiah 1–39*, 105–6) consider it to refer to a second act of judgment against the northern provinces. The translation "he made heavy" is entirely possible. See the excellent study and bibliography in J. A. Emerton, "Some Linguistic and Historical Problems in Isaiah viii. 23," *JSS* 14 (1969) 151–75.

[6]A conjecture. For the translation "their joy" the Hebrew has "the nation not," which is clearly a defective text. Read *haggîlâ* for *haggōy lōʾ*.

[7]For the "Day of Midian" see my essay "Non-Royal Motifs in the Royal Eschatology," in *Israel's Prophetic Heritage* (B. W. Anderson and W. Harrelson, eds.; New York: Harper & Row, 1962) 149–53.

Shall be only for burning,
only fuel for the fire.

The Child-King: 9:5

For a child is born for us,
a son is given to us.
The governance shall be on his shoulder,
and his name be called,
"Wonder-Planner,
Hero-God,
Eternal Father,
Prince of Peace."[8]

The Kingdom: 9:6

Of the increase of governance,
and of peace,
there shall be no end,
Upon the throne of David
and on his kingdom,
Upholding and sustaining it,
by justice and by righteousness,
from now until for ever.
The zeal of the LORD of hosts—
it is doing this!

FORM

The poem is most similar to psalms of thanksgiving addressed to God in the cult, expressions of praise for acts of deliverance and mercy. Here, the situation is not in doubt: God has broken the hold of the enemy, has provided deliverance through divine intervention, and is even now setting up, or preparing to do so, the newly designated king upon David's throne whose kingdom will exercise peaceful rule throughout the land forever. The psalm of thanksgiving for deliverance seems to have been a regular feature of celebrations in which the king of Israel took the lead. See especially Psalm 18 (= 2 Samuel 22). The prophet is using the psalm of thanksgiving, however, out of its immediate cultic context in order to engender hope and confidence in the people in their time of distress.

SETTING

What is this time of distress? The difficulties are enormous in reaching a decision. I am convinced that the setting is the period 734–732 B.C.E., when North Israel lost the northern provinces to Tiglath

[8]Wildberger's treatment of the names is excellent: *Jesaja,* 381–84.

Pileser III and then had to prepare for further resistance against Assyria by helping to form a coalition of local states, including Syria. Judah's refusal to participate in the coalition led to the Syro-Ephraimitic war, an effort by Syria and North Israel to force Judah to take part in the resistance as their ally. In Isaiah 7 and 8 this particular event is in view, and it seems that Isa 8:23–9:6 is best located at the same time. The contrast is being drawn between the gloom that has settled upon North Israel, and especially upon the regions of Galilee, the Transjordan holdings, and perhaps also the Plain of Sharon, south of the Carmel Range, along the Mediterranean. Our psalm of thanksgiving for God's coming deliverance with its oracle of impending salvation affirms that the new ruler set up in Zion by God will transform the darkness and gloom of this time into rejoicing and peace, into a situation where warfare and war-mongering come to an end.[9]

THE IMMEDIATE MESSAGE

Isaiah's message for Ahaz and for the people of Israel is clear enough. Already in chaps. 7 and 8, Isaiah had been in frequent conversation with Ahaz about the course of faith that God purposed for the king. In 7:1–9, emphasis falls upon the demand that Ahaz and the people place their full trust in the LORD, rather than in North Israel and Syria and their coalition against Assyria. The situation is less clear in 7:10–25, where we may have an ironic promise of fertility and blessing, gained only by means of a massive devastation of the entire land. Any survivors would live well, but how few would be survivors! Yet, the sign of the child named Immanuel was a sign of hope and confidence in God.

In chap. 8, Isaiah deals again with the Syro-Ephraimitic war, apparently without being able to succeed in calling king and people to place their trust in God. The prophet may have withdrawn from the public scene as a result (see Isa 8:16–18). Then there follows our psalm of thanksgiving to God for the birth of a child that will lighten the people's darkness. The child referred to in Isaiah 8 is the prophet's son; this child, however, seems to have greater similarity to the child mentioned in 7:10–25. A descendant from David's family must be intended, but it would seem unlikely that the reference is to Hezekiah personally, assuming that Hezekiah is about to be born or has recently been born. According to 2 Kgs 18:2, Hezekiah was twenty-five years of age when his reign began, in 715 B.C.E.,[10] which would place his birth in 740 B.C.E., five years before Ahaz assumed the kingship. The chronology of Ahaz is

[9]See Wildberger, *Jesaja*, 368–71; Gottwald, *All the Kingdoms of the Earth*, 148–62.

[10]On the difficult question of the dates of Ahaz's reign see H. B. MacLean, "Ahaz," *IDB* 1. 64–66.

very difficult to reconstruct, and we probably should not place great reliance upon the ages or the length of reign in his case or in that of Hezekiah. Even so, the passage must be either anticipating the actual birth of a potential heir to Ahaz or be portraying, in faith, the future of a child recently born to Ahaz. Hezekiah can not be ruled out.

The message is not so much about a child's birth, however, as it is about the triumph of God's purposes for the people, the whole of Israel. Isaiah's interest is in North Israel as well as in Judah. The loss of provinces to the northern kingdom is a loss of Israel's promised heritage. The very division of the kingdom into Israel and Judah is probably a great tragedy to him, one that God will bring to an end. The kingship God purposes has its seat in Jerusalem; it encompasses the land once belonging to David's kingship. When the hero-king here promised comes to the throne, peace will come to the entire region. It will no longer be a matter of choosing Assyria over the local coalition, even as the lesser of two evils, for God's covenant zeal will establish the *divine* rule in Jerusalem.

For the years 732 B.C.E. and following, then, the prophet calls king and people to take note of a divine intervention now occurring, the result of which will be a fresh set of political developments that will usher in an extraordinary change in the life of the people of the land. Dispirited and anxious folk, including the king (see Isa 7:1–9), may confidently lay aside their fears, for the danger they face will be averted.

Did Isaiah not, however, wish the people to bear fully in mind that this laying aside of anxiety was to be accompanied by the *practice* of the covenant faith? Those who were busy joining house to house and field to field, until they were left alone in the land, possessors of a vast landholding that had been put together by the destruction of their neighbors (Isa 5:8), were called to account. Jerusalem, the once-faithful city that had become a harlot-city (Isa 1:21), could not persist in its evil. God's day of deliverance would be a day of woe and lamentation for all who were desecrating the divine covenant by their conduct (Isa 2:6–3:15). The promise of deliverance through the mysterious child whom God would raise to the throne of David was tied to the critical message of the prophet during these years.

THE MESSAGE FOR DAYS SOON TO DAWN

The prophet does expect, however, that the situation faced by the people will shortly be radically transformed by political actions even now taking root. The child referred to may be born, but the child has not yet claimed the kingship. Ahaz is king, and Ahaz will remain king for many years to come. The great shattering of the forces of warfare is coming, but it has not come as yet. When it comes, the deliverance will be like that on the day of Midian—an apparent reference to the scattering of the Midianite forces by Gideon through a stratagem described in Judg 7:1–23. That overwhelming victory of Gideon with only 300 men pitted against the Midianite hordes seems to have been used by Isaiah to remind the people that God's raising up of the new descendant of David would be of such a sort that normal acts of warfare, normal battle-strategies, and normal acts of diplomacy and treaty-making would be of no consequence at all in the establishment of the peace God had in store for the people. Here is where the magnificent imagery of the destruction of battle-sandals and the burning of blood-flecked clothing stand out so clearly. And in this connection too we have the five-fold names of the new king, imagery borrowed from Egypt, it seems, and the language used on occasions of the accession of the Pharaoh to the throne, which makes our king to come the product of miraculous divine interventions, a peacebringer who makes warfare into a shabby and pointless thing.

Isaiah thus offers a promise to the people of Judah, Jerusalem, and North Israel that the intervention of God to bring peace and blessing to the entire land is soon to come. Whether or not the prophet first presented this message on some occasion when the situation in fact was marked by hope is of little or no consequence. We would like to know, of course, if that were in fact the case. But the prophet's message is about a time sure to come very soon, the import of which is great indeed, here and now. The people of the covenant *have* hope, for this promise will surely come to birth, the prophet insists. They also can feel the judgment upon their life then and there, as they live not in accordance with this purposed life in peace and righteousness, but faithless to the covenant, not now living as appropriate subjects of a king with such titles and with such a mission from God. And they probably were able, as communities of faith in subsequent times have been, to feel the weight and the drawing power of such a vision that is finding realization.[11] Thus the passage portrays a future, one that has a chronological dimension to it, into which they are being drawn by processes already at work within their midst. This is not just the cultic joy and transformation that a worshiping community can revel in as the earthly king is re-installed and the power of God the king is recognized to be focused in him. This is a picture of change under way in the historical and political existence of the people, set in motion by God at a particular time, and sweeping the people along toward the day of its consummation, its public display.

[11]For the ways in which eschatology probably functioned in the life and cult of the people of Israel, see Walter Harrelson, *From Fertility Cult to Worship* (Scholars Press reprint; Chico: Scholars Press, 1980) 137–51.

PROMISE ON THE WAY TO REALIZATION

The passage is also to some extent realized already in the life of the community of Isaiah's day. This assertion cannot be proved, but it seems to me highly probable. The very use of verbs in the so-called "prophetic perfect" is somewhat supportive of the idea. More importantly, the continued use of these promises, in changing circumstances that never fully bring about the reality promised, but which do not lead to despair and abandonment of faith—the continuing preservation and elaboration of these promises, supports the view that their existential import for all times and generations was high. I recognize that the faith of Israel is focused upon the future day of consummation when publicly this promised reality will be evident to all, and that the introduction of "Christian" notions of realized or being-realized eschatology would be inappropriate. Christian faith does talk about consummation in Jesus as the Christ in ways inappropriate for these texts from the Hebrew Scriptures in their own day. My point is that the prophet, the disciples of the prophet, and also others within each generation are very likely to have held to these promises of God in such a way that the consummation broke in upon them before the actual day of consummation had arisen. I am not speaking of a merely subjective feeling of peace or liberation or the sense of being a part of a righteous community when unrighteousness is everywhere to be seen. I am speaking rather of the interior, depth-quality of a life in faith, a recognition that that which God has disclosed about our future is a reality being anticipated in our community before it finds public display.[12]

Look at our text in this light. God is identifiable as the one who breaks the hold of the oppressors, who has no further use of warriors or their armaments, whose designated ruler leads the community surefootedly and confidently to the destiny awaiting. Military might cannot prevail against God and the king raised up. But the scene that meets the eye is not of carnage wrought by God or the agent of God. Rather, it is a scene of public justice, equity, peace, security, blessing. We are even now in the care and custody of the God who is transforming the darkness into light. We are citizens of the light, belong to the light, and are partaking of the peace and righteousness and wholeness of a transformed social existence.

My chief point is that this passage has for ancient Israel, in all probability, much of the meaning that the later Christian community will assign to it when it claims that the promise finds its fulfillment in

[12]See the suggestive remarks of von Rad, *Old Testament Theology*, 2. 118–19. In my view, they are not carried far enough.

Jesus as the Christ. Christians have a right to read the passage in the light of the revelation that they discern in Jesus Christ. Jews have a right to read the passage in light of the continuing promise of the Messianic age that is yet awaited. But all human beings drawn to this text have a right to savor its existential power, its capacity to present a faith and a hope that seem to have the power to adumbrate that which is promised, that for which hearers are invited to hope.[13]

[13]I am happy to offer this study to George E. Mendenhall, a respected colleague and friend, whose interest in the actual experiencing of religious faith is always nearby as he carries on his investigations into the literature, language and thought of the ancient world.

The Divine King and the Human Community in Isaiah's Vision of the Future

J. J. M. Roberts
Princeton Theological Seminary

Isaiah's inaugural vision of the divine king seated on his exalted throne dominates the prophet's conception of the future as indeed it dominates all his theology.[1] In the words of the refrain to his powerful vision of Yahweh's coming day of judgment, "Yahweh alone will be exalted in that day."[2] Judgment, deliverance, and future bliss are all focused in the divine initiative. Yahweh may use human agents as his tools for working out the future, but Isaiah leaves no doubt that the plan and its execution are Yahweh's plan and Yahweh's work. Within this impressively theocentric theology, therefore, it may be profitable to look at the role of the human community. What, if anything, remains as human responsibilities?

JUDGMENT

Yahweh's judgment of his people is provoked by their rebellion. The people as a whole,[3] their political and religious leaders,[4] including

*It is a pleasure to contribute this study in honor of a scholar whose creative treatment of the Old Testament has remained a stimulating influence on me since I first read his *Law and Covenant* almost twenty years ago.

[1]Isa 6:1. The attempts by Jacob Milgrom (*VT* 14 [1964] 164–82) and others to treat this chapter as a later commissioning during Isaiah's prophetic career is unconvincing. It does show close similarities to the Micaiah ben Imla episode in 1 Kings 22, but it also has certain features in common with the call narratives that are absent from 1 Kings 22. The fiery cleansing of Isaiah's sins, centered on his lips, is surely to be understood as enabling him to take up the prophetic task, and as such it is analogous, though not identical, to the divine actions in Jer 1:9 and Ezek 2:8–3:3. The literary placement of Isaiah 6 is no argument against this interpretation, as the placement of Amos's call narrative demonstrates (Amos 7:10–16). Moreover, the evidence of Isa 1:5–9 shows that Isaiah's oracles are *not* arranged in chronological order.

[2]Isa 2:11, 17.

[3]Isa 1:3–4.

[4]Isa 1:10, 23; 2:12–15.

even the royal house[5]—though Isaiah seems curiously reticent to attack the Davidic kings—and the women of means,[6] are all forced to bear the blame for God's impending judgment. As an agent of judgment Yahweh had used Aram,[7] the Philistines,[8] Ephraim and Manasseh against themselves and both against Judah,[9] and he threatened to use Assyria as his staff to punish both Israel and Judah.[10] But Assyria's role was to be a limited one, and any transgression of those limits, any attempt to elevate themselves and rival Yahweh, would be crushed by God.[11] Yahweh alone will be exalted.

DELIVERANCE

While God's plan to judge his people had its human agents, it is far more difficult to find any human agents for Yahweh's deliverance of the remnant, symbolized in his deliverance of the city of Jerusalem. In Isaiah's early oracles from the period of the Syro-Ephraimitic war it is true that Assyria is mentioned at least once and perhaps several times as the agent that would remove this northern threat,[12] but other passages which may date to this period simply speak of Yahweh frustrating the plan of Judah's enemies without naming any historical agent for Yahweh's deliverance.[13] The ultimate source of this deliverance is far more important to Isaiah than its proximate source, and the demand he places on his hearers is for faith in God's promises, not for confidence in his analysis of the external political situation.[14]

In his later prophecies from the period of the Assyrian crisis there is no attempt to point to the human agent of Judah's deliverance.[15] In fact,

[5]Isa 7:13.

[6]Isa 3:16–4:1; 32:9–14.

[7]Isa 9:11.

[8]Isa 9:11.

[9]Isa 9:20.

[10]Isa 10:5ff.; cf. 5:26–29.

[11]Isa 10:12, 15ff. I remain unconvinced by Hermann Barth's (*Die Jesaja-Worte in der Josiazeit* [WMANT 48; Neukirchen-Vluyn: Neukirchener Verlag, 1977]) and R. E. Clement's (*Isaiah and the Deliverance of Jerusalem* [JSOTSup 13; Sheffield: JSOT, 1980] and *Isaiah 1–39* [New Century Bible Commentary; Grand Rapids: Eerdmans, 1980] 5–6) attempts to redate most of the oracles against Assyria to the Josianic period.

[12]Isa 8:4. See also 7:18, 20.

[13]Isa 7:7–9, 16; 8:9–10; 17:12–14.

[14]Isa 7:9

[15]Some recent scholars have again defended an eighth century date for the references to the Elamites and the Medes in chapters 13, 21, and 22 (Seth Erlandsson, *The Burden of Babylon* [Coniectanea Biblica, OT Series 4; Lund: CWK Gleerup, 1970]; and the more limited and nuanced work of A. A. Macintosh,

the prophet quite explicitly denies that God will use any human agent: "Assyria shall fall by a sword, not of man; and a sword, not of man, shall devour him."[16] The deliverance is portrayed as pure miracle, as due to the direct intervention of Yahweh himself.[17]

In view of this emphasis, it is important to note the relatively secondary role the Davidic ruler plays in the *inauguration* of this era of salvation. Neither in Isaiah 9 nor 11 does the messianic king overthrow the foreign enemy. Rather, in both cases, he inherits and enhances the results of Yahweh's prior intervention. This is especially clear in 11:1 where the growth of the messianic shoot is immediately preceded by Yahweh's lopping off of the arrogant, overbearing forest of Jerusalem's enemies.[18] It is less clear in chapter 9, but one should note that Yahweh's smashing of the enemy power (9:3) precedes the prophet's comments on the rule of the Davidic monarch, and the whole section is concluded with the statement: "The zeal of Yahweh of hosts shall accomplish this."[19]

Nonetheless, this messianic figure is not totally passive. He judges, he reproves, he smites the earth, he slays the wicked—in short he exercises royal rule in justice and righteousness.[20] While he apparently does this in response to the prior deliverance of Yahweh, the king still plays an active role, and that forces one to ask about the role or task of the human community in the coming age of salvation.

AGE OF SALVATION

While Jerusalem's deliverance may be attributed to the intervention of Yahweh alone and human participation in that deliverance be reduced to mere obedient faith in God's promise,[21] a more active role is assigned

---

Isaiah xxi: A palimpsest [Cambridge: Cambridge University, 1980]), but whatever one's response to their argument, it does not affect my point. The Medes and Elamites do not deliver Judah from Assyria in these passages if they are read in an eighth century context.

[16]Isa 31:8.

[17]Isa 10:16–17, 25–27, 33; 14:24–27; 29:6–8; 30:31–33; 31:4–9; 33:10–12.

[18]Isa 10:32–34. The common critical insistence that Isa 11:1 begins a new oracle, and should therefore be read in antiseptic isolation from its present literary context, is a bit puzzling. Not only does the image of the hacked-down forest provide a meaningful setting for the image of new growth, but this decimated forest imagery appears elsewhere referring both to Assyria's downfall (10:17–19) and to Judah's restoration through and after judgment (29:17; 32:15–19).

[19]Isa 9:6.

[20]Isa 9:6; 11:3–4.

[21]Isa 7:9; 30:15. I use the term "obedient faith" because Isaiah is speaking of a confidence in God that expresses itself by turning away from frantic attempts

to the human community in the coming age of salvation. Isa 32:1–8 provides a good framework for the discussion of Isaiah's point of view:

See, a king will reign in righteousness,
And ministers will govern with justice.
Everyone of them will be like a refuge from the wind,
A shelter from the rainstorm,
Like streams of water in a desert,
Like the shade of a massive rock in a weary land.
Then the eyes of those who see will not be closed,
And the ears of those who hear will listen attentively,
The minds of the thoughtless will attain understanding,
And the tongues of the stammerers will speak fluently.
No longer will the villain be called noble,
Nor will "gentleman" be said of a knave.
For the villain speaks villainy,
And his mind plots treachery:
To act impiously,
And to advocate disloyalty against Yahweh.
To leave the craving of the hungry unsatisfied
And deprive the thirsty of drink.
As for the knave, his weapons are evil.
He devises wicked schemes
To destroy the poor with lies
Even when the plea of the needy is just.
But the noble plans noble actions,
And he is constant in noble deeds.[22]

Since many modern critics regard this passage as secondary, it is necessary to treat that question before one can use this text as a source for Isaiah's vision of the future. The arguments against Isaianic authorship are actually not very impressive. Wildberger, while admitting the weakness of the arguments, nonetheless rejects the passage on the basis that "for Isaiah the שׂרים would hardly have had a place next to the Davidide in such a vision of the future."[23] But this judgment flies in the face of the clearly Isaianic 1:26, where Yahweh, following his refining judgment on Zion, promises to restore her judges and counselors as at the beginning. Isaiah's vision of the future included a place for royal

---

to achieve security by oppressive political and military planning, and concentrates instead on easing the oppression of the poor (Isa 28:12; see my note on this passage in *HTR* 73 [1980] 49–51).

[22]The translation is the author's, though heavily influenced by the RSV and the new JPS rendering.

[23]Hans Wildberger, *Jesaja* (BKAT X; Neukirchen-Vluyn: Neukirchener Verlag, 1978) 1253.

officials, and it is not surprising to find them mentioned here.[24] R. E. Clements argues that 32:1 does not foretell the advent of the king who rules justly, but simply describes him as a present figure,[25] but against him one must insist that vv 1–5 are all clearly construed in the future. Moreover, the oracle is placed in a context where it follows Yahweh's deliverance of Zion, just as 11:1 follows Yahweh's destruction of Zion's enemies.[26] The oracle may originally have been independent of its present context, but it had a context, and I see no reason to fault the ancient editor, who apparently understood the oracle to refer to the era of salvation after Yahweh will have destroyed Assyria.

Hermisson, who accepts 32:1–2 as genuine, rejects vv 3–5, since these verses deal with the altered nature of humans or particular human types in the age of salvation. He cannot see any connection between a change in human nature and the coming kingdom.[27] Wildberger similarly claims that Isaiah envisioned a particular political-social action of Yahweh, not the creation of a new humanity.[28] Both of them miss the point. In his critique of his contemporaries Isaiah had blamed the leaders for misleading the people.[29] The political and religious leadership were largely responsible for Judah's blindness, deafness, and folly.[30] The promise is that when the leaders rule justly, these defects will fall aside. It is precisely the political-social establishment of just government which will lead to a transformation of society. This is not an individualistic vision of a transformed humanity, but a vision of transformed society!

[24]Cf. Hans-Jürgen Hermisson, "Zukunftserwartung und Gegenwartskritik in der Verkündigung Jesajas," *EvT* 33 (1973) 67; J. Skinner, *Isaiah* (The Cambridge Bible for Schools and Colleges; Cambridge: University, 1925) 255; Bernh. Duhm, *Das Buch Jesaia* (HzAT; Göttingen: Vandenhoeck & Ruprecht, 1892) 210–11.

[25]R. E. Clements, *Isaiah 1–39*, 259.

[26]Moreover, 31:9 contains the fire imagery so dear to Isaiah for describing Yahweh's deliverance through judgment that leads to a renewed community (cf. 1:25–26; 10:17; 30:33; 33:10–14).

[27]Hermisson, "Verkündigung Jesajas," 57, n. 12.

[28]Wildberger, *Jesaja*, 1252.

[29]Isa 3:12.

[30]Their refusal to look to the Holy One of Israel (5:12; 22:11), their desire not even to hear of him (30:9–11), ultimately led to the loss of their wisdom (29:9–14). Precisely what the "tongue of the stammerer" refers to is not clear. The word "stammerer" (*ᶜlg*, 32:4) occurs nowhere else in the OT. The closest parallel is in the expressions *blᶜgy śph*, "by those of strange lips" (28:11), and *nlᶜg lšwn ᵓyn bynh*, "who stammer in a tongue you cannot understand" (33:19). In 32:4, however, the stammerer is not a foreigner, but an Israelite.

If my argument for the authenticity of at least 32:1–5 is sound,[31] what kind of framework does this passage provide for exploring Isaiah's vision of the future king, his officers, and the populace as a whole?

King

The role the king plays in this passage's portrayal of the future is similar to the function of the messianic king in Isaiah 9 and 11. All these passages give expression to the very ancient ideals of Davidic royal theology. Isa 32:1, though it uses a different verb, resembles in thought and expression the demands that Yahweh imposed on the human king in his covenant with David as recorded in the "Last Words of David": "Rule over men in righteousness, rule in the fear of God."[32] Isa 11:1–5 is full of phraseology that can be paralleled in the royal Psalms. It is particularly close to Psalm 72. In Isaiah the king is equipped for his task by the "spirit of Yahweh" which rests upon him, so in Psalm 72 it is God's gift of his own divine justice and righteousness that enables the king to fulfill his task. In both passages that task is defined as primarily judicial in nature. The king judges the poor in righteousness and reproves the humble of the earth in equity (*wšpṭ bṣdq dlym whwkyḥ bmyšwr lᶜnwy ᵓrṣ*; Isa 11:4a). He judges God's people in righteousness and his humble ones in justice (*ydyn ᶜmk bṣdq wᶜnyyk bmšpṭ*; Ps 72:2). In both passages his vindication of the poor involves the slaying of the wicked (*whkh ᵓrṣ bšbṭ pyw wbrwḥ śptyw ymyt ršᶜ*; Isa 11:4b; "and he crushes the oppressor," *wydkᵓ ᶜwšq*, Ps 72:4). On this point compare also Ps 2:9: "You will shatter them with an iron staff, you will smash them like a potter's vessel" (*trᶜm bšbṭ brzl kkly ywṣr tnpṣm*), and Ps 101:8: "Each morning I will destroy all the wicked of the land, cutting off all the evildoers from the city of Yahweh" (*lbqrym ᵓṣmyt kl ršᶜy ᵓrṣ lhkryt mᶜyr yhwh kl pᶜly ᵓwn*). The staff with which the king smashes the evil is a staff of equity (*šbṭ myšr*, Ps 45:7), and he establishes his throne by justice and righteousness (Isa 9:6; cf. Prov 20:28; 25:5).

It is important to recognize that in all these activities not only is God at work (Isa 9:6), but the king is participating in what is really the work of the divine king. Yahweh judges the peoples (Isa 2:4), including

[31]The authenticity of 32:6–8 is more seriously questioned, but I am not convinced that even these verses are secondary. They have a wisdom flavor to them, but Isaiah's contacts with wisdom are well established, and he could well have adapted wisdom material to make his point. These verses are not central to my argument, however.

[32]2 Sam 23:3. Reading *mšl* with 4 QSam[a] and vocalizing as an imperative following G[L]. See F. M. Cross, *Canaanite Myth and Hebrew Epic* (Cambridge: Harvard University, 1973) 235–36, n. 70; and E. C. Ulrich, Jr., *The Qumran Text of Samuel and Josephus* (HSM 19; Missoula: Scholars Press, 1978) 114.

the poor (Ps 10:18), in righteousness (Pss 9:8–9; 67:5; 96:13; 98:9). He slays the wicked (Pss 9:6; 129:4; 145:20), and the foundations of his throne are righteousness and justice, while mercy and truth stand before him (Ps 89:15; cf. 9:8; 97:2). In other words, the human king is simply the regent of the divine sovereign, participating in what is ultimately the divine rule. His authority comes from God and rests in the conformity of his human rule to the divine will, a view of kingship adumbrated in the ancient Davidic covenant.

Isaiah's vision of the future is controlled by the ancient concept even though it was never fully realized in the past and the monarchs of his own day fell woefully short of the ideal. Despite that experience, Isaiah could not, or at least did not, conceive of a future without a power structure centered in a human king, and he assigned that king the same day to day tasks of judicial administration that the monarchs of his own day were botching.

Ministers

It is worth noting, however, that the portrayal of the age of salvation in Isa 32:1 includes a role for ministers or officers alongside the role of the king. This corresponds to the Isaianic promise in 1:26 that God would restore Jerusalem's judges as at the first and her counselors as in the beginning. The reference here is clearly to the idealized Davidic period, and it indicates that just as Isaiah could not envision a future for his people without a monarch, so he could not envision monarchical rule without the royal officials to carry out royal policy. In that sense his vision for the future is very much tied to history and to this world.[33]

Even more interesting, however, is the imagery used to characterize the role of king and ministers in Isa 32:2. The metaphors found there are elsewhere in the Old Testament associated primarily with Yahweh's role. The word *mḥbᵓ*, "refuge," does not occur again in a similar context, but *str*, "shelter," is used most often of God as the place of refuge for his people (Pss 27:5; 32:7; 61:5; 91:1; 119:114), and *mḥsh*, a synonym of *mḥbᵓ*, is similarly used of Yahweh (Ps 61:4; Isa 25:4). Though the expression *plgy mym*, "streams of water," is not elsewhere used as a metaphor for Yahweh (see, however, Ps 1:3),[34] it calls to mind the numerous passages that do compare Yahweh to water or the source

[33]If Isa 8:23–9:6 originated as an enthronement oracle for Hezekiah as a number of scholars think, that would underscore just how closely Isaiah's glorious hopes could be tied to mundane realities. His concrete threats to Shebna and promises to Eliakim (22:15–24) might also provide a paradigm of how Isaiah himself understood this business of restoring just officials.

[34]The expression is used of a human king in Prov 21:1, but the meaning of the metaphor is quite different there.

of water (Jer 2:13; 17:13; 18:14–15; Isa 33:21; Pss 42:2; 63:2). The use of *ṣl*, "shade," as an image for Yahweh's protection is widespread (Pss 17:8; 36:8; 57:2; 63:2), as is also the metaphor of Yahweh as the rock (Pss 18:3; 31:4; 42:10; 71:3). The closest parallel to Isa 32:2 is found in the Isaiah apocalypse, where a number of the same elements are picked up and applied to Yahweh:

> For you will be a refuge to the weak,
> A refuge to the needy in his affliction,
> A shelter (*mḥsh*) from the rainstorm (*zrm*), a shade (*ṣl*) from the heat. . . .
> (Isa 25:4)

The continuation of this text, with its interpretative identification of the "winter rainstorm" (*zrm qr*[35]) and "heat in the desert" (*ḥrb bṣywn*) as the "spirit of the ruthless" (*rwḥ ᶜryṣym*), suggests that it is dependent on Isa 32:2. If so, it simply underscores the degree to which metaphors appropriate to the deity have been applied to the human king and his human ministers in Isa 32:2.

In short, in the age of salvation, king and ministers alike will participate in Yahweh's salvific activity. Yahweh's vindication of the needy among his people will be the concern of his human agents, and when that takes place, when Israel's leaders truly pursue justice, the moral blindness and hypocrisy which marred the society of Isaiah's contemporaries will cease to exist.

People

That brings one to the role of the people in the age of salvation. If just monarchical rule is truly to strip away pretense and sham, if reality is again to be called by its true name, if Zion is once again to be known as the faithful city of righteousness (Isa 1:26), this drastic change in Judean society must demand something of God's people as well as its leaders. Just as a radical purging of corrupt officials and their replacement by righteous judges appears as a prerequisite for the unfolding of the age of salvation, so the rest of society must also experience the purging effect of God's judgment. It is through judgment that Jerusalem is to be saved, and that judgment involves both the death of sinners and the transformation of those who survive (Isa 1:27–28).[36]

[35]The correction from *qyr*, "wall," to *qr*, "cold," is suggested by the contrast with *ḥrb*, "heat." *Qyr* is probably the result of a mistaken vocalization of a form written in a defective orthography.

[36]Those scholars who regard the "remnant" as a purely negative motif in Isaiah must not only delete these verses as secondary, they must also dismiss them as a misinterpretation of Isaiah's message. But the interpretation of 1:21–26

Isaiah sees this transformation arising out of the glorious yet terrifying experience of Yahweh's deliverance of Jerusalem. This theme is touched on in a number of passages, but nowhere is it more clearly stated than in Isa 33:10–16.[37] After describing how he would rise up to punish his enemies and deliver Jerusalem, Yahweh calls upon people far and near to observe what he has done. Then he describes the impact of that experience on the inhabitants of Zion. The sinners and impious in Zion are thrown into a panic. God's devastating judgment on his enemies forces them to raise the question, "Who among us can sojourn with such a devouring fire?" The response comes in the form of an entrance torah similar to those in Psalms 15 and 24.[38] The kind of

---

offered by such modern critics is not as convincing as the ancient one found in 1:27–28. How can one speak of purifying and restoring a city, if there is to be no continuity between the present and future inhabitants? Hermisson argues for a continuity focused totally on the city as an institution, ignoring its population, and he claims that the contrary view rests on rationalistic considerations (*EvT* 33 [1973] 68, n. 38). This rigid distinction between city and people appears unbiblical and a bit artificial, not to say irrational, however. Had Moses used similar logic, there would have been no Israel (Exod 32:9–14), and one might hope that interpreters could be as sensitive to the implications of a divine action as Moses was. Moreover, one cannot cut away every passage which sees a positive future for a segment of the people without appearing to trim the evidence to fit the theory (cf. the judicious remarks of Joseph Jensen in "Woe and Weal in Isaiah: Consistency and Continuity," *CBQ* 43 [1981] 167–87). A righteous remnant is clearly presupposed by 14:32: "For Yahweh has founded Zion, and in it the humble of his people will find refuge."

[37]Cf. 4:3–4; 10:20–23; 29:17–21; 30:18–26; 30:27–33; 31:4–9. Unfortunately most of these passages, including 33:10–16, are generally dismissed by modern scholars as non-Isaianic and therefore ignored in treatments of Isaiah's view of the future. The question is too complex to treat in an article of this scope—see my study of Isaiah 33 in the forthcoming Festschrift for Noel Freedman and the more limited treatment of 30:18–21 in "The Teaching Voice in Isaiah 30:20–21," *Christian Teaching: Studies in Honor of LeMoine G. Lewis*, ed. Everett Ferguson (Abilene: Abilene Christian University, 1981) 130–37—but I do not share the prevailing judgment. Some of the passages appear to have been glossed or to have otherwise suffered in the course of textual transmission, but the underlying theology is thoroughly compatible with that of Isaiah. One might attribute some of this material to close disciples, but to assign it to the postexilic or even Josianic period and then set up sharp contrasts between it and Isaiah's own, very narrowly construed, thought, is utterly unconvincing.

[38]Since Psalm 24 most likely dates to the very early monarchic period (Cross, *Canaanite*, 91–94), this form was certainly at home in Jerusalem prior to Isaiah's time. That he should adapt it for his own use is no more surprising than his use of the Zion tradition or his references to festival processions (30:29) in the course of which such liturgies apparently had their place.

person who will live in the purified Jerusalem with Yahweh, this never-dying fire, is

> The one who walks in righteousness,
> Who speaks uprightly,
> Who refuses the profit from oppression,
> Who shakes out his hands from taking a bribe,
> Who closes his ears from participating in plots to shed blood,
> Who shuts his eyes from looking at evil (33:15).

The moral transformation of Zion's surviving remnant is expressed here in very traditional Israelite categories. In this, as in his description of the messianic king and his enlightened ministers, Isaiah remains very much a man of his time, rooted in ancient tradition. But the catalyst behind this transformation is a new experiential awareness of God's character, a new openness to his activity in history. As Isaiah's inaugural vision of the awesome, holy, divine king transformed the prophet, so the people's vision of Yahweh's terrifying judgment and awesome deliverance would transform their lives. When that experience forced them to hallow the Holy One of Jacob and stand in awe of the God of Israel, a change in behavior would follow (29:23–24).

SUMMARY

In Isaiah's vision of the future the initiative belongs to Yahweh. Whether in judgment, deliverance, or the following age of salvation, Yahweh remains the dominant actor. In Isaiah's description of the age of salvation, however, something is expected of all segments of the transformed human society. It is a transformed society, not because the form of the society is changed—Isaiah foresees a monarchical community basically similar to the one he knew—but because its experience of divine judgment and deliverance has been so profound that king, official, and commoner alike are motivated to realize the ancient ideals for their station.

Imperial Dream: Text and Sense of Mic 5:4b–5

DELBERT R. HILLERS
THE JOHNS HOPKINS UNIVERSITY

In a book as full of textual and critical problems as Micah, 5:4b–5 seems rather easy, and commentators have with some reason treated it as such. But at a key point the text is unsatisfactory, and as a result the sense of the whole passage has seemed vague or even mysterious. This note attempts to present a reading that is in detail more satisfactory linguistically and historically, and which yields a more precise general sense.

REVISED TEXT

4b אשור[a] כי יבוא בארצנו וכי ידרך באַדְמָתֵנוּ[b]
והקמנו עליו שבעה רעים ושמנה נסיכי אֲרָם[c]
5 ורעו את אשור[d] בחרב ואת ארץ נמרד
בִּפְתִיחָה[e]
והִצִּילוּ[f] מאשור כי יבוא בארצנו
וכי ידרך בגבולנו

TRANSLATION

As to Assyria—when they come into our land,
When they tread on our ground,
We will raise against them seven rulers,
Eight Aramaean chiefs.
They will rule Assyria with the sword,
The land of Nimrud with a dagger.
They will deliver us from Assyria
When they come into our land,
When they tread on our territory.

TEXTUAL NOTES

(Most of the departures from MT here, or decisions in favor of MT in disputed cases, are of an unremarkable sort and will be dealt with only briefly.)

a Many have thought that this passage is a direct continuation of the preceding Messianic section not only in theme, but grammatically, so that beginning at אשור the grammar is altered in various ways to join it in a sentence with והיה זה שלום.[1] The view taken here is that this phrase is a title of the Messianic king: "The One of Peace,"[2] so that there is no grammatical connection of 4b to 4a.[3]

b Cathcart has vigorously defended MT 'our palaces,'[4] but unconvincingly. It seems clear that MT has arisen by a common scribal error, and that LXX ἐπὶ τὴν χώραν ἡμῶν preserves the correct reading (thus many commentators).

c All commentators seem to have been content with MT נסיכי אדם, rendering it 'princes over men' or 'human princes,' but investigation reveals difficulties. What is the sense of 'human princes'? What other kind is there? At a pinch this might be an appropriate phrase in a contrast between something like 'divine rulers,' and 'human princes,' but such a sense would be acutely inappropriate here. The alternative 'princes over men' also encounters the objection that it is hopelessly flat: what else is there for a prince to rule over? The evidence from usage also makes this phrase suspect. In several hundred occurrences of אדם no closely comparable phrase occurs.[5] There is no *מלך אדם or *שׂר אדם or anything of the sort.

A change to אֲרָם 'the Aramaeans' involves the assumption of a very common sort of scribal error. To the resulting phrase compare נְסִיכֵי צָפוֹן Ezek 32:30. Aside from the few other biblical occurrences (Josh 13:21; Ps 83:12), this term (in the form *nasīku*) is used frequently in neo-Assyrian and neo-Babylonian inscriptions—precisely and exclusively of Aramaean chiefs.[6]

d MT ארץ אשור 'land of Ashur'; the shorter reading, attested in LXX, fits the parallelistic style better.

[1]For a convenient summary of proposals of this sort, see W. Rudolph, *Micha-Nahum-Habakkuk-Zephanja* (KAT 13/3; Gütersloh: Mohn, 1975) 91.

[2]A recent exposition of this view, rich in references to previous treatments, is Kevin J. Cathcart, "Notes on Micah 5, 4-5," *Bib* 49 (1968) 511-14.

[3]It is rather common for the subject of a temporal/conditional clause beginning כי to precede the conjunction; see the examples in *BDB*, 473. This observation seems necessary in view of the assertion by James Mays that "In the present MT 'Assyria' stands outside any expected syntax," in his *Micah* (OTL; Philadelphia: Westminster, 1976) 119.

[4]Kevin J. Cathcart, "Micah 5, 4-5 and Semitic Incantations," *Bib* 59 (1978) 38-48.

[5]Prov 15:20 and 21:20 כְּסִיל אָדָם 'foolish man' and Gen 16:12 פֶּרֶא אָדָם 'wild ass of a man' seem to me somewhat similar, but neither is very close.

[6]See J. A. Brinkman, *A Political History of Post-Kassite Babylonia 1158-722 B.C.* (An Or 43; Rome: Pontifical Biblical Institute, 1968) 272-75.

e MT 'in its entrance/gates' is unsatisfactory in sense, and as a parallel to 'sword.' פְּתִיחָה 'dagger' (approximate, exact sense unknown) occurs in Ps 55:22 (in plural) and the verb פתח is used with חֶרֶב in Ps 37:14 and Ezek 21:33. Some such sense can also claim the support of various minor ancient versions. Although sg is suggested above, a pl might equally well have been conjectured. Many commentators since Wellhausen have favored approximately the solution given here.

f MT has sg, probably influenced by connecting this passage closely with the preceding, and its single Messianic deliverer.

SENSE

In the time of David, Israel's empire was conceived as reaching, ideally, from the Euphrates to the boundary with Egypt, and to some degree this ideal was realized. Israel could think of herself as adjoining Mesopotamia, but protected from that side by subject Aramaean states. In later times, down to the fall of Damascus, the successors to the Davidic empire, confronted by threats to their land by Assyria from the 9th century on, could think of their security as lying in alliance with the Aramaean states that lay between. Whatever the real strength of the states between her and the Euphrates (Israel might at times not even be *primus inter pares*), Northern and Southern kingdom alike, we may suppose, maintained an old notion about the extent of 'our land' and the function of the Aramaeans as her tools.

'When the Assyrian comes into our land' in this historical and ideological context means 'when the Assyrian army crosses the Euphrates.' Israel will in such a situation 'raise up' the intervening subject-states, who will conquer and rule Assyria with the sword, i.e., military might and violence. Thus Israel will be saved.

Elements of such a vision persist into later periods of Israel's history. 'Assyria' could be read as a name for Babylon, or the Seleucid empire, or any enemy of the kingdom of God, and the people might hope for inviolate preservation of the boundaries of that kingdom. But the peculiar formulation of that hope, involving buffer states in Syria, seems most likely to have originated before the destruction of Samaria—in fact, before Tiglath-Pileser's removal of the shield of states that separated Israel and Judah from direct confrontation with their destroyer. A later time may have interpreted the seven shepherds as the "helpers of the Messiah," but the origin is not in the mythological sphere, but in a geopolitical situation.

The relation of this passage to the book of Micah must be reserved for discussion elsewhere; on the basis of the reading suggested here, one can only note that the material is archaic enough to be an early component of the book.

Discourse on Prophetic Discourse

DAVID NOEL FREEDMAN
UNIVERSITY OF MICHIGAN

THIS paper examines a problem in the interpretation and even more basic understanding of prophetic oracles in the Hebrew Bible. While we must always consider the literary context, the social and cultural setting, as these affect meaning and sense, the immediate question is more narrowly linguistic in character: do we understand a certain configuration of words found in the Bible and attributed to a certain prophet, and can we render it into appropriate comprehensible English? This is the common challenge for translators of texts in other languages, but for the Bible there are particular if not peculiar aspects and ramifications, owing to its antiquity, which require special consideration. The Bible itself contains a wide range of materials, of different literary types and correspondingly varying degrees of comprehensibility. Much of it is written in straight-forward prose, which aside from a manageable number of scribal errors can be read and interpreted quite easily. The content often is unusual, and sometimes shocking, but that is a function of cultural and temporal distance and is not a linguistic difficulty. Standard Biblical Hebrew prose has its grammar and rules, its normal structures and patterns, and with rare exceptions it follows them.

The same may be said for its poetry, with the proviso that the rules as well as the vocabulary are different. In the nature of the case, poetry is more evocative and emotive, it relies more on impact, whether visual or audile, in the arrangement of words and phrases and the sequence of sounds. It also has a more complex, often confusing, grammar and syntax, along with a penchant for unusual words. The mastery of Hebrew verse comes only after much study, not to speak of pain and prayer, and even then we suspect that much of its subtle sophistication, its multiple meanings and larger senses, escape our notice. Our penetration into the subtleties and complexities of poetic usage and our grasp of its varieties and tonalities are limited indeed. Some significant progress has been made through the investigation of cognate languages and literatures, and the patient and intensive study of the surviving biblical texts. Using the tools and weapons forged by modern linguists, and recognizing the special devices universally used by poets to enhance the senses, disguise features, and compound meanings, we are making headway in the face of many obstacles. The rewards, however, are great, and contested terrain, once seized, will not be lost in the future.

When it comes to prophetic discourse, we are dealing with another distinctive phenomenon, a *tertium quid* that defies even the acute reasoning of Molière: while it shares in the aspects and specific features of prose on the one hand and poetry on the other, not infrequently it cannot be described as belonging wholly to either camp but remains defiantly in the no-man's land between them. Sometimes we are faced with ordinary narrative or declarative prose, and sometimes with poetry in the classic mode, but often there is an admixture not easy to analyze or describe, with lines of prose interlaced with those of poetry, or occasionally a kind of poetic prose or prose poetry that cannot be broken down into constituent elements of either kind. Whether in the end the problem of classification is more with our categories than with the Hebrew prophets is a question we can beg, and then escape. Even when we hit upon this middle ground between prose and poetry, we have not resolved an issue of long standing in the traditions of scholarship in this discipline. For many centuries the prophetic literature was read and copied as prose, that is, like the rest of the Hebrew Bible, except for a few poems identified as such and certain books recognized as poetic. Then in the 18th century, Bishop Lowth, Professor of Literature at Oxford, transformed scholarship by identifying much of the prophetic corpus as poetry, and contributed everlastingly to the understanding and appreciation of those oracles as poetic compositions of the highest merit. Now we must modify the latter judgment somewhat in the direction of the former tradition, and allow that much of this literature falls between the poles, with its own rhetorical forms and expressions.

There is another persistent problem in the understanding and interpretation of prophetic discourse. I refer to the question of textual integrity. On the one hand, errors in transmission are inevitable, as a comparison of manuscripts demonstrates; or I should say differences show up, and scholars have procedures for identifying probable mistakes and eliminating them. Recovery of an accurate original or at least an earlier text is an appropriate and necessary objective, and much time and effort have been expended by scholars, as was the case with editors and scribes of an earlier time, to preserve or restore the best possible text. On the other hand, indulging in the restorative process always risks compounding or creating errors and so producing a new text that has little or nothing in common with the original author's work. It is one thing to choose among readings preserved in different manuscripts; it is quite another, and much more risky, to restore a text that is not attested in any manuscript. Steering a middle course between excessive restraint whereby we preserve and enshrine errors as canonical, and excessive freedom whereby we emend away the particular expression of the author because it seems or is so strange, is no easy task, and yet it is essential. It cannot be avoided by some dogmatic presupposition about the nature of the text and the way it is to be treated (e.g., regarding the biblical text as divinely inspired, hence inerrant, or necessarily conforming to 19th century rules governing diction, grammar, and syntax, hence emendable).

My approach to the Hebrew text has become increasingly conservative, beginning with a practical consideration having to do with scholarly consensus. Since for much of the Hebrew Bible the text base is narrow and supports only one well-attested reading, there is very little chance that another reading, no matter how brilliantly devised, will win more than a few adherents. Even if the received text bristles with difficulties it makes more sense to cope with it than with a text no one else accepts. Over the years it has become clear that some features of Biblical Hebrew have been preserved in the text but not recognized by grammarians, medieval or modern. Gradually we are learning to accept these features, thus preserving and clarifying the text, without resorting to the surgery of emendation. From an esthetic point of view this is much more satisfying than the kind of ruthless assault practiced by an earlier generation of scholars. It is akin to the difference between finding and fitting the right but elusive piece in a jig-saw puzzle and forcing the wrong but handy piece into the configuration, thereby guaranteeing an imperfect solution.

Focusing this concern, I will treat two substantial passages from the book of Micah. Why the book of Micah? Because it illustrates in a dramatic way the problem described, and because it is the subject of my current research. Scholars concede two passages, from chaps. 3 and 1 (in that order), to be from the prophet himself and part of the original work. One of these, the oracle in chap. 3, is quite readable and comprehensible. It is poetic and exhibits the standard features of classic Hebrew verse. It poses no particular problems of analysis or interpretation, and there is a prevailing consensus on its structure and meaning. The other passage, in chap. 1, is a nightmare of confusion and incoherence described by the illustrious Paul Haupt as the most corrupt passage in the Hebrew Bible. That verdict has not been altered substantially in the years since. The recently published Stuttgart Bible has as a footnote on this unit the following comment: *omnia mutilata sunt.*

Assuming that this judgment is correct—which in spite of its longevity and universality may not be tenable—then how can one explain the absolute contrast in the history of the transmission of different parts of the same text? While the distribution of scribal errors is hardly uniform, it follows a determinable pattern, and by its nature has an important random component. Thus we would expect a sprinkling of trivial errors throughout the material (in chaps. 1–3), many of which could be corrected in the framework of the established text. The point here is that if the great bulk of the text is clear and comprehensible and there is widespread agreement that it is in order, then occasional aberrations can be identified and corrected in accordance with the usual rules governing such matters. The ratio of wrong to right readings should be low, and the passage as a whole should be generally understandable. Difficulties arise when the ratio apparently rises, and when there is doubt about the context and the passage as a whole. Emendation becomes a matter of guesswork, and the end result may be worse than the reading in the text. When it requires changing one word after another until an entirely new text is created, not only has the editor exchanged roles with the author, but the whole effort becomes an exercise in creative irresponsibility. Although this has been, in fact, the usual procedure over the years, it has become increasingly clear that the results are unacceptable and unusable. What we may call progressive emendation and transformation of a text are self-defeating examples of literary ingenuity. Certainly the approach did not develop in a vacuum, but was a serious response by dedicated and often brilliant scholars to a genuine problem, that of trying to recover the meaning of a text. Even if we reject the results of a free-wheeling text manipulation and management, we freely concede occasional brilliancies and successes. Rejecting the solution doesn't by itself change the status of the problem. At best we are back where we began, and unless we abandon the scholarly enterprise, we must try again. In what follows, we will try to define both the problems and the ground rules and come up with a new set of proposals for these passages in Micah.

First we will assume that the text is mostly all right, that is, that it is a faithful reproduction of what the prophet said, or what he or, more likely, his scribe or editor wrote down. We will not try to distinguish between the two, and will be quite satisfied to arrive at the more modest objective of recovering as much as possible of the sense of the written edition. Second: at the same time we will concede the presence of errors, and will make some effort to identify and correct them. This can only be done successfully if the text is basically and generally sound and the error a technical slip falling into one of the well-established categories: haplography, dittography, metathesis, and the like. Even then we cannot claim certainty, and we are left with a paradox or anomaly: the more certain the correction is, the less important it is likely to be, while the more important the correction is, the less convincing.

Now we will look directly at the two passages and compare the original text with one or more translations. With respect to the first passage (Micah 3:1–8) we will try to show how simple and understandable the text is and how reliable the transmission has been. Then following the same procedure with the second passage (Micah 1:10–16, but mentioning 2–9) we will see how difficult and troublesome another unit from the same source can be. When we have done our best, while avoiding the temptations of progressive emendation, we will have resort to a new hypothesis to explain the radical difference.

MICAH 3:1–8

The first part (3:1–3) is consistent and intelligible. The imagery is vivid if somewhat distasteful, but there are no serious problems in the text. There is only one obvious difficulty in the passage: in v 3 the Hebrew text has *kʾšr*, "as," so that we would render:

> And they break (them) in two as in the pot
> And like flesh in the midst of the caldron.

That is not impossible, but as poetry it limps and the parallelism is imperfect. What apparently has happened is that *kʾšr* was written accidentally for *kšʾr* which means "meat" or "flesh" and is a perfect parallel to the word in the second colon: *kbśr*, "like meat" or "flesh." Both of these words occur in the preceding verse, enhancing the possibility of confusion. The error itself is one of the most common, as any writer or typist can attest: metathesis. The correct reading is confirmed by the OG, which has *hōs sarkas*, "like meat" or "flesh." That shows that the error in the Hebrew text occurred rather late in the course of transmission, after the time when the Greek rendering was made (generally thought to be in the late 3rd or 2nd century B.C.E., long after the original composition of the book).

Verse 4 contains a shift in person and subject, but it serves as a fitting conclusion to this unit:

> Then they all cry out to Yahweh,
> But he won't answer them;
> And he will hide his face from them at that time,
> Since they have committed such wicked crimes.

Once again the general sense is quite clear, although the grammatical and syntactical connections are somewhat looser than would normally be true of prose. The first and last clauses are linked by a common subject and common verb form (3 m. pl.), while the subject of clauses two and three is 3 m. s. (Yahweh). This sort of envelope construction is quite common, especially in poetry and prophetic discourse, and we may infer that the final clause, which is the reason for the negative response of God, may also be the occasion if not the reason for their crying out to God.

The next section, vv 5–8, deals with false prophets, a special thorn in the flesh to a true prophet such as Micah. It is similarly perspicuous, requiring very little in the way of analysis or interpretation.

Essentially the text is clean and the message and meaning are clear. We may examine special features which mark the structure and admire the sublety and sophistication of the poet in the arrangement of words (e.g., the envelope construction in v 6 bound by "night" and "day" in that order) or the interlocking of terms in v 8, combining the mighty spirit of Yahweh with the power of authority in judgment, the role of the true prophet, but these should not detain us from our principal task.

MICAH 1:2–9

We may now turn to chap. 1 for a study in contrasts. The first unit, vv 2–9, forms the general introduction and makes reasonably good sense. There are some soft spots, but not out of line with what we have already seen. These may be minor slips, or else peculiarities of style and structure with which we are not familiar.

The oracle begins with a summons to the peoples of the earth to hear and pay attention to the testimony forthcoming, testimony concerning the guilt of Israel and Judah which makes them worthy of ultimate judgment, and liable to condign punishment. There follows a description of a theophany, the awesome power of God as he manifests himself in the violence of nature, here as the God of storm and quake (vv 2–4).

There follows a brief characterization of the basic sin, the central theme of the oracle:

> For the transgression of Jacob is all this
> (and) for the sins of the House of Israel.

Immediately after this comes the question:

> What is the transgression of Jacob?

and its answer:

> Is it not Samaria?

with its parallel:

> And who (what) are the high places of Judah? Is it not Jerusalem?

The first response fits with the previous statement quite well, at least with respect to the names or terms. The initial reference to the "transgression of Jacob" is picked up by the question "What is the transgression of Jacob?" The answer is consistent in that the capital city of the northern kingdom is cited. The root of the trouble lies there, and while the statement is elliptical and elusive the sense is that Samaria, the head of the kingdom, is responsible for the violation of fundamental covenant commitments. We are reminded of a similar correlation in Isaiah, in a contemporary situation:

> The head of Ephraim is Samaria and the head of Samaria is Ben-Remaliah (the king) (Isa 7:9).

The next pair diverges substantially. Where we (probably) would have expected "Who is responsible for the sins of the House of Israel?" we have instead: "Who (what) are the high places of Judah?" that is, who is responsible for them? The two changes suggest that something is out of order, and the usual procedure is to restore the presumed original on the basis of the preceding pattern. Both the response to the rhetorical question and what follows make it clear that either the shift was deliberate on the part of the speaker or author, or any earlier version which may have conformed to expectations has been effectively supplanted. There is nothing to be done except to cope with the surviving text.[1]

It is clear, first of all, that the theme of these introductory utterances, as already intimated in the heading, 1:1, is the guilt of both kingdoms represented by their capitals, Samaria and Jerusalem, and the catastrophic punishment decreed for them by the divine judge of all human behavior. That Judah and Jerusalem in this passage are correct and in balance with Jacob (which here is equivalent to Israel or, more precisely, Ephraim) is confirmed by v 9 where the same terms are used in describing the threatened judgment. What of the high places? Clearly this term is not parallel with "transgressions" used with Jacob, and some other interpretation of the usage must be sought. What we have discovered is that parallelism is only one way and hardly the most common by which a Hebrew poet relates terms in a balanced arrangement.

A more frequent procedure is to separate for prosodic reasons terms that belong together and help to define or precise each other. Thus we suggest that transgression properly combines with high places to form the phrase "the transgression of the high places," which applies equally to north and south and evokes the monotonously repeated charge of the Deuteronomistic historian against the kingdoms: both kingdoms are condemned for conducting unacceptable worship at the high places. The formula for northern kings, that they continued the practice initiated by the first king of north Israel, Jeroboam, whose activity in establishing the illicit worship of the golden calves at Bethel and Dan and at the high places, is described in 1 Kgs 12:25–33 (esp. 30–32). The kings of Judah are routinely condemned for not removing the high places, the building

[1]LXX tries to smooth things out.

of which is attributed in the first instance to Solomon, who dedicated them to foreign gods, and their proliferation to the Judahites of the days of Rehoboam, the heir and successor of Solomon. According to the biblical text, the first king to dismantle the high places was Hezekiah, who reigned from 715–687 (after the fall of Samaria in 722 B.C.E.). It would seem clear, now, that Micah's prophecies concerning the high places in Israel and Judah, and the charges levelled at central administration, must date from a time before the fall of Samaria and the removal of the high places in Judah, which goes well with the other information in the book and related sources. We conclude: who is responsible for the transgression of the high places in Jacob (i.e., Ephraim) and Judah? The government leaders in Samaria and Jerusalem, certainly.

There follows in v 6 a vivid account of the imminent overthrow of Samaria, including specifically the destruction of all of its idols and images. There is a break at the end of v 7. With v 8 the prophet introduces himself as the official mourner for the demise of the northern kingdom. He speaks of his distress and distraction, his uncontrollable grief and his ululation, like the caterwauling of the jackals and the high-pitched shrieks of the ostrich's offspring. This verse serves then as a transition to Judah and Jerusalem, and the threat hanging over the southern kingdom. It may also help to explain the more hysterical and incoherent utterances that follow. Clearly the fate of Jerusalem and Judah is closer to the heart of the prophet, and even though he recognizes the common evil and hence the equivalent consequences for the two nations, he is more impassioned and less comprehensible in his outpouring for his own people as compared with his more dispassionate response to the fate of the north. Finally in v 9 the section closes with the ominous pronouncement that the disaster has entered the country (presumably in the form of an enemy army), that the mortal blows are raining on the weakened city—in short, that the ultimate divine enemy is pounding on the gate of Jerusalem itself.

While the going has not been easy, still we are able to follow the prophet as he begins his oracle of doom. So far at least, the procedures and devices are within the bounds of syntax, and the rules of grammar, if strained, are not yet broken. Even without emendation we are able to follow the text, or stay within reasonable or reachable range of the prophet in his utterance.

MICAH 1:10–16

Now, however, in vv 10–16, we come to a passage that breaks through these limits, one which has effectively baffled commentators and interpreters. After a very brief introduction, the prophet runs down a list of towns and villages guarding the southern and southwestern approaches to Jerusalem, the classic route of invading armies, to be followed by the infamous Sennacherib within a generation. He binds all together in a litany of disaster giving a kaleidoscopic view of various scenes of frantic defense and panicky response, impending and occurring ruin, the folly of resistance, and the fate of the defeated, an unrelenting tragedy which ends in the conquest of the land and the death and exile of its citizens. At the center is Jerusalem, Daughter of Zion, a bereaved mother wailing for children lost in war, banished to captivity.

Immediately noted features of the passage include the extensive use of paronomasia and the profusion of different pronominal elements, creating both intensification and confusion, if not incoherence. Presumably the passage expresses the previously mentioned grief and hysteria of the prophet. The passage is built around a series of place-names, cities and villages which belong to the region of Jerusalem. There may be as many as 14 such names including the central city: Jerusalem, Daughter of Zion. Under the threat and reality of military invasion, the cities, symbolic of their populations, are described in various postures of despair, while being encouraged to lament their fate. Aside from the elaborate paronomasia and the introduction of unusual or unique terms, the general idea can be captured, and the meaning seems to be consistent with the use of word-play. There are, however, other threads running through the material, elements which complicate the picture, are not readily classified, and put intolerable strains on ordinary, or even poetic grammar and syntax.

Following the basic principle of parsimony and in accordance with the practice of paleoanatomists in bone sorting, we will group grammatically congruent components. The opening line has verbal forms in the 2nd m. pl.: "Do not announce . . . do not weep." These m. pl. people are not identified in the section, but their presence may be noted not only in v 10 but also in v 11, twice in prepositional constructions. Who they are may remain a mystery, but we are obligated to look for an appropriate antecedent. The only one which commends itself is the subject of the initial summons and command in 1:2: "Hear O peoples (all of them), pay heed O earth (in its fullness)."[2]

Whether or not this analysis is correct, there can be no doubt about the grammar; 2nd m. pl. people are addressed in v 10a, whereas v 10b shifts abruptly to 2nd f. s., an unusual and archaic verb form. Here the subject is apparently the personified city, represented by several or many of the names preceded by the term *inhabitant* or *daughter* to justify the f. s. form. (The dramatic shift from 2nd m. pl. to 2nd f. s. is obscured in English, where we use the same word *you* for all four forms, m. and f., s. and pl.) The verse can be rendered:

[2]Note in passing the anomaly of the combination of 2nd and 3rd person forms: "Hear peoples all of them; pay heed earth and its fullness," literally.

In Ga'h do not you tell (it)
In Bǝ κο [?] do not you weep.
In Beth-le-aphrah roll thyself in the dust

In v 11 we have the curious phenomenon of double direct address, which can hardly be expressed intelligibly in English, or in Hebrew, for that matter. Put literally, we have "You pass by [imperative 2nd f. s.] for you [2nd m. pl.]." The latter must be the same people as addressed in the opening line but different from the 2nd f. s. people (against RSV, which equates them, erasing the distinction in the Hebrew), while the former is identified as the city of Shaphir, presented as a woman. Behind this town is the central city of Jerusalem, Daughter Zion, but the notion of simultaneous direct address to different parties is difficult to accommodate either grammatically or conceptually. Clearly it must be considered unless we either identify the groups under different figures or eliminate one as an error in transmission. Actually the messages are in conflict if not in contradiction, since the instruction to the 2nd m. pl. group is not to proclaim, not to weep, whereas the mandate for the city is to roll in the dust, a vivid image of mourning and self-abasement in the face of tragedy. In short, outsiders are not to be sympathetic, because the punishment is thoroughly deserved.[3] The inhabitants, the participating group, however, must give full expression to grief or self-laceration for precisely the same reason. Only by a show of remorse and repentance can the guilty victims make a proper response to the judgment of their angry God.

The 2nd m. pl. forms occur through v 11 and then cease. We have identified these people as outsiders, spectators of the scene of devastation and catastrophe, who are admonished not to spread the news or weep in mourning. We can reach back to v 2 for an appropriate antecedent: "the peoples of the earth." In v 10 the meaning is fairly clear: "Tell it not—do not weep." The topical references may be unrelated and belong rather to the central scene (in Gath, in Bako?). The significance of the prepositional phrases in v 11 is less clear: "for you" and "from you." In neither case does the immediate context offer much help, although the entanglement in the action of the 2nd f. s. forms indicates that the 2nd m. pl. people are near the scene. "For you" may have purely ethical connotations, i.e., "for your benefit or advantage": "do not weep for

[3]The opening clause is reminiscent of the famous lament of David over Saul and Jonathan (2 Sam 1:19–27), "Tell it not in Gath," except for a slight change in the order of the words. In neither poem is the subject (2nd m. pl.) of the verb identified. In the Davidic dirge, the instruction is given so as to preclude or postpone the inevitable rejoicing of the Philistine women over the defeat of the Israelites. In the passage in Micah the circumstances are less clear, and the reason correspondingly more obscure.

yourselves." The 3rd m. s. forms refer to different people: perhaps the subject is God or an agent of God, or the construction may be impersonal, while the suffixed pronoun may refer to the person for whom mourning normally would be appropriate, i.e., the king; but in Jer 22:10–19 there is an interdict against mourning for a dead king. The ban on mourning, which is associated with Beth Haezel, would fit with the initial prohibition against audible wailing.

Now we must grapple with the 2nd f. s. forms which dominate the unit. The central figure or person clearly is Jerusalem (Daughter of Zion), vv 12–13. This image is frequent in the prophets especially of the 8th century B.C.E.: Jerusalem/Zion is portrayed as a woman or girl who represents the city as a whole, its population, or various groups. Along with Jerusalem/Zion, Micah mentions about a dozen cities or villages in the surrounding area, mainly in the southwest environs along a major military route. The most common designation of these "inhabitant(s)" is *yôšebet* plus the name of a city, with collective force similar to the phrase Daughter of Zion. The expression *yôšebet* plus city name occurs five times in the passage:

yôšebet šāpîr	(11)	inhabitant of Shaphir
yôšebet ṣaʾănān	(11)	inhabitant of Zaanan
yôšebet mārôt	(12)	inhabitant of Maroth
yôšebet lākîš	(13)	inhabitant of Lachish
yôšebet mārēšâ	(15)	inhabitant of Mareshah

The apparent gap between the last two members of the list is actually filled by a similar-sounding but different expression, *môrešet* ("possessor" perhaps, or "possession, territory"), which is joined to the city-name *gat* to produce Moresheth-gath. It is a common practice of the poets and prophets of Israel to vary a sequence of repetitions by a single change in a long list. At first glance this may seem anomalous, but the practice of varying from a norm, or avoiding monotony, is well known, and in the case of biblical poetry this variation itself has become a principle. I have collected a number of examples which only need be listed here without additional comment:

Amos 1–2: *wĕšillaḥtî ʾēš* (1:4, 7, 10, 12; 2:2, 5) varied by *wĕhiṣṣattî ʾēš* (1:14).

Jer 51:20–23: *wĕnippaṣtî bĕkā* (51:20, 21 [2], 22 [3], 23 [3]) varied by *wĕhišḥattî bĕkā* (51:20).

Gen 49:25–26: *birkōt* (49:25 [3], 26 [2]) varied by *taʾăwat* (26).

The parallel passage in Deut 33:13–16 has the same feature: *mimmeged* (33:13, 14 [2], 15, 16) varied by *mērōʾš* (15).

Micah contains a second example, only the pattern itself is more complex and elaborate. Each of the repeated words is balanced by a parallel expression or paraphrase; in the last case the initial term of the pair is also changed:

5:9	*wĕhikrattî*	—	*wĕhaʾăbadtî*
10	*wĕhikrattî*	—	*wĕhārastî*
11	*wĕhikrattî*	—	*lōʾ yihyû—lāk*
12	*wĕhikrattî*	—	*wĕlōʾ—tištaḥăweh*
13	*wĕnātaštî*	—	*wĕhišmadtî*

Returning to Mic 1:10–16 we can count probably twelve different city-names, not including the pair Jerusalem/Daughter of Zion, which is obviously the focus of attention. The twelve serve as attendants or subordinate associates: suburbs and exurbs of the capital. The passage is organized around the names of the cities: the occurrences of the repeated expression *yôšebet* (and its substitute *môrešet*) form a framework within which the other names are inserted. After the introductory pair, introduced by the preposition *bĕ*,[4] the remaining twelve city-names are grouped in units of four:

1) vv 10–11:

bĕbêt lĕʿaprâ
yôšebet šāpîr
yôšebet ṣaʾănān
bêt hāʾēṣel

Here we have an envelope construction in which the outer pair is characterized by the prefixed term *bêt*, literally "house," and often used as part of the names of places (e.g., Bethel, Bethlehem, etc.). The inner pair is already familar from its use of *yôšebet* indicating the population of the towns named.

2) vv 12–13:

yôšebet mārôt
yĕrûsālēm

[4]The second term *bākô* was interpreted by the Massoretes not as the name of a city but as a form of the verb *bkh*, a so-called infinitive absolute, which goes with and strengthens the main verb: *tibkû*. A literal rendering would be: "Weeping, do not weep!" Cf. RSV, "Do not weep at all." The Massoretes may well have missed a word-play concealing the name of a city (perhaps *Bōkeh*); a similar play on words occurs in Judg 2:1–5 where the verb *bkh* is associated with the place name *Bōkîm*. No place with a similar name is known in the area described by Micah, but that is true of several of the city-names in his list.

yôšebet lākîš
lĕbat ṣîyôn

Here the pattern is an alternating one, in which the first and third terms are characterized by the familiar *yôšebet,* while the second and fourth are parallel terms for the capital city, Jerusalem/Daughter of Zion, that is, two expressions for the same place.

3) vv 14–15:

ᶜal môrešet gat
bāttê ᵓakzîb
yôšebet mārēšâ
ᶜad—ᶜădullām

Here the structure is less precise, but a mixture of the two preceding patterns can be discerned. The alternating sequence can be observed in the pairs *môrešet gat // yôšebet mārēšâ* and *ᵓakzîb // ᶜădullām.* At the same time the use of the prepositions *ᶜal* and *ᶜad* with the first and last cities shows that an envelope scheme is also to be observed. Thus *ᶜal môrešet gat* and *ᶜad-ᶜădullām* belong together, while the remaining pair seems to have in common the absence of prepositions and the status of objects rather than subjects. This unit remains obscure and difficult; several divergent arrangements and analyses are possible.

Looking at the assemblage it seems clear that the association of verbs and cities is occasioned by various forms of paronomasia rather than historical or functional considerations. Lachish is instructed to harness the horses because the word used for horse, *rekeš,* sounds like *lākîš,* although it is quite likely that steeds were quartered there. Likewise one rolls in the dust at Beth-le-aphrah because the word for dust, *ᶜapār,* is very similar to the last element in the name of the city, *ᶜaprâ.* Other word-plays are more or less obvious: e.g., *ᵓakzîb* and *ᵓakzāb, yōrēš* and *mārēšâ, lōᵓ yāṣĕᵓâ* and *ṣaᵓănān.* The conclusion, perhaps drastic, is that all the cities together represent the single entity Judah, or more specifically the capital Jerusalem, which they guard, and which stands also for the country. In similar fashion, the activities ascribed to the separate localities together add up to the frenzied and hysterical behavior of the inhabitants of the invaded country and besieged city in the last throes of desperate struggle before the final collapse of resistance, followed by destruction, desolation, captivity, and mourning. These activities are glimpsed haphazardly as the eye of the prophet wanders over the scene of anguish and devastation, picking out individual figures and settings at different stages of the disaster. The lack of overall clarity reflects the confusion of battle and destruction, but of the overarching tragedy there can be no doubt. Binding the passage as a whole are the repeated 2nd f. s. verbs and vocatives. The referent is in some cases our ubiquitous *yôšebet* and in others Jerusalem/Daughter of Zion, while in the remaining ones the subject is not specifically identified but must be the population seen collectively as a female figure: the city and its inhabitants.

Three prepositional phrases, all with the 2nd f. s. suffix, provide a key to understanding the sweep of the prophet's vision:

1) v 13: "For in thee (*bāk*) are found the trangressions of Israel."
2) v 15: "Yet again I will bring the dispossessor to thee (*lāk*)."
3) v 16: "Strip and shave thyself over thy delightful sons / Make extensive thy baldness like the vulture / For they have gone into captivity from thee (*mimmēk*)."

In sequence, the three clauses give the rationale and the reality of divine punishment. Judgment has come upon Judah because the sins characteristic of the northern kingdom (spelled out at length elsewhere) have been imported into and adopted in Judah, so that the latter will share the destiny of the former. As a consequence, God (speaking through the prophet in the first person) has brought, is bringing, or will bring the conqueror to the land. In the third sentence the end of the drama is portrayed: they (thy sons) have gone away into exile. The immediate associations with individual locales are subordinated to the overall picture with its focus on the central city and on the consequences spread out through the vicinity.

We may note that the 2nd m. pl. forms which are prominent in the opening verse (10) are balanced by the 2nd f. s. forms in the closing verse (16). Curiously the same prepositional phrases with 2nd m. pl. suffixes occur in the beginning as occur with 2nd f. s. suffixes toward the end: *lākem* in v 11 (2nd m. pl.) balancing *lāk* in v 15 (2nd f. s.), and *mikkem* at the end of v 11 matching *mimmēk* at the end of v 16. Exactly how to interpret the 2nd m. pl. forms remains obscure, but the matching pattern suggests that the text is sound and that the pairing is intentional.

While I believe it is impossible to make coherent sense out of the passage as it stands, it is possible to isolate the central theme and to group elements that seem to belong together. Thus we can follow the prophet's message through its various embodiments and representations to some kind of conclusion.

The major theme is to be found in vv 12–13, which is also the midpoint of the passage. In v 12b we read: "For evil (harm) has come down from the Lord to the gate of Jerusalem." This theme has already been expressed in Mic 1:9: "For it has come as far as Judah; he has struck at the gate of my people, as far as Jerusalem." Parallel to v 12b is v 13b (the interlocking structure has already been described), which we try to render literally: "The first (or chief) of sin (was) she for the Daughter of Zion, because in thee were found the transgressions of Israel." The opening and closing lines of this unit express clearly the intention of the prophet: Judgment in the form of military disaster has been decreed by Yahweh; the underlying reason is the transgressions of Judah, which has imitated Israel in this respect. The background and connections are explained earlier by the prophet himself (1:2–7) and confirmed elaborately by the Deuteronomistic editor of 2 Kings (chaps. 16–18). The middle clause is different, but the "she" who constitutes the chief sin is not identical with Daughter of Zion / Jerusalem, but someone or something in the city. The f. s. pronoun here suggests that the figure is an image of the chief goddess of Canaan, Asherah, whose worship in Israel is mentioned often in the historical and prophetic books. There are specific references to this figure in Israel, and the implication here is that the same goddess is now being worshipped in Judah, and especially in Jerusalem. The parallelism between Samaria and Jerusalem is affirmed in Mic 1:5, so we cannot be far off the track. There is another intriguing feature of the two passages: In 1:5 we have *pešaᶜ* (s.) "transgression" matched with *ḥaṭṭoʾt* (pl.) "sins," whereas in 1:13 the reverse is the case: *ḥaṭṭāʾt* (s.) is paralleled with *pišᶜê* (pl.). The meaning is hardly affected, but the forms are carefully arranged in chiastic and interlocking fashion.

We may now turn to the list of activities linked with the inhabitants of the various cities and gather from them glimpses of the frenzied hysteria which gripped the country in its time of peril. On historical grounds we believe that the Micah oracle reflects the period when Judah was invaded by Israel and Aram around 735 B.C.E. and when, according to the account in Kings and Chronicles, much of Judah was overrun, its armies routed, and many of its citizens taken captive by the victorious Israelites and Arameans. The armies of the latter invested Jerusalem and laid siege to the city, which with its suburbs was apparently the only surviving territory of Judah. In this emergency, Ahaz, the king of Judah, appealed to Tiglath-pileser III, the great king of Assyria, for help. The crisis is depicted by the prophet Isaiah in a notable passage (chap. 7); while he adamantly urged calm reliance on Yahweh for succor, the king understandably turned to a somewhat more visible source of aid. In our passage, the prophet Micah, with his omnitemporal eye, fusing past, present, and future into a single picture of disaster, speaks of the crisis and impending doom.

We have already observed that the dirge over Judah begins with a warning to the peoples of the world (Mic 1:2) not to waste tears or sympathy; routine divine justice is being administered to the sinful nation. Then he turns to the targeted victim: she (or they) is not only permitted to mourn, but commanded to do so; "roll in the dust" is a typical if exaggerated form of grief.[5] The next element is exposure,

[5]The verb here in the original text (the written form, *kethib*) may be described as a precative perfect, not the expected imperative (which is preferred by the oral form, the *qere*). In the passage a wide variety of verbal forms is used, perhaps to convey omnitemporality, along with the avoidance of repetition.

nakedness coupled with shame. This is a common consequence of defeat which especially symbolizes the humiliation and degradation of women. "Pass by in shameful nakedness," is a reflex, perhaps, of captives going into exile. The following line speaks of the seclusion associated with mourning, but neither expression is clear.

V 12a is obscure, but perhaps the expectation of or waiting for "the Good" is antithetical to "the Bad" which Yahweh has decreed from heaven (v 12b). Coupled with the vain waiting for "the Good" is the presumably ironic instruction to harness the chariots to the horses (or vice versa), perhaps for battle, perhaps flight, either of which will be futile.

Beginning with v 14 matters become somewhat more confusing, but a structural analysis may help to untangle themes or threads which can be made to yield meaning. In v 14 we recognize an envelope construction linking 14aA and 14bB: "Therefore you shall pay tribute [parting gifts, i.e., to buy off the invader] . . . to the kings of Israel"; perhaps then, as part of the same structure, payment is to be made from the store-houses of Akzib, used here symbolically as a link to the next word, which means "to the false or deceptive one." This last word may well be another designation of the "dispossessor," namely, the "glorious one," the king(s) of Israel. The plural "kings" is strange since the other three forms are all singular. We must hesitate before emending the text, otherwise an attractive option. Perhaps the plural here refers to a group of Israelite kings in this period or, as seems more likely, to a dual monarchy or co-regency arrangement, the existence of which is confirmed more than once in the history of these kingdoms. There also seems to be a play on ᵓ*akzāb*, "false," and *kābôd*, "glory," since they share similar consonants: "the false or deceptive glory."

V 15 offers a fairly clear frame of reference:

Again will I bring to thee a dispossessor—
the glory (glorious one) of Israel will come.

It seems clear that the conqueror is the glorious one of Israel, presumably the king of that country currently leading the invasion of Judah.

The closing brings us back to the central theme in terms of its ultimate consequences: unceasing grief for the loss of the manhood of the country. The survivors are taken away in exile as the passage ends: "They have gone away into captivity from thee."

What is still needed is some explanation of the radical confusion and disorientation of the text. The lack of agreement among verbs, nouns, and pronouns, the leaping about from subject to subject, and the incoherent variety of circumstances go far beyond the normal range of scribal (i.e., inadvertent) error. Patching up the piece to make it read like ordinary poetry or prose would require extensive rewriting and would not help. Is it possible to account for the product without either appealing to the emendatory recourse or consigning the passage to oblivion? Perhaps a look at the prophetic experience will help.

In the examination of the material from and about the prophets we find in effect two traditions. One, already discussed, is fairly standard and consistent; prophets are poets or very close to them. Their oracles fall into well-known patterns, and given the general difficulties of dealing with poetry of any language or period, we can make reasonable headway and come out with satisfactory results. Here we assume conscious composition by the prophet with a certain amount of arranging and editing by disciples and later editors.

In the present case (chap. 1 as over against chap. 3) such an approach won't work, so we must look again at the tradition. Some, perhaps most, prophets were ecstatics, and presumably gave utterance under the power of the spirit. Micah affirms this explicitly in 3:8, "But as for me, I am full of the mighty spirit of the Lord, with power and judgment." So we may suggest that the oracle in 1:10–16 was uttered during an ecstatic seizure occasioned by his almost hysterical grief at what he foresaw to be the fate of his beloved country and people (cf. 1:8, "On account of this I am grief-stricken and wail inconsolably. I howl like the jackals, and lament like young female ostriches").

In a paroxysm of anguish, sharpened by a panoramic vision of desolation and ruin, the prophet pours out in fits and starts, in bits and pieces, his woe. Then we may suppose that the words which came forth were recorded by a scribe who simply set down what he heard, or what he could make out in words and sentences of what was uttered. Apparently little or no effort was made to reconstruct a sensible or comprehensible speech, but what was preserved and transmitted were the key words, the basic clues to the inmost feelings and uppermost thoughts of the distraught prophet. If it is possible to probe into the psyche of this prophet, then here are the essential data, requiring not reconstruction or rewriting, but rather analysis and response. On another occasion, the prophet, in a calmer frame of mind, reflecting on the same situation, might well have organized his thoughts along normal lines of poetic expression such as we have found in chap. 3 and very frequently in the prophetic literature. Here in 1:10–16, we seem to have the raw product straight from the soul of the prophet, who could not restrain the torrent of words (or sounds), an almost incoherent speech forced from his lips by the spirit of God. This could be a striking example of things said in a moment of ecstatic inspiration, about which we read in different parts of the OT and NT (cf. Jer 20:7–9, and 1 Corinthians 12–14). Mic 1:10–16 might well belong to the category of semi-coherent ecstatic utterances characteristic of certain classes of prophets. There also seems to be a family resemblance to the glossolalia which swept through the Christian churches in the days of the apostles.

One word of caution should be added. Our investigation has shown that the passage cannot be analyzed or parsed according to the common rules of Hebrew syntax and grammar. At the same time, the more carefully we examine the components the more connections and structural patterns emerge. It is possible that such features are an aspect of the prophet's subconscious, expressed in the involuntary speech of an ecstatic experience. It is also possible that the passage in question is the result of a carefully planned presentation, which resembles ecstatic utterance but is deliberately designed that way. Our sense of its incoherence may be a reflection of our ignorance, or failure to recognize more intricate patterns and arrangements, which differ from standard usage but have a subtle system of their own. Perhaps we will finally discover that the interaction of ecstatic experience and intellectual planning is adequate to explain the whole range of prophetic poetic utterance.

At present and perhaps for the foreseeable future, we will not be able to answer the questions we have raised about prophetic oracles generally, and this one in particular. If we cannot now discern motivation and intention, we nevertheless have the inescapable obligation to deal with the finished product and to analyze and interpret the text which has come down to us. In short, we must respond to what we find and leave always open the question of just what the prophet had in mind. We may conclude with the following observations.

All texts are corrupt in some measure, and it is the task of scholarship to correct corrupt texts. The better the text the easier it is to correct errors, and the less important the process becomes. The worse the state of the text, and the more imperative the interpretive obligation, correspondingly the more difficult to achieve satisfactory results, or even modest progress. Put another way, the more difficult the text, and the more important it is to clarify, the harder it is to come up with anything useful.

Studies in the Structure of Hebrew Verse: The Prosody of the Psalm of Jonah

FRANK M. CROSS
HARVARD UNIVERSITY

I

IN a recent paper, a companion to the present study, I have discussed in some detail the character of the complex verse form commonly called "*qînâ* meter" (despite the fact that the lament is only one genre among many in which the verse form is used).[1] The acrostic laments in the Book of Lamentations have figured prominently in the early isolation and description of such verse, and in the study referred to above I analyzed prosody in Lamentations 1. For the fundamental units or building blocks of Hebrew poetry, including "*qînâ*," commonly labeled 3 and 2 in stress notation, I prefer to label neutrally *l* (*longum*) and *b* (*breve*), a notation which leaves open the question of auditory (stress or quantitative) rhythm. According to my analysis, the verse form under study, of which the Psalm of Jonah is a superb example, follows the patterns *l:b::l:b, l:b::b:l, b:l::l:b,* etc. In the classical stage of this verse, as in Hebrew verse generally, poetic artifice consists fundamentally of binary correspondences of word and phrase (semantic parallelism), complemented by intricate grammatical parallelism at every level. Grammatical and semantic binarism in the complex verse of the Psalm of Jonah is chiefly between corresponding bicola. However, internal parallelism between the asymmetrical (or mixed) cola is not infrequent. Hence our notation or some similar notation is required to describe the full complexity of the verse structure.

The Psalm of Jonah, Jonah 2:3–10, is, in its present form, a typical example of the genre labeled "the individual thanksgiving." Vv 3–7 contain archaic material. The imagery of these verses picture death, or the approach to death, alternately as entrance into the underworld, or as engulfment in cosmic waters. In the Semitic mythological lore which underlies this language—much of it perhaps vague or forgotten in later

[1] "Studies in the structure of Hebrew Verse: The Prosody of Lamentations 1:1–22," forthcoming in the Freedman volume. I am pleased to dedicate this pair of papers to two colleagues, both my friends and coworkers since our school days at Johns Hopkins.

Israel—are conceptions of an entry into the underworld at the "sources of the two rivers, the fountains of the double deep," at the foot of the cosmic mountain(s). This appears to have been the place of the river ordeal, where one enters *ʾereṣ*, "the underworld," or Sheol, etymologically "(the place of) questioning" (or judgment). Or one may speak of entering into the mouth or maw of Môt (Death) on one's way to becoming a denizen of Môt's city "Ooze, Decay the seat of his enthronement, Slime the land of his heritage."[2] The mingling of images of the realm of the dead seems confused and illogical. The underworld in one image is a monstrous power with gaping jaws and insatiable belly, in another a realm of chaotic waters, in a third a swampy city presided over by Death himself. These images are now better understood, thanks to rich parallels in Babylonian hymns and Ugaritic mythology. These have been collected most recently by Ruth Rosenberg, and need not be recited here.[3] The imagery in the Psalm of Jonah is also paralleled in biblical poetry: Ps 40:3; 42:8; 69:2, 3, 15, 16; 88:5–8; Job 38:16–17, and most closely in 2 Sam 22:5–7 (= Ps 18:5–7).[4]

Canaanite myths known from the texts of Ugarit and from their residue in the Bible provide us with complementary accounts of the basic conflict between order and chaos, life and death. These "alloforms" of cosmogonic conflict include the battle of Baᶜl, lord of fertility (life), with Prince Sea/Judge River (the latter title presumably reflecting his role in the ordeal); the conflict with Môt, lord of death, Baᶜl's defeat and descent into the underworld, and return to life; and variously the defeat of Lôtān/Leviathan or Tĕhōm/Tiāmat, the primordial sea or her monstrous *alter ego*. The mythic approach to reality is thus expressed in multiple or complementary models whose logical relationship is left unresolved. The manifestation of the power of death, sterility, or chaos may be described as the attack of Sea or River, or as the attack of Death, or as the attack of their agents, including the rivers and breakers of Sheol. Thus the rich poetic language used in speaking of the life and death of man, or of the manifestation of death or danger in life, may draw on images which stem from mythic geography, and, in some instances, democratized versions of Semitic cosmogonic myths.

The prosodic structure of Jonah 2:3–7 reflects an oral-formulaic style. There is an extraordinarily low density of prosaic particles. The

[2]CTA 5.2.2–4, 15–16; cf. 4.8.12–14.

[3]"The Concept of Biblical Sheol Within the Context of Ancient Near Eastern Beliefs" (unpublished Ph.D. dissertation, Harvard University, 1980).

[4]On the reconstruction of the text underlying 2 Samuel 22 and Psalm 18 see F. M. Cross and D. N. Freedman, *Studies in Ancient Yahwistic Poetry* (SBLDS 21; Missoula: Scholars, 1975) 125–58; and "A Royal Song of Thanksgiving: II Samuel 22 = Psalm 18," *JBL* 72 (1953) 15–34.

article is absent.[5] The prefix conjugation (without *waw*), used in the past narrative sense, is found in v 4 (*ysbbny* parallel to *ʿbrw*), and v 6 (*ysbbny* parallel to *ʾppwny*). The form *wtšlykny* introducing v 4 is read *tšlykny*, i.e., without the conjunction, in the OG, no doubt correctly, giving a third instance.[6] Thus in vv 3–7 the conjunctive *waw* is not used to introduce a bicolon save in the instance of *wtʿl*, v 7b, and the originality of this form may be questioned.[7] In contrast vv 8–10 show few traits of early style either in poetic structure or in syntax, and prosaic particles intrude.

II

In the following analysis of the structure of the Psalm of Jonah, it will be useful to indicate the positions of elements in a colon by dashes, for example, *qrʾty-* (first element) *-mṣrh-* (middle element) *-ly* (final element). We have numbered the cola in the right column according to the larger units of the poem, followed by our notation of colon type (*l*/*b*), and in parentheses we have then supplied syllable counts in (reconstructed) early pronunciation.

קראתי מצרה לי	(7) *b*	[v 3]	1. I called out of my distress
אל יהוה ויענני	(7) *l*		2. To Yahweh and he answered me.
מבטן שאול שועתי	(7) *l*		3. Out of the belly of Sheol I cried;
שמעת קולי	(5) *b*		4. You heard my voice.
תשליכני במצולת ים	(9) *l*	[v 4]	5. You cast me into the depth of Sea;
נהר יסבבני	(7) *b*		6. River encircled me.
כל משבריך	(5) *b*		7. All your breakers
וגליך עלי עברו	(9) *l*		8. And all your waves engulfed me.

Poetic license has been taken in the first bicolon for structural reasons described below. The caesural pause is placed unnaturally. Further, the colon length (seven syllables) is borderline, capable of being read *l:b* or *b:l*. One suspects that the original reading of the first colon was *ʾqrʾ mṣrh ly*, giving the expected contrast *b:l*. Cf. *bṣr ly ʾqrʾ yhwh* in 2 Sam 22:7 (= Ps 18:7). In this case the use of the prefix tense for

[5]*hʾrṣ* in v 7 appears without the article in the OG, a reading we take to be original.

[6]See the discussion of David A. Robertson, *Linguistic Evidence in Dating Early Hebrew Poetry* (SBLDS 3; Missoula: SBL, 1972) 7–55.

[7]See Cross and Freedman, *Studies in Ancient Yahwistic Poetry*, 127–28, and Table, 161–68. The *waw* of *wʾny* (vv 5 and 10) is a special usage. It introduces a *casus pendens*, a construction already found in Ugaritic poetry.

narrative past (used freely in vv 4 [bis] and 6) has been suppressed in favor of the standard perfect.

In colon 5 we are inclined to see a conflation of ancient variants, both stock phrases: *mṣwlt ym* and *blbb ymym*. In colon 6 similarly there is evidence of variants: *nhr* and *nhrym* (or *nhrwt*). OG reads *ym* in colon 5 (θαλασσης), *nhrym* in colon 6 (ποταμοι).[8] We prefer the singular with its mythological redolence in each colon. The conjunction beginning colon 6 is to be suppressed in view of its rarity elsewhere in the poem in this position, and the notorious tendency for its introduction in the course of textual transmission.

The four bicola form a quatrain of interlocking structure: *b:l::l:b—l:b::b:l*. As reconstructed, the sequence of bicola is both cyclic and chiastic. Primary parallelism is between the bicola 1–2 and 3–4, a couplet within the quatrain, and 5–6 and 7–8, the second couplet of the quatrain. But there is also "internal" parallelism between cola in these bicola, and long-range correspondences which bind the whole into a quatrain.

In the first bicolon note the following structures: *qrʾty-* / *-wyᶜnny* in chiastic correspondence, as well as *-ly*/*ʾl-*. On the other hand there is grammatical parallelism between *-ly* and *-ny*. In the second bicolon we find chiastic order again, *-šwᶜty*/*šmᶜt-*, an assonant pair. The binary correspondences between the two bicola are more dramatic:

qrʾty- (1)
-šwᶜty (3)
-yᶜnny (2)
šmᶜt- (4)

Here there is synonymous parallelism in chiastic order. The elements *-mṣrh ly* and *mbṭn šʾwl-* are also parallel and in chiastic order, both introduced by the preposition *m-*. The elements *-ny* and *-qwly* complete the parallelistic structures linking the bicola.

In the third bicolon, the formulaic pair *-ym*/*nhr-* is arranged chiastically as are the verbs

tšlykny-
-ysbbny

giving to the bicolon "internally" structured parallelism.

[8]The *kaíge* text from Naḥal Ḥever reads [ποτα]μος, correcting to the Hebrew. See provisionally, D. Barthélemy, *Les Devanciers d'Aquila* (Leiden: Brill, 1963) 170.

In the fourth bicolon the caesural pause must be placed after *mšbryk,* separating it from *glyk,* the second member of the formulaic pair, in *b:l* structure, lending the bicolon internal parallelism and chiasm:

-mšbryk
wglyk-

The second couplet exhibits complex parallelism. Note the following:

tšlykny-
-ysbbny
-ᶜly ᶜbrw

The chiastic placement of the first two verbal elements is complemented by *ᶜly ᶜbrw,* parallel semantically to *ysbbny,* but contrasting grammatically (*yqṭl/qṭl*); *ᶜly ᶜbrw* also is in chiastic relation to *tšlykny.* The reverse relationship exists with the elements

-ny
-ny
-ᶜly-

The formulaic pairs also bind the second couplet in extended parallelism and studied chiasm:

-ym
nhr-
-mšbryk
wglyk-

The two couplets present two images, one of death reflected in the parallel elements *mṣrh ly* and *mbṭn šʾwl,* the other in the expressions *mṣwlt ym* (or *lbb ym*) and its complements *nhr, mšbryk,* and *glyk.* In the traditional pairing of the images of Death and Sea, the maw of Death, and the watery or mucky abyss, the sequence of images in the two couplets resonates semantic parallelism. It is hardly chance that there is the assonant series beginning with *mṣ-, mb-, bmṣ-*:

-mṣrh ly
mbṭn šʾwl-
-bmṣwlt ym

The four bicola are then suitably described as a quatrain or a pair of couplets in interlocking structure: *b:l::l:b—l:b::b:l.*

ואני אמרתי	(6) *b* [v 5]	1. As for me, I said
נגרשתי מנגד עיניך	(8) *l*	2. "I am driven from your sight."
איךְ אוסיף להביט	(7) *l*	3. "How shall I look again
אל היכל קדשך	(6) *b*	4. Upon your holy temple?"

The couplet is to be understood as part of the description of the poet's plight, not, at this point in the thanksgiving song, an expression of hope or trust. Thus we are not to read ᵓ*ak,* but ᵓ*êk(ā),* with most commentators. Theodotion reads πως, ᵓ*yk* or ᵓ*ykh.* The frequent use of ᵓ*ak* in laments, to introduce an affirmation of confidence, may have triggered the misreading.

The couplet stands alone, preceded and followed by a quatrain. Its structure is *b:l::l:b.* The caesural pause in colon 1 naturally follows ᵓ*mrty.* There is little strict parallelism between the bicola. There is polar correspondence between *mngd* ᶜ*ynyk* and *lhbyṭ* ᵓ*l.* However, note the phonetic parallelism (assonance) in the repetition of ᵓ*alep*:

ᵓ*ny* ᵓ*mrty* (colon 1)
ᵓ*yk* ᵓ*wsyp* (colon 3)

and the sequence: *-êkā* (colon 2), ᵓ*êkā* (colon 3), and *-ekā* (colon 4). The expression ᵓ*l hykl qdšk* also echoes ᵓ*l yhwh* (v 3).

אפפוני מים עד נפש	(7) *l* [v 6]	1. The waters encompassed me, reaching my throat;
תהום יסבבני	(7) *b*	2. The deep surrounded me.
סוף חבוש לראשי	(6) *l*	3. Seaweed enwrapped my head
לקצבי הרים	(6) *b* [v 7]	4. At the roots of the mountains.
ירדתי ארצ[9]	(4) *b*	5. I went down into the netherworld;
ברחיה בעדי לעולם	(9) *l*	6. Its bars (locked) behind me forever.
ותעל משחת חיי	(6) *l*	7. But you brought my life up from the pit,
יהוה אלהי	(5) *b*	8. O Yahweh my god.

The structure of the quatrain is *l:b::l:b—b:l::l:b.* In the first bicolon there is internal parallelism, semantic and grammatical. The formulaic pair *-mym-/thwm-* is used, and the verbal elements, one suffixal, one prefixal, are arranged chiastically:

ᵓ*ppwny-*
-ysbbny

The first two bicola also reveal parallelistic structures. *ʿd npš* corresponds to *lrʾšy*, and *ḥbwš*, "enwrapped," echoes *ʾppwny* and *ysbbny*. The series:

-mym-
thwm-
swp-
-hrym

is subtly related in semantic field. *mym* (sea-)water and *swp* (sea-)weed in cola 1 and 3 evoke complementary images, and both are monosyllabic. *thwm* and *hrym* form an alternate formulaic pair to *mym* and *thwm*, in their polar correspondence. The couplet abounds in the repetition of *m*, *n*, *b*, and *p*, nasals and bilabials. One may also raise the question as to whether the poet is playing on the elements

-lrʾšy
lqṣby-

literally "to my top" and "to the feet." If so, the chiastic arrangement is to be noted.

The second couplet exhibits strong parallelism between the two bicola. The polar pair *yrdty-/wtʿl-* introduce the bicola. Note also the formulaic pair *-ʾrṣ*, "underworld," and *-šḥt-*, "pit (of the underworld)." The theme of encompassing, surrounding, binding (*ʾppwny, ysbbny, ḥbwš*) is continued in the expression *brḥyh bʿdy* alluding to imprisonment, linking the bicola into a quatrain.

In the first quatrain (vv 3–4), the couplets were linked by the image "the belly of Sheol" (first couplet) over against images of water: Sea/River (second couplet). In this quatrain (vv 6–7), the couplets are linked by images of water (*mym, thwm*) in the first couplet over against images of the netherworld (*ʾrṣ, šḥt*) in the second couplet. This may be visualized as follows:

Quatrain 1: underworld : cosmic waters;
Quatrain 2: cosmic waters : underworld.

This is an exquisite example of cyclic construction. The cyclic construction and combination of images of cosmic waters and the underworld is closely paralleled in 2 Sam 22:5–6 (= Ps 18:5–6):[10]

1. אפפוני משברי מות
2. נחלי בליעל יבעתוני

[9]On this reading, see n. 5.

[10]For this reconstruction, see the references in n. 4.

3. חבלי שאול סבבוני
4. קדמוני מוקשי מות

In this quatrain (*l:l::l:l*) one notes chiastic structure:

ᵓppwny-
-ybᶜtwny
-sbbwny
qdmwny-

While each couplet places its parallel elements in chiastic order, colon 1 and 4, and colon 2 and 3 are linked with parallel elements forming a quatrain in cyclic structure:

-mšbry mwt	(colon 1)
-mwqšy mwt	(colon 4)
nḥly blyᶜl-	(colon 2)
ḥbly šᵓwl-	(colon 3)

Vv 3–7 of the Psalm of Jonah form an intricately structured complex of traditional poetry. Oral formulae abound. Chiastic and cyclic figures ornament bicola and quatrains and the whole. The overall structure can be pictured as follows:

quatrain	couplet	quatrain
b:l::l:b	*b:l::l:b*	*l:b::l:b*
l:b::b:l		*b:l::l:b*

III

The final section of the Psalm of Jonah yields on analysis far less sophisticated and intricate verse. The verse form is the same, but monotonously repeats without variation: *l:b::l:b*.

בהתעטף עלי נפשי	(8) *l*	[v 8]	When my soul fainted within me,
את יהוה זכרתי	(6) *b*		I remembered Yahweh.
ותבוא אליך תפלתי	(10) *l*		And my prayer came unto you,
אל היכל קדשך	(6) *b*		To your holy temple.
משמרים הבלי שוא	(8) *l*	[v 9]	Those who care for vain things (gods),
חסדם יעזבו	(5) *b*		Forsake their (source of) mercy.
ואני בקול תודה	(7) *l*	[v 10]	As for me, with a voice of thanksgiving
אזבחה לך	(5) *b*		I will sacrifice unto you.

אשר נדרתי אשלמה	(9) *l*	That which I vowed I will pay.
ישועתה ליהוה	(7) *b*	Salvation is of Yahweh.

Study quickly reveals that these last verses yield little internal or long-range structure. Oral formulae do not appear. Only in v 9 do we find a faintly chiastic figure in contrast to its extensive use in vv 3–7. Grammatical parallelism including assonance is rare. Prosaic elements, wholly missing in vv 3–7, appear and are difficult to expunge (*ʾt* in v 8, *ʾšr* in v 10). The language gives no appearance of early features; indeed the use of pseudo-cohortatives (v 10) is late as is the language of v 9.

The contrast in the language and prosody of vv 3–7 and vv 8–10 requires explanation. I do not believe that the sections can stem from the same poet or from the same time. Rather it appears that vv 3–7 derive from an old thanksgiving song (or lament) when traditional-oral skills were flourishing. Vv 8–10 appear to be a stock cultic ending of later date welded on to the older traditional verses. I am not suggesting that the author of Jonah has spliced together a thanksgiving hymn to fit his purposes. The standard cultic ending of the psalm of thanksgiving fits no better—and no worse—than vv 3–7—into the narrative concerning the prophet.

IV

Archaeology and History

The Use of Ethnography in an Archaeological Research Design

Albert E. Glock
Birzeit University

The process of decoding cultural trace elements and reconstructing patterned human activity is a major aim of much research today into ancient and modern lifeways. The mental maps of ancient artisans, farmers, merchants, housekeepers and priests are fossilized in artifacts and architecture, waste debris and decayed installations. The cognitive maps of archaeologists are embedded in field procedures, laboratory analyses and excavation reports. The subtle and powerful biases inculcated by social, religious and political education have shaped the forms of both types of cultural expression. To find the past that is truly dissimilar from the present, but at the same time to be aware that the inquiry into the past serves modern needs, requires a deliberate consideration of the intellectual form and social function of the archaeological enterprise. This essay is an attempt to define the intellectual framework necessary for the recovery of a usable past.

Decisive gains in archaeology today include the requirement of an explicit statement of conceptual modes that define research aims, focus on the discovery of adaptive strategies, and foster a new modesty, born of an awareness of the limits of a fragmented past, as well as a sensitivity to the distance between our questions and those questions relevant either to the ancients or to their modern descendents *in situ*, and our answers which do not satisfy our limited tests for truth which derive from our limited research tools. Following two decades of effort to apply the techniques of "cognitive anthropology" to the interpretation of excavated materials, Manfred Eggert identified four major epistemological fallacies in research designs and concluded that we do not have the procedures to research ancient cognitive maps in archaeological data.[1] In the context of modern archaeology, however, such a sobering conclusion leads not to despair but to continued search for more manageable objectives. Indeed, precisely this has happened to the ethnographic component of the more complete archaeological research design.

[1]M. K. H. Eggert, "Prehistoric Archaeology and Cognitive Anthropology: A Review." *Anthropos* 71 (1976) 508–24. See also the same author, "Prehistoric Archaeology and the Problem of Ethno-Cognition," *Anthropos* 72 (1977) 242–55.

Before turning to the use of ethnography by archaeologists, a further word about the research design is in order.[2] Perceived of as an intellectual structure rather than a technician's tool, the research design exists on two levels (macro and micro), has two dimensions (time and space), and four stages (data base, analysis, reconstruction of adaptive systems, and working models for each sub-system and for all systems conjoined), in addition to a series of procedures appropriate for each stage, dimension, and level of investigation. For example, if we consider the data stage where ethnography belongs together with environment, survey, excavation, and existing literature, two procedures are basic. First, in order to determine the quantity and quality of "facts" and the form of analysis, it is necessary to decide what ceramic, social or technological systems are to be reconstructed and why. If we wish to reconstruct a craft tradition, we must first decide what "facts" we are to collect if we are to have any assurance that the data will be usable. A second procedure is equally exciting. Assuming that the main intellectual task of archaeology is "explanation," the key two-step procedure is hypothesis formation and testing, the borderland where data patterns are interpreted as reflections of human behavior. We may agree that "explanation" is the goal of the archaeological inquiry and that a model or hypothesis is a proposed possible explanation for a specific set of archaeological phenomena. But there may be a divergence of view on *what* is to be explained and how we measure what is a satisfactory explanation. Indeed, how does data collection on a contemporary ethnographic horizon contribute to the ultimate aim of explanation?

The inclusion of ethnographic information in the data base, the first of the four stages in the research design, has two important philosophical implications. First, ethnoarchaeology is built on the assumption that the present is the key to the past. This uniformitarian view is derived from 18th-century English natural science. Social scientists have had a long struggle attempting to employ this principle, and they still find the unique and particular in human culture, i.e., in areas of ideational and symbolic behavior. How do we avoid the criticism that the interpretation of the patterns in the archaeological record based on the ethnographic present means that one cannot know more about the past than one already knows about the present? Second, the form of the argument based on the uniformitarian assumption, viz., the argument of

[2]One of the better examples of a research design is W. W. Fitzhugh, *Environmental Archaeology and Cultural Systems in Hamilton Inlet, Labrador*. (Smithsonian Contributions to Anthropology 16; Washington, D.C.: Smithsonian Institution, 1972) 1–11. In the Middle East an early example not yet superseded is F. Hole, K. V. Flannery and J. A. Neely, *Prehistoric and Human Ecology in the Deh Luran Plain* (Memoirs of the Museum of Anthropology, University of Michigan, No. 1; Ann Arbor, 1969) 1–9.

analogy, *can never prove anything*; at best it will offer a degree of probability. Based on the degree of biophysical proximity to the source of the archaeological material, two categories of analogy can be distinguished: the one, world-wide or discontinuous, the other, regional or continuous—also known as "direct historical" analogy.[3] Ascher's injunction twenty years ago remains valid, "Seek analogies in cultures which manipulate similar environments in similar ways."[4] Perhaps the most satisfactory solution to the problems posed is to assume that the uniformitarian view is more valid for human behavior dependent on the natural world than for the interpretation of activity flowing form ideology and embedded in symbols. The problem of the argument from analogy is best handled by treating "potential analogies as hypotheses to be tested, not as ready-made interpretations of archaeological data."[5] Ethnographic data collected at an early stage of research provide grounds for hypotheses which facilitate interpretation of the archaeological data at the end of the study.

There are two archaeological consequences for the research design with the introduction of ethnographic data. First, the chronological framework is reduced to a fine-line grid, and second, research topics emphasize continuity in a sociological context. Both shifts of emphasis can conveniently be illustrated by a single example, viz., the archaeological study of *tradition*. Most studies of tradition have dealt with symbol-producing or ideational literature and almost never with the material correlates—which is where archaeology begins the study of tradition. In the Middle East there remain pockets of traditional culture in the villages, albeit rapidly disappearing. In 1875, Clermont-Ganneau was convinced that the villages of Palestine contained much that could be traced to the Iron Age.[6] He also speculated that the traditions of the women were older than those of the men, though he had no way to find out. Today I think we can find out, not only by the conceptual structure

[3]The terminology belongs to R. A. Gould, "Some Current Problems in Ethnoarchaeology," *Ethnoarchaeology* (ed. C. B. Donnen and C. W. Clewlow, Jr., Institute of Archaeology, University of California, Los Angeles. Monograph 4; Los Angeles, 1974) 29–48. Also J. H. Steward, "The Direct Historical Approach to Archaeology," *American Antiquity* 7 (1942) 337–43.

[4]R. Ascher, "Analogy in Archaeological Interpretation," *Southwestern Journal of Anthropology* 17 (1961) 319. Reprinted in *Man's Imprint from the Past* (ed. J. Deetz; Boston: Little, Brown and Co., 1971) 262–71. See esp. p. 265.

[5]P. J. Watson, *Archaeological Ethnography in Western Iran* (Tucson: The University of Arizona, 1979) 3.

[6]Clermont-Ganneau, "The Arabs of Palestine," *PEFQS* (1875) 199–214. Reprinted in *Survey of Western Palestine IV. Special Papers.* (London: PEF, 1881) 315–30.

that seriously integrates ethnography into archaeological research design, but also by field work and laboratory analysis.

A fundamental assumption in the search for ethnographic connections with the archaeological record is the poweful linkage with the past reflected in tradition. The external traits of tradition are a transmission system, continuity in time and sometimes place, social consensus, and integrated innovation. The content of tradition is beliefs, social attitudes and organizational behavior, knowledge of environmental resources, and technological skills—all supported by the authority of past experience. Living traditions experience constant adjustments due to internal and external pressure, but attempt to curb massive change. In summary, a research design incorporating an ethnographic component has the capability of searching for the specific parameters of tradition, social, economic or technological, in archaeological data.

Let pottery serve as an example. For the student of ancient cultures the chief function of the study of the sociology and technology of living traditional potters is the formulation of testable hypotheses to explain archaeological data. There is always the possibility of great antiquity to at least elements of living traditions. According to Reina and Hill, the Indian women potters of Guatemala vary little in their forming techniques and shapes from their Mayan ancestors.[7] Balfet thinks that Maghreb pottery technique is at least 2000 years old.[8] Lister speaks of hand-built native Nubian pottery tradition as more than 5000 years old.[9] Mackay regards the pottery tradition in Balreji, near Mohenjo Daro, as dating to the third millennium B.C.[10] There is a heavy hand-made red or gray burnished fabric we have found in the Jenin area which I call Yabad Ware. It seems to begin in the early Mamluk period in Palestine, though the inexperienced may mistake it for Early Bronze. (Bowls sometimes have ledge handles!) The ware is still manufactured in Yabad, southwest of Jenin. In order, however, to increase the probability of statements about the antiquity of ceramic traditions, it is necessary to collect and analyze three types of evidence: 1) materials, tools, and artisan action, from collecting and preparing clay, to firing a finished

[7]R. E. Reina and R. M. Hill II, *The Traditional Pottery of Guatemala* (Austin: The University of Texas, 1978) 21–25, 273–75.

[8]H. Balfet, "Ethnographical Observations in North Africa and Archaeological Interpretation," in *Ceramics and Man* (ed., F. R. Matson; Chicago: Aldine Publishing Co., 1965) 161–77.

[9]F. C. Lister, *Ceramic Studies of the Historic Periods in Ancient Nubia* (Anthropology Papers No. 86, University of Utah, Department of Anthropology; Salt Lake City, 1967) 73–77.

[10]E. Mackay, "Painted Pottery in Modern Sind: A Survival of an Ancient Industry," *Journal of the Royal Anthropological Institute* 60 (1930) 127–35.

pot;[11] 2) the distribution, use and reuse of a vessel;[12] 3) its symbolic value, location and mutation in the archaeological record.[13] The segment of this trait complex of special interest to us here is the technical rather than the social network. Within the technical we will consider only forming and firing, with special attention to fuel. The source of our information is the traditional women potters working in five non-industrial villages on the West Bank, viz., Yabad, Qusra, Sinjil, Beit Anan, and el Jib.[14] The descriptive data will be confined to the technique for forming cooking pots and the firing system.

Though there are three different techniques for forming the *qidreh* or cooking pot in these five villages, there are many features that are similar. All are hand-built of yellow or white clay mined nearby, tempered as much as 50% with calcite, also from nearby. The shapes are similar: rounded bottoms, sharply incurved shoulder, opposing handles usually higher than the rim. Walls are generally ca. 1 cm thick. On the other hand, in Yabad, Qusra and el Jib, cooking pots are made in as many different routines. In the first two places the pot is formed in a morning, while at el Jib the process requires three or four days, depending on the weather. At Yabad the base begins as a patty on a straw tray

[11]Important examples of such studies are O. S. Rye and C. Evans, *Traditional Pottery Techniques of Pakistan* (Smithsonian Contributions to Anthropology No. 21; Washington, D.C.: Smithsonian Institution, 1976); M. Centlivres-Demont, *Une communauté de potiers en Iran* (Beiträge zur Iranistik; Wiesbaden: Dr. Ludwig Reichert, 1971); and B. Saraswati and N. K. Behura, "Pottery Techniques in Peasant India" (Anthropological Survey of India, Memoir 13; Calcutta: Anthropological Survey of India, 1966).

[12]Unfortunately the difficulties of tracing the varied life of a pot have deterred any systematic study of the subject so far as I am aware. For ceramic ethnographers, emphasis on the process of manufacture has left little energy for examination of primary and secondary use or discard patterns. There are other reasons for neglect. Interest in the subject is displayed in J. Birmingham, "Traditional Potters of the Kathmandu Valley: An Ethnoarchaeological Study," *Man* 10 (1975) 370–86.

[13]B. L. Fontana, "The Cultural Dimensions of Pottery: Ceramics as Social Documents," in *Ceramics in America* (ed. I. M. G. Quimby; Winterthur Conference Report, 1972; Charlottesville: University of Virginia, 1973) 1–13.

[14]A review of earlier literature may be found in A. E. Glock, "Ceramic Ethno-techniculture" (First International Conference on the History and Archaeology of Jordan, Oxford, England, March 1980. In press). In 1973 the Taanach Excavations began a study of traditional potters in the West Bank and Gaza in connection with the study of Bronze Age pottery of Taanach from a technological perspective. The ceramic technologist was Owen S. Rye. In 1975, John Landgraf entered the work, dealing largely with women potters. In the meantime I have continued to collect data on both women and men potters. It is hoped that soon Rye will be able to publish a more complete study of the traditional potters of Palestine.

sprinkled with sand, at Qusra the base of an old cooking pot becomes a convex mold when covered with a wet cloth, and in el Jib the vessel is shaped as a deep bowl around the left forearm before it is thrust into a shallow bowl filled with *tābūn* ash (*sakan*) and resting on a wooden block. In Yabad the pot is built up with coils forming a heavy cylinder, the lean and sticky clay continually smoothed by hand. The inverted rim is only slightly thickened and rounded. At Qusra the bowl-shaped base is turned upright and placed in a basket filled with *tābūn* ash, after which the interior is smoothed with a convex side of a wooden spoon before the rest of the pot is fashioned with slabs formed from flattened coils. Clay is added to thicken the rim exterior while the top of the rim is flattened with the thumb. At el Jib, after the pot has dried over night, the rim is formed from the uneven edge, but no clay is added. At Yabad the vessel dries in the sun for two or three hours before the heavy coil handles are added. The next day the base is trimmed with a knife, the body wet-smoothed. Three or four days later the pot is wiped with red slip inside and out. At Qusra the handles are attached and strengthened with a fillet at the lower side of the join points. The handles of the el Jib cooking pots are fixed to the point of widest diameter, while at Yabad the handle is on the upper shoulder.

Before we turn to an analysis of these data I want to present a brief description of open firing of cook pots by the women potters in these villages. There are two different systems, distinguished in the main by different fuels as well as the non-plastic tempers added by the potter of the clay. Farm wastes as well as dried grasses and weeds are the most common fuels. Among these we will consider two, a spiny shrub that grows in the shallow soil on treeless rocky mountain slopes, in Arabic *netish* (*Sarcopoterium spinosa*), and various animal manures. The first is used to fuel the firing of calcite tempered cooking pots largely because calcite can withstand the thermal shock of rapid rise and fall of temperatures. *Netish* fire temperatures leap at ca. 150°C per minute, in contrast to dung which averages between 2°C and 7°C per minute. In 10–15 minutes *netish*-fueled open firings reach 400°C. This level is maintained and exceeded by 50 to 80 degrees only with the addition of more fuel each five minutes for 25 to 30 minutes, the average heating period. Cooling is also rapid, dropping to 150°C in 40 minutes. The entire process, from excavating the shallow pit and loading the pottery (9 or 10 vessels), to carrying the pots home, lasts from two to three hours. This process was observed at el Jib and Qusra. At Yabad, where cooking pots were fired with platters and a brazier (*mōqadeh*), the main fuel was dung and the entire firing process never exceeded two hours.

The second major type of open firing uses mostly dung (cow, donkey, sheep or goat) as fuel. The temperatures generally reach 100°C higher than *netish*-fueled firings, the rate of increase to the peak is slower and longer (2 to 5 hours). Variability is due to humidity, density of fuel pack, and the care with which all exposed surfaces are continually kept covered with dung. This last important step is generally supported by a cover of burlap bags over the top of the pile and an edging of scrap metal, both designed to keep the dung cakes in place. The pottery repertoire is mostly jars, bowls, drinking jugs and various specialized vessels, such as a strainer or foot bath. Most of the clay from which these pots have been formed is grog tempered, preferably with sherds from an ancient site. As with cooking pot firings, a shallow pit may or may not be excavated. The area is covered with a layer of *tābūn* ash (*sakan*) and then a layer of dung. The large jars (*zīr*, sg) are placed on their sides, facing east (leeward). Dung pads are placed between the pots and on top. Smaller vessels are also placed in the space between large vessels, sometimes inside. Not enough measurements have been taken to be sure that the thermocouples have registered meaningful variables. Thus, in one such firing, after 45 minutes the temperature increased 20°C per minute for ten minutes and then dropped to 1.5°C increase per minute for the next 90 minutes. Sometimes it has been recorded that cooling occurred at the same rate as heating, while in another instance the cooling was three times more rapid. (These data were collected at Yabad, Beit Anan and Sinjil.) Major firing catastrophes are rare but it is common for about one-fourth of the fired pots to develop cracks on rim or base. These cracks can be mended easily.

From the point of view of *tradition* the apparent diversity of forming techniques for producing essentially the same or similar forms requires explanation. Are we seeking one, two, or three different forming traditions? One hypothesis that the data suggest is that behind Qusra and el Jib techniques there is a common technique (sequence system), which today appears as a *divergent tradition* (diagrammed as an inverted Y→⅄), while at Yabad the system is sufficiently dissimilar that we may have an example of a *direct tradition* (diagrammed as a vertical line).[15] The second body of selected data dealt with the intensive exploitation of environmental resources relating to pyrotechnology. One is always amazed that such seemingly haphazard and simple firing methods consistently succeed. Hidden in the tradition are specific kinds of knowledge not easily accessible. Among the women, for whom pottery making is a dying craft, an oral "explanation" is sometimes offered to replace a long forgotten technical understanding. In any case, the

[15]The only serious attempt to view tradition from an archaeological point of view is E. W. Haury, et al., "An Archaeological Approach to the Study of Cultural Stability," *Seminars in Archaeology: 1955* (ed. R. Wauchope; Memoirs of the Society for American Archaeology, No. 11, 22/2; Salt Lake City, 1956) 31–57.

evidence as presented suggests the hypothesis that the correlation between pottery and fuel used in firing is systematic, that this correlation is mainly between fuel burning rates and levels and the clay body, chiefly the non-plastics.

Both of these hypotheses require testing at two levels, technical and historical (or stratigraphic). Both require, for testing, replication in the laboratory and excavation in earlier phases of the archaeological record. We have not experimented with women potters, but men working on a wheel are very willing to illustrate the possible ways to throw a vessel.[16] Failing such an informant it is necessary to work with a potter forming by hand, to determine the probable methods used to shape round-based vessels, whether indeed the mold-made and hand-formed round base are close enough to be regarded as off-shoots of the same system. Criteria for reconstructing firing techniques are well-known to ceramic technologists and need not be discussed here.[17] Experimental replication of thermal shock on clay samples and non-plastics from the village potters' resources will provide an adequate test revealing at least elements of the technical knowledge hidden in the potter's tradition. Testing at the historical (stratigraphic) level is more troublesome. Ethnographic data are mostly horizontal, a tradition in space. The archaeologist's interest, however, also requires a diachronic dimension based on a stratigraphic sample from successive chronologic periods. Unfortunately, one of the least-known periods is the immediately preceding Ottoman Period, a 400-year long link to the slightly better documented Mamluk period. It is imperative that this gap be filled if testing of connections with the ethnographic present at the historical-archaeological level is to gain in force.

In sum, the use of ethnographic data in an archaeological research design enlarges the archaeologist's vision of the explanatory task and increases his capability to find probable interpretations by making visible the connections between people and place, a cultural tradition and its environment. The use of hypotheses is a reflection of an awareness of the variety of truthful explanations possible. No single explanation

[16]In two of the five villages it was necessary to pay the potter to encourage her to make pots. Some may regard this procedure as "replication." The use of metals and plastics for containers has long threatened the existence of the potters' craft and its traditions. Wonder is that anything has survived alive. For an adaptation of a cognitive model to replicate the process of pottery making see J. R. Sabloff and R. E. Smith, "Ceramic Wares in the Maya Area: A Clarification of an Aspect of the Type-Variety System and Presentation of a Formal Model for Comparative Use," *Estudios de Cultura Maya* 8 (1970) 97–115.

[17]The best recent work is O. S. Rye, *Pottery Technology: Principles and Reconstruction* (Manuals on Archaeology 4; Washington, D.C.: Taraxacum Inc., 1981).

contains the total truth. Indeed, we have found that a romance with a hypothesis, indeed with two hypotheses, is more exciting than marriage to an illusion, at least intellectually.

Social Stratification and Cultural Continuity at Alalakh[1]

ALBERTO R. W. GREEN
RUTGERS: THE STATE UNIVERSITY

I

THE 15th century B.C. literary sources from Alalakh IV have furnished us with lists of individuals which reveal an alignment in that society according to classes and sub-groups along with their corresponding functions. The groups most frequently mentioned are *maryanne, eḫele, ḫaniaḫḫe, ḫupšu, ṣabē-nāmē,* and *ḫapiru*. The texts from Alalakh VII in the 18th century, however, while they also reveal various groups of individuals fulfilling different functions, give no specific indication of a cultural stratification at this time. In general, unlike the later 15th century sources, these texts provide us with relatively little information about these earlier groups or the interrelationship between them.

The Late Bronze Age Alalakhian society is described as Hurrian, while that of the Middle Bronze Age is referred to as Old Babylonian, with a "Dark Age" of approximately two centuries between. It is the

[1]The following special abbreviations are used in this investigation: A = Tafelsignatur des Archäologischen Museums in Antakya, Turkey. AHw = *Akkadisches Handwörterbuch*. AT = D. J. Wiseman, *The Alalakh Tablets* (London: British Institute of Archaeology at Ankara, 1953). CAD = *Chicago Assyrian Dictionary*. DL = M. Dietrich and O. Loretz, "Die soziale Struktur von Alalaḫ und Ugarit," I: *WO* 3 (1966) 188–205; II *WO* 5 (1969) 57–93; IV: *ZA* 60 (1970) 88–123. GHL = F. W. Bush, *A Grammar of the Hurrian Language* (Ph.D Dissertation; Ann Arbor, 1966). GS = H. Klengel, *Geschichte Syriens im 2. Jahrtausend v. u. Z.* (Berlin: Akademie, 1965–70), 3 vols. HHA = A. E. Draffkorn, *Hurrians and Hurrian at Alalah: An Ethno-Linguistic Analysis* (Ph.D. Dissertation; Ann Arbor, 1959). NPN = I. J. Gelb, P. M. Purves, and A. MacRae, *Nuzi Personal Names* (Chicago: University of Chicago, 1943). PRU = J. Nougayrol, *Le palais royal d'Ugarit; III: Textes accadiens et hourrites des Archives Est, Ouest et Centrales* (Mission de Ras Shamra, VI; Paris, 1955), 2 vols. UT = C. H. Gordon, *Ugaritic Textbook* (Rome: Pontifical Biblical Institute, 1965). WUS = J. Aistleitner, *Wörterbuch der ugaritischen Sprache* (Berlin: Akademie, 1963).

purpose of this investigation to trace that process of social stratification revealed in the 15th century texts back to its earlier roots in the 18th century community, notwithstanding the "Dark Age" which separates them. Methodologically, this process of cultural continuity at Alalakh will be pursued by way of a re-examination of the patterns of cultural distribution first in the 15th century society, and subsequently a comparison of the results with available data on the earlier 18th century society.

This investigation of the cultural continuity in this region recognizes, of course, certain inherent problems. On the one hand the written sources may not always reflect the prevailing cultural situation. In documents primarily of an economic nature, one may only presume certain relationships between individual groups if such relationships are not explicitly stated in the texts. On the other hand the administrative texts, decrees, proclamations, and treaties assume an extensive foreknowledge on the part of the ancient reader, and thus can only be reconstructed through inference. Finally, there are the linguistic problems involving the usage of Hurrian terms with reference to certain groups. The role of these groups and the meaning of the terms applied to them has to be determined on the basis of contemporaneous usage, the historical context, and ultimately, against the background of external forces affecting the region and the Fertile Crescent as a whole during these periods. Notwithstanding these problems, the Alalakh texts, which originate from both the public and the private sectors, provide us with good source material for an investigation into the process of cultural continuity of the city-state during the 18th through the 15th centuries B.C., incomplete though this picture may be.

All the inscriptional material from this early period ends with the devastation of Alalakh VII by Hattusilis I during his second campaign in the last half of the 17th century B.C.[2] Levels VI and V represent a

[2]Most scholars who have dealt with the archaeological findings from Level VII at Alalakh have dated this destruction to MB IIB towards the last third of the 17th century B.C. See discussion by W. F. Albright, "Stratigraphic Confirmation of Low Mesopotamian Chronology," *BASOR* 144 (1956) 69; "Further Observations on the Chronology of Alalakh," *BASOR* 146 (1957) 30; H. J. Kantor, "Syro-Palestinian Ivories," *JNES* 15 (1956) 158; L. Woolley, *The Forgotten Kingdom* (London: Max Parish, 1959) 64–82; A. Kempinski, *Canaan, Syro-Palestine During the Last Stage of the Middle Bronze Age IIB 1650–1550 B.C.* (Jerusalem: Hebrew University, 1974) 44–47. A recent study has fixed the destruction more specifically to the twenties of the 17th century B.C. See N. Naᶜaman, "A New Look at the Chronology of Alalakh Level VII," *Anatolian Studies* 26 (1976) 140–41. The "Low Chronology" has allowed some 50 years between the destruction of Level VII and the destruction of Aleppo by Mursilis I.

"Dark Age" of about two centuries in the city's history.[3] The Level IV period is better known than any other phase in its occupation. In addition to the tablets deriving from this level, the recovery of the autobiography of King Idrimi inscribed on his statue has provided substantial information on the city during the reign of Idrimi, Niqmepa, and Ilimilimma II. There has been considerable discussion of the chronological limitations of this period; however, the period covering ca. 1550-1473 has generally been accepted as the most likely for Alalakh IV.[4]

North Syria was dominated in the 16th–15th century B.C. by the Mitannian kings Parattarna, Saushtatar, and Shutarna, to whom the local rulers of Alalakh owed their allegiance. Indicative of this Hurrian political and cultural domination during the Level IV period is the four-to-one Hurrian to West Semitic ratio in personal names,[5] compared to the earlier three-to-five Hurrian to West Semitic ratio during the Level VII era.[6] Hurrian names such as Kabia, Aki-Tesup, Takuhli, and

---

So, for example, M. B. Rowton, "Ancient Western Asia," in *CAH* 1/1, 3rd ed., 212–14; and J.-R. Kupper, "Northern Mesopotamia and Syria," *CAH* 2/1, 3rd ed., 30–32. If, however, this fifty year chronological span between the two events is acceptable, then General Zukraši, who appears in both the Alalakh Tablets and the Annals of Hattusilis I, could not figure within the period of Hattusilis I's campaigns where he rightfully belongs, though Zukraši at AT 6 is the same person mentioned in the king's annals which describe the events during his reign. Under these circumstances, the "Low Chronology" would be unsuitable for Alalakh VII. The translation, study, and dating of the "Annals," "Acts," or "Autobiography" of Hattusilis I has been variously treated by H. Otten, *MDOG* 91 (1958) 73–84); A. Goetze, *JCS* 16 (1962) 24–28; H. G. Güterbock, *JCS* 18 (1964) 1–6; O. Carruba, *ZDMG* Supp. 1 (1969) 231–34; A. Kammenhuber, *KZ* 83 (1969) 264–65, 282; F. Imparati and C. Saporetti, *Studi Classici e Orientali* 14 (1965) 40–85; and most recently, H. C. Melchert, *JNES* 31 (1978) 1–22.

[3]Woolley's earlier analysis of a 200 year span between Levels VI and V was based on the theory that Saushtatar is to be dated after the campaigns of Thutmose III and his son Amenophis II in Syria, dating the beginning of Level IV to ca. 1435 B.C. It is generally accepted, however, that both Parattarna and Saushtatar are to be dated toward the end of the 16th century and the beginning of the 15th, prior to the campaigns of Thutmose III in Syria. On this basis, Idrimi, who was a contemporary of Parattarna, would be dated toward the end of the 16th century. See also Albright, "Low Mesopotamian Chronology," 26–28; and *GS* 2, 175–77, 185, 209, 211.

[4]So W. C. Hayes, "Chronology," in *CAH* 1/1, 3rd ed., 211–16; B. Landsberger, "Assyrische Königsliste und 'Dunkles Zeitalter'," *JCS* 8 (1954) 53ff.; and *GS* 2, 227–41.

[5]*HHA*, 17, 117.

[6]I. J. Gelb, "The Early History of the West Semitic Peoples," *JCS* 15 (1961) 31. Draffkorn has noted that three-quarters of the population bore Hurrian names at this later level V, three-eights during the earlier period; *HHA*, 17.

Takuwa, occur in numerous texts in the 15th century (AT 68, 85, 87, 91, 152, 169, 187).[7] It is possible that the Hurrians, who had established themselves qualitatively as an influential minority in the 18th century, by the time of the Niqmepa in the 15th century had become a majority of the population at Alalakh, and in the process had come to exercise considerable political power.

There is indication of a substantial increase in use of Hurrian vocabulary in the 15th century. A good example of this trend is the common use of Hurrian terms with the occupational formative *-uḫli*,[8] as in *ḫāšeruḫli* (AT 269:22), *kubšu-ḫuli* (AT 263:18), *purkullu-ḫuli* (AT 227:8), and others (AT 136:41, 148:55, 172:7, 193:23, 199:33, 200:17, etc.).[9] The use of Hurrian names for months such as *nigaše* and *šumulalše* (AT 309–318)[10] may be an indication that the Hurrian calendar was also in use in Alalakh at this time. The prominent role of Hurrian deities Tesub and Khepa in official treaties and contracts, the regular mention of other Hurrian gods as Aštapi, Kuppa, Šauška (AT 126-127), along with the use of the Hurrian ritual term *azasḫi*, and names given to certain festivals (AT 269) are attestations to the strength of the Hurrian influence in the cult of Alalakh at this time.

Our most important source material on the social structure of Alalakh IV, however, derives from an analysis of the different groups given Hurrian technical designations, and their respective functions within the society. The following, will focus on this problem.

II

The Maryanne

The Census Lists tablets are particularly useful in their treatment of the *maryanne* and other groups at Alalakh (AT 128–178). The tablets catalogue several hundred persons of whom 101 are specifically identified as persons of the *maryanne*, 38 of whom owned chariots (AT 128–34, 136–39, 143, 144, 148–150, 152–55).[11] The term *maryanne*, explained in light of its Vedic source, is taken to mean young men or retainers who

[7]In her study of the name types, Draffkorn has listed a total of 410 positively identifiable Hurrian names and 211 name-types of known Hurrian derivations; *HHA*, 20–118, esp. 117–18.

[8]For an adequate discussion see *DL* I, 188–97, 201–5, also E. A. Speiser, "The Alalakh Tablets," *JAOS* 74 (1954) 20; note also *HHA*, 216–18; *JESHO* 5 (1962) 130; *AHw*, 314; and *CAD*, *Ḫ*, 57.

[9]Speiser, "The Alalakh Tablets," 20; *HHA*, 216–18; and *DL* I, 201–5.

[10]Wiseman, *AT*, 5.

[11]*DL* II, 89.

were really "chariot-warriors," both in cuneiform and Egyptian texts.[12] The interpretation of the term as a reference to a chariot-warrior class is confirmed from a study of the social structure of the kingdom of Mitanni where individuals of high rank were especially associated with chariotry.[13]

This warrior class was prominent in both Canaan and Mitanni during the New Kingdom period in Egyptian history.[14] Initially, the *maryanne* relationship with chariotry seems to have been the common denominator in these regions as well as the 15th century society of Alalakh (AT 131:55).[15] Many of the chariot owners bore Hurrian names. After the names of certain members of this group was written "own chariots," or "do not own chariots" in the case of nine others.[16] Such

[12]The term *maryannu* as noted in contexts of earlier Egyptian and cuneiform historical sources translates as "hero, young man, retainer." See H. Winckler, "Die Arier in den Urkunden von Boghazköi," *Orientalistische Literaturzeitung* 13 (1910) cols. 289–301. It is also to be explained as the Indic accusative plural *maryan* plus the Hurrian termination *-ni*, and in real meaning interpreted as "young men" who were really "chariot-warriors." See, in addition, Albright, "Mitannian *maryannu* 'chariot-warrior' and the Canaanite and Egyptian Equivalents," *AfO* 6 (1930) 217–21; A. Alt, "Bemerkungen zu den Verwaltungs und Rechtsurkunden von Ugarit und Alalach," *WO* 2 (1956) 235-36; H. Reviv, "Some Comments on the Maryannu," *IEJ* 22 (1972) 218–28; *AHw*, 611–12. For a new approach to the question of origins, see M. Mayrhofer, *Die Indo-Arier im Alten Vorderasien* (Wiesbaden: Harrassowitz, 1966) 41ff.; and A. Kammenhuber, *Die Arier im Vorderen Orient* (Heidelberg: C. Winter, 1968) 213.

[13]There are some 80 personal names of primarily Indo-Aryan origin, a number of which are associated with horses, horse-training, and chariots. They are essentially individuals of high rank. R. T. O'Callaghan, "New Light on the *Maryannu* as 'chariot-warrior'" *Jahrbuch für Kleinasiatische Forschung* 1 (1950) 309; and more recently Reviv, "Some Comments on the Maryannu," 218–20.

[14]W. F. Albright, "Mitannian *maryannu* 'chariot-warrior'," 218; K. Galling, "Hyksosherrschaft and Hyksoskultur," *ZDPV* 62 (1939) 110ff.; R. Engberg, *The Hyksos Reconsidered*, SAOC 18 (Chicago: University of Chicago, 1939) 23, 44; Y. Yadin, "Hyksos Fortifications and the Battering Ram," *BASOR* 137 (1955) 23–25; S. Lowenstein, "Notes on the Alalakh Tablets," *IEJ* 6 (1956) 219–20; J. Van Seters, *The Hyksos: A New Investigation* (New Haven: Yale University, 1966) 186–87; *DL* II, 85, 89, 93; A. F. Rainey, "The Military Personel at Ugarit," *JNES* 24 (1965) 19-21; Reviv, "Some Comments on the Maryannu," 220–21; and *PRU* 234.

[15]At Ugarit the *maryannu* is assumed to render service in the chariotry. A list of these individuals is included on a roster of chariots from serveral cities; *PRU* 193 (12.34, 24, 30). See also Wiseman, *AT*, 11; and Y. Yadin, *The Art of Warfare in Biblical Lands* (New York: McGraw-Hill, 1963) 86–88.

[16]Note, for example, *AT* 131, 132, 153; and *DL* II, 1:62–64; 8:28, 33–36, 38, 39.

statements tend to imply that the association of this group with chariotry could have been one of the identifying characteristics of the *maryanne*.

If one of the main criteria for defining the *maryanne* as a select group at this time was its association with chariotry,[17] these chariot-owning groups could have been much more numerous than those listed exclusively under the *maryanne* names,[18] and their roots may also be traced back to the emerging warrior groups of the earlier 18th century society who are listed as possessing chariots.[19] Ehli-adu and his sons and Akkati (AT 205–206) would fall into this category.

In the 18th century sources there is no reference to a designated *maryanne* class. For that matter, we have no evidence of Indo-Aryan names at this early period. This may mean that Indo-Aryans had not yet penetrated this far south into Syria. The omission of a designated *maryanne* class may also be due to other factors. There is the problem of the political instability of the region deriving from the interstate rivalries which enveloped western Asia, rivalries involving among others the Syrian kingdoms of Mari, Qatna, Yamhad, Aleppo, and the Mesopotamian kingdoms of Assyria, Babylon, and Eshnunna. In addition, there is also the evidence of the Asiatic Hurrians expanding to the south and west.[20]

It can be reasonably assumed that during the ensuing "Dark Age" between Levels VII and IV, the 18th century Hurrian population was constantly reinforced with fresh arrivals creating, in the process, a more Hurrianized society. The term *maryanne* did not come to be applied as a technical designation to a certain group of the chariot-warrior category until this Hurrian culture was later joined by small, vigorous Indo-Aryan groups from the far north or east, who, by reason of their superior armament in the form of the use of the light war-chariot, were able to impose their leadership upon the Hurrian-speaking majority, becoming in the process the predominant influence of a later period.[21] While the

[17]*DL* II, 89–90. This is of the total of 101 *maryannu* names on the Census Lists.

[18]Note the names and associations with chariotry from some tablets which are not of the Census Lists; *AT* 183, 189, 193; *DL* IV, 8:13, 9:33.

[19]For individuals specifically listed as owning chariots, see *AT* 205–6.

[20]The Hurrian settlement into northern Mesopotamia and Syria proper may be dated from the time of Zimri-Lim of Mari. Reference is made to Hurrian rulers in Ursim and Haššim. There is also evidence of early Hurrian penetration into the region around Chagar Bazar and Dilbat. See J.-R. Kupper, "Un gouvernement provincial dans le royaume de Mari," *RA* 41 (1947) 81–83; *GS* 2, 138–51; C. J. Gadd, "Tablets from Chagar Bazar," *Iraq* 7 (1940) 22–26; and A. Ungnad, *Beiträge zur Assyriologie* 5 (1909) 8–21.

[21]See especially Yadin, *The Art of Warfare*, 74f., 86ff., 196.; Stuart Piggott, *Prehistoric India* (Harmondsworth: Penguin Books, 1950) 273ff.; Goetze, *Hethiter*,

term *maryanne* is of Indo-Aryan etymology, as noted earlier, there is no evidence of Indo-Aryan names. The word *maryanne* is likewise absent from the epigraphical sources of the 18th century city. It can, therefore, be concluded that the designation of *maryanne* as the elite chariot-warrior was diffused through northern Syria via the Hurrians, and only as the Indo-Aryan superstructure fused itself with the Hurrian Alalakhian society did this technical term emerge in the texts of this period.

Aside from being chariot owners, the *maryanne* of the late 15th century have also been identified as landowners (e.g., AT 128–32, 134–39, 152–155, 183, 193–198), and as bureaucrats.[22] This leads to two reasonable assumptions. First, the association of certain individuals with chariotry was more factual and descriptive than the more technical designation "*maryanne*." The designation of these chariot-warriors as a *maryanne* class was the result of Indo-Aryan influence diffused through Hurrians when the kingdom of Mitanni was organized. On this basis, it could be concluded that chariot-warrior groups were known and identifiable as such already during the 18th century.[23] Second, all identifiable names of these Level VII chariot-warriors are non Indo-Aryan. This suggests that whereas the Level VII groups could have been non Indo-Aryan, in view of the fact that chariot-owning is the primary characteristic of the chariot warriors of both the 18th and the 15th century groups, the *maryanne* of the 15th century may be seen as continuous with earlier warrior groups of the 18th century.

The term *maryannu* does not appear in the literary texts of 14th century Ugarit, nor is it found in the Keret Legend which describes the preparation for a military campaign.[24] The reference to the chariot in the Keret text is to its use as a ceremonial vehicle.[25] The legend of Aqhat describes the chariot as a vehicle used only by the Rephaim.[26] The

---

Churriter und Assyrer: Hauptlinien der Vorderaisatischen Kulturentwicklung im II. Jahrtausend v. Chr. (Leipzig: Harrassowitz, 1936) 85; H. Schmökel, *Geschichte des Alten Vorderasien* (*Handbuch der Orientalistik*, 2/3; Leiden: Brill, 1957) 160.

[22]It is assumed that the "royal *maryannu*" (*maryannu šarri*) at Ugarit who were exempted from military service were essentially "non-chariot owners" engaged as bureaucrats in specialized functions or positions for the crown; *PRU* 80 (16.239, 17); Reviv, "Comments on the Maryannu," 219–20. At Alalakh, aside from being chariot owners, some were identified as scribes and mayors; *AT* 129, 138, 150, 155; *DL* II, 3:21, 5:33, 18:25, 29:8.

[23]There is philological indication that the earlier Mitannians had competence in the use of the chariot in warfare, and a few Amorite names of Level VII are also associated with horses and chariots. See discussion in Goetze, "Warfare in Asia Minor," *Iraq* 25 (1963) 124–26; and Yadin, *The Art of Warfare*, 36ff., 74ff.

[24]*UT*, Krt: 85–105.

[25]*UT*, Krt: 56, 286.

[26]*UT*, 121:II, 1–9.

contexts in these literary texts in which references to chariots are found may well represent a much earlier state in the growth of the Ugaritian society when the chariot was still a rare vehicle. In the 18th century Alalakhian texts, the historical references to the possession of chariots by certain members of a warrior group may similarly be a reflection of an earlier period in the Alalakhian society when the chariot was still a rare vehicle comparable to that alluded to in the Ugaritian literary texts. In both contexts, however, the association of chariotry with warrior groups is indicated. It may be assumed on this basis that the warrior groups of the earlier period inferred in the Ugaritian literary sources, and those mentioned in the 18th century Alalakhian society, would have gone through a similar evolutionary stage prior to the migration of Indo-Aryan tribes under whose influence their technical designation as *maryanne* began to emerge in both regions two centuries later.

The evidence relating to the *maryanne* at Alalakh in the 15th century, and the *maryannu* at Ugarit in the 14th century, indicate that the members of this class were not restricted to one ethnic group. While there is no direct linguistic evidence, it is very possible that in its initial stages, chariotry was in the sole possession of a small, exclusive Indo-Aryan aristrocracy, and as such, *maryannu*-ship would be confined to this elite ethnic minority. Later, in 15th century Alalakh and 14th century Ugarit, and presumably in other areas in northern Syria, our documents reveal that the persons comprising the *maryannu* class in their majority carry Hurrian and Semitic names.[27]

In 15th century Alalakh, Kabia was elevated to *maryanne*-ship and to the priesthood, making him eligible for royal rations (AT 15, 91).[28] His elevation and functions as a priest in the service of the king in the 15th century society follow a pattern very similar to that of Nakkasse, the priest and royal aviarist (AT 126), Zadamu (AT 279), and other priests of Ishtar (AT 270), who in the 18th century society served the king as royal

[27]*Maryannu*-ship was a rank originally associated with chariotry by the Indo-Aryan elements among the Hurrians; however, when it took root in the Near East, it was not confined to one ethnic group. See Schmökel, *Geschichte des Alten Vorderasien*, 160–61; O'Callaghan, "New Light on the Maryannu," 320–21; Rainey, "The Military Personnel at Ugarit," 19–22; and Mayrhofer, *Die Indo-Arier im Alten Vorderasien*, 41ff. In the Census Lists of Alalakh all of the *maryanne* names of the village of Alime are Hurrian; see *DL* II, 1:56–65; *AT* 313.

[28]Even though a *maryanne*, he is registered as a non-chariot owner. Two groups are distinguishable among this element in the Alalakh tablets: the chariot-owning *maryanne*, and those who did not own chariots; see *DL* 85, 89, 93; and Reviv, "Comments on the Maryannu," 219–20. In the Census Lists, however, there is no specific differentiation between the groups; see, for example, *AT* 130, 132, 136, 144, etc.; *DL* II, 7:11ff., 8:27–30, 6:32ff., 3:14ff.

functionaries and fulfilled similar technical duties. With the emergence of the technical designation *maryanne*, under Hurrian influence, officials of rank already fulfilling certain bureaucratic functions could be elevated to *maryanne*-ship. Such development was evident at Ugarit in the case of Abdu, who was designated a "royal *maryannu*." The later sources at Alalakh and those from Ugarit apparently indicate a two-tiered *maryanne* structure. There were the non-chariot owners such as Kabia, Abdu, and Adal-senni,[29] wealthy and influential persons who were elevated to the *maryanne* ranks, exempted from service in the chariotry, and allowed special privileges as royal functionaries.[30] On the other hand, there were the chariot owners who, as members of the *maryanne*, only served in the military. However, since they did not fulfill any additional special royal function in the king's court, it would appear that they did not enjoy a status of social elitism comparable to those *maryanne* who served as royal functionaries.[31]

In the 18th century such a two-tiered division among the chariot-warrior groups and those serving as royal functionaries is not indicated. The societal distribution was more fluid. There is no indication that Ehli-adu, his sons, Akkati, and possibly others, were directly in the king's service, even though the priests Nakasse, Zadamu, and others presumably served at the king's pleasure.

In 15th century Alalakh, the designation of *maryanne* included individuals of rank from various ethnic origins. This would indicate that citizens who wielded military or religious power could be elevated to such a status. Our evidence has shown that the personal names on the *maryanne* lists are derived from different linguistic strains;[32] however, the common denominator of the *maryanne* was generally his association with chariotry.

Our sources on the *maryanne* at Alalakh during the 15th century, and those from Ugarit a century later, have portrayed this class of individuals as a *corps d'elite* around the royal family. There is ample

[29]These men were exempted from military service and were elevated to *maryannu* status; *PRU* 81 (16.239, 31–33); 84 (16:157, 22–23); 86 (16.250, 17–19), etc. See also Rainey, "The Military Personnel at Ugarit," 19, n. 40; and Reviv, "Comments on the Maryannu," 224.

[30]Examples include references to mayors (*DL* II, 3:19, 5:33, 29:8); a royal scribe (*DL* II, 3:21); or even a royal tanner (*DL* II, 18:25).

[31]*DL* II, 89–93. Note especially Reviv, "Comments on the Maryannu," 221–22.

[32]The names of the members of this class are predominantly Hurrian in so far as can be analyzed, but a respectable number are also Semitic, Indo-Aryan, or of an unknown ethnic strain; see *HHA*, 248–49; *NPN*, 245, 276; and O'Callaghan, "New Light on the *Maryannu*," 320-21; for an opposite view, see Speiser, "The Alalakh Tablets," 21.

indication that the *maryanne* function at this time could represent the continuation of an earlier 18th century societal trend of the rising elitism of the emerging chariot-warrior class of individuals around the king. As a "created class," the religious functions of some of its members were probably only a continuation of like functions of individuals in a similar position in the 18th century. This continuing professional function in the service of the king logically carried with it the status of social elitism and, in the 15th century, was technically designated with the title *maryanne*, with all the additional prerogatives and rights inherent in that rank.

The Eḫele

Within the social structure of Alalakh, the *eḫele* occupy a place next in rank to the *maryanne*. There are many references to this group in the 15th century texts. The word *eḫele*, from the Hurrian root *eḫli-*, *eḫal-*, conveying the feudal sense "to free" or "to rescue,"[33] would indicate that the *eḫele* represent a group or groups which had been freed.[34] The *eḫelena*, therefore, are members of a social class of persons who were freed from a feudal status, hence, literally "freedmen."

More than 100 names on 14 Census Lists make reference to this group (AT 129, 131–33, 138–139, 143–144, 149, 157, 186, 197, 200, 202). On two of the tablets 13 *eḫele* names are also listed as *šūzubu* (AT 131, 143).[35] The contextual implication is that these two terms may be essentially equivalent. On another tablet other than the Census Lists, 53 *purena* are also called *eḫelena* (AT 192),[36] as are 31 *šūzubūtu* listed on two additional tablets. If the *eḫelena*, *šūzubūtu*, *purena* refer to the same category of individuals, then it would appear that the total *eḫele* class would number a few hundred.

Several features of this class are evident from the texts. On the *eḫele* lists, the profession of every second person is given. Among the listed occupations are grooms, shepherds, gardeners, herdsmen, a scribe, a mayor, tanners, etc. (AT 129, 130, 134, 135, 136, 138, 148, 150).[37] The *eḫelena* own houses (AT 189);[38] however, in none of these references are

[33]The plural *eḫelena* (the adjective *eḫel* + the plural suffix *-ena*).

[34]*DL* II, 85, 92; *AHw*, 191; *CAD, E*, 51; *HHA*, 119, 152, 162, 248; Landsberger, "Assyrische Königliste," 57.

[35]*DL* II, 60, 68, 88, 89.

[36]Akkadian *pūru*, land obtained by lot, or reference to holdings; a designation for land originally acquired by lot as opposed to inheritance. At Alalakh *bitāti purena* would correspond to houses belonging to the Nuzi *bēl puri* and *bitāti ṭuppatinena* (houses by deed) to a *bēl zitti*. Houses belonging to *purena*: *AT* 189; 194:1, 32; 190; 195. See also *AHw*, 881–82; *HHA*, 195.

[37]*DL* II, 88, 89; *DL* IV, 115, 117–19.

[38]*DL* IV, 117–19.

they associated with the military or given military designations. The Census Lists reveal that certain individuals belonging to this class also held fiefs and in some cases were settled on lands of the king (AT 187).

The term *šūzubu*, "freedman,"[39] used to designate certain groups among the *eḫelena* (*mārē*^{meš} *eḫelena ana šūzubu* AT 143), is a reference to free persons who had no feudal obligations. According to the Census Lists, the members of this class are portrayed in a non-military role, freedmen owning parcels of land in surrounding villages and maintaining a livelihood as professionals, artisans, and craftsmen, some of whom even held important state offices.[40] Proportionately, they represent a significant percentage of the names on the Lists.

The designations *eḫele, šūzubu,* and *purre,* as the designation *maryanne,* do not occur in the 18th century texts. There is evidence, however, of individuals during this earlier era within the Alalakhian society whose societal functions were similar to those of the later *eḫelena* class.

A number of the earlier residents are listed as freedmen who practiced their crafts and professions.[41] They appear to have had no feudal obligations.[42] Some are depicted as affluent citizens who own land and other valuable property. This class is not included in the administrative personnel as are the previously discussed *maryanne*-type individuals. They do not appear on the king's ration lists. As a class during this earlier period, some of these individuals were competitive with the king's family, with whom they also conducted economic transactions (AT 52, 53, 54, 61, 76). Like their later counterparts, the *eḫelena,* many of them resided in the surrounding villages.[43] Loans and contracts are associated with a number of the individuals in this category during the 18th century, but there is no specific reference to persons of the later *eḫelena* class securing loans by *mazzazānūtu* transactions.[44] Even though there is no direct evidence of loans at this later time, we must presume, nevertheless, that people of this economic level would engage in similar

[39]From the verb *ezēbu,* "to release, abandon, leave." See also Speiser, "The Alalakh Tablets," 21; *AHw,* 1295; *DL* II, 83, 85, 88, 90, 92.

[40]Wiseman, *AT,* 11.

[41]*AT* 19, 20, 32, etc.

[42]Compare *eḫelena* in *AT* 131, 143, 189, from the later period with the earlier inhabitants of the villages of Alama, Taradi, Igbar, Šipte, Ure, Erirambi (*AT* 42, 55, 56).

[43]See references to inhabitants of Alama (*AT* 42) and similar villages of the earlier period, and those of the later list of *eḫelena* villages and property holders in *AT* 202:46; 192:28; 200; and 211.

[44]For a comprehensive treatment of the *mazzazānūtu* type contracts and their function as a principle of personal antichretic security in the traditions of Mesopotamian law, see B. L. Eichler, *Indenture at Nuzi* (New Haven: Yale University, 1973) 49–88.

business practices as their predecessors. None of these individuals in the 18th century society, like their *eḫelena* counterparts, are listed as members of the military personnel. Numerically, on the basis of the Census Lists, the late *eḫelena* class appear to be proportionately fewer in number than their earlier counterparts.

An analysis of the available data from both periods points to a continuation of this social class of free citizens from the 18th century into the now technically designated *eḫelena* class of the 15th century in the Alalakhian region. This social trend seems to be a natural development and need not be attributed solely to Hurrian influence, even though an application of the technical term *eḫelena* to this class of people was the result of Hurrian influence.

The Ḫaniaḫḫe

Ḫaniaḫḫe is the name given to another important group to which frequent reference is made in the 15th century texts. The term derives from Akkadian *ḫanū* and the Hurrian adjectival ending *-ḫḫe* (pl. *ḫaniaḫḫena*), hence the Hurrian loan word for "out of Hana."[45] Linked with this term is also the Akkadian *ekû*, "indigent, impoverished," used at times to describe the former.[46] The contexts of these references would imply that the *ḫaniaḫḫena* were a class of people "coming out of Ḫana."

In a number of references the occupations of the *ḫaniaḫḫena* are listed as weavers, tanners, potters, musicians, shepherds, blacksmiths, grooms, etc., (AT 132, 136, 138, 139, 148).[47] One text contains a list of 18 *ḫaniaḫḫena* living in villages owned by the king (AT 187),[48] and there is also an additional list of 18 *ḫaniaḫḫena* on a roster of the *ṣabē-nāmē*. There is one isolated reference to a *ḫaniaḫḫe* who owns a chariot (AT 198:47). Some of the *ḫaniaḫḫena* owned houses and small plots of ground (AT 187, 190, 198, 200, 202), and lived in the rural areas around the villages and towns (AT 143, 148, 198). In many respects the social functions of the *ḫaniaḫḫena* are very similar to those of the *eḫelena*. The identity and functions of this class can be ascertained more closely through an analysis of additional data outside the Alalakh texts.

A theory which has received general acceptance is that the *ḫaniaḫḫena* were essentially semi-nomadic tribal people who roamed through

[45]*Ḫanu* may be associated with ᶜ*ănâ* (Gen 36:2–29; 1 Chr 1:38, 41) and may perhaps be related to ᶜ*ny*, "destitute, humble," given its use as an appellative for a lower class. See also *CAD*, *Ḫ*, 82; *DL* IV, 115, 119, 121–22; and *AHw*, 321.

[46]The *ḫaniaḫḫe* are also described as *ekūtu*; Speiser, "The Alalakh Tablets," 21; *AHw*, 195; *DL* II, 91, 92.

[47]*DL* II, 84, 87, 88, 91, 92.

[48]*DL* IV, 113–14.

the regions around Mari,[49] living in encampments called *nawûm*. They also settled in the towns and villages as semi-nomads who recognized the authority of the king of Mari, and periodically furnished him with military assistance. They were connected with the region of Hana near Tirqa in the Mari area proper.[50] Both Yahdun-Lim and Zimri-Lim called themselves "King of Mari, Tuttul, and the country of Hana." The fact that Yahdun-Lim fought seven sheiks of Hana could be an indication that Hana was a part of either Mari or the region immediately adjacent to it. Viewing the *ḫaniaḫḫena* as nomadic or semi-nomadic groups fits in with the general theory that these were one of the numerous West Semitic groups which occupied the territory of Mari during and immediately after the "Lim-era."[51] If elements of this group settled in the vicinity of Alalakh during the Mari era and subsequently became a part of it, it is of interest that no reference is made to them until the 15th century texts. Several factors could be responsible for this silence.

The political instability of north Syria was one of the contributing factors which led to the organization of the state of Alalakh within the kingdom of Yamhad. The 18th century texts reveal that the early kings of Yamhad expanded and consolidated the state's boundaries through judicious purchases and exchanges of adjacent lands.[52] There is the possibility that the numerical strength of the *ḫaniaḫḫena*,[53] who had settled earlier in the region, had brought certain areas under their control, rendering those areas off limits to the rulers of Alalakh. Under such circumstances, this territory would not be under the jurisdiction of Alalakh, and the hostile character of the group would preclude any sort of contact between the *ḫaniaḫḫena* and the kings of Alalakh, hence the silence in the texts.

[49]At times the general meaning of "nomads" has been applied to the word *ḫanū* as indicative of a people who roam the steppes and grasslands; Kupper, *Les nomades en Mésopotamie au temps des rois de Mari* (Paris: Société d'Edition "Les Belles Lettres," 1957) 1–46. See also Gelb, "West Semitic Peoples," 37; *AHw*, 770–71.

[50]Kupper, *Les nomades*, 30; and "Benjaminites and other Nomads," in *CAH* 2/1, 3rd. ed., 24–25.

[51]Gelb, "West Semitic Peoples," 36–37, 45; and *GS* 3, 138–40, 143–44, 146–47.

[52]Draffkorn, "Was King Abba-An of Yamhad a Vizier of the king of Hattusa?" *JCS* 13 (1959) 94–97; W. G. Lambert, "A Vizier of Hattuša? A Further Comment," *JCS* 13 (1959) 132; Wiseman, *AT*, 2–3; D. Collon, *The Seal Impressions from Tell Atchana/Alalakh* (AOAT 27; Neukirchen-Vluyn: Neukirchener; 1975) 139–40; *GS* 1, 151–62; and *AT* 1, 6.

[53]They were established in strength in the Euphrates and Khabur valleys. In the Terqa district alone they numbered several thousand. So Kupper, *Les nomades*, 32–34; and "The Benjaminites," 26–27.

Another plausible theory would be that during the earlier period, the *ḫaniaḫḫena* were not fully sedentarized and did not really make an economic impact or exert any significant social influence upon the young state of Alalakh. It should be noted in this regard that, of the 178 tablets deriving from Level VII, only seven deal specifically with legal matters involving the historical foundation of the state (AT 6–10, 12, 78), and only one, which treats the history of Alalakh vis-à-vis the king of Yamhad, makes any reference to political matters which may have a bearing on the external politics of Alalakh (AT 1). The main thrust of these documents is economic rather than political. If the *ḫaniaḫḫena* were settled in the region as early as the 18th century, we may presume some reference to them in the texts only if they posed a political threat or were economically important in the emerging state. It should also be noted that, aside from the warriors and the *ḫapiru,* no other groups are specifically differentiated in the earlier texts. Given this pattern, the *ḫaniaḫḫena* class individuals of the 18th century society fall into the same anonymous category as the previous groups. In certain circles, as one of several groups at Alalakh they have been assumed to occupy a place in the societal structure second only in importance to the *maryannena.*[54] On the other hand, the *ḫaniaḫḫena* have also been made a sub-group of the *ṣabē-nāmē,* while the *eḫelena* have been placed next in rank to the *maryannena.*[55] Another theory, which emphasizes the impoverished nature of the *ḫaniaḫḫena,* places this group third on the social ladder, slightly above the *ṣabē-nāmē.*[56]

A study of the various contexts in which the *eḫelena* and the *ḫaniaḫḫena* appear would suggest that in certain respects they both carried out similar functions at Alalakh. Both were excluded from the military listing, except in one case where a group of *ḫaniaḫḫena* were listed along with the forces of the SA.GAZ (AT 226). Both own houses and plots of land in the villages and towns. Both are mentioned as professional artisans and craftsmen, although the majority of the professional listings are among the *eḫelena.*

One way to explain this similarity in function but difference in technical designation is that the *eḫelena* may represent the original native population of the area who owned plots of ground in and around Alalakh, while the *ḫaniaḫḫena* were later arrivals who were able to settle farther away on the outskirts during the times of unrest when the borders of the state were not well defined. This latter group subsequently

[54]See Wiseman, *AT,* 11; Gelb, "West Semitic Peoples," 36–37; and Kupper, *Les nomades,* 44–45.

[55]Especially Speiser, "The Alalakh Tablets," 20–21; I. Mendelsohn, "On Slavery at Alalakh," *IEJ* 5 (1955) 65–72; and *HHA,* 119.

[56]*DL* II, 90–92.

became permanent settlers on the land they had occupied and were later identified with the permanent residents of the region, becoming in the process an integral part of the society.

With the development of a more stable political situation under Hurrian suzerainty, the *eḫelena* and the *ḫaniaḫḫena* came to appear as one social class almost similar in their social functions, but retaining their respective traditional designations by which they were later identified by the Hurrians. The *eḫelena*/*ḫaniaḫḫena* may, therefore, represent the cultural continuity of certain resident peoples who were in the region as early as the 18th century and who, in the later 15th century social structure, were then characteristically identified by their traditional names. It cannot be demonstrated so far that either the *eḫelena* or the *ḫaniaḫḫena* were sub-groups of the *ṣabē-nāmē*, although some of them lived in villages belonging to the king.

The Ṣabē-nāmē

The designation *ṣabū* (group of "people") of the *namû*/*nawû* (Hebrew *nāweh*), pasture-ground or uncultivated land on the outskirts,[57] as a social class could be given to the rural poor of Alalakh.[58] The term is applied to the largest and most complex of all the classes at Alalakh. Thirty tablets make reference to this group,[59] with the Census Lists alone providing a total of more than 500 names.

One of the difficulties involved in the precise identification of this class is that all the other classes and sub-groups, except the *maryannena*, at one time or another, are also equated with the *ṣabē-nāmē*. Illustrative of the problem is the following: the *ṣabē-nāmē* are equated with *ḫupšena* on three tablets (AT 131, 136, 152), with the *eḫelena* on two tablets (AT 133, 152), and with the *ḫaniaḫḫena* on nine tablets (AT 129, 131, 132, 135, 139, 140, 143, 148, 149). The *ṣabē-nāmē* are also equated with the *ḫupšena* on a number of tablets other than the Census Lists (AT 197–182, 186–197, 202, 211), the largest number mentioned at one time on a tablet being 1,446 persons. Since the *ḫupšena* are equated more frequently with the *ṣabē-nāmē*, the problem here is the nature of the relationship between the *ṣabē-nāmē* and the *ḫupšena* on the one hand, and the connection between these and the other classes on the other.

The various contexts seems to indicate that in function the *ṣabē-nāmē* and the *ḫupšena* were roughly equivalent in the Alalakhian society. The designation *ṣabē-nāmē* would imply that this class resided primarily around the villages in the rural areas of the state. A profile of the *ḫupšena*, however, can best be studied from areas outside Alalakh.

[57]For Akkadian *ṣabū*, see *AHw*, 1072; *CAD*, Ṣ, 46–55.

[58]*DL* II, 90–91.

[59]Wiseman, *AT*, 64–68.

The term *ḫupšu* (Hurrian, *ḫupšena*) is the Semitic designation for certain persons of a lower social status.[60] In various areas of the Near East outside Alalakh they are subject to military conscription. It is clear, however, that they were not entirely free-born persons. In many places around Assyria they appear as people of low social status who were mainly engaged in agricultural work as day-laborers, share-croppers, or tenant-farmers.[61] At Alalakh, however, there are a few isolated references to *ḫupšena* owning houses (AT 186, 187, 202:45, 211, A83/22).[62] Since there is no reference to any *ḫupšena* among the artisans or craftsmen, it may be implied that the primary function of this segment of the population was agricultural and tenant-farming. At Ugarit the *ḫupšu* is time and again portrayed as a militarily draftable tenant-farmer living off the land.[63] Only in the Nuzi texts is the term specifically associated with weavers.[64]

Both the *ṣabē-nāmē* and the *ḫupšena* fulfill a similar role in the Alalakhian structure. Both groups reside in the rural areas where they are employed in tenant-farming and animal husbandry. The few references to other occupations are found exclusively among the *ṣabē-nāmē*. Such occupations include a tanner, a potter, an attendant, a weaver, a blacksmith, etc. (AT 131, 132, 136, 143, 148, A81/32, A49).[65] On the lists dealing with this class, there is a ratio of 18 names with specific occupations to every 542 names. On this basis both of these groups should be considered collectively as an agricultural class. The texts show that neither the *ṣabē-nāmē/ḫupšena,* nor the *eḫelena/ḫaniaḫḫena* are listed among the military personnel;[65] however, unlike the latter, in only

[60]Among other sources outside of Alalakh, the term *ḫupšu* appears in the Amarna Letters, Nuzi texts, Ugaritic texts, Middle Assyrian Laws, Late Assyrian texts, the Old Testament, etc. The *ḫupšu* are referred to in general as people who abandoned towns in search of grain, weavers (only at Nuzi), and persons in the army and subject to corvée labor, or people belonging to the lower classes (in Assyria, Syria, and Palestine). See Mendelsohn, "New Light on the *Ḫupšu*," *BASOR* 139 (1955) 9–11; *WUS*, 1071; CAD, *Ḫ*, 241–42; and *DL* II, 91.

[61]Mendelsohn, "The Canaanite Term for the Free Proletarian," *BASOR* 83 (1941) 36–38; E. R. Lacheman, "Note on the Word *ḫupšu* at Nuzi," *BASOR* 86 (1942) 36–37; C. J. Gadd, "Hammurabi: The End of His Reign," in *CAH* 2/1, 3rd. ed., 196–97.

[62]*DL* II, 91; IV, 115.

[63]Rainey, "Military Personnel at Ugarit," 24–25.

[64]Lacheman, "*Ḫupšu* at Nuzi," 36–37.

[65]See also *DL* II, 86–87, 89–91.

[66]At Ugarit and in the Amarna Letters they are listed in the infantry contingents; Rainey, "Military Personnel at Ugarit," 25; *AHw*, 357.

a few isolated cases are the *ṣabē-nāmē*/*ḫupšena* identified as householders. In most cases they possess agricultural implements and a few texts imply that some of them own cattle.[67]

Due in part to the similarity in roles between the *ṣabē-nāmē* and the *ḫupšena*, it is possible to ascertain the approximate function of this complex group as the largest class within the social structure. The *ṣabē-nāmē*/*ḫupšena* were essentially non-freeborn tenant-farmers who stood between the artisan/professional *eḫelena*/*ḫaniaḫḫena* class and the slaves. If the figures given on the various lists are a guide, they were more numerous than any other class at Alalakh. As tenant-farmers, even though their names are absent from the military roster, they would be subject to military draft in the service of the king or village owner, as at Ugarit.

The permanent residence of this class, and of certain members of the other classes, was primarily in the rural areas of the state. The mention of a number of *ḫaniaḫḫena* and *eḫelena* in association with the *ṣabē-nāmē*/*ḫupšena* need not be interpreted to make the former sub-groups of the latter. Our texts indicate that the *eḫelena*/*ḫaniaḫḫena* represent a certain category of people who fulfilled specific functions at Alalakh which were quite different from the functions carried out by the masses of the *ṣabē-nāmē*/*ḫupšena*; hence, it would seem incorrect to consider them as sub-groups of the latter. The references which convey the impression that the *eḫelena*/*ḫaniaḫḫena* were sub-groups of the *ṣabē-nāmē*/*ḫupšena* seem rather to be pointing mainly to the rural residence of certain members of the *eḫelena*/*ḫaniaḫḫena* class, which was in the same general location as the *ṣabē-nāmē*/*ḫupšena*. This could be a plausible explanation for the census listing of a number of *eḫelena*/*ḫaniaḫḫena* as part of the totals of both the *ṣabē-nāmē* and the *ḫupšena*.[68]

The terms *ṣabē-nāmē* or *ḫupsěna*, as the other previously discussed technical designations, do not appear in the 18th century texts. However, in a general sense there is a close similarity between the functions of the *ṣabē-nāmē*/*ḫupšena* and the lower class persons of the Level VII society.

Much of the territory in the 18th century state was privately owned by the king's family and a few affluent members of that society (AT 35–41, 52–56, 76, 97–98a). Under these circumstances most of the indigenous inhabitants of the surrounding region were essentially tenant-farmers. Such is the status implied in certain texts like the following: "Irpa-ada buys from Labbina the villages of Sallun . . ." (AT 56; cf. 52–55, 75, 76–80). There is a list of approximately twenty such

[67]The phrase "has no cattle" beside a few of the names would imply that some did own cattle. See *AT* 136; and *DL* II, 7:1–31.

[68]As *AT* 133, 152. See also *AT* 129, 131, 135, 139, 140, 143, 148, 149.

villages under the ownership of affluent individuals.[69] This class of tenant-farming people living in villages owned by specific individuals comprised the majority of the population.

On the matter of military conscription in the early society there is a similar type of involvement as during the later period. The texts specifically indicate that the owner of a village would draft its residents into his army (AT 54, 55).

It may correctly be assumed that with the continued Hurrianization of Alalakh from the 18th century onward, this rural, poor tenant-farming class of people who traditionally comprised the majority of the population, due in part to the place of their residence, their occupation, and their role in society, were later in the 15th century texts specifically referred to as *ṣabē-nāmē* and *ḫupšena*.

The Ḫapiri/SA.GAZ[70]

The role of the *ḫapiru* in the 15th century is brought to light in a number of tablets (AT 164, 180, 184, 226, 350). These references indicate that the *ḫapiru* were organized militarily and controlled certain areas in the state. A number of texts list the components of each *ḫapiru* group under its leader (AT 180–184). The total of the combined *ḫapiru* is in excess of 2000 (AT 226). It is also evident that they exercised considerable influence on the society as a whole.

The term *ḫapiru* is probably of West Semitic origin, and has denoted a social element,[71] as first pointed out by Landsberger.[72] There is virtual unanimity of opinion on this view. The *ḫapiru* are represented in various sources as vagrant elements with no single language scattered among the peoples of Western Asia.[73]

[69]Listed in Wiseman, *AT* 52–58, involving sales; and note *AT* 76–80, exchange of villages.

[70]The Sumerian term SA.GAZ, to which the West Semitic *ḫapiru* corresponds, is equated with the Akkadian *ḫabbātu*, "bandit, robber, or raider." Hence the SA.GAZ as a social element of predatory bands or gangs of bandits are equivalent to the *ḫapiru*. See also *AHw*, 301–04; *CAD, Ḫ*, 13–14; also J. Bottéro, *Le problème des Ḫabiru* (Cahiers de la Société Asiatique 12; Paris, 1954) and M. Greenberg, *The Ḫab/piru* (AOS 39; New Haven, 1955) 3–8.

[71]*AHw*, 322; *CAD, Ḫ*, 84–85.

[72]Landsberger, "Ḫabiru and Lulaḫḫu," *Kleinasiatische Forschungen) 321ff.*

[73]Among the more recent studies on the *ḫapiru* problem are G. Buccellati, "*ᶜApirû* and *Munnabtūtu*—The Stateless of the First Cosmopolitan Age" (*JNES* 36 [1977] 145–47), in which the *ᶜapirû* are compared to the politically displaced *munnabtūtu*; and especially M. B. Rowton, "Dimorphic Structure and the Problem of the *ᶜApiru—ᶜIbrîm*" (*JNES* 35 [1976] 13–20), where the role of the *ᶜapirû* is discussed within the dimorphic structure and typology of the history of Western Asia. See also Bottéro, "Le problème des Ḫabiru," *RLA* 4 (1972) 14–27.

The roster of the *ḫapiru* in these texts includes individuals from every social class and group except the *maryanne*. There is also the inference that their military organization included leaders who were equivalent to warrior chieftains.[74] In the census listing of this class the *LU SA.GAZ* of each village referred to is a person of importance (AT 180–182). In addition to the charioteers and the chariots (AT 180, 182, 226), the ranks of the *ḫapiru* also included regular bowmen, soldiery, and the *ṣabē-šanannu* (AT 145, 183, 350).[75] In other places certain *ḫapiru* also owned houses (AT 202, 350). Elements representing this large group are also listed in 43 localities around Alalakh.

The reference to the *ḫapiru* in AT 58 is the only occurrence in the 18th century texts; however, the chronological and political context of its appearance at Alalakh coincides with the earliest use of the word in Western Asia and with the general disruptions caused by the penetration of Amorite and other groups in the urban areas of Upper Mesopotamia and Syria.[76] Given this association between the emergence of the term *ḫapiru* with the ethnic movements and tribal disintegration in these areas, it has recently been argued that the usage of the term takes into consideration the process of tribal disintegration and hence includes reference to certain local elements of tribal origin.[77] Such developments have been noted to a significant degree in the Mari texts.

The emergence of *ḫapiru* influence in Alalakh at this time lends support to the idea that in a tribal society the *ḫapiru* probably also included elements of the detribalized, since, in effect, it is they who constitute the economically and socially uprooted.[78] The 18th century Alalakh texts indicate that the *ḫapiru* included, among others, elements

---

Other earlier studies of importance are the previously mentioned Greenberg, *The Ḫab/piru*, and Bottéro, *Le problème des Ḫabiru*. These two works have investigated more than 200 citations dealing with the *ḫapiru*, and provide excellent bibliographies.

[74]The occurrence of LÚ *ḫapiri* twice between LÚ *bîti* and *mâr šarri* (*AT* 164) could very well suggest the individual's rank within the *ḫapiru* structure. See also *AT* 145, 180, 183, 185, 202, 301.

[75]Probably a type of bowman. See Albright, "The Early Alphabetic Inscriptions from Sinai," *BASOR* 110 (1948) 6–22; Rainey, "Military Personnel at Ugarit," 22-23; *DL* IV, 117; *GHL*, 274ff.; *AHw*, 78; and *HHA*, 237.

[76]For the earliest occurrence of the term in the Cappadocian region within the general period of Amorite infiltration in Babylonia, see Bottéro, *Le probléme des Ḫabiru*, 8–9; and Gelb, *Inscriptions from Alishar* (OIP 27; Chicago, 1954) 24–27.

[77]Rowton, "The Problem of the *ᶜApiru—ᶜIbrîm*," 17–18.

[78]Kupper, "Northern Mesopotamia and Syria," 24–28; and J. T. Luke, *Pastoralism and Politics in the Mari Period* (Ph.D. Dissertation; Ann Arbor, 1965) 272–75.

which lacked sufficient resources to sustain themselves, who abandoned their tribes to seek a living otherwise.

The important status of the *ḫapiru* within the newly organized kingdom of Alalakh is highlighted in AT 58. This document from the 18th century society makes reference to the sale of the village of Annase to Talmammu ". . . in the year Irkabtum the king made peace with Semuma and the *ḫapiru*."[79] The *ḫapiru* group led by Semuma would have contained elements like those which have been previously discussed. These elements, welded together in the vicinity of the state of Alalakh, could command considerable power. They were sufficiently autonomous and important to have Irkabtum of Yamhad, the suzerain of Alalakh, conclude a treaty with them. Probably the power they wielded around Alalakh would explain why such a treaty of coexistence was necessary.[80]

The emergence of the *ḫapiru* within the political context of the 18th century society correlates well with the political changes taking place at this time, changes precipitated by the migrations of diverse ethnic groups during the 19th and 18th centuries.[81] During this period of political instability around Syria, there is ample documentation of the gradual rise of strong Amorite, Hurrian, and *ḫapiru* influence in the area.[82] It is probable that Semuma's *ḫapiru* held the balance of power

[79]Irkabtum of Yamhad is the successor of Niqmepah of Yamhad. Both were contemporaries of Yarimlim II of Alalakh. See *AT* 7, 52, 95, 96; and N. Naᶜaman, "New Look at Chronology," 136–37.

[80]Greenberg, *The Ḫab/piru*, 19–20, 64.

[81]This involved the rise of Babylon in the south, the kingdoms of Mari and Assur in the west and north, and the continued pressure of the semi-nomadic groups such as the Benjamites, Haneans, and Sutians. It also involved the expansion of the Hittites south and eastward from Anatolia, the spread into the Fertile Crescent from Upper Mesopotamia and the ever present threat of *ḫapiru* groups upon such Amorite states as Eshnunna, Yamhad, Qatna, and others. See Kupper, "Northern Mesopotamia and Syria," 3ff.; and Speiser, "Ethnic Movements in the Ancient Near East," *AASOR* 13 (1931–32) 38–44.

[82]The correspondence of Zimri-Lim notes in effect that "no king is powerful by himself." He indicates that ten or fifteen kings follow Hammurapi of Babylon, a similar number follow Rim-Sin of Larsa, an equal force follow Ibalpiel of Eshnunna and Amutpiel of Qatna, and some twenty follow Yarimlim of Yamhad. The letter is a clear indication of the rise of the Amorites during this period; see G. Dossin, "Les archives epistolaires du Palais de Mari," *Syria* 19 (1938) 117. A few of the Hurrian princes like Adalšenni of Burundum and Šukrum-Tešub of Elakhut appear in the Mari documents, indicating their political ascendancy at this time; see A. Finet, "Adalšenni, roi de Burundum," *RA* 60 (1966) 17–20. On the influence of the *ḫapiru* at this time, see also Kupper, *Les nomades*, 249–53; "Sutéens et *Ḫapiru*," RA 55 (1961) 197–200, and n. 2. On Hurrian penetration see Speiser, "The Hurrian Participation in the Civilization of Mesopotamia, Syria, and Palestine," *JWH* 1 (1956) 311–27.

around Yamhad and Alalakh. Under such conditions during these early periods the kings of Yamhad and Alalakh were probably dependent upon the support of such groups in order to retain power.

With the crystallization of monarchic rule in Syria in the late Middle Bronze and the Late Bronze Ages and the gradual withdrawal of certain "*maryanne*" from their traditional role as elite chariot-owning nobility and their resultant integration into civilian life as an important part of the state bureaucracy, there is the apparent trend by monarchies to assign individuals from other social classes into the *maryanne* ranks. The chariot-warrior function of the *maryanne* in the 15th century society thus gradually began to include individuals from other classes who traditionally were not members of the socially elite. This social and political change is implied in the 15th century texts. They show individuals from such towns as Zalaki, Anzakar, and Marmaru who were *ḫapiru* "chariot-warriors" but are not listed as *maryanne* (AT 180–182, 189, 192, 198).

In view of the meaning of the term *ḫapiru*, it is to be expected that even chariot-warriors and charioteers would be numbered among their ranks. A study of the list of the armed forces (AT 180–184) reveals that *ḫapiru* contingents were found in most villages. Whether or not this implies that they were under royal control,[83] or that they were independent forces supporting the crown, cannot be fully ascertained from available data. Their increase in numerical strength is a logical social and political development which would be due in part to the periodic acceptance into their ranks of fugitive elements from other classes in society.

A reasonable conclusion, then, is that emerging *ḫapiru* elements, which exerted considerable influence since the 18th century, continued to develop during the subsequent "Dark Age" during which period *ḫapiru* groups became resident populations in and around certain cities such as Alalakh. With the re-emergence of Alalakh in the 15th century, it seems reasonable to expect representative *ḫapiru* peoples as a recognized social and political class not only in Alalakh, but also in other urban centers around Western Asia. The marked increase in the *ḫapiru* population at Alalakh at this time was, therefore, a process which continued to develop from the 18th century through the "Dark Age," and was well entrenched as a part of the social structure of the subsequent Late Bronze Age city.

III

The socio-cultural process in progress at Alalakh during the 18th/17th century is indicative of a trend which developed in Syria and

[83]Reviv, "Comments on the Maryannu," 222–23.

Mesopotamia during the Middle Bronze Age. The political changes and ethnic movements around Syria during the ensuing "Dark Age" did not, however, affect to any appreciable degree the cultural process at Alalakh which began during the earlier centuries of the second millennium B.C. The results of this continuing trend of class stratification may be observed in the social distribution which was apparent when the city emerged from its almost two centuries of silence. Certain ethnic elements, social patterns, and political forms, which were only incipient during the 18th century, had taken root during the "Dark Age," and had subsequently emerged in the 15th century as permanent forms.

The documented societal pattern revealed in the epigraphic sources appropriately illustrates this process of cultural continuity. The emerging social structure of the earlier 18th century did not change; rather, it congealed and under Hurrian socio-political influence was given technical designations in accordance with the existing social structure. The earlier chariot-warrior elements and certain affluent merchant types gradually merged into the elite *maryanne*; the non-affluent free artisan/professionals of the earlier period evolved into the constituted *eḫelena/ḫaniaḫḫena* class; the stateless *ḫapiru* of the 18th century proliferated during the "Dark Age," and due in part to the political influence of their numbers, became an integral part of the 15th century society; and the impoverished tenant-farmer of the 18th century is later referred to as the tenant-farming *ṣabē-nāmē/ḫupšena* of the 15th century.

The evidence of an overwhelming percentage of Hurrian personal names and lexical terms in the 15th century sources makes it reasonable to believe that these people, who were already a representable proportion of the population in the 18th century, were being continually infused with fresh arrivals during the "Dark Age," and subsequently emerged as the dominant political and cultural force at Alalakh. This dominance of Hurrian power and influence is well documented in the available sources from the Hurrian kingdom of Mitanni. While the mere attestation of onomastic evidence on any given ethnic group may not by itself constitute an index of that group's cultural impact, the consistent usage of terms acros the cultural spectrum, along with the onomastic evidence, would be an indication of its overwhelming influence upon the society. The usage of Hurrian or Hurrianized terminologies to describe social classes and their functions at Alalakh point to a society which may qualitatively be described as being dominated by a Hurrian superstructure.

This study has shown that a Hurrian superstructure essentially gave technical Hurrianized designations to an existing cultural pattern in North Syria which continued from the 18th century through the 15th century in Alalakhian society. Even though certain points remain obscure and some conclusions must remain tentative, nevertheless, the evidence from Alalakh contributes to our increasing awareness of the cultural processes at work in Syria during the second millennium B.C.

What is a Temple? A Preliminary Typology

JOHN M. LUNDQUIST
BRIGHAM YOUNG UNIVERSITY

As we attempt to determine what constitutes a temple and its ritual in the ancient Near East, it becomes evident that the temple of Solomon can serve as a paradigm for the kinds of problems we might face.[1] On the one hand it is *par excellence* an archaeological problem, one which involves us in architecture, interior and exterior furnishings, ritual installations, arrangements of courtyards, and relationships to other buildings; and yet, there are no archaeological remains of Solomon's temple.

On the other hand the accounts of Solomon's temple present us with philological or text problems. We can expect to find in the Bible descriptions of building procedures and descriptions of the cult carried out within the temple. And yet here also the Biblical material that we have at our disposal is beset with problems: it is diffuse, separated chronologically, and in some cases contradictory within itself, as is the case with the descriptions given in 1 Kings and 2 Chronicles of various

Additional Abbreviations used in this article not found in the *JBL* list:

AAA	Annals of Archaeology and Anthropology (Liverpool University).
CRRA	Compte rendu de la . . . Rencontre Assyriologique Internationale.
RlA	Reallexikon der Assyriologie und vorderasiatischen Archäologie.
SAK	F. Thureau-Dangin, *Die Sumerischen und Akkadischen Königsinschriften*, Leipzig, 1907.

[1]I am not going to discuss the meaning of the term "temple" itself. For a rather standard definition of the term see W. B. Kristensen, *The Meaning of Religion* (The Hague: Martinus Nijhoff, 1960) 369. It should be noted that the Greek root *temnō*, from which *temenos* derives ("a piece of land marked off from common uses and dedicated to a god, precinct," *LSJ* 1774), has a predecessor in Sumerian, *temen*, "Erdaufschüttung" (Anton Deimel, *Sumerisch-Akkadisches Glossar* [Sumerisches Lexikon 3/1; Rome: Verlag des Päpstl. Bibelinstituts, 1934] 206), which appears, for example, in the inscriptions of Gudea of Lagash. See SAK 76 (= Statue C III 8), 78 (= Statue E II 13). For a discussion of Babylonian equivalents of "temple" see Edmond Sollberger, "The Temple in Babylonia," *Le Temple et le Culte* (CRRA 20; Istanbul: Nederlands Historisch-Archeologisch Institut, 1975) 31–34.

architectural details.[2] Rare indeed is an instance anywhere in ancient western Asia where we have the union of standing or excavated temple remains and texts which can be unequivocally related to the ritual practices of that temple.[3] When we face these deficiencies with regard to the temple of Solomon we are led inevitably to the comparative method, according to which we attempt to relate architectural remains and ritual texts from surrounding cultures to those descriptions given in the OT.[4] As unsatisfying as the comparative approach often is, it can yield positive results if kept "within closely adjacent historical, cultural or linguistic units," and if "the comparison be between a total ensemble rather than between isolated motifs."[5]

Essential to the comparative method is the issue of cultural continuity versus discontinuity. In the light of the extraordinary cultural disruptions in the ancient world documented so ably by George Mendenhall,[6] it is important to note that there were areas of equally extraordinary cultural, historical and religious continuity.[7] I believe that the temple as an institution and the cult associated with it constitutes one of the most interesting examples of such continuity.[8] The following list of motifs attempts to focus on this continuity. It does not purport to be a complete motif list (hence the word "preliminary" in the title), nor to have identified all examples to which a given motif may apply. Nor is it my intention to claim that a common "pattern" can be applied indiscriminately to all ancient Near Eastern temples without regard to time, space, and cultural uniqueness. The full extent to which such a list can

[2]For an excellent discussion of the various problems related to the study of the temple of Solomon see Jean Ouellette, "The Basic Structure of Solomon's Temple and Archaeological Research," *The Temple of Solomon* (ed. J. Gutmann; Missoula: Scholars Press, 1976) 1–20.

[3]Such is not the case with Egypt, where a prominent example can be found in E. A. E. Reymond. *The Mythological Origins of the Egyptian Temple* (Manchester/New York: Manchester University Press/Barnes and Noble, 1969).

[4]Th. A. Busink, *Der Tempel von Jerusalem von Salomo bis Herodes; eine archäologisch-historische Studie unter Berücksichtigung des westsemitischen Tempelbaus* (Leiden: E. J. Brill, 1970) 1, *Der Tempel Salomos.*

[5]Jonathan Z. Smith, *Map is Not Territory* (SJLA 23; Leiden: E. J. Brill, 1978) ix.

[6]George E. Mendenhall, "'Change and Decay in all around I see': Conquest, Covenant and the Tenth Generation," *BA* 39 (1976) 152–57.

[7]Mendenhall has also been in the forefront of documenting such continuity: see "The Ancient in the Modern—and Vice Versa," *Michigan Oriental Studies in Honor of George G. Cameron* (ed. Louis L. Orlin; Ann Arbor: Department of Near Eastern Studies, The University of Michigan, 1976) 227–53.

[8]Arvid S. Kapelrud, "Temple Building, a Task for Gods and Kings," *Or* 32 (1963) 56–62.

be applied to various temple traditions is a task worthy of continued research.[9]

Proposition 1. The temple is the architectural embodiment of the cosmic mountian.

Discussion: This theme is extremely common in ancient Near Eastern texts. See SAK 113 (= Gudea Cylinder A XXI 23), 141 (= Gudea Cylinder B XXIV 9); "Hymn to the Ekur," *ANET*, 3rd ed., 582–83 ("The great house, it is a mountain great/ The house of Enlil, it is a mountain great/ The house of Ninlil, it is a mountain great," etc.). From the time of Sargon II onwards the cult room of Aššur in the temple of Aššur, *É ᵈAššur*, was *É.ḪUR.SAG.GAL.KUR.KUR.RA*, "House of the Great Mountain of the Lands." See G. van Driel, *The Cult of Aššur* (Assen: Van Gorcum, 1969) 34–36. This perception is very common in the OT, as is well known and is seen in such passages as Isa 2:2 and Ps 48:2. These conceptions of Zion as a holy mountain go back ultimately to the inner-Israelite experience at what is probably *the* holy, cosmic mountain of religious literature, Sinai. The temple of Solomon would seem ultimately to be little more than the architectural realization and the ritual enlargement of the Sinai experience.

One must not be dealing with an actual building in order to be in what I would call a "temple" setting in the ancient Near East (Kristensen, *The Meaning of Religion*, 257–58). Ancient religious texts are permeated with temple symbolism. In many cases the texts describe an encounter between the deity and a person which did not take place within a building, and yet bears all the earmarks of the "temple" relationship. Basic to temple ideology is the act of appearing "before the Lord." As Menahem Haran states it: "In general, any cultic activity to which the biblical text applies the formula "before the Lord" can be considered an indication of a temple at the site, since this expression stems from the basic conception of the temple as a divine dwelling-place and actually belongs to the temple's technical terminology." See Menaham Haran, *Temples and Temple Service in Ancient Israel* (Oxford: Clarendon, 1978) 26. In spite of the many vagaries involved in the textual analysis of Exodus 19–24 (see Martin Noth, *The Laws in the Pentateuch and Other Studies* [Edinburgh/ London: Oliver and Boyd, 1966] 36–41), it would seem that in this case the "temple at the site" is the mountain itself. Geo Widengren compares the Sinai theophany with the text describing the enthronement of Enmeduranki of Nippur in the temple of Ebarra: ". . . ascension to God, a meeting between Moses and God and a handing over to Moses of the tablets belonging to God." He further mentions the

[9]In compiling the following list of motifs I have learned much from Hugh Nibley, *What is a Temple? The Idea of the Temple in History* (Provo: Brigham Young University, 1968).

sacral meal which Moses and the elders ate in the presence of God (Exod 24:11) following the sealing of the covenant with blood of Exod 24:8 (*The Ascension of the Apostle and the Heavenly Book* [King and Saviour III; Uppsala: A. B. Lundequist, 1950] 24).

Proposition 2. The cosmic mountain represents the primordial hillock, the place which first emerged from the waters that covered the earth during the creative process. In Egypt, for example, all temples are seen as representing the primeval hillock.

Discussion: The Eninnu temple, built by Gudea, is depicted as arising up out of the primeval waters (*apsu*) and raising its head to heaven in SAK 113 (Cylinder A XXI 18–27). This same temple is called the "foundation of the abyss" *temen abzu* in SAK 113 (Cylinder A XXII 11), and the "house of the abyss," in SAK 127 (Cylinder B V 7). The Gudea Cylinders are filled with the motif of the house (= mountain) rising up out of the primordial waters. Indeed it seems to me that the Gudea Cylinders are social and religious documents of inestimable value. They provide us the full scenario of temple building as it must have been perceived by many ancients. Parts of this scenario can be attested elsewhere (Kapelrud, "Temple Building"), but perhaps nowhere else in such complete form. See also A. Falkenstein and Eva Strommenger, "Gudea," *RlA* 3 (1971) 676–87.

For Egypt, see E. A. E. Reymond, *The Mythical Origin of the Egyptian Temple*, 46, 47, 59, 266, 305. See also J. A. Wilson, in *ANET* 4 n. 7. "Practically every temple or shrine of this period [Late Period] was considered a replica of the first temple, built upon the primaeval mound in the midst of the water of the Nun. . . ."; see A. J. Spencer, "The Brick Foundations of Late-Period Peripteral Temples and Their Mythological Origin," *Glimpses of Ancient Egypt* (Fs. H. W. Fairman; ed. John Ruffle et al.; Warminster: Aris and Phillips, 1979) 133. See also M. el-Din Ibrahim, "The God of the Great Temple of Edfu," *Glimpses of Ancient Egypt*, 170–73.

Proposition 3. The temple is often associated with the waters of life which flow forth from a spring within the building itself—or rather the temple is viewed as incorporating within itself or as having been built upon such a spring. The reason such springs exist in temples is that they are perceived as the primeval waters of creation, Nun in Egypt, Abzu in Mesopotamia. The temple is thus founded on and stands in contact with the primeval waters.

Discussion: "At every hierocentric shrine stood a mountain or artificial mound and a lake or spring from which four streams flowed out to bring the lifegiving waters to the four regions of the earth"—so Hugh Nibley, "The Hierocentric State," *Western Political Quarterly* 4 (1951) 235. Geo Widengren connects the water, tree, temple basin and a sacred grove in "Early Hebrew Myths and their Interpretations," *Myth, Ritual and Kingship* (ed. S. H. Hooke; Oxford: Oxford University, 1956) 168. For this theme at Ras Shamra see Richard Clifford, "The Temple in the Ugaritic Myth of Baal," *Symposia* (ed. F. Cross; Cambridge: American Schools of Oriental Research, 1979) 145. For an Egyptian example see H. W. Fairman, "Worship and Festivals in an Egyptian Temple," *BJRL* 37 (1954-55) 177. The theme occurs in Ezek 47:1 and, in all probability, in Psalm 29.

Proposition 4. The temple is built on separate, sacral, set-apart space.

Discussion: Anton Moortgat, *The Art of Ancient Mesopotamia* (London/New York: Phaidon, 1969) 20 (the Temple Oval at Khafaje), 19 (fixing the building immovably in the earth by means of foundation figures). Joan Oates notes the practice documented in the excavations of Eridu, Uruk and in the Diyala Valley of incorporating the foundations of earlier temples into the platform of later ones. This practice was achieved by filling in the surviving chambers of the earlier temple with mud brick. See Joan Oates, "Ur and Eridu, the Prehistory," *Iraq* 22 (1960) 45. This same practice has been documented more recently in Syria. See G. van Driel, "De Uruk-Nederzetting op de Jebel Aruda: een Voorlopig Bericht (Stand eind 1976)," *Phoenix* (Vooraziatisch-Egyptisch Genootschap "Ex Oriente Lux") 23 (1977) 46. Mount Moriah, the place where Solomon built his temple, carried of course the association of Abraham's sacrifice of Isaac. But another association, that of the threshing floor, which David purchased from Araunah the Jebusite, may carry overtones more significant for the erection of a temple. Ad de Vries points out that "the threshing floor is an omphalos, at once a navel of the world (with the hub of ears in the middle) and a universe-emblem (a round piece of earth, with the earth in the middle, and the sun-oxen going round)"; see *Dictionary of Symbols and Imagery* (2nd ed.; Amsterdam/London: North-Holland Publishing Company, 1976) 464. (I am indebted to Michael Lyon for suggesting this latter connection.)

The process of excavating an enormous trench, which is then filled with sand, the whole serving as the foundation for the temple, is known not only from Early Dynastic Mesopotamia (the Temple Oval at Khafaje), but also in Late-Period Egypt. Late-Period Egyptian texts give the mythological rationale behind this practice: the bed of sand represents the primeval mound, which is founded in the primeval waters of Nun; see A. J. Spencer, "The Brick Foundations," 133. A similar "mythological" setting for the practice documented at Khafaje would seem to be present in the temple of Enki at Eridu which was also believed to have been founded in the primeval waters, in this case *Abzu*; see E. Douglas Van Buren, "Foundation Rites for a New Temple," *Or* 21 (1952) 293, and the discussion of Proposition 7. As Spencer states: "The effect of religious beliefs on architecture were not, as some have claimed, a vague symbolism, but were an important part of the construction of the temples, necessary for the buildings to fulfill their symbolic role"; see Spencer, "The Brick Foundations," 133.

Proposition 5. The temple is oriented toward the four world regions or cardinal directions, and to various celestial bodies such as the polar star. As such it is, or can be, an astronomical observatory where sightings are made, the purpose of which is for those who come to the temple to orient themselves in the universe. The buildings might face the sun at its rising or other celestial bodies.

Discussion: For an example of a long maintained tradition of orienting the corners of temple buildings to the cardinal directions see the prehistoric temples of levels 11 through 6 at Eridu (Tell Abu Shahrain) and the partly contemporaneous northern Ubaid period temples of levels 14 through 12 at Tepe Gawra; see Ann Louise Perkins, *The Comparative Archaeology of Early Mesopotamia* (SAOC 25; Chicago: University of Chicago, 1949) 67–70, 87. The burials discovered in the Ubaid period cemetery at Eridu were oriented in the same direction as the temples; see Max Mallowan, "The Development of Cities from Al-'Ubaid to the End of Uruk 5," *CAH*; 3rd ed.; 1/1 347. For the possibility of a temple observatory at Akkad in the time of Sargon the Great see John D. Weir, *The Venus Tablets of Ammizaduga* (Istanbul: Nederlands Historisch-Archeologisch Instituut, 1972) 40–47. For an extensive discussion of possible cosmic symbolism in the temple of Solomon see W. F. Albright, *Archaeology and the Religion of Israel* (5th ed., Garden City: Doubleday, 1968) 144–50. For an interpretation of evidence from Egypt and Mesopotamia in this light see Andrzej Wiercinski, "Pyramids and Ziggurats as the Architectonic Representations of the Archetype of the Cosmic Mountain," *Katunob* 10 (1977) 71–87. (I am indebted to Professor John Sorenson for this reference.) For the orientation of the Ziggurat of Nanna at Ur see Anton Moortgat, *The Art of Ancient Mesopotamia*, 56. A Seleucid period tablet for a temple ritual at Uruk reads in part, in A. Sachs' translation: "In the first watch of the night, on the roof of the topmost stage of the temple-tower of the Resh temple, when the star Great Anu of Heaven rises and the star Great Antu of Heaven rises in the constellation Wagon, (he shall recite the composition beginning? . . . .") And further on in the same text, "Upon seven large golden trays, you shall present water (for washing) hands to the planets Jupiter, Venus, Mercury, Saturn, Mars, the moon, and the sun, as soon as they appear"; see *ANET* 338. For a discussion of the cosmic orientation of the Israelite tent shrine see Hugh Nibley, "Tenting, Toll, and Taxing," *Western Political Quarterly* 19 (1966) 603–5. For an attempted refutation of the view that Solomon's temple was oriented toward the sun see

H. Van Dyke Parunak, "Was Solomon's Temple Oriented Toward the Sun?" *PEQ* 110 (1978) 28–33.

Proposition 6. Temples, in their architectonic orientation, express the idea of a successive ascension toward heaven. The Mesopotamian ziggurat or staged temple tower is the best example of this architectural principle. It was constructed of three, five or seven stages or levels. Monumental staircases led to the upper part of the tower, to a small temple which stood at the top.

Discussion: SAK 77, 79 (Gudea Statue D II 11, Statue E I 16 = "*e.PA*, Temple of the seven zones," but see A. Falkenstein, *Die Inschriften Gudeas von Lagaš* (AnOr 30; Rome: Pontificium Institutum Biblicum, 1966) 132–34, who casts doubt on the traditional meaning (that is, a seven tiered building) ascribed to these and similar passages. For the *gigunû* as the most holy and secret sanctuary of the sacred marriage, placed atop the seven staged ziggurat, see E. Douglas Van Buren, "Foundation Rites for A New Temple," 301–2. And for a Sumerian sacred marriage text expressing the imagery of an ascent toward the chapel which stands atop the ziggurat see Thorkild Jacobsen, *The Treasures of Darkness* (New Haven/London: Yale University, 1976) 126.

Proposition 7. The plan and measurements of the temple are revealed by God to the king, and the plan must be carefully carried out. Nabopolassar stated that he took the measurements of Etemenanki, the temple tower in the main temple precinct of Babylon, under the guidance of Shamash, Adad, and Marduk, and that he kept the measurements in his memory as a treasure.

Discussion: For Nabopolassar's text see S. Langdon, *Die neubabylonischen Königsinschriften* (Vorderasiatische Bibliotek 4; Leipzig: Hinrichs, 1912) 62–63. And see E. Douglas Van Buren, "Foundation Rites," 293 for an explanation of the "ordinances and ritual of Eridu," the "precisely ordained rites" which must be carried out in the construction of a temple in Mesopotamia. Gudea's well known dream, which he received while in the temple of Baga, revealed to him the plan of the temple to Ningirsu which he was to build. He was shown a lapis-lazuli tablet with the temple plan on it, and was given a sacred brick mould which contained the bricks to be used in the building. See SAK 89–97 (= Cylinder A I–VII). See also Widengren, *Ascension of the Apostle*, 30. Moses was given the plans for the building of the tabernacle directly by God (Exod 25:9), and God appeared to Solomon at Gibeon before the building of the temple commenced (1 Kgs 3:4–15), and after it was finished (1 Kgs 9:3–9). Although the text does not say so explicitly, Kapelrud interprets the passages concerning Solomon in the light of the dream/revelations of Gudea, and assumes that the plans of the temple must have been revealed to Solomon on the first occasion; see Kapelrud, "Temple Building," 59–61.

Proposition 8. The temple is the central, organizing, unifying institution in ancient Near Eastern society.

Discussion: See Solomon's dedicatory prayer for the Jerusalem temple in 1 Kgs 8:22–54 for an extraordinarily clear expression of this idea. The same concept comes through clearly in the Gudea Cylinders, as for example SAK 101–3 (= A XI 18–27), and SAK 123 (= B I 10). J. Z. Smith, referring to *m. ᵓAbot* 1:2, "on three things the world stands: on the law, on the temple service, and on piety," adds the comment that "The temple and its ritual serve as the cosmic pillars or the 'sacred pole' supporting the world. If its service is interrupted or broken, if an error is made, then the world, the blessing, the fertility, indeed all of creation which flows from the Center, will likewise be disrupted"; see *Map is Not Territory,* 118. For an excellent discussion of the economic and social role of the Mesopotamian temple see J. N. Postgate, "The Role of the Temple in the Mesopotamian Secular Community," *Man, Settlement and Urbanism* (ed. P. J. Ucko, R. Tringham, and G. W. Dimbleby; Cambridge: Schenkman, 1972) 811–25.

Proposition 8a. The temple is associated with abundance and prosperity, indeed is perceived as the giver of these.

Discussion: In addition to the discussion under Proposition 8, see SAK 101 (= Gudea Cylinder A XI 1–27), where one reads that abundance shall come from heaven when the foundation of the temple is laid, that there will be a fullness of water, oil, wool, and that harmony and light will influence people's lives.

Proposition 8b. The destruction or loss of the temple is seen as calamitous and fatal to the community in which the temple stood. The destruction is viewed as the result of social and moral decadence and disobedience to God's word.

Discussion: These ideas are seen quite clearly in Lamentations and Haggai, and in the Sumerian "Lamentation over the destruction of Sumer and Ur" (*ANET* 3rd ed., 611–19), where, however, the destruction brought on Sumer and her temples and people is caused not so much by the people's wickedness as by a decree of Enlil that political power be shifted to another people. See *ANET* 3rd ed., 646 n. 6. The Sumerian historiographic poem "The Curse of Agade" is another well-known example of the view that the desecration of a temple by a king (in this case Naram-Sin) brings destruction on his entire people. See *ANET* 3rd ed., 646–51.

Proposition 9. Inside the temple images of deities as well as kings, temple priests and worshippers are washed, anointed, clothed, fed, enthroned and symbolically initiated into the presence of deity, and thus into eternal life. Further, during the New Year rites texts are read and dramatically portrayed which recite a pre-earthly war, the victory in the war by the forces of good, led by a chief deity, the creation and establishment of the cosmos, cities, temples, and social order. The sacred marriage is also carried out at this time.

Discussion: For the manufacture, washing, anointing, clothing and initiation of images see Sidney Smith, "The Babylonian Ritual for the Consecration and Induction of a Divine Statue," *JRAS* (1925) 37–60; O. R. Gurney, "Babylonian Prophylactic Figures and their Rituals," *AAA* 22 (1935) 31–96; Edmond Sollberger, "The Temple in Babylonia," 33, and H. W. Fairman, "Worship and Festivals," 173, 180. The clothing of the goddess in a "priestly garment" is described in the "Blessing of Nisaba by Enki," in W. W. Hallo, "The Cultic Setting of Sumerian Poetry," *CRRA* 17 (1970) 129. The washing and clothing of Inanna in "garments of power" in preparation for the sacred marriage rite, and of Shulgi in the *me* garment along with a "crown-like wig" are described by S. N. Kramer in "The Dumuzi-Inanna Sacred Marriage Rite: Origin, Development, Character," *CRRA* 17 (1970) 136–40. For the washing, anointing, and clothing in priestly garments (including the Urim and Thummim, which Widengren associates with the Tablets of Destiny of Babylonian traditions [*Ascension of the Apostle*] 27) of the Aaronide priests of Israel see Exodus 29, Leviticus 8 and 16. The "people" are involved in washing and clothing rituals at Sinai, just as they are involved in the covenant ceremony that follows the giving of the Law. See Exodus 19 and 24.

The question of the temple as a locus of initiation into divine life, something that has long been associated with Egyptian religion, is a question intertwined with the issue of the temple as a locus of vicarious cult drama. That such was the case in Egypt is well established. See the texts in *ANET* 4–6 and 329–30, and H. W. Fairman, "Worship and Festivals," 193–96. It has long been assumed that the *enuma elish* was the "text" of the Babylonian New Year's festival carried out in the Esagila temple and in the *akītu* festival house, that is, that it was *recited* there, as we see in *ANET* 332. That it was the text of a dramatic presentation, a dramatic recreation of the war in heaven, Marduk's victory, the creation of mankind and the organization of the cosmos and of the earth, has been assumed by some and doubted by many others. See Svend Aage Pallis, *The Babylonian Akītu Festival* (Copenhagen: Bianco Lunos, 1926) 248–67. See also W. G. Lambert, "The Great Battle of the Mesopotamian Religious Year, The Conflict in the Akitu House," *Iraq* 25 (1963) 189–90. An Assyrian building inscription of Sennacherib (K. 1356) states that the *bit akītu* festival house in Aššur had bronze door plates on the central entry way which depicted the battle between Aššur (taking Marduk's place) and Tiamat. Sennacherib is himself identified as a substitute for Aššur in the battle.

Pallis affirms that the "king acts the part of the leading deity in the battle drama," and that "we cannot doubt that a religious battle drama took place in *bit Akītu* during the *Akītu* festival, in which the king acted the part of the divine victor." He further emphasizes that to assume that the bronze door plates described above are "a mere artistic decoration, independent of the cult, is out of the question here"; see *The Babylonian Akītu Festival,* 260–65, and Walter Andrae, *Das Wiedererstandene Assur* (Munich: C. H. Beck, 1977 [reprint; orig. 1938]) 223. H. Sauren attempts to demonstrate that the Gudea Cylinders form the text for a seven day "mystery play," carried out each year at the temple dedication feast. He assumes that groups of actors, perhaps extending beyond priestly circles, would have been carefully chosen for each year's enactment. See H. Sauren, "Die Einweihung des Eninnu," *CRRA* 20 (1975) 95–103.

The view has been fairly widespread that the Baal cycle from Ras Shamra, found along with the other mythological texts in the library or scribal rectory on the temple acropolis, was used by the priests of Ugarit as the text of a dramatic presentation carried out in the temple of Baal. For a recitation of the views of many scholars who held this or similar views, see Ivan Engnell, *Studies in Divine Kingship in the Ancient Near East* (2nd. ed.; Oxford: Blackwell, 1967) 103–5. The presence in the Baal texts of the themes of council in heaven, battle between deities, creation, temple building and sacral meal, among others, when coupled with the find spot of the tablets and the analogies with *enuma elish* and its role in the Babylonian New Year's festival, would seem to point in this direction. But as Richard Clifford has stated, we cannot certainly decide such an issue; see Richard Clifford, "The Temple in the Ugaritic Myth of Baal," 145; see also Loren R. Fisher, "Creation at Ugarit and in the Old Testament," *VT* 15 (1965) 313–24. And for a very important Ugaritic text which combines the themes of enthronement, mountain (temple), creation, ritual battle and sacred marriage, among others, see Loren R. Fisher and F. Brent Knutson, "An Enthronement Ritual at Ugarit," *JNES* 28 (1969) 157–67. It seems to me that the Ur III and earlier cylinder seals which depict the "presentation, by an intermediary, of a worshipper to a god or a deified king," would prove to be a most interesting study from the point of view of their ritual setting. See Anton Moortgat, *The Art of Ancient Mesopotamia,* 68. It is possible that the last preserved part of the Seleucid tablet from Uruk may be relevant in this regard; see *ANET* 339. For an extensive discussion of the themes of baptism, anointing, clothing, enthronement and initiation into divine life in Mandean religion, and the Syrian and Mesopotamian background of such customs, see Widengren, "Heavenly Enthronement and Baptism, Studies in Mandaean Baptism," *Religions in Antiquity, Essays in*

Memory of Erwin Ramsdell Goodenough (Studies in the History of Religions, 14, ed. Jacob Neusner; Leiden: Brill, 1968) 551–82. Finally, for the sacred marriage drama in an Egyptian temple, see H. W. Fairman, "Worship and Festivals," 196–200.

Proposition 10. The temple is associated with the realm of the dead, the underworld, the afterlife, the grave. The unifying feature here is the rites and worship of ancestors. Tombs can be—and in Egypt and elsewhere are—essentially temples (cf. the cosmic orientation, texts written on the tomb walls which guide the deceased into the afterlife, etc.). The unifying principle between temple and tomb is resurrection. Tombs and sarcophagi are "sacred places," sites of resurrection. In Egyptian religion Nut is depicted on the coffin cover, symbolizing the cosmic orientation (cf. "Nut is the coffin").[10] The temple is the link between this world and the next. It has been called "an antechamber between the worlds."

Discussion: For the Hittite sphere see O. R. Gurney, *Some Aspects of Hittite Religion* (Schweich Lectures; Oxford: Oxford University, 1977) 61–63. For Egypt see H. W. Fairman, "Worship and Festivals," 200. One of the chapels in the Eninnu temple was called "é.nì.ki.sè 'the house in which one brings offerings for the dead'." It carried the further description "it is something pure, purified by *Abzu*"; see A. Falkenstein, *Die Inschriften Gudeas von Lagaš,* 131. For a discussion of a sepulchral chamber to Marduk in Etemenanki in Babylon see Pallis, *The Babylonian Akītu Festival,* 104–5, 108–9. There is an intimate connection between burials and temples VIII and XI at Tepe Gawra, the latter of which, according to Tobler, "attracted considerable numbers of burials to its precincts"; see Arthur J. Tobler, *Excavations at Tepe Gawra* 2 (Museum Monographs; Philadelphia: University of Pennsylvania, 1950) 98–101. At Ur, however, where we might expect spectacular support for such a connection, Woolley is at pains to dampen such speculation; see C. L. Woolley, *Ur Excavations 2, The Royal Cemetery, Text* (Publs. of the Joint Exped. of the Brit. Mus. and the Mus. of the Univ. of Penn. to Mesopotamia; New York: Trustees of the Two Museums, 1934) 12–14. Isa 65:3–4 would seem to be relevant here. But see the discussion of W. Boyd Barrick, "The Funerary Character of 'High Places' in Ancient Palestine: A Re-assessment," *VT* 25 (1975) 565–95. He does not, however, discuss this passage.

Proposition 11. Sacral, communal meals are carried out in connection with temple ritual, often at the conclusion of or during a covenant ceremony.

[10]Kristensen, *The Meaning of Religion,* 372–73.

Discussion: Having attempted to establish the "temple" background of Exodus 19–24 above in discussing Proposition 1, I would like now to introduce 24:11, the meal which directly follows the covenant ceremony of Exod 24:8, as the parade example of this point. The Gudea Cylinders end with the conjunction of a festive meal attended by all of the gods and the fixing of the destinies; see A. Falkenstein, *Die Inschriften Gudeas von Lagaš*, 120. Pallis states that "the *akītu* festival was concluded by a great sacrificial meal of which all, the gods, the king, the priests, and the people, partook" (*The Babylonian Akītu Festival*, 173). *Enuma elish* III 128–38 contains the account of the gods entering the sacred chamber where the destinies are decreed, at which time they partook of a festive banquet; see *ANET* 65–66. We have the recurring theme here of formal act and sacral meal, the same phenomenon that we see in 1 Kings 8 where, following Solomon's dedicatory prayer for the Jerusalem temple (a prayer carried out "with the hands spread up to heaven"), the king held a feast. This prayer fits in remarkably well with the form and the religiosity expressed in the Babylonian psalm cycle *šu-ila;* see Erich Ebeling, *Die Akkadische Gebetsserie 'Handerhebung'* Berlin: Akademie Verlag, 1953. See also Geo Widengren, *The Ascension of the Apostle,* 24. For a Hittite text which conjoins the themes of blood, sacral meal and covenant, see O. R. Gurney, *Some Aspects of Hittite Religion,* 29–30.

Proposition 12. The tablets of destiny ("tablets of the decrees"[11]) are consulted both in the cosmic sense by the gods, and yearly in a special chamber, in the Eninnu temple of Gudea's time.[12] It is by this means that the will of the deity is communicated to the people through the king or the prophet for a given year.

Discussion: Note *enuma elish* IV 22. The association of sacred meal and setting of the destinies in *enuma elish* and in the Gudea Cylinder B has been pointed out above in discussing Proposition 11. Widengren has an excellent discussion in which he interprets the association of heavenly council, enthronement, and tablets of destiny. He writes that "the tablets of Law, as well as the Urim and Thummim, play the same role as the tablets of destiny in being the instrument by which the will of the deity is communicated to the leader of the people, be it Moses or the king" (*The Ascension of the Apostle,* 27). Both the Urim and Thummim and the tablets of destiny are fastened in a pouch on their possessor's chest; see Widengren, "Early Hebrew Myths," 167; see also Pallis, *The Babylonian Akītu Festival* 193–94.

Proposition 13. There is a close interrelationship between the temple and law in the ancient Near East. The building or restoration of a

[11]Jacobsen, *The Treasures of Darkness,* 178–79.
[12]Falkenstein, *Die Inschriften Gudeas von Lagaš,* 141–42.

temple is perceived as the moving force behind a restating or "codifying" of basic legal principles, and of the "righting" and organizing of proper social order.

Discussion: Martin Noth writes that the OT "clearly associates the conceptions of 'covenant' and 'law' with one another in a definite relationship" (*The Laws in the Pentateuch*, 39). I would add "temple" to this pair. The act of Moses' appearing "before the Lord" in Exodus 19–24 produced the law, or rather what Mendenhall would call "policy" (Mendenhall, "Ancient Oriental and Biblical Law," *BAR* 3, 3). The action which gives rise to the "codification" of the ancient collections of "royal judgments," or "just laws" (see F. R. Kraus, "Ein zentrales Problem des altmesopotamischen Rechtes: Was ist der Codex Hammurabi?" *Genava* 8 [1960] 285–88), is, in my opinion, rebuilding or rededicating of a temple, or the appearance of the king in the temple early in his reign. The Prologue of the Code of Hammurabi places great emphasis on his concern for the temples and cult centers under his sway, and finally states, just before the "laws" proper begin: "When Marduk commissioned me to guide the people aright, to direct the land, I established law and justice in the language of the land. . . ."(*ANET* 165). This commission from Marduk would presumably have come to Hammurabi in Esagila, where in fact a stela containing the laws was placed; see *ANET* 178. The Epilogue also states that "I, Hammurabi, am the king of justice, to whom Shamash committed law" (*ANET* 178). This is not to revive the largely outmoded ideas of Henry Maine and others that law derives from religion (William Seagle, *History of the Law* [New York: Tudor Publishing Co., 1946] 117–30), it is simply to look more carefully at what the texts themselves say, which is, I believe, that the impetus by the king to *compile* the existing body of judicial precedents (see Mendenhall, "Ancient Oriental and Biblical Law," 11) was seen to come as a result of duties connected with the temple.

Proposition 14. The temple is a place of sacrifice.

Discussion: The ubiquity of this aspect of temple worship in the ancient Near East is such that its mention here may seem superfluous. And yet sacrifice has been one of the most difficult, least understood and most discussed of all religious phenomena. For an excellent summary of the *status questionis* see Kristensen, *The Meaning of Religion*, 444–52 and 458–96. For a selection of sacrificial practices over a widespread geographical area, see, for Egypt, H. W. Fairman, "Worship and Festivals," 178, 180–84, 191, 198–202; for Assyria, G. van Driel, *The Cult of Aššur*, 86–119; for Asia Minor O. R. Gurney, *Some Aspects of Hittite Religion*, 24–43; and for northern Mesopotamia the recent excavations at Tell Chuera in northern Syria, which have yielded one of the most important archaeological evidences for a sacrificial practice in ancient times. The Akkad period *Nord-Tempel* yielded remains of an offertory stairway at the east entrance along with what appeared to be an offering table and an adjacent *Wanne* which would have received the blood of the offerings. The excavators of Tell Chuera compare the remains of this installation with the well-known scene of the White Obelisk of Assurnasirpal I, which shows an elaborate cult installation of sacrificial offering in front of a temple. See Anton Moortgat, *Tell Chuera in Nordost Syrien, Vorläufiger Bericht über die dritte Grabungskampagne 1960* (Wiss. Abh. der Arbeitsgem. für Forsch. des Landes Nordrhein-Westfalen, 24; Köln/ Opladen: Westdeutscher Verlag, 1962) 13–14, with Plan II and Abb. 9–10. See also Dennis J. McCarthy, "The Symbolism of Blood and Sacrifice," *JBL* 88 (1969) 166–76.

Proposition 15. The temple and its ritual are enshrouded in secrecy. This secrecy relates to the sacredness of the temple precinct and the strict division in ancient times between sacred and profane space.

Discussion: Exod 19:12–13, 21–24 apply here: there are certain precincts that are "off limits." To trespass sacred precincts, or to approach sacred objects without being ritually prepared, can result in disaster (1 Sam 6:19–20). A second century A.D. Aramaic inscription from Hatra invokes "The curse of Our L[ord] and Our Lady and the Son of our Lord and Shaharu and Baasham[en] and Atargatis (be) on [anyone] who enters past this point into the shr[ine]"; see Delbert R. Hillers, "*Mškn*ʾ 'Temple' in Inscriptions from Hatra," *BASOR* 207 (1972) 54–56. The Neo-babylonian tablet which describes the ritual for the consecration and induction of a divine statue concludes with the warning "Let initiate instruct initiate, he shall not let the uninitiated see: it is a thing forbidden of Enlil, the elder, [and] Marduk"; see Sidney Smith, "The Babylonian Ritual for the Consecration and Induction of a Divine Statue," 51–52.

The problem of secrecy relates of course to the question of who was allowed access to the temple precincts, or, rather, to what extent the general populace was allowed access to the temple ritual. A series of inscriptions on doors of the Ptolemaic temple at Edfu in Egypt relates access to the temple to moral worthiness: "Everyone who enters by this door, beware of entering in impurity, for God loves purity more than millions of possessions, more than hundreds of thousands of fine gold." And again, "Do not come in sin, do not enter in impurity, do not utter falsehood in his house. . . ." And the admonition to secrecy: "do not reveal what you have seen in the mysteries of the temples." See H. W. Fairman, "Worship and Festivals," 201. Of course, these admonitions are directed to priests, for, as Fairman writes: "It is clear that for the majority of the people there was not direct contact with either daily service or with many festivals, and no participation in any intimate or sacred rites" (Fairman, 201). During the ceremonies connected with the New Year festival and the rededication of the temple, "the doors of the temple were shut while they were being celebrated, and no member of the general public witnessed them" (Fairman, 187). In Egypt, as well as in Israel and Mesopotamia, the primary way that the general populace would have taken part in temple ritual was through attendance at the great processionals, and the public banquets which would take place at the end of a ritual period; see Fairman, 202–3; J. N. Postgate, "The Bit Akiti in Assyrian Nabu Temples," *Sumer* 30 (1974) 57–62; and 1 Kgs 8:62–66. But all Israelite males were commanded to "appear before the Lord God" three times during the year (Exod 23:17; 34:23), and this was expanded to include all members of the family, as we see in Deut 16:11, 14 and 31:11–12. See also Menahem Haran, *Temples and Temple Service,* 290–94. Inscriptions on the south gate of the temenos of the Edfu temple give further insight into what access the common people would have had to the temple, and what role it would have played in the religion of the people: "It is the standing place of those who have and those who have not in order to pray for life from the Lord of Life. . . . The place for hearing the petitions of all petitioners in order to judge Truth from Falsehood. It is the great place for championing the poor in order to rescue them from the strong. . . . The place outside which offerings are made at all times consisting of all the produce of the servants" (Fairman, 203).

The Epilogue of the Code of Hammurabi states that a stele containing the Code was placed in Esagila, where any oppressed person could read the pertinent passages of the laws and thus understand his cause. But as Wiseman writes, it is unlikely that common Babylonians could have come into the sacred precincts of Esagila to examine the stele; see D. J. Wiseman, "The Laws of Hammurabi Again," *JSS* 7 (1962) 166. Copies of the stele would presumably have been available elsewhere. Yet another insight into the extent to which common people would have had access to temples comes from the countless votive sculptures which archaeologists find in the excavation of temple ruins. Such statues, meant to represent their human offerers, often inscribed, and presumably manufactured in a temple workshop and available for purchase by the donor, would be placed in the temple, presumably by priests, and stationed on benches in the sanctuary, in an adjoining room, or in a courtyard. The statue would then stand perpetually before the effigy of the deity, representing the blessings the offerer hoped to obtain. See Henri Frankfort, *Sculpture of the Third Millennium B.C. from Tell Asmar and Khafajah* (OIP 44; Chicago: University of Chicago, 1939) 10–11. The Early Dynastic temples in the Diyala Valley give us classic architectural examples of temple precincts that are successively cut off from their immediate surroundings and made inaccessible to passersby by means of thick walls and elaborate series of courtyards; see Anton Moortgart, *The Art of Ancient Mesopotamia,* 20–25.

"Your Father Was an Amorite" (Ezek 16:3, 45): An Essay on the Amorite Problem in OT Traditions

J. Tracy Luke
Alma College

I

This essay seeks to reappraise our understanding of the Amorite problem in the OT traditions, avoiding as much as possible a restatement of the familiar elements of the so-called "Amorite Hypothesis" and not retreating more than absolutely necessary into the technical details of my description of the tribal pastoralists of the Mari Kingdom.[1] After a minimal presentation of such material, I will turn to the OT traditions themselves in order to see whether any of the ambiguities of the understanding of "Amorites" can be clarified. Initially I will review how Amorite territorial distribution can be reconstructed from the traditions in light of later tribal areas and the politics of the early monarchy. At the end of the study I will attempt to associate a theological strand in the work of the Yahwist and later traditions with Old Babylonian sources which I consider either Amorite or influenced by Amorites. In the process, I will seek to identify and understand pre-Iron age and non-Palestinian elements in the OT traditions.

There are various ways in which George Mendenhall's work influences this essay. In his remarkable study *Law and Covenant in Israel and the Ancient Near East*,[2] Mendenhall drew attention to the international suzerainty treaties as the model for the Mosaic covenant, and his thesis is a masterpiece of the comparative historical method. His work remains pivotal in OT interpretation, and its implications for our understanding of the kingship of Yahweh and the ideology of the tribal

[1]J. T. Luke, "Pastoralism and Politics in the Mari Period: A Re-examination of the Character and Political Significance of the Major West Semitic Tribal Groups on the Middle Euphrates, ca. 1828–1758 B.C." (Ph.D. dissertation, University of Michigan, 1965). See also my study, "Abraham and the Iron Age: Reflections on the New Patriarchal Studies," *JSOT* 4 (1977) 35–47.

[2]G. E. Mendenhall, *Law and Covenant in Israel and the Ancient Near East* (Pittsburgh: The Biblical Colloquium, 1955).

league in the period of the Judges, as well as the controversies related to Israel's attempts to form a monarchy, are manifest. This discovery would have been impossible without the use of historical analogy and cross-cultural comparison, and Mendenhall instills in his students and readers a sense of how essential this approach is to any historical method that hopes to break new ground.

In recent years a new school of literary criticism of the OT has emerged, emphasizing structural analysis of literary components, with particular interest in themes or motifs, and insisting either on the general lateness of the same traditions or that these traditions were created for their own time of redaction and are scarcely reliable sources for the history of earlier times. The rise of this method has included a vigorous attack on the comparative historical approach.[3] I have tried to think through the assumptions of this methodology and to appraise my own assumptions in light of that critique.

Mendenhall's most recent major work, *The Tenth Generation: The Origins of the Biblical Tradition*,[4] clearly demonstrates the comparative historical method. His insistence that the culture of ancient Israel be viewed within the larger ancient Near Eastern setting, that archaeological, linguistic, and textual data be appraised without a priori assumptions about what will not be important, and what will, and his openness to interdisciplinary theoretical insights are the key elements. That volume also illustrates a subtle aspect of the historian's craft, viz., selectivity and discrimination—the ability to sense what is essential or significant amid numerous alternatives.

II

To convey some sense of the variety of analytical questions this essay asks let me begin with the very late texts from which the title of this study is taken. Ezekiel writes:

> Son of Man, make known to Jerusalem her abominations, and say, "Thus says the Lord God to Jerusalem: Your origin and your birth are of the land of the Canaanites; your father was an Amorite, and your mother was a Hittite." (Ezek 16:2–3)

And lest one think this an isolated image in Ezekiel, notice that later in the same chapter he shifts the symbols slightly but reuses the theme:

[3]Especially T. L. Thompson, *The Historicity of the Patriarchal Narratives* (BZAW, 133; Berlin: de Gruyter, 1974), J. Van Seters, *Abraham in History and Tradition* (New Haven: Yale University, 1975).

[4]G. E. Mendenhall, *The Tenth Generation: The Origins of the Biblical Tradition* (Baltimore: Johns Hopkins, 1973).

> Have you not committed lewdness in addition to all your abominations? Behold, every one who uses proverbs will use this proverb about you, "Like mother, like daughter." You are the daughter of your mother, who loathed her husband and her children; and you are the sister of your sisters, who loathed their husbands and their children. Your mother was a Hittite and your father was an Amorite. (Ezek 16:43b–45).

What shall we say about Ezekiel's description of the origins of Israel? In fairness let us note that these harsh verses appear at the beginning and near the end of a scathing condemnation, which Ezekiel resolves with a proclamation of restoration and hope in 16:53–63. However harsh and condemnatory the language is, we have heard it before. Prophetic language of this quality abounds, and we know that Ezekiel draws on a rich prophetic tradition going back at least to Amos. But what of his claim that Jerusalem has an Amorite father and a Hittite mother? What are his sources or referents? We must assume that his sixth century B.C. audience would have understood this language, or that he thought they would, yet we know that neither Hittite nor Amorite were contemporary political labels of this era. His images are historical in requiring a recollection of a known past or a literature telling of this past. Does Ezekiel intend "Amorite father" and "Hittite mother" as poetic methaphors, as precise historical references, or as both? The Assyrian king Adad-nirari III (810–783) could still speak of the Khatti and Amurru country as the locus of his foes in Syria. Does Ezekiel call forth no deeper or more specific recollection of the people's background than that? We might speculate that Ezekiel is trying to draw on some Jerusalem-Hittite-Amorite association and that he thinks of Bathsheba whose husband was Hittite and became involved in abomination in Jerusalem with David. But David has no Amorite connection that we know of, and this association seems far-fetched and unlikely. Moreover, from Ezekiel's vision of hope for a new Davidic king (Ezek 34:23–24; 37:24–25), he would scarcely imagine David as a source of the people's abomination.

Perhaps an adequate explanation is that throughout the Pentateuchal sources and derivative passages Hittites and Amorites are listed among the iniquitous enemies of Israel in the land. Ezekiel's metaphors may only draw on that strong negative attitude, asking the people to apply it to themselves. But since in the Pentateuchal references the Israelites are consistently differentiated from the Amorites and Hittites, the "father" and "mother" aspects of the metaphors would still not be explained. As another possibility, Esau had two Hittite wives and we are told that they made life bitter for him (Gen 26:34–35). Yet even though Esau might be thought of as an Amorite, he is an unlikely candidate for the "father" and has no significant connection with Jerusalem. There is also the possible association with Sarah and Abraham. Whether she was Hittite or not we will pass over, but the field and cave for her burial were purchased from a Hittite, and Abraham is the perfect candidate for the "father," as progenitor of all Israel, and is associated with Melchizedek the king of Salem, traditionally taken as Jerusalem. Outside of Genesis, Sarah is mentioned only in Second Isaiah, who cites Abraham and Sarah as father and mother of the people (Isa 51:2), though not at all in a condemnatory setting. In suggesting that Ezekiel has Abraham and Sarah in mind when he thinks of an Amorite father and a Hittite mother, we have at least a plausible association. But we need to go further and note what we have failed to resolve. Surely Ezekiel would not want literally to think of Abraham and Sarah as sources of abomination and lewdness; he draws on another aspect of Amorite-Hittite attitudes within the tradition for this, as we will see.

Finally, there is for the historian perhaps the most intriguing question of all: did Ezekiel know anything about ancient Amorites and did he identify Abraham as Amorite? As a parenthetical concern for those who wrestle with methodological questions and try to determine what counts as evidence in an attempt to establish "historicity," the question is, does Ezekiel's apparent opinion that Abraham was an Amorite lend any significant support to the similar opinion of the historian?

Recent attempts to discredit the so-called "Amorite hypothesis" succeed, I think, only by an appeal to extremely rigid notions of historical verification (in contrast to plausibility) and by ignoring several very important kinds of evidence. The scholarly literature is quite extensive now that demonstrates linguistic cognates between biblical Hebrew and the Amorite dialect attested especially through the Akkadian texts from Mari. The presence of Amorite-type names not only in the early narratives of the OT but in extrabiblical sources as well from the Middle Bronze age into the Late Bronze age strongly suggest either the movement of these people from Syria into Palestine, Transjordan and Egypt, or that they had been there for some time and suddenly became socio-politically involved to such an extent that they emerge in the records. As a paradigmatic example of Mesopotamian Amorites who also appear in western Syria, Palestine, and Egypt, we may cite the Suteans. They are well known in the Mari texts, which suggest that they were residents farther south and were encountered by the officials of Mari while they were in transit through the Kingdom.[5] Also, in the early second millennium B.C. they are mentioned in the Egyptian Execration Texts in a passage that may relate them to Transjordan and possibly the region of (later) Zebulun.[6] The Suteans were still active in the west

[5]Luke, "Pastoralism and Politics," 105–38.

[6]J. R. Kupper, *Les nomades en Mésopotamie au temps des rois de Mari* (Bibliothèque de la Faculté de Philosophie et Lettres de l'Université de Liège, 142; Paris: Société d'Edition "Les Belles Lettres," 1957) 83–145, esp. 141–42.

during the Late Bronze age, as we know from both Alalakh and the Amarna letters.[7] The Suteans were either a significant enough problem or a familiar enough sight to the Egyptians, that the name Sutu became a common Egyptian term for "Asiatics."[8] Whether biblical Seth is related to Amorite Sutu need not be determined in this essay, but the correlation has been suggested.[9] In the Late Bronze age we know of at least several small political states and a variety of kings in western Syria from the Orontes River southward through Transjordan which are given the label Amorite.[10] Since the Mesopotamian origin of the name Amurru is scarcely in doubt, and "western" rarely makes literal sense from the vantage point of the Syro-Palestinian texts that speak of these states and individuals, the westerly displacement of the name if not the people seems rather obvious.

In the first half of the second millennium B.C. the kingdom of Mari is on occasion called Amurru by others, but that is not the designation which the court scribes at Mari use for their own country.[11] The term *amurru* occurs in the Mari texts in the personal disignations *rabi Amurre* and *tupšar Amurre,* which may suggest that these persons are from farther west, but we do not know. A certain Hanean clan is also called *Amurru,* but we are unable to locate the group with any precision.[12]

The primary uses of the name *Amurru* from the late third millennium B.C. Dynasty of Akkad through the early second millennium B.C., point to the sweeping Syrian steppe lands and uplands, from the Euphrates River to the Mediterranean coast. We have observed that Amorites are also attested from the early second millennium B.C. through the Late Bronze age, in a range southward from northern Syria along the arc of the Fertile Crescent that bends toward Egypt. At some point in the Late Bronze age, the name Amorite begins to yield to "Hatti land" and "Aḫlamu/Aram" as primary designators for the old Amorite regions in Syria. We do not need to speculate about the Amorite homeland, or to imagine great waves of Amorites invading the southeast and southwest,

[7]Ibid., 96–101.

[8]R. T. O'Callaghan, *Aram Naharaim: A Contribution to the History of Upper Mesopotamia in the Second Millennium B.C.* (AnOr, 26; Rome: Pontifical Biblical Institute, 1948) 94.

[9]L. Hicks, "Seth," in *IDB*, 4, 294.

[10]Kupper, *Les nomades,* 178–81.

[11]The Iahdun-Lim inscription offers the possibility that a preferred name for the kingdom was "Hana land," after the Haneans whose villages were located close to the capital; see Kupper, *Les nomades,* 30.

[12]Kupper, *Les nomades,* 191–94. For the Amorite Haneans and the lack of evidence for their activity in the far west, see Luke, "Pastoralism and Politics," 148–49.

but we do need to recognize that Amorite people were widely distributed and politically significant in the second millennium B.C.

In the stories of early Israel, from the prelude to the Conquest to the fall of the United Monarchy, the Transjordanian states of Bashan and Heshbon are consistently viewed as Amorite. The area dominated by Heshbon became known as Ammon, with its capital at Rabbah. Our attention is drawn to this phenomenon here because the story of the origin of Ammon and the high number of names from this region that relate to Mari Amorite names suggest Amorite influence that may be of long standing.

The incestuous story of Lot and his daughters (Gen 19:30–38) provides the basis of direct descent from the Abrahamic–Lot family to the Ammonites. Ben-ammi (a rather fitting name given the circumstances!) is the offspring who fathers the Ammonites. We do not miss the point that the Ammonites have not endeared themselves to the teller of this tale, yet the incest image may have a double meaning. "Inbred" we may take to imply "extremely Amorite," which would match our impression of the region from other biblical references.

Before we turn to a thorough examination of other Amorite references in the OT, a series of observations on Mari pastoralism and a few notations of long-standing issues in the semi-nomadic model for the Patriarchs may serve as a helpful background. After 1945 the distinction between semi-nomadism and Bedouin life-style was becoming firmly introduced into OT interpretations, so that there was a diminishing use of Bedouin analogies. Nevertheless, this shift had not resulted in a careful thinking through of two elements in nineteenth century nomadic theory: 1) evolutionary sedentarization, and 2) the assumption that pastoralists were more violent than villagers. The Mari texts provided important correctives for both of these opinions, at least regarding Amorite pastoralists. From the Yahdun-Lim inscription we learn that the Iaminite groups (earlier called Benjaminites) had very old territorial claims in the Mari region.[13] They were not nomads pouring into the Mari Kingdom only to meet superior urban force and thus be sedentarized. Instead, they constituted an established tribal confederation, with numerous subdivisions and well-established claims to villages and pasture lands.[14] I would emphasize that the combination of village life and sheep pastoralism is firmly evidenced for the Mari Iaminites and for

[13]The first publication of the Iahdun-Lim inscription was G. Dossin, "L'inscription de fondation de Iaḫdun-Lim, roi de Mari," *Syria* 32 (1955) 1–28.

[14]The Iaminites frequented pasturelands in the "Upper Country" north of Mari proper, north roughly of a line from the mouth of the Baliḫ River in the west to Qattunan in the east, and south of a similar line from Carchemish east to Harran; see Luke, "Pastoralism and Politics," 69–77.

the Haneans as well.[15] The evolutionary notion that herding is closer to hunting-gathering involves a reversal, since it appears now that utilization of the seasonal steppe pastures is an economic speciality that develops in the village setting. While this may seem a minor issue, it lends much clarity to the OT stories in which tribal pastoral groups seem to move with great ease from village to pastoral settings, or from living in houses to living in tents. This life style is quite appropriate to the Amorite (and certainly other) groups from the second millennium B.C. on, and, no doubt, earlier.

J. R. Kupper, in his outstanding study of Mari pastoralism, tended to evaluate the various tribal groups according to their degree of sedentarization and correlated level of violence, i.e., the more nomadic, the more violent.[16] This has led to some views that are misleading, especially the view that the Iaminites were quite violent.[17] As a group, sheep pastoralists are not great perpetrators of violence for rather obvious reasons; small villages are highly vulnerable, and sheep are slow. While I have no desire to idealize or romanticize the Iaminites, their raids and hostile misadventures in the Mari texts seem primarily reactions to urban intrusions into their life ways, especially the attempts by the rulers to limit their seasonal movements, take censuses, and conscript them into military or corvée work.[18] On the other hand, we do not have to search far to discover why the rulers of Mari continually tried to control the Iaminites[19] (and succeeded somewhat better with the closer-

[15]The evidence of Iaminite and Hanean villages is quite extensive and Kupper's work as well as my own notes this, though we understand the significance quite differently. Conveniently, for examples of Iaminite villages, see *ARM* II.102, and G. Dossin, "Signaux lumineux au pays de Mari," *RA* 35 (1938) 174–86.

[16]Kupper's treatment of the Suteans reveals this approach; see Kupper, *Les nomades*, 83–145.

[17]Texts describing or alluding to Iaminite raiding practices include *ARM* V.81, and those discussed by G. Dossin, "Benjaminites dans les textes de Mari," in *Mélanges syriens offerts à M. René Dussaud* (Bibliothèque archéologique et historique, 30; Paris: Geuthner, 1939), 2, 981–96. An example of the assumption that all Benjaminites were thus violent can be noted in K. Elliger, "Benjamin," *IDB*, 1, 383.

[18]Iaminite census or *tēbibtum* is the subject of *ARM* I.6; III.21. Iaminites resist conscription in *ARM* VI.30. Seasonal migration was interfered with in *ARM* II.92. Iaminite villages were confiscated by Haneans (!) according to a text cited by Dossin, "Benjaminites," 984.

[19]A text from the reign of Zimri-Lim indicates that official concerns were real. The king of Mari had reports that the Iaminites would join the kings of Zalmaqum in an attack on Tuttul; see Dossin, "Benjaminites," 987.

to-hand Haneans[20]). The seasonal pasturing of the Iaminites took them north into regions where the kings of Mari lacked political power, and the Iaminites were not above forming alliances with political enemies of the kings of Mari.[21]

The Amorite-style names of the Patriarchs, along with the place names in the genealogy of Genesis 11 and 12 that interchange as personal and place names and that occur in subsequent Genesis stories, are well known as a primary basis for associating the Patriarchs with Mesopotamia. Haran and Nahor are the most remarkable examples in comparison with Mari evidence. Both towns are located in the heart of Iaminite pasture lands.[22] In the OT, outside of Genesis, Haran is mentioned a half-dozen times, but Nahor is mentioned only in the retelling of the story of the fathers in Joshua 24. So Nahor, at least, was of no interest to the later writers except in their recollections of the Patriarchs. If the Genesis stories of returning to these towns or the region are viewed as mere literary constructs, the theory of repetition of theme would minimize the emphasis that Genesis gives this activity. This is a subtle and difficult question, because the wife-sister stories certainly reveal literary repetitive traits. And we must allow that the real or idealized prohibition against marrying foreign women is thematic to the stories of return to the northern (Mari) region. But why to this precise region? And why are these stories so rich in semi-nomadic details? The intentionality and description of locale and life-style does not seem drawn from fantasy, nor accidental. And repetition is so common to religious rite and daily human behavior (not to mention, going home) that the reduction of repeated stories in any tradition to a singular idea, motif, or literary intent, surely runs some dangers of error.

The donkey caravaneer or ass nomadism model for understanding the Patriarchs, offered by W. F. Albright, is not impossible; this economic speciality was practiced in the Middle and Late Bronze ages. Yet reservations to this suggestion stem from the assumptions involved in viewing *ᶜāpiru* as meaning "dusty" and thus "caravaneer," and the difficulty of imagining this highly specialized activity as a life mode for the patriarchal tribes as a whole. We need not review the debate about references to camels in patriarchal stories. Albright's long held view that domestication did not reach a level of specialization at which substantial

[20]I agree with Kupper that the Haneans were more fully integrated into the political and economic life of the Mari Kingdom, but they continued their old life ways and sometimes resisted; see Luke, "Pastoralism and Politics," 266–69, which notes *ARM* II.48 in which Haneans resist the authorities.

[21]Luke, "Pastoralism and Politics," 269–72.

[22]Dossin, "Benjaminites," 986. The Iaminites concluded a formal alliance with the kings of Zalmaqum in the temple of Sin at Harran. Nahor, while not positively identified, is certainly nearby in the Iaminite pasturelands.

groups could use the camel as a primary animal in their economy, until the end of the Late Bronze age, remains substantially accurate.[23]

Parallels between designations of tribal subgroups and leaders at Mari and in the OT have also been widely noted and need not be reviewed here, though three leadership terms which could be important in our subsequent examination of biblical references merit discussion. The early equating of Mari *dawidum* with the name David has long been rejected; the term does not seem to be a title for a leader at Mari. The most common designation for a tribal "chief" at Mari is *sugāgum*, but there is no direct parallel to this term in the OT. Perhaps the greatest success of the Mari kings was their ability to control tribal leadership to some degree by requiring payment for *sugāgu*-ship. This could be viewed as a tax, but it alludes more to a tactic of urban appointment and thus control.[24] The common and well-known Akkadian word for king, *šarru*, is used at Mari to refer to high tribal leaders. This may seem surprising, but it is helpful to our understanding of the derivation of Hebrew *śar*, "prince."[25] That this usage was early in Palestine is assured by the occurrence of a feminized form in Judg 5:29.

III

Can we clarify any of the ambiguities in the usage of the term Amorite in OT traditions? We begin with Genesis 14, where Abram with his family and presumably a group the size of a clan (he has as many soldiers as the kings of Mari normally tried to conscript from a single Iaminite subgroup[26]) are sojourning at the Oaks of Mamre, or Hebron (Gen 14:13). Mamre is explicity called an Amorite; and he and his brothers become Abram's allies. This group in turn is bound by covenant to Melchizedek, king of Salem/Jerusalem. Lot, who has separated from Abraham, is living in Sodom with a similar relationship to the king there, as the meeting in Gen 14:17 indicates. We notice that Abram does not own land, and when he does purchase it (Genesis 23), it is not from Mamre, but from Ephron the Hittite. In this act, Abram ceases to be a sojourner (*gēr*), and the purchase is carried out in the best spirit of the law: one law for citizen and for sojourner.

We have noted that Lot is linked to Amorite Transjordan by the story of the birth of the Ammonites, and Genesis 14 is the closest that the biblical traditions come to declaring Abram an Amorite, although the

[23]W. F. Albright, *Yahweh and the Gods of Canaan* (Garden City: Doubleday, 1968) 179.

[24]See above, n. 18.

[25]Exod 2:14; Numbers 21–23; and Judg 5:15, 29; 8:6, 14; and 10:18 are significant examples.

[26]See *ARM* I.42; 200 or 300 men are taken from Iaminite clans.

patriarchs generally fit with what is known of the early history of the Amorites. Interestingly, it is in Gen 14:13, and only here, that he is called a Hebrew. For some scholars this will suggest the lateness of the entire tale, but the usage is appropriate, i.e., Abram was an *ᶜāpiru* from Haran, i.e., someone who had intentionally withdrawn from a sociopolitical structure. Nor would the writers of the monarchy lack interest in this, since David had once been in the status of an *ᶜāpiru* (1 Sam 29:3), began his reign at Hebron, and we certainly know from Ps 110:4 that the Davidic traditions picked up the Jerusalem-Melchizedek association.

But what happens to Abraham's Amorite affiliation suggested in Genesis 14? Why is it that Abraham, who from this story and so much extrabiblical data should appropriately be called "Abraham the Amorite," apparently becomes known as "a wandering Aramean" in Deut 26:5?

Here then are some initial assumptions and setting of parameters of our inquiry. Genesis 14 intimates that Abram is an Amorite, while the Mari texts exhibit a large Amorite tribal group bearing a name obviously related to the later biblical tribal name, Benjamin. Will the biblical traditions support at all the possibility that the biblical Benjaminites are a remnant Amorite element in the Israelite confederation? And if that might be established, why is such an innocent item of information so hidden in the traditions as they now appear?

We look with great difficulty for friendly comments about Amorites in the remainder of the OT, once we leave the story of Genesis 14. 1 Sam 7:14 mentions a period of peace between Israel and the Amorites, but the comment is not elaborated upon and does not yield much sense. David, according to 2 Samuel 21, gave seven men from the house of Saul to the Gibeonites, who are called "a remnant of the Amorites" protected or spared by Israel, but this story may be misleading.[27] We do not know what violent act David charges Saul with having carried out against the Gibeonites, and to some degree this story may contradict the claim in 1 Samuel 7 noted above. More troublesome is the way this story shifts to the Gibeonites the responsiblity for killing a segment of Saul's house under the guise of reparation for blood guilt incurred by Saul. The killings as well as the shifting of the responsiblity are very much in David's self-interest, and we should not infer from this story that David is a great friend of some Amorite group.[28]

The dealings of the United Monarchy with Amorites do not end with these two references in Samuel. Solomon claims to have resolved

[27]Could Gibeon be an error for Gibeah? Saul was there as the events began, leading to the killing of the priest of Nob. Otherwise, we not not have information on the background to this story.

[28]Nor would we expect him to be; see the conclusion of this section.

the problems between Israel and the Amorites, as well as the other non-Israelite peoples of the land, by forcing them to serve in a corvée of slaves.[29] The note in this same context that he did not make slaves of the Israelites may seem like hairsplitting when we remember the subsequent Israelite forced labor on his building projects, which contributes more than a bit to the political decline of the United Monarchy. How seriously, therefore, we should entertain the contrast he makes between his dealings with Amorites and his dealings with Israelites is unclear, but here at least is a claim of resolution of Amorite affairs. Before leaving this passage we will want to note two important views concerning Amorites in traditions of the United Monarchy. First, they are disassociated from Israelites (though 1 Kgs 9:20 also implies that the Israelites in part came from these people). Second, the Amorites of the land of Canaan are simply mixed in or listed among a larger group of non-Israelites, which includes Hittites, Perizzites, Hivites, and Jebusites. This familiar type of reference has in the past discouraged any attempt to sort out or trace the references. In its fullest and most idealized form the list includes ten names and claims that these people are spread from Egypt to the Euphrates (Gen 15:18–21). A shorter form of this list, usually six or seven names, is common to the JE source and to D.[30]

The book of Kings also identifies two other significant themes about Amorites. The Transjordanian kingdoms of Heshbon and Bashan are mentioned, and the former is again termed Amorite in 1 Kgs 4:19. We also notice a highly charged negative opinion of Amorites in the narrative about the reign of Manasseh. Amorite-style "abominations," in which this king apparently delighted (2 Kgs 21:11), are focused on in order to generate resurgence of anti-Amorite feeling. This was probably known to Ezekiel, and it may well have contributed to the metaphors examined earlier. It is not unusual for individuals or groups to displace their rage on handy and obvious targets, but religious fanaticism can be built on more humble or deeper foundations than a king's bad religious habits or an ongoing alienation from Transjordanian Amorite folk. So we will look for another thread to lead us to an earlier intertwining of Israelite socio-political struggles.

In the OT traditions, the Amorite element is clearly predominant among the Transjordanian people. We cannot examine all the references to Amorites in this region; these are both numerous and repetitive. But whether we think of Sihon of Heshbon and Og of Bashan, of Gilead, of the precise definition of the territory between the Arnon River and the Jabbok as Amorite, or of the later state of Ammon, there are continuing Amorite associations. The picture is quite consistent and is reminiscent

[29]1 Kgs 9:20–21.

[30]Exod 3:8, 17; 13:5; 23:23; 34:11; Deut 7:1; etc.

of the Egyptian story of Sinuhe, which describes this general region in the early second millennium B.C., and exhibits a similar high level of semi-nomadic activity together with some more formalized town or urban political life.[31] The region may have been more highly controlled by urban centers in the Late Bronze age, but the general image is otherwise remarkably consistent. This same picture continues on into the Iron age in the biblical traditions.

The Deuteronomic tradition visualizes the Transjordanian Amorite region as farther to the south and as extending west toward the Mediterranean Sea so as to include Kadesh-barnea.[32] Here we may have a curious turn of influence in which the earlier tradition placing Abraham in the area of Kadesh (Gen 20:1) apparently colors the impression of Amorite whereabouts in this later understanding. Some interesting lines of investigation are raised by this Genesis reference, but we cannot pursue them here.

Returning to the tradition of the Amorites in Transjordan, we discover a key source of anti-Amorite feeling in the stories of Numbers 21 that report the battles with Sihon of Heshbon and Og of Bashan, the Amorite kings who blocked the route of the Israelite tribes as they moved toward Jericho and entry into the land of Canaan. These stories, long remembered and recited, would make definitive disassociation between Israelites and Amorites, were it not for some curious details which come from surprising sources. In Judges 11, Jephthah, who as a Gileadite is probably of Amorite stock himself, sent a statement to be read to the Ammonite king. The statement begins by asking why they cannot make peace (an appropriate inquiry from one Amorite to another).[33] The communication moves on to retell the story of the Israelite struggle for Transjordan. It is full of theological claims to possession, hinting that this story is something other than a simple early rendition. Yet in the midst of this we find a remarkable question posed by Jephthah to the king of Heshbon:

> While Israel dwelt in Heshbon and its villages, and in Aroer and its villages, and in all the cities that are on the banks of the Arnon, three hundred years, why did you not recover them within that time? (Judg 11:26).

Of course, this question may be nothing more than a piece of impatient political rhetoric, but it might also be a recollection of ancestors of Israel, living long ago and for a long time, precisely where the traditions place the Amorite land.

[31]See the translation by J. A. Wilson in *ANET*, 18–22.

[32]Deut 1:19.

[33]Judg 11:12; but notice that the Ammonite king has his reasons!

Jephthah as a Gileadite reminds us that the northern region of Transjordan is given in part to the Israelite tribe of Manasseh, suggesting that we may want to inquire as to whether the Joseph tribes are involved in our inquiry. But before we attempt to relate the Amorite problem to Israelite tribal genealogy, we need to follow out our final lead with regard to Amorite territorial location by returning to ask if we can make better sense of the picture of Amorites in Palestine proper, i.e., in the western hill country.

Sketchy as it may be, the evidence of Amorite distribution in the western hill country of Palestine is very fascinating. We began with Genesis 14, with Abraham and his claim in the area of Hebron. This location is supported by Deut 1:24, 27, which tells of spies sent to the valley of Eshcol (i.e. Hebron) who report that an attack would lead to defeat: "because the Lord hated us he has brought us forth out of the land of Egypt, to give us into the hands of the Amorites, to destroy us."

The book of Joshua distinguishes between Canaanite kings on the sea coast and Amorite kings in Transjordan generally,[34] but in Joshua 10 the story informs us that after Joshua's defeat of Ai, five Amorite kings (from Jerusalem, Hebron, Jarmuth, Lachish, and Eglon) attack Gibeon because it has made peace with Joshua. We have already noted that 2 Sam 21:2 calls the Gibeonites remnant Amorites, so we assume that this attack is not upon an enemy, but against an ally who has joined the enemy, thus violating an alliance. A further interesting question is raised by Josh 11:19, where the Gibeonites are called Hivites. Is it possible that the Hivites are also Amorites? For the present we will simply note that once more we have a specific claim that central Palestine was Amorite. Other sources describe Jerusalem as Jebusite-Canaanite, so that this claim that it was Amorite is important. We need to face the possibility, of course, that our sources are not as discriminating as we would wish, and that the labels Amorite and Canaanite can be mixed with no intent of changed meaning. But for the moment let us imagine that this reference is intentional. The list of cities in Joshua 10 defines an area from north of Jerusalem to south of it and westward. Could this area, together with Hebron, once have been Amorite?

As a transition from this survey of references to Amorite territory in the western hill country of Palestine to our brief investigation of tribal genealogy, especially the Joseph tribes, we look briefly at Jacob's blessing of Joseph, as Jacob, father of the Israelite tribes nears death:

[34]Josh 5:1. Presumably the writer, by "beyond the Jordan," means Transjordan, but this reference could be read differently; if the writer imagines himself in Transjordan, the Amorite kings "beyond the Jordan to the west," would be in the central hill country, and that may be the better sense of it in light of Joshua 10.

> I have given to you rather than to your brothers one mountain slope (Shechem) which I took from the hand of the Amorites with my sword and with my bow. (Gen 48:22)

Jacob's association with Shechem is well attested in Genesis 33–34, and it has been widely noted that the group associated with Shechem, the *bĕnê Ḥămôr* ("sons of the ass," Josh 24:32), suggests an Amorite covenant-making ceremony known from the Mari texts.[35] Perhaps we do not press these references too far by suggesting that OT traditions remember at least two Amorite regions: one in Transjordan, which was consistently so described, and one in the western hill country from Hebron to Schechem, that for some reason is nearly forgotten. Could it be that later divisions between north and south made this definition of an old Palestinean Amorite territory something of an embarrassment?

Many of the references utilized in this reconstruction are from sources typically viewed as late and northern. It is important to notice that even the D source is not free of anti-Amorite sentiment,[36] which I take as an indication that this tradition (and perhaps E as well) is not fully aware of shifting emphases in the development of Amorite attitudes in an earlier time. It would seem that some of the linkages traced here have survived in spite of, not because of, vested interest within a literary tradition.

If the associations suggested here between the reconstructed Amorite territories and the Jacob-Benjamin-Joseph tribes seem far-fetched, they improve with a reading of the story of Jacob's journey to Transjordan and Palestine, because it now will not seem accidental that it includes stops in Gilead (Gen 31:25), Succoth, farther south in Amorite Transjordan (Gen 33:17), then Shechem (Gen 33:18), then south to Bethel (Genesis 35), and on to Mamre or Hebron (Gen 35:27) after a stop to bury Rachel at Ephrath (Bethlehem). This itinerary reads like a guided tour of the two Amorite territories we have reconstructed from a variety of sources.

If we compare the later Israelite tribal boundaries with the Amorite territories reconstructed here, noting as we have that the Joseph tribes of Ephraim and Manasseh, plus Benjamin, should be associated with these lands, we would need add only Gad and Reuben to account for the occupation of all the old Amorite lands except the most southerly part around Hebron, the home territory of David.

Benjamin, loved by Joseph, becomes the object of an Israelite massacre (Judges 20), which seems an excessive response to the rape of the concubine (the rationale offered in Judges 19, is a story that has as its

[35]See G. E. Mendenhall, "Mari," in D. N. Freedman and E. F. Campbell, Jr., eds., *BAR* 2 (Garden City: Doubleday, 1964) 18.

[36]Deut 1:27; 7:1.

background a similar incident at Sodom; cf. Genesis 19). The reparations to the Benjaminites in Judges 21 do not overcome the intent to exclude the Benjaminites from full status in Israel (Judg 21:18). This is intriguing in terms of Israelite leadership. Saul was a Benjaminite. And if one rereads the book of Judges it is quite remarkable how many of the early judges, including Abimelek, who tried to become king at Shechem, were residents of the old Amorite territories, the lands of the Joseph tribes and Benjamin.[37]

This line of argument brings us to the interesting possibility that it was the rise of the Davidic-Solomonic monarchy, with its origins in Hebron and its need to diminish the inheritance of the Benjaminite, Saul, that created the conditions for reworking of the Amorite traditions. Old stories of wars with Transjordanian Amorite kings provided a convenient source of anti-Amorite sentiment and disassociation of the Israelites from the Amorites, while the old Amorite territory in the western hill country from Shechem to Hebron, vastly enlarged by monarchical successes, had at its very heart a bad memory which insisted upon redefinition. For from that territory came a different history of tribal unity, and the view that Joseph, not Judah, should be "prince."[38] Since the Amorite tradition had been carried by the Joseph tribes and Benjamin, which may in fact have had old Amorite roots, the assault on the traditions of Saul caught the Amorite traditions in the same whirlwind, and they were whipped into dusty corners of the larger and newer traditions from which we have sought to recover them.

As it turns out, anachronism may be the wrong term by which to describe the process through which the Amorite patriarchs came to be called Arameans. It is of course convenient that at the time that the label Amorite was no longer desirable, Aramean could be used to identify the same region, the same towns, and the same ethnic stock. Even the J source could preserve the memory of tribal heritage, but avoid the identification of the fathers directly with the Amorites.

IV

The entire question of patriarchal origins, the literary and historical questions involving so much debate about methodology, would be of only modest interest if we could conceptualize ancient Israel and her culture as an isolated phenomenon, entirely comprehensible from within biblical literature. We know that such a concept is historically impossible, and thus we continue to ask questions about how the faith and life of

[37]Gideon is called at Ophrah in Benjaminite territory (Judg 6:11), and Abimelech is Gideon's son (Judg 8:31). Jephthah has been discussed above. Note also Ehud (Judg 3:15).

[38]Deut 33:16.

Israel, as expressed in her literature, relate to what we know about her neighbors. Whether Abraham was an historical figure is not a very important issue, but whether the Genesis stories do or do not indicate early associations with the Syrio-Mesopotamian culture that we call Amorite is an extremely important question. Thus I will conclude with a comment on one element of Israelite theology that seems to me very early and Mesopotamian in origin, to the degree that we can imagine we know the origin. This theological element is exhibited at the heart of urban Mesopotamian theology, yet has its imagery drawn from peasant-pastoral experience. I am referring to the concept of the *gēr* or "sojourner." The understanding of the *gēr* is certainly older than the Yahwist, and would seem to have its roots fully in uprooted tribal peasant life. It is clearly a theology arising from experience, and not from the fantasies of kings. (Kings would always do well to reflect on their limitations, but they tend to think about eternal dynasties instead, as did the writers of the royal theology of David and Solomon.)

The extensive influence of Mesopotamian mythology on the book of Genesis is clear, including particularly the Yahwist (the Eden story, the tower of Babel, and of course the Flood, which not only shows absolute signs of Mesopotamian borrowing in details, but of theological borrowing as well, since God's promise is Ishtar's lament, and his rainbow—in P—is her string of jewels in the sky).

The patriarchs are repeatedly called sojourners, indicating an early dependence on others in the process of moving from being *ᶜāpiru* to becoming new citizens. The patriarchal experience became the companion paradigm for the Egyptian bondage theology. Exod 12:49 exhibits the fundamental socio-legal spirit of early Israel (at the community's best):

> There shall be one law for the native and for the stranger who sojourns among you.

It is Deut 10:19 that epitomizes the combined traditions in perhaps the finest rationale for religious conviction, viz., the recollection of personal experience:

> Love the *gēr* therefore; for you were *gērîm* in the land of Egypt.

The semi-nomadic life of antiquity with all its uncertainty created the context for kindness to others, even strangers (related to later laws of hospitality), which continued into urban life because of the inescapable importance of anti-narcissistic qualities in life and religion. This, I believe, is an old Mesopotamian idea which begins to emerge also in the

J source of the Old Testament.[39] Abraham himself is an important anti-narcissistic symbol, though we may miss this in our emphasis of the engrandizing monarchical images that are related to Abraham. The name Abram ("lofty father") shifts to Abraham ("father of many"), as self-centeredness gives way to generativity. Abraham's remarkable faith or righteousness turns out to be trust and humility, and this symbolic father who is "blessed" and "to be a blessing," leads us to recall that Hebrew *bārak* basically means "to bend the knee," i.e., to lower oneself.

Thus, however we decide to approach the stories of the emergence of early Israel with regard to historicity, mythology, story, and remembrance, it is necessary to conclude that life experiences and religious ideas stemming from those experiences condition early understandings of *ᶜāpiru* and *gēr*. Israel was born of the struggles and hardships of semi-nomadic village-peasant life, not of royal ease, and her stories and theology were early on imprinted and enriched by these realities. Yet her traditions have long processes of development and great complexity. So it is that Ezekiel, from one vantage point, looked back upon Amorite origins through one lens of the tradition and saw a birth of abomination. Yet within this same literature a Psalmist could write, looking back very differently:

> Hear my prayer, O Lord,
> and give ear to my cry;
> hold not thy peace at my tears!
> Because I am a sojourner (*gēr*) with you,
> a temporary dweller (*tôšâb*) like all my fathers.
>
> (Ps 39:13)

[39]During this past winter I was privileged to spend a sabbatical semester at the Menninger Foundation in Topeka, Kansas, and engage in research of ancient Near Eastern mythology with the eminent psychologist of religion, Paul W. Pruyser. The focus of our joint research was the Gilgamesh epic, which we now view as a central ritual drama of the Babylonian New Year's Festival. The primary theme of this story is not the problem of death, but the epic is an anti-narcissistic story of a mighty and problematical king who becomes shattered by the death of his "brother" and thus driven out on a journey in order to discover that the magical solution to life he seeks is not available. He must return, resigned to find meaning in his life as it contributes to the life of the city, Uruk. Thus humbled, the king is appropriately prepared (and hopefully the worshippers too) for the sacred marriage, and the beginning of a new year. See our study, "The Epic of Gilgamesh," *American Imago* 39 (1982) 73–93.

Heshbon: The First Casualty in the Israelite Quest for the Kingdom of God

LAWRENCE T. GERATY
ANDREWS UNIVERSITY

ONE of the dominant themes in George Mendenhall's writing has been the nature of the Israelite "conquest" traditions. His initial reconstruction[1] was completed before the archaeological excavation of Tell Ḥesbân, the site in Jordan long associated with biblical Heshbon, the "capital" of Sihon's Amorite kingdom. According to biblical tradition, Heshbon was the first city to fall to the Israelites. This essay outlines some of the approaches that may be taken in an attempt to relate the well-known biblical and recently-discovered archaeological material.

I

Methodologically, it seems better to look first at the biblical information on Heshbon. These written traditions can then provide the framework for interpreting the artifactual data. As Mendenhall himself has said, "Though any historical thesis must be compatible with archaeological evidence, nevertheless, unwritten artifacts alone cannot produce a history. The biblical traditions need not be rejected."[2]

[1]George E. Mendenhall, "The Hebrew Conquest of Palestine," *BA* 25 (1962) 66–87; reprinted in *BAR* 3, 100–120. Later, in his book *The Tenth Generation: The Origins of the Biblical Tradition* (Baltimore: Johns Hopkins University, 1973), Mendenhall comments, "The message of a new element in human history, associated with the miraculous escape from Egyptian contol, and reinforced by the defeat of attacks by Sihon and Og (both almost certainly newcomers to political and military power in Transjordan) must have been extremely attractive to the people of the region" (p. 22).

[2]*Tenth Generation*, 19; cf. Max Miller, *The Old Testament and the Historian* (Philadelphia: Fortress, 1976): "When written sources are utilized alongside (non-written) archaeological findings it is generally the written evidence which provides the framework for interpreting the artifactual data, and not the reverse" (12).

If we examine the OT in its present arrangement,[3] the first reference to Heshbon is in Num 21:21–25 (cf. Deut 2:16–37)—the familiar account already referred to of Israel's conquest of the kingdom of Sihon the Amorite. A straightforward reading of this passage yields the following information: Traversed by the King's Highway, the boundaries of the Amorite kingdom extended from the Jabbok in the north to the Arnon in the south, from the Jordan on the west to the Ammonites on the east.[4] The actual battle took place at Jahaz (Hebrew *yāḥĕṣâ*), whose location is uncertain[5] except that to get there from Heshbon, Sihon had to go eastwards "to the wilderness" (v 23).

The following verses (Num 21:26–31) are an apparent attempt to justify Israel's occupation of territory claimed at various times by Moab. This passage claims that at least the southern half of Sihon's kingdom, the geographical tableland known in the OT as the Mishor,[6] had indeed been Moabite, but that earlier Sihon had wrested it from Moabite control.[7] As proof, the so-called "Song of Heshbon" (Num 21:27b–30), ostensibly an Amorite war taunt, was inserted in the narrative. The Israelite argument thus was that though Moabite territory was forbidden to them, the Mishor was an exception because it had been in Amorite hands during the conquest.

This claim was again made in Judg 11:12–28, where Jephthah denies the Ammonites their claim to the region between the Jabbok and Arnon on the basis that it was from the Amorites and not the Ammonites that it was originally taken by Israel.[8]

[3]Cf. W. Vyhmeister, "The History of Heshbon from Literary Sources," *AUSS* 6 (1968) 158–77, which is a condensation of the same author's B.D. thesis on the subject at Andrews University.

[4]Cf. Josh 12:2; 13:10; Judg 11:22.

[5]Y. Aharoni, *The Land of the Bible* (Philadelphia: Westminster, 1967) 187, suggests Khirbet el-Medeiyineh, though due east of Madaba, on the Desert Highway, there is the modern settlement of Al Jīzah.

[6]From the Wadi Ḥesbân in the north to the Wadi Mojib in the south, or "from Heshbon as far as Dibon" (Num 21:30; cf. Deut 2:36).

[7]How long before is not indicated, but it is clear from the biblical sources that the Mishor was closely associated not only with the Amorites (Deut 4:46) but also with the name Moab; to quote Vyhmeister, "Even after the defeat of Sihon by Moses it is said, (a) that the plain on the eastern side of the Jordan River, across from Jericho, was called 'plains of Moab' (Num 22:1; 31:12; 33:48; 36:31); (b) that Balak's and Balaam's intervention took place in Sihon's former territory (Num 22:24); (c) that 'the people began to commit whoredom with the daughters of Moab' (Num 25:1) in the plains of Moab, across from Jericho; and (d) that Moses died and was buried 'in the land of Moab' (Deut 34:5, 6)" (159).

[8]It is strange to find Jephthah attributing Chemosh, the Moabite god, to the Ammonites, in Judg 11:24, unless the Ammonites were in league with the Moabites at this juncture.

After the original defeat of the Amorites, Num 32:1–6 informs us that the tribes of Reuben and Gad requested the territory that had been encompassed by Sihon's kingdom for their tribal allotment, on the basis that it was good for their cattle. Verse 37 goes on to say that it was actually Reuben that built Heshbon and other nearby towns which were (according to the difficult and cryptic next verse) "changed as to name . . . and they called by (other?) names the names of the cities which they built." Josh 13:15–23 confirms the allotment of Heshbon to Reuben, though vv 24–28 indicate it was contiguous to Gad's allotment. In fact, later, when in Josh 21:34–40, Heshbon finally becomes one of the Levitical cities, it is even classed there as a city of Gad. If there is no outright confusion here, our sources may suggest that Reuben, like Simeon, soon lost its tribal identity and was absorbed, in this case, by Gad.[9]

Though Heshbon is not mentioned by name in connection with the history of the United Kingdom, 1 Kgs 4:19 puts "the land of Gilead, the country of Sihon king of the Amorites," in Solomon's twelfth district. In Cant 7:4 (Hebr. v 5), of uncertain date, we read, "Your eyes are like [with the versions] pools in Heshbon, by the gate [plural in LXX and Vg] of Bath-rabbim." So Heshbon apparently had pools and gate(s) worth referring to in poetry!

By the close of the 8th century and into the 7th century, Heshbon appears to be back under Moabite control, for it figures in both extant recensions of a prophetic oracle against Moab (Isa 15:4; 16:8, 9; and Jer 48:2, 34, 35), where its fields, fruit and harvest are mentioned. By this time it may have been a steep *tell*, for fugitives stop in its shadow (Jer 48:45).

In Jer 49:3, Heshbon appears again in the oracle against the Ammonites; perhaps it had changed hands again.

Heshbon's final biblical mention is in Neh 9:22, where it is part of an historical allusion to the Israelite conquest.

To summarize this (which to some may be an "uncritical"[10]) overview of the biblical data on Heshbon, we might conclude then that the site, probably a prominent Iron Age *tell*, with notable pools and gate(s), should lie near the northern edge of the Mishor, west of the wilderness, in the vicinity of Elealeh, with which it is most often associated, as well as other towns such as Jahaz, Medeba, and Sibmah.

[9]Cf. 1 Chr 6:81. Vyhmeister ("History," 160–61, n. 22) assembles the views of commentators on this problem.

[10]I am not unaware of the complexities of the biblical tradition, but I feel justified in my approach by the conclusions reached in the study referred to in n. 19.

When this geographical information is coupled with an acceptance of the biblical traditions with regard to time,[11] one would also conclude that the site should be settled at least as early as the Amorite Period of Sihon—presumably to be associated with the Late Bronze Age—and certainly in the period of the Judges—sometime in Iron 1. Apart from the uncertain time frame for the Canticles allusion, no later occupation at the site is required until the late 8th to early 6th centuries B.C.

To summarize what we know about Esbus-Ḥesbân from post-biblical literary sources, we would expect the site to be occupied in the following periods:

Hellenistic (2nd-mid 1st century)—perhaps moving from Ptolemaic/Nabatean control to Maccabean.

Early Roman (late 1st century B.C.-early 2nd century A.D.)—Herodian fortress, later sacked by Jews.

Late Roman (2nd century)—Ptolemy giving site's exact location.
(3rd century)—locally minted coins.
(4th century)—Eusebius' *Onomastikon*'s site location.

And all through this period—milestone evidence.

Early Byzantine (4th-5th century)—Christian council evidence.

Late Byzantine (6th-7th century)—Continuing bishopric.

Thereafter our evidence is skimpy until the Mamluk period, when once again the site enjoys importance.[12]

II

This sketchy review of the biblical and post-biblical literary data for Heshbon-Esbus-Ḥesbân can now serve as a framework against which we may mention the non-written archaeological data from Tell Ḥesbân which have been uncovered since 1968. The significant results have all been published in a series of preliminary reports[13] and are too well-known to be repeated here. A careful perusal of these reports will demonstrate, I think, that the literary and archaeological data correlate well, both for the geographical location of the site as well as the nature of its occupation for just about every period till we get back to the earliest period. The only substantive non-correlating data appear to be the biblical allusions to the date, nature, and location of Sihon's Amorite capital, and the archaeological evidence that human occupation at Tell Ḥesbân did not antedate ca. 1200 B.C.

[11]Starting with such passages as Num 33:38; Deut 1:3, 4; Judg 11:26; 1 Kgs 6:1.

[12]This summary of the evidence depends entirely on Vyhmeister.

[13]Boraas and Geraty, *Heshbon 1976* (Berrien Springs: Andrews University, 1978); see the first footnote and the bibliography.

III

What are our options? Let me outline briefly at least eight that come to mind. Since we started with the biblical data, let us look at those again first.

Option 1 could be that my treatment of the OT passages is too "uncritical" and therefore too simplistic. It does not take into account the complex nature of the traditions involved nor utilize the many helpful approaches to such literature that modern biblical scholarship has developed. After a century of literary-critical study it is obvious that the OT traditions are late, unhistorical, and therefore untrustworthy for any scholarly historical reconstruction. In its most extreme form, this could be taken to suggest that there was no such thing as an exodus-conquest. Negative archaeological results at Jericho, Ai, and Gibeon were enough, but now negative evidence at Heshbon, too, simply corroborates the results of literary-critical analysis.

Typical to such an approach to the Sihon passage is the recent study of John Van Seters, "The Conquest of Sihon's Kingdom: A Literary Examination,"[14] in which he concludes that Num 21:21–35 is a conflation of two deuteronomistic versions of the same event (Deuteronomy 2 and Judges 11)—that included the reworking of a taunt against Moab—rather than a conflation of the older pentateuchal sources J and E or so-called oral traditions.[15] To quote Van Seters, "This means that the account in Numbers is post-deuteronomic and must be regarded as late-exilic at the earliest. Furthermore, it can offer *no* independent witness to the antiquity of the Sihon tradition. . . . On the historical level the conquest of the kingdoms of Sihon and Og must be regarded with grave suspicion. The oldest accounts in the literary tradition are the rather late deuteronomistic ones and they have a highly ideological character which makes these episodes historically untrustworthy."[16]

Maxwell Miller seems essentially to agree with Van Seters, though his conclusions are more cautiously stated. After discussing Num 21:21–35 and like passages, he says, "The diversity and inconsistencies of the relevant passages suggest that more than one stage of Deuteronomistic compilation and/or redaction was involved. It is difficult to assess the historicity of the reports . . . since these reports are clearly influenced by Deuteronomistic ideology and in conflict with each other."[17]

[14]Van Seters, *JBL* 91 (1972) 182–97.

[15]Van Seters, "Conquest," 189, 195.

[16]Van Seters, "Conquest," 196, 197.

[17]J. Maxwell Miller, "The Israelite Occupation of Canaan," in *Israelite and Judaean History* (ed. J. H. Hayes and J. M. Miller; Philadelphia: Westminster, 1977) 227.

This type of approach to the biblical data makes correlation with the archaeological data at Tell Ḥesbân much easier: since Numbers is late-exilic, Sihon was a late literary creation; he probably never lived at all, and certainly not in the Late Bronze Age. Thus there is no conflict with the archaeological datum that Tell Ḥesbân was not settled before 1200 B.C. However, Miller himself has said, "In evaluating written sources, ancient or modern, it is rarely a matter of deciding *whether* a particular document is trustworthy for historical reconstruction, but of determining its *degee of credibility* and the *kind of historical information which legitimately can be derived from it*."[18] So the fact that the Sihon episode is there, however it came to be there, deserves to be taken more seriously. This leads us to our next option.

Option 2, after paying due attention to literary-critical concerns, would still accept the priority of the Sihon account in Numbers 21 and interpret the story as an essentially historical description of the conflict between Israelites and Amorites from the early conquest-settlement period.[19] This is the position of most scholars who have studied the question—both literary critics and historians—though they ignore or reinterpret biblical statements and consistently date the conquest-settlement period to the 13th or 12th centuries B.C.

Paul Hanson is among those who have argued strongly for an early (13th century) dating for the poem in Num 21:23–35.[20] After presenting a very convincing analysis of the poem, Hanson concludes, "The evidence thus interpreted supports the thesis that the Elohist incorporated into his narrative an authentic Amorite Victory Song of the thirteenth century to document his historical note in Num 21:26. The Song is a very useful historical source for us as well, corroborating and supplementing the knowledge we have from other sources of the events in the Trans-Jordanian area during the pre-Conquest and Conquest period."[21] Hanson sees no reason to doubt that the Amorites were in this region in the period of the conquest, since the combined witness of the biblical tradition is that Sihon was an Amorite king. If one does doubt this, one has to disregard the position of the poem in the context of the conquest narrative.

[18]Miller, "The Patriarchs and Extra-Biblical Sources: A Response," *JSOT* 2 (1977) 65 (emphasis mine).

[19]For a thorough analysis and critique of scholarly positions on the Sihon tradition see Arthur J. Ferch, "A Review of Critical Studies of Old Testament References to Heshbon," forthcoming, in the series of final Heshbon excavation reports.

[20]Paul D. Hanson, "The Song of Heshbon and David's *Nîr*," *HTR* 61 (1968) 297–320.

[21]Hanson, "Song," 307.

The main problem in correlating this view with the archaeological finds at Tell Ḥesbân is that the latter do not begin till 1200 B.C.—*after* a 13th century "conquest." Thus George Mendenhall is now suggesting the "founding" of Sihon's kingdom as a new socio-political entity at Heshbon between 1200–1175 B.C., with Sihon's defeat at the hands of the Transjordanian tribes about 1175 B.C.[22] He supports this suggestion with biblical genealogical data. Though this view has the advantage of taking seriously the archaeological evidence from Tell Ḥesbân, it is difficult to correlate with the mention of Israel on the Merneptah Stele a generation earlier.

Option 3 could suggest that references to Heshbon in the Bible are misunderstood if they are taken to refer to a city instead of a region, at least initially.[23] Parallel region-city relationships in Late Bronze–Iron Age Palestine include Gilead (Ramoth-Gilead), Amman (Rabbat-Ammon), Moab (Kiryat-Moab), Damascus, Samaria, etc. Og, king of Bashan (region), is regularly paralleled with Sihon, king of Heshbon (region?).[24] Even today the name Ḥesbân refers to a broader region than merely the tell, as is shown by the names Wadi Ḥesbân and ᶜAin Ḥesbân (both at some distance north and east). However, Sihon's Heshbon is called a city (*ᶜîr*).

Because the biblical traditions are indeed complex, it is possible that one of these options which seeks to reinterpret the biblical data may prove most useful, but I am bothered by the subjectivity of most such attempts—a subjectivity that Miller claims is inevitable: "Any attempt to evaluate these sources [for Israel's occupation of Canaan] with regard to their historical implications necessarily involves a significant degree of subjective judgment."[25] Till more rigorous controls can be devised, however, it seems methodologically sounder to take the biblical data as historically reliable unless forced to do otherwise by clear, universally-recognized contradictory evidence.

This leads us away from new interpretations of the biblical data to options involving the archaeological data. Thus *Option 4* might suggest that our interpretation of the archaeological evidence is faulty. Non-archaeologists often wonder about the accuracy of digging techniques, ceramic typologies, etc. There is certainly room for error in these

[22]Mendenhall, "The Chronology of the Israelite 'Conquest' of Palestine," unpublished paper presented on Feb 22, 1982, at the Midwest Region SBL Meeting, Evanston, Illinois.

[23]Cf. Larry G. Herr, "History and Settlement of the Ḥesbân Region in the Iron Age," unpublished paper, and Siegfried H. Horn, *Heshbon in the Bible and Archaeology* (Occasional Paper, Horn Archaeological Museum at Andrews University, 1982).

[24]Cf. Deut 29:7; Josh 9:10.

[25]Miller, "Israelite Occupation," 264.

matters, but in the periods with which we are dealing at Tell Ḥesbân, such e ror is in the magnitude of decades, not centures. Through comparative stratigraphy from scores of ancient excavated sites, the dating methods of Palestinian archaeology have become remarkably accurate. Therefore to the "initiated," at least, this alternative is not very attractive.

Option 5 could suggest that our understanding of the process of sedentarization for the period in question is faulty. If Sihon's Amorites were semi-nomadic pastoralists, then perhaps they did not leave the kind of artifactual and occupational evidence that archaeologists customarily find at town sites. While we know from many recent studies that such could theoretically be the case, we also have contemporary sedentary occupation within the region at sites like Jalul, Umeiri, and Madaba.

Option 6 might be that Amorite Heshbon is at Tell Ḥesbân but it has not been found yet in the limited exposure of five digging seasons. While such an option always remains a theoretical possibility until the entire area of human occupation is excavated to bedrock, it becomes increasingly less likely with each season of work that discovers no trace whatsoever of pre-Iron I occupation, despite a conscious attempt to sample the occupation history of the site as widely as possible. In addition to the concentrated effort on the acropolis of Tell Ḥesbân, during the last three seasons the Andrews University expedition carried out eighteen additional soundings and test trenches in all sectors of the site, yet without finding any evidence for settlement before Iron I. The lack of pre-Iron Age surface ceramic evidence, coupled with the lack of occupation depth in remaining sectors of the mound, also argues against this option.

Option 7 might then be that Tell Ḥesbân is not biblical Heshbon, despite the linguistic equivalence of the names. Since there is a problem correlating their earliest history, perhaps the original name migrated to the present site from some other *tell* in the vicinity. Though this may at first appear to be an attractive suggestion, it becomes less so when one considers that Tell Ḥesbân's precise location and prominence make it the most likely topographical candidate for biblical Heshbon—indeed a likelihood unquestioned in the history of scholarship. This is especially true when Ḥesbân is seen as the sister city to Khirbet el-ᶜAl (Elealeh), with which it is often coupled in the OT. And as we have noticed, the correlation of literary and archaeological data seems excellent from Mamluk times all the way back to the Hellenistic period, at least, and perhaps even into the Iron Age. So although there is no "proof," Tell Ḥesbân's identification with Greco-Roman Esbus, at least, seems to receive additional support from coin and milestone evidence and such geographical specifications as required by Ptolemy and Eusebius. Its identification with Iron Age Heshbon is supported not only by the huge water reservoir within the city, as required by Cant 7:4 [Hebr. v 5] but also by the ostracon found there in 1978, whose first line Frank M. Cross translates, "To Heshbon . . ."[26]

Option 8 suggests that Tell Ḥesbân is probably Greco-Roman Esbus and Iron Age Heshbon, but that the name moved to this site when the Amorite site somewhere in the vicinity declined in importance or was abandoned. The occasion for this transferral of name may be alluded to in Num 32:34–38, wherein Reuben builds and names Heshbon. This option has the disadvantage of postponing the solution to our problem or perhaps solving it, in a sense, by another unknown, but it has the advantage of yielding to the full weight of the evidence for Esbus (Heshbon back to the Iron Age) while attempting to harmonize both the biblical and archaeological data for the earlier Late Bronze Age. Such a migration of names in Palestine was a common phenomenon—Jericho and Lachish being obvious examples. Such an option is not altogether a solution by positing an unknown. In 1976 a survey team combed a region of 250 square km. within a radius of 10 km. of Tell Ḥesbân and turned up a possible candidate for Amorite Heshbon, in terms of this option. Jalul—10 km. south-east of Ḥesbân, between Madaba and Al Jīzah—is unquestionably the largest *tell* on the Mishor (in fact it is a true *tell* in a sense which Ḥesbân is not) and intensive sherding of its surface produced 27,000 sherds, of which the majority belonged to the Bronze and Iron Ages with only a sprinkling of later periods represented. This option would then suggest that we have the Amorite capital at Jalul, a location which fits admirably all the biblical requirements for Heshbon, and that although an Iron Age city continued at that site the Reubenites built the *new* Heshbon at Tell Ḥesbân. After the exile, perhaps under Maccabean patronage, and certainly by Roman times, Tell Ḥesbân became the more important site preserving the old name on what became the crossroads for the north-south Via Nova and the east-west Jericho-Livias-Esbus highway. This reconstruction does justice to all the literary data and is "non-falsified" (to use a recent term)[27] by the archaeological evidence.

IV

I am not entirely happy with any of the options presented. Options 1, 4, 6, and 7 seem the least likely. It is possible that I could be persuaded by some form of option 2 eventually, but as Arthur Ferch says, "When one considers the number of secondary explanations offered and the fact

[26]Cross, "An Unpublished Ammonite Ostracon from Ḥesbân," forthcoming in the Horn Festschrift.

[27]S. M. Warner, "The Patriarchs and Extra-Biblical Sources," *JSOT* 2 (1977) 53.

that more evidence has to be explained away than can be called upon to support these theories it becomes apparent that they offer little advantage over the interpretation . . . that Num 21:21–31 and its later elaborations in Deuteronomy and Judges describes an Israelite victory over Sihon during the conquest period and incorporates an Amorite poem (Num 21:27–30) in early Hebrew orthography commemorating an earlier Amorite conquest of Moab."[28] At the present moment I would see this happening sometime within the Late Bronze Age. Options 3 and 5 may hold keys to the resolution of our problem. Option 8 can perhaps be tested by the proposed series of excavations at Tell Jalul.

I am certainly open to other options, however, because I have more serious thinking to do about the historical interpretation of our finds at Tell Ḥesbân. I agree with George Mendenhall, who recently wrote, "Granting that an excavation report can hardly be expected to have the last word on the interpretation of the finds, it seems to me a gross dereliction of duty to assume that the excavator can leave that to others."[29]

[28]Ferch, "References to Heshbon," conclusion.

[29]George E. Mendenhall, in a letter to the author, dated Dec 5, 1977.

V

Biblical Ideology

Magic, Monotheism and the Sin of Moses*

JACOB MILGROM
UNIVERSITY OF CALIFORNIA, BERKELEY

I. THE SIN

DOWN through the ages, the sin of Moses, as described in Num 20:1–13, has been regarded as one of the Gordian knots of the Bible. The punishment is clear. But what is the crime? At least ten explanations given by the medieval Jewish commentators deserve our serious attention. They can be subsumed under three different aspects of the biblical account:

1) Moses' action, striking the rock: (a) instead of speaking;[1] (b) following his choice though the people wanted another;[2] (c) twice instead of once.[3]

2) His character, shown by: (a) his blazing temper;[4] (b) his cowardice;[5] (c) his callousness.[6]

3) His words: (a) which in the form of a question were misconstrued

*An earlier form of this paper was delivered at the annual meeting of the SBL, 1959.

[1]The most commonly accepted explanation, e.g., Rashi, Rashbam, Arama, Luzzato, Malbim, ad loc. Cf. also the Midrash: *Yal.* I, 763–64. Moses' transgression is also universally regarded as unintentional, but God "holds the righteous accountable even for (the deviations of) a hair" (Rashbam).

[2]Based on the words "this rock" and מרים, interpreted as "instructors" (v. 10). Cf. *Oraḥ Ḥayyim*, Hayyim Ben Moses ʿAṭṭar (1696–1743) for the complete argument. Cf. Midrashic sources: *Yal.* I, 763–64; II, 879 (on Ps 78) and *Leqaḥ Ṭov* on Num 20:10.

[3]In addition to the commentators cited above, cf. Ibn Ezra on v 11.

[4]Manifested both by his words and action. Maimonides, *Introduction to* ʾAbot; Ibn Ezra, ad loc.; cf. *Midr. Deut. Rab.* 2:2; *Tanḥuma* Buber IV, 210, etc.

[5]In fleeing for refuge to the sanctuary (v 6) instead of facing the people with unflinching trust in God. Albo, *Book of Principles*, IV, 22; *Biur* of Moses Mendelsohn, ad loc.

[6]In mourning for Miriam while his people were dying of thirst. Based on vv 1, 2 and on *Yal.* I, 763; *Leqaḥ Ṭov* on Num 20:6.

as doubting God;[7] (b) actually doubting God;[8] (c) calling Israel "rebels";[9] (d) **נוציא**, "shall we draw forth . . ."[10]

We shall begin, however, with an eleventh theory—that offered by the consensus of the modern critics, latter day Alexanders, who cut through the knot by claiming that the sin of Moses has been lost[11] or deliberately obscured so as not to detract from the glory of Israel's founder.[12] An agrument *e silentio* is, of course, rarely satisfactory, particularly if the text itself can be made to disclose Moses' sin, as we shall soon discover. As for the notion that Moses' transgression was excised from the narrative, it requires a severe mutilation of the text to accomplish this purpose.[13] Moreover, such a motive is not in keeping with what we find elsewhere in the Bible. The biblical editors have no respect for halos; they delight in tarnishing them. David's historian, for example, was fiercely loyal to him and his seed, recounting that God would "establish the throne of his kingdom forever" (2 Sam 8:13, 16). Yet he spared no pains to castigate his hero for the sin with Bathsheba (2 Sam 12:1–14). The pentateuchal narratives are equally hard upon Judah, the ancestor of David, not to speak of Levi, the ancestor of Moses, and Noah, the ancestor of mankind (Gen 9:21; 34:30; 38; 49:5–7).

Of the ten arguments, we focus first on the popular contention that Moses' irascibility was the source of his sin (2a). Ramban's rebuttal leaves little to be desired: (1) God's condemnation: "You did not trust Me . . . you disobeyed My command" (Num 20:12, 14) cannot refer to anger; (2) Aaron was not guilty of anger.[14] Why was he singularly punished? (3) Most important of all, our text is not an isolated case of Moses' petulance; e.g., Moses was wroth with his army officers (Num 31:14) without provocation.[15] Ramban's apt illustration has Moses venting his spleen only on Israel; we add that it could border on heresy

[7]Rabbi Meir Hakohen (13th century), quoted in *Oraḥ Ḥayyim*, ad loc.; cf. *Yal.* I, 763 and Ramban, ad loc.

[8]Cf. midrash: *Tanḥuma* Buber IV, 121–22; *Midr. Deut. Rab.* 19:13–14.

[9]An unpardonable slight. Cf. Ibn Ezra, ad loc.

[10]See discussion below.

[11]E.g., A. H. McNeile *Numbers* (Cambridge Bible; Cambridge: Cambridge University, 1911), ad loc.

[12]E.g. A. Ehrlich, *Randglossen zur hebräischen Bibel*, 7 vols. (Leipzig: Hinrichs, 1908–14), ad loc.; G. B. Gray, *Numbers* (ICC; New York: Scribner's, 1903) 258.

[13]Cf. the reconstructions cited by Gray, *Numbers*, 258, 261–62.

[14]He never was. The figure of Aaron in Rabbinic literature as peacemaker and compromiser is based solidly on the text (e.g., Exod 32:22–24; Lev 10:36).

[15]The slaughter of the female Midianites was not commanded.

when directed to God.[16] As for his alleged cowardice (2b), we note that Moses was prone to desperation and paralysis for which, however, he never incurred punishment (e.g., Exod 14:15; 15:25; 17:4; Num 14:5; 16:4). His alleged callousness (2c) cannot be derived either from our texts or anywhere else.[17]

In dealing with the category of action—striking the rock—we can immediately discount (1b) and (c).[18] But we must cope seriously with the claim which carries the greatest weight in the tradition, that Moses incurred God's wrath by striking the rock rather than speaking to it (1a). Ramban, again, is most effective in refuting it: (1) when Moses addressed Israel, "Listen, you rebels," he was also speaking to the rock and therefore fulfilling God's command; (2) how are we to understand that Moses failed to "sanctify" God (Num 20:12; 27:14; Deut 32:51) in striking the rock when it is as much a miracle to draw forth water by striking as by speaking?; (3) why would Moses be told at the beginning of our text to "take the rod" (v. 7) if not for the purpose of using it? Indeed, wherever the rod is employed, smiting is either specifically mentioned or implied.[19]

Particularly instructive is Exod 17:5–7 where a similar incident is reported. Moses is commanded "take . . . your rod . . . in your hand . . . strike the rock, and water shall issue from it." Similarity is more than just in content but, as the quoted passage indicates, also in language. Here we can justifiably ask: if Moses was told once before to obtain water out of the rock by striking it, how could he not but strike again when asked to repeat the miracle, particularly as he was instructed to "take the rod" with him (cf. Exod 7:15, 17)? Furthermore, if the transgression lay in striking, why are we told that God was not sanctified "in the sight of the Israelite people" (v 12a)? The Israelites could not have been aware that a desecration had occurred since they knew

[16]E.g., Exod 5:22b, which phrase is inflated to one of unbridled insolence in Num 11:11–15, 21–22.

[17]Particularly in the face of his unflinching intercession on behalf of his people: Exod 30:11–13; Num 12:13; 14:13–19; Deut 9:18–20, etc.

[18]These are farfetched. There is no indication that when Moses previously employed the rod on water (Exod 7:17, 20; cf. 17:5), on earth (Exod 8:12) or on rock (Exod 17:5–6), he struck but once. Indeed, when after Elisha commands Joash "strike the ground," he does so only three times, the prophet upbraids him for striking minimally (2 Kgs 13:18–19). In fact the consequence of Moses' double blow is that "much water" gushed forth (v 11b). Clearly, the striking was effective and, hence, legitimate. As for the choice of rock (n. 2), cf. Ibn Ezra's refutation, ad loc.

[19]E.g., Exod 7:17, 20; 8:12; 17:5–6, where the specific verb "strike" is employed in connection with the rod; cf. the previous note.

nothing about the order to speak to the rock and since their previous experience would have led them to expect Moses to strike it again.

The remarkable parallels between Exodus 17 and Numbers 20 in both context and style have led most critics to posit two variant accounts for the same incident.[20] This possibility was not lost upon one of the medieval Jewish exegetes, Joseph ben Isaac of Orleans, France, known as Bekhor Shor.[21] He postulates the existence of duplicate narratives in our text not just for the rock incident but also for the stories about the manna and the quail. The three episodes are each related twice, once in Exodus and once in Numbers.[22] Evidently, it is the duplication of the quail incident that leads Bekhor Shor to propose his radical solution. For, he asks: "If Moses saw that the quail arrived in sufficient quantities the first time, how could he on the second occasion doubt: 'Could enough flocks and herds be slaughtered to suffice for them?'" (Num 11:22).

With this initial clue given to us by Bekhor Shor, we can press the case on our own. Deut 33:8b reads, "Whom you tested at Massah, Challenged at the waters of Meribah." Since a poetic line consists of parallel clauses, Massah and Meribah must refer to the same incident. The Psalms also interchange the names.[23] Ps 78:15–31, in particular, which reviews the triad of rock-manna-quail, serves to corroborate the entirety of Bekhor Shor's thesis. Here, the incident of the quail is mentioned as occurring once. Furthermore, each reference to the rock speaks of it being struck. Lastly, since it is the Numbers version of the quail that is reported here,[24] the psalmist might also have recounted the Numbers version of the rock, and yet he speaks of the rock only as being struck! Perhaps the clearest evidence is that of Deut 9:22, "Again you provoked the Lord at Taberah, and at Massah and at Kibroth-hattaavah."

[20]Among the reasons given are the same locus, Meribah, and etiology, e.g., Exod 17:7b parallel to Num 20:13aβ.

[21]He was one of the last of the French exegetical school (end of the 12th century) distinguished by its emphasis on the literal, rational approach to the text. On our problem Bekhor Shor not only anticipated modern Bible critics, but, as we shall see, goes far beyond them in approaching the correct solution.

[22]Of course, he would not ascribe the duplications to different editors, as the present documentary hypothesis would hold. He simply regards the Numbers versions correct chronologically whereas they were repeated in Exodus to teach how God supported Israel with manna, quail, and water.

[23]Ps 95:8–9: "Harden not your heart as at Meribah, as in the day of Massah in the wilderness, when your fathers tried me. . . ," again repeating the parallelism of Deut 33:8b. That Meribah refers to Meribah of Numbers 20 is evident from Ps 81:8b. Note the identical root, בחן.

[24]The psalm speaks of God's wrath and punishment following the quail episode, found only in the Numbers version: Num 11:20, 33–34.

But the first and third sites are reported in Numbers (Num 11:3, 34), whereas Massah is the name given to the rock in Exodus (Exod 17:7)![25] It agains stands to reason, in the words of Bekhor Shor, that "the two are one." Finally, attention should be paid to the final verse in the Numbers pericope: "Those are the waters of Meribah—meaning that the Israelites quarreled with the Lord . . ." (20:13). The wording indicates that the name "Waters of Meribah" has been given previously. And indeed it has, in Exod 17:7, "The place was named Massah and Meribah, because the Israelites quarreled, and because they tried the Lord." Here, then, is another indication that the two water-from-rock incidents are one and the same. Further support for their identity is the mention in this verse of Israel's quarrel with the Lord. However the quarrel is not with the Lord but with Moses and Aaron (20:2). It is only in the Exodus version that Meribah receives its name because of Israel's "quarrel with the Lord" (Exod 17:7).

Thus the possibility exists that the two episodes of Moses' drawing water from the rock in Exodus 17 and Numbers 20 are but variants of the same tradition. Yet they cannot be equated, because of one major difference: in Exodus Moses is told to strike the rock; in Numbers he is to speak to it. Ramban suggests two ways of eliminating this difference. First he proposes that **אל**, "to," should be understood as **על**, "of," citing Jer 27:19 as a precedent, with the result that Num 20:8 now reads, "You and your brother Aaron take the rod and assemble the community and before their very eyes speak *of* the rock so that it will yield its water." Alternately, Ramban suggests a transposition of **ודברתם** and **אל הסלע** with the result that the verse now reads, "You and your brother Aaron take the rod and assemble the community *at* the rock and speak in their presence so that it will yield its water." Thus, according to either rendering Moses and Aaron are not to speak to the rock but to the assembled Israelites to inform them of the coming miracle, that the Lord will provide water from the rock as soon as Moses will strike it. Indeed some oral explanation is always required in advance of a miracle so that the people will know that it was the work of God and not an accident of nature. Such advance explanation is not only logically expected but is always attested (e.g., the plagues: Exod 7:16–19, 26–29; 8:16–19; 9:1–4, 13–19; 10:3–6; 11:4–8; the sea: Exod 14:13; the wilderness: Exod 16:6–8; Num 11:18–20; Sinai: Exod 19:7, 10–11, 15–16; Korah: Num 16:16–17, 28–30; 17:16–20).

Ramban's second interpretation is supported by the oft-attested usage of **אל** meaning "by," "at," "in the vicinity of," particularly with reference to natural objects, e.g., place (Deut 16:6; 1 Kgs 8:30b), sky (1 Kgs 8:30b), water (Jer 41:12), hill (Josh 5:3), and particularly by the

[25]Also note that the name is Massah and Meribah—a clear conflation.

evidence in this pericope itself. As it stands, v 8 contains God's command; v 9–10a describe its execution. Since, as demonstrated, Moses' sin lies not in the execution of God's command, the two parts—command and execution—should not vary from each other ever so slightly, either in context or language. But this is not what we find. V 10a gives the fulfillment of God's order as follows: ויקהלו משה ואהרן את הקהל אל פני הסלע ואמר להם . . . "Moses and Aaron assembled the congregation in front of the rock and he said to them." Thus the fulfillment passage clearly states that the gathering is *at* the rock and the speaking is *to the people*. Since these conditions should also obtain in the command (v 8), we therefore conclude that אל הסלע here too is the object of the verb הקהיל and means "at the rock," and that the command ודברתם, "you shall speak," like ויאמר להם (v 10), is directed to the people and not to the rock.

It may be conjectured that originally Num 20:8a read as follows: קח את המטה והקהל את העדה אתה ואהרן אחיך (ודברתם) אל הסלע [והכיתם את הסלע] לעיניהם ונתן מימיו "You and your brother Aaron take the rod and assemble the community before the rock and strike the rock in their presence so that it will yield its water." That striking with the rod must take place before those on whom the ensuing miracle must make an impression is clear from the plague narrative where the same vocabulary occurs: ויךְ את המים . . . לעיני פרעה ולעיני עבדיו "he struck the water . . . *in the presence* of Pharaoh and *in the presence* of his servants" (Exod 7:20; cf. 9:8b). Even more striking is the occurrence of this vocabulary in the Exodus version of the water-rock story: והכית בצור . . . ויעש כן משה לעיני זקני ישראל "and strike the rock . . . So did Moses *in the presence* of Israel's elders" (Exod 17:6). Thus it is extremely possible that the original text of Num 20:8a contained the command "strike the rock," which, however, accidentally fell out because of homoioteleuton, and that subsequently ודברתם "and speak" was (incorrectly) inserted on the grounds that the fulfillment passage does relate that Moses did speak (20:10b).

A third, more radical, approach is to postulate that the original text called for Moses to strike the rock because an act was needed to bring the Word into fulfillment, but was altered to speaking to the rock according to the alleged later view (reflected in Genesis 1) that God's word was inherently effectual and required no human gesticulation.[26]

In any event, even if we are not disposed to accept the suggested, drastic textual change or either of Ramban's renderings, but follow the accepted interpretation that Moses and Aaron were ordered to speak to the rock, we cannot gainsay the evidence that the rock was also struck

[26]F. Kohata, "Die priesterschriftliche Überlieferungsgeschichte von Numeri," *Annual of the Japanese Biblical Institute* 3 (1977) 3–34.

with the rod, and thus their sin lies not in their action, but in the only remaining alternative—in Moses' words.[27]

Arguments 3a, 3b, and 3c are easily dismissed. As to the question in v 10b, implying either unintentional (3a) or deliberate doubt (3b) of God's powers, this is not a first for Moses (e.g., Exod 4:10–14; 5:22–23; esp. Num 11:11–15, 21–22). The answer given by the midrashim that elsewhere Moses' doubts were uttered in private is unconvincing. Moses' recurring failure of nerve, another form of doubt, subject to divine censure, occurred at times under full public scrutiny (e.g., Exod 14:15 and our own text, v 6). Finally, since v 10b is addressed to Israel, not to God, it is most likely not a question but rather an exclamation of Moses' brittle impatience.

Regarding the use of the word "rebels" as unbecoming (3c), it is apparently not too unbecoming for the Deuteronomist to harp on it (Deut 1:26, 43; 9:7, 23–24; 31:27), for Ezekiel to favor it in chastising Israel (e.g., Ezek 20:8 et passim), and for its repeated use by the psalmist (Pss 78:17; 106:33; 107:11). Indeed, if God Himself had earlier dubbed the Israelites as "rebels" (Num 17:25), why should Moses not have availed himself of this divine precedent?

We are left with argument 3d: נוציא. On this word Bekhor Shor has a single terse comment which points to the resolution of our enigma: "the sin resulted from saying נוציא 'shall we draw forth,' and they (Moses and Aaron) should have said יוציא 'shall He draw forth,' meaning God." Bekhor Shor is not original. This interpretation was proposed earlier by Rabbi Hananel ben Hushiel of Kairawan (ca. 980–1056), and is cited with approval by Ramban (cf. also Ibn Ezra on Ps 106:33). Rabbi Hananel explains Moses' sin by comparing the circumstances of Meribah (Numbers 20) with Massah-Meribah of Exodus 17. At the latter place God stood upon the rock before the seventy elders, which for Hananel means the cloud of God's glory. But at the former there was no visible evidence of God's presence. Hence, when Moses said "shall we . . . " there was the clear implication that what followed was his miracle not God's.[28]

[27]Ibn Ezra (on Num 20:8) cites R. Moses Hakkohen, the Spaniard, who also points to Moses' words as the source of his sin, but Ibn Ezra rejects his thesis on the grounds that Aaron too was punished though he did not speak and that the antecedent of "(they vexed) his spirit" (Ps 106:33) is the Lord, not Moses; but cf. below.

[28]E. Arden, "How Moses Failed God," *JBL* 76 (1957) 50–52, followed by M. Margaliot, "The Transgression of Moses and Aaron at Mey Merivah," *Beth Mikra* 58 (1974) 374–400 (Heb.), independently reached the same conclusion: the use of "we" by Moses is blasphemous in that "Moses in his anger takes it upon himself that God is exasperated too," and since there is no evidence of God's

Thus the nature of Moses' sin, far from being obscure or unjustified, is now projected with startling clarity. Moses' sin was not an ordinary transgression. His defiance of God was not merely a countermanding of His order but a denial of His essence. In the sight of the assembled throngs of Israel Moses and Aaron missed the opportunity to "sanctify" God—לא קדשתם—"before the eyes of the children of Israel" (Num 20:12; 27:24; Deut 32:51). Instead they showed no trust, לא האמנתם (Num 20:12a), acting treacherously, מעלתם (Deut 32:51), rebelling against God, מריתם פי (Num 20:24; 27:14; "you changed My words"—Ramban's rendering), setting themselves up in His place, arrogating to themselves the divine power to draw forth the water miraculously from the rock.

Thus all prior incidents of Moses' petulance and doubt pale before the magnitude of this sin. For now, in a direct address to his people, Moses ascribes miraculous powers to himself and Aaron. Indeed, by broadcasting one word, נוציא, "we shall bring forth," Moses and Aaron have made themselves into God.

Considering that Moses' generation had hardly been weaned from the bondage of Egypt, his error was neither slight nor pardonable. Israel had to be released from more than chains; it still had to be purged of its pagan background. In being redeemed from Pharaoh, it had yet to be bound to its God.

II. ITS CONSEQUENCES FOR ISRAEL'S MONOTHEISM

Y. Kaufmann, in his monumental work, *The History of the Religion of Israel,*[29] has shown that all polytheistic systems can be reduced to one common denominator:

> The gods are not ultimately sovereign; they emerge out of a pre-existent realm and are subject to a transcendent order . . . (which) entails the imposition of natural or supernatural compulsion upon the gods . . . .

---

displeasure with Israel, Moses thereby "destroys the hallowed moment God had so clearly intended." Beginning with the correct clue Arden veers to the "blazing temper" argument, refuted above. The "we" indeed is blasphemous, not because Moses falsely attributed anger to God—which still leaves this punishment incommensurate with the crime—but because it indicates that Moses and Aaron publicly usurped the role of God, as explained anon. Furthermore, the interpretation put forth by both Arden and Margoliot that "we" refers to Moses and God is completely unwarranted. In v 8 both perform it; and in v 12 both are condemned for it. Finally, Aaron's complicity in the crime is left unexplained.

[29] 4 vols. (Jerusalem: Dvir, 1937–56) (Heb.). The first three volumes have been abridged and translated by M. Greenberg as *The Religion of Israel* (Chicago: University of Chicago, 1960), and the fourth volume has been translated in its entirety by C. W. Efroymson (New York: Ktav, 1977).

> (Hence) the magical character of the pagan cultus. Magic is an art whose purpose is to move occult powers to act in a desired manner. It utilizes means which are automatically efficient, irrespective of the will of the gods . . . . The power of magic transcends the gods: they themselves employ it, for they too are in need of this almighty instrument which is independent of them and their will . . . pagan religion sees the cult as activating the transcendent source of power upon which both the gods and the world depend.[30]

For our purpose it is important to qualify Kaufmann's perception of the magical nature of polytheism by one consideration. Pagan magic may or may not involve a manual act, but it always involves the use of words. In Egypt, as A. H. Gardiner has shown, "the magical rite is always two-fold and comprises (1) an oral rite, consisting of certain words to be recited, and (2) a manual rite, consisting of certain actions to be performed." In the oral rite, the aspect which primarily interests us, the divine force "is treated personally, being commanded, persuaded, cajoled, warned, threatened, or cursed, just like a human being." Gardiner also dwells upon the extensive use of images and amulets in Egyptian magic but remarks, "images were not immediately potent of themselves, but had to be charged with magical power in one way or the other. The oral rite is usually recited over them."[31] Thus the oral rites, the use of incantations, charms, curses, and threats—are indispensable elements of Egyptian magic (see also *ANET*, 6–7, 12a, 12–14).

Mesopotamian magic reveals the same characteristics: "the act of casting a spell of divine power probably consisted of uttering words extended by conventional movements of the hands,"[32] i.e., a combination of incantation and gesticulation. "Le rituel d'exorcisme comprenait à la fois des *legomena,* tous designés par le terme *chiptou* ("incantation") . . . et des *dromena,* c'est à-dire l'action rituelle,"[33] again a combination of incantation and gesticulation, though the oldest material at times contains incantations without ritual.[34] Thus the oral formula is the indispensable ingredient in pagan magic. (For Mesopotamian examples of rituals comprising incantations and manual acts see *ANET*, 335–38; for Hittite examples, see *ANET*, 346–56).

The Bible contains a striking confirmation of this two-fold nature of pagan magic. The pagan general Naaman is angry that the prophet Elisha did not treat his leprosy as would one of his own magicians: "I

[30]Y. Kaufmann, "The Biblical Age," *Great Ages and Ideas of the Jewish People* (ed. L. W. Schwartz; New York: Random House, 1956) 9–10.

[31]*Encyclopedia of Religion and Ethics,* s.v. "Magic, Egyptian" 262–69.

[32]S. Langdon, ibid., s.v. "Expiation" 639a.

[33]E. Reiner, "La magie babylonienne," *Le Monde du Sorcier* (Sources orientales, 7; Paris: Editions du Seuil, 1966) 8.

[34]Ibid., 74–76.

thought," he said, "he would surely come out to me, and would stand and invoke the Lord his God by name, and would wave his hand toward the spot, and cure the affected part" (2 Kgs 5:11). Once again, magic is effected by a combination of incantation (invoking the deity) and gesticulation (waving the hand).

It is only with this background in mind that the Mosaic period as reflected in the Torah can be properly understood. In contradistinction to the Egyptian priest or magician who compelled the gods through verbal formulae, Moses performs his miracles in dead silence. In the instance of the plagues, Moses not only acts without speech, but on four different occasions when he accedes to Pharaoh's plea to ask for their cessation, he leaves Pharaoh's presence and prays to God alone, that he not be taken for a heathen magician (Exod 8:8, 25–26; 9:29, 33; 10:18; cf. Num 23:3–7, 15–17). Also Moses' intercessory prayers for Israel are always in private, again to dissociate him from his pagan counterpart (e.g., Exod 5:22; 32:11–13, 30–31; 33:7–11).

Thus we see that the measures taken by the pentateuchal narrators to distinguish Moses from his Egyptian counterpart are extreme. But only now can we appreciate their acute sensitivity to the role of Moses. He personified the essential distinction between Israel's new religion and that of its environment. Moses is only the agent of the supreme God. He is not the initiator of the miraculous but only its executor. He is a prophet. "These nations which you are about to dispossess do indeed resort to soothsayers and augurs. To you, however, the Lord your God has not assigned the like. The Lord your God will raise up for you a prophet from among your people; him shall you heed" (Deut 18:14–15).

Central to his prophetic role, Moses must sever Israel from its idolatrous seductions. To help him, God shows Israel authenticating "signs" of His power: He performs miracles. But to make certain that Israel understands their origin in divine will and not as a coincidence of nature, God repeatedly instructs Moses to describe the miracle in advance and designate the precise moment of its occurrence through a specific manual act. Thus for example, "Moses says to Pharaoh: 'You may have this triumph over me; for what time shall I plead' . . . 'For tomorrow,' he replied. And [Moses] said: 'As you say—that you may know that there is none like the Lord our God'" (Exod 8:5–6). Rabbi Samuel ben Hofni (cited by Ibn Ezra) suggests that the reason why Pharaoh did not request Moses to stop the plague immediately was that he suspected Moses "the magician" knew by the stars that the plague was destined to cease at once. Therefore, to trick him, he asked that the plague be removed the next day. In any event, Moses makes sure that the time of the miracle is fixed in advance (even allowing Pharaoh to fix it), so that there can be no doubt that God is performing it (see also Exod 9:5, 18; Josh 11:8). It is precisely here that the danger of mistaken identity can occur. The

Israelites, steeped in their experience of Egyptian sorcery, might easily attribute the marvel not to God but to the craft of Moses. (Might not even Moses make a similar mistake?) Hence the gulf between Moses and his Egyptian counterpart is made as wide as possible. Moses offers no incantations, recites no formulae, intones no esoteric names: he makes a commonplace gesture—strikes with his rod, pours water, throws up soot (Exod 4:9; 9:8), puts his hand in his shirt, or raises his arm high (Exod 4:6–7; 17:11)—and through it all, remains silent.

The dialogue between Elisha and Naaman, referred to above, offers a striking analogy. Elisha's act has none of the incantations and gesticulations expected by Naaman, who is told merely to bathe seven times in the Jordan (2 Kgs 5:10), an act so ordinary, and (from Naaman's point of view) incapable of influencing the divine, that he walked away in a frustrated rage (vv 11–13). This of course is the hallmark of Israel's prophet: just the ordinary gesture—and no incantations.

Y. Kaufmann has demonstrated that the priests of the First Temple performed their ritual in silence.[35] To this view we must add that in the Torah, this holds true for the prophet (i.e. Moses) too. The prophet's function, in distinction from that of the priest, is to intercede in prayer for his charges, and if through his agency a miracle comes to pass, he must be silent during its occurrence. Thus Moses and all his prophetic successors differed sharply from their pagan counterparts when they acted as vehicles of the divine might. They gestured—albeit a common gesture—in order to designate the precise moment of the miracle, but they gestured in silence lest the community of observers attribute the miracle to the power of their words rather than to the power of God.

This backdrop of pagan magic should suffice to explain why it is impossible to believe that Moses was commanded to draw forth water from the rock by speaking to it. In addressing the rock, he would have committed the quintessential heresy: his assembled people would have taken his words as an incantation and him as a magician who performed the miracle by his own powers rather than by divine agency. Most critics aver that speaking to the rock represents a later tradition which has rejected the allegedly cruder rock striking tradition.[36] To the contrary, it is speaking to the rock in the sight (and hearing) of the Israelites which constitutes the grand heresy that Moses commits, and to ascribe this act to the Lord's command is to vitiate all the pentateuchal passages which impose a uniform silence upon Moses during his initiation of all the miracles.

[35]*History*, vol. 2, 476–78.

[36]Cf. Kohata, "Numeri xx 1–13"; J. Koenig, "Sourciers, thaumaturges et scribes," *RHR* 164 (1963) 17–38, 165–80.

The sin of Moses now stands out in its proper perspective. Against the backdrop of the pentateuchal sensitivity to man's usurping of God's powers, Moses' act is manifestly shocking. Even if we consider the Numbers version authentic, that unique among his acts he was to have spoken to the rock, the heresy lies in what he and Aaron said ("shall *we* . . ."). It is our understanding, however, that the striking of the rock was to have been the same mute performance that characterized his other miracles. As final proof that this is the correct reading of the sin of Moses, we submit the testimony of the psalmist: "they (the people) rebelled against Him and he (Moses) spoke rashly" (Ps 106:33). The text reads literally, "he expressed with his lips," i.e., "he blurted out," indicating that his sin may not have been in what he said, but in the bare fact that he spoke at all.

Keeping in mind the unrelenting vigil of the Torah in denying man any share in the manipulation of divine power, we are startled by the contrasts found in the Former Prophets. The Elijah-Elisha narratives, for example, confront us with at least five instances when the prophet performs a supernatural act without the previous consent or command of God, and takes full credit for the ensuing miracle without even attributing his power to God (1 Kgs 17:1; 2 Kgs 1:10, 12–14; 2:8, 9; 4:2–7; 13:21). Other instances can be cited, all of which illustrate the independent power of the prophets. For example, both Moses and Elisha cast wood into water, but whereas the Torah states, "The Lord showed him a piece of wood and he threw it in the water" (Exod 15:25), the Former Prophets state "He (Elisha) cut off a stick and threw it in" (2 Kgs 6:6). Similarly the oath to Caleb, according to the Former Prophets, is given by Moses (Josh 14:9), but in the Torah Moses says nothing, for the oath is made by God (Num 14:21–24, 28–30; Deut 1:34–36). Again, a miraculous birth announcement stems from Elisha in the Former Prophets (2 Kgs 4:16) but from the Lord in the Torah (Gen 18:10; cf. v 13). In the post-pentateuchal narratives, therefore, there is a blurring of the sharp demarcation between the power of man and God, a nonchalance which contrasts dramatically with the puritan zeal of the Pentateuch.

Finally, the remaining bloc of prophetic narratives in Chronicles and Daniel brings us back to the pentateuchal climate. In Chronicles, as distinct from Kings, the prophet is shorn of all wonder-making powers. All miracles are performed by God. Even going further than the Pentateuch where the prophet at least was permitted a manual act, albeit in silence, the prophet of Chronicles never lifts a finger. He is only a mouthpiece for the Almighty's message. In Daniel as well, we find miracles scrupulously attributed to God and punctuated by homiletic perorations of man's need to trust Him.

How are we to account for the difference in point of view between the folk narratives in the Former Prophets, on the one hand, and the Torah and the Chronicles-Daniel literature, on the other? Surely we cannot say that the Torah was recast by the Bible editors in order to fit the point of view of the later literature, for if so, why did they leave the Former Prophets untouched? We can only conclude that each narrative group accurately reflects a different historical period which was entered unrevised into the Canon.

What circumstances can account for the sensitivity found in the Torah and for the contrasting laxness in the narratives of the Former Prophets? Only one answer is possible. The Torah is religiously militant because it was forged in a period of ideological stress: the monotheistic revolution. This is clearly conveyed by the pentateuchal narratives: not only must a pagan Pharaoh be convinced of God's omnipotence but stiff-necked Israel itself.

The narratives of the Former Prophets, on the other hand, show themselves to be relaxed and undisturbed concerning theological issues which pique the pentateuchal narrators. This is exactly what we would expect from our knowledge of that era. It was self-confident and unreflective. It was marked by a creeping syncretism (e.g. Baal names, household gods, wonder-working prophets, etc.). These borrowings from Canaanite religion, however, were only external—form and not content. Just as the profusion of theophoric names compounded with Baal in the Saul–David era is no indication of wholesale defection from pristine Mosaism—all accounts agree that loyalty to the Lord was uncompromised in that age—so must we understand that other syncretistic forms did not meet the opposition of the prevailing spiritual leadership, priestly and prophetic alike, because the latter did not regard them—or were unaware of them—as possible threats to the Covenant faith.

The golden calves of Dan and Beth-El serve as an excellent case in point. Their worship is not condemned even by zealots like Elijah and Elisha. Only Hosea, one hundred years later, and he alone of the eighth century prophets, regards the calves as sinful (Hos 8:5–6; 10:5–6; 13:2). But standing at the threshold of North Israel's decline, Hosea is the prescient forerunner of that soul-searching, cathartic later age which sought an explanation for the destruction of Israel's national life such as we find in the homiletical historiosophy of the editor of Kings. Similarly, we note that the existence of pillars (1 Kgs 14:23), אשרים (1 Kgs 14:15), sodomite enclaves (1 Kgs 14:24; 15:12), and גללים (1 Kgs 15:12) which were built "on every high hill and under every leafy tree" did not incur the wrath of Elijah and Elisha and other early prophets. In these instances too, the syncretic tendencies among the superstitious-prone masses were tolerated.

Hence, by the same token, the belief that miraculous powers were vested in the prophets is but another instance of the unconscious osmosis characterizing the penetration of external pagan notions into Israelite life during this generally unreflective and carefree period.

In Josh 10:12–14 we are given a quotation from the Book of Jashar to the effect that Joshua commanded the sun and moon to stand still. The editor goes on to say that this miracle, performed "in the presence of the Israelites," is unparalleled since "neither before nor since has there ever been such a day, when the Lord acted on words spoken by man." This editorial comment leads us to the following observations: (1) The Book of Jashar, just as the Elijah-Elisha block, has no compunctions ascribing to man the power to initiate miracles. Since this book comprises the poetic compositions at least for the period between the Conquest and the United Kingdom (see 2 Sam 1:15; 1 Kgs 8:13 LXX), it fits in with our general conclusion that the monotheistic revolution took place in the pre-conquest era, and that afterwards there crept in a more tolerant attitude regarding the wonder-working of the prophet. (2) Still, the editor was disturbed by the implication of the poem. Indeed he might well be. It was not only the magnitude of the Gibeon miracle that startled him but especially its inception: Joshua did not request but commanded—the nearest we come in the Bible to the polytheistic concept of man controlling the divine. Yet we note how the editor dealt with his material. He did not change it. Rather, he recorded the miracle tradition dutifully and allowed himself the luxury of the comment that this event was unique—but never again to be repeated. Thus, our confidence in the authenticity of the biblical narratives receives a new source of support. (3) Finally, we have a clear standard by which to measure Moses' sin. What was disturbing and unique about the miracle at Gibeon was that man and not God evoked a particular supernatural event, for which the editor found he had to apologize. Moses was guilty of a similar incident in commanding the rock to give forth water. But he went far beyond Joshua. He attributed the power to himself. He left the border of effrontery and entered the domain of heresy. And for this he was commensurately punished.

In arriving at the nature of Moses' sin we have also staked our claim to ancillary conclusions, as follows:

1. With the help of Bekhor Shor, we have lent strength to the hypothesis that duplicate accounts of the wilderness period exist in Exodus and Numbers.

2. The ideal prophet in Israel, as exemplified in Moses, was constrained to speechlessness during the performance of a miracle, a practice which contrasted sharply—deliberately so—with the wonder-workers of other nations.

3. The enforced silence of Moses during a miracle is matched by his reticence in its initiation. Both characteristics of Moses clash with the behavior of his successors as related in the prophetic legends, and they cleave the Torah and the Former Prophets into two independent blocks of narrative material, reflecting, in general quite accurately, the theological climate of the periods they describe. In the case of the Torah, this can only mean that the monotheistic revolution was a product of the Mosaic age.

One final observation. If correct, we have uncovered the true pathos in the personal tragedy of Moses. Israel's teacher is condemned for revealing the very failing which he tried to rectify in his charges. There was a promised land also of the spirit to which he successfully brought his people, but which he himself failed to reach.

Qoheleth and the Reformation of Wisdom

Frank Anthony Spina
The School of Religion
Seattle Pacific University

R. B. Y. Scott has underscored the difficulty involved in interpreting Qoheleth by remarking that it is not only the "strangest" book in the Bible but also the one whose presence in the sacred canons of Judaism and Christianity is the "most inexplicable."[1] In large part this appraisal, which is by no means confined to Scott, stems from the cynical and perhaps even nihilistic outlook which characterizes the book.[2] Its apparently negative stance toward all of life and the created order seems to be at considerable variance with the central themes of the Hebrew Bible, especially those having to do with Yahweh's gracious self-disclosure to Israel and His providential and passionate involvement in Israel's history. To be sure, the wisdom tradition generally has often been viewed as peripheral to, if not at odds with, orthodox biblical thought in that wisdom is seen as "humanistic" or "secular" rather than "religious."[3] It follows that if wisdom is regarded as tangential to what is central in the biblical tradition, then Qoheleth is twice removed. While wisdom may be humanistic or secular in the sense that man is left more or less on his own to work out his life in the world, which at least says something positive about human ability and the possibility of a meaningful life, Qoheleth does not even go that far. Religious or secular, wise or foolish is immaterial to Qoheleth—in the final analysis everything is "vanity" and a "striving after wind." Thus, if the wisdom tradition is difficult to fit into the framework of classical biblical

[1]R. B. Y. Scott, *Proverbs, Essclesiastes* (AB 18; Garden City, NY: Doubleday, 1965) 191.

[2]See e.g. H. W. Hertzberg, *Der Prediger* (KAT 17/4–5; Gütersloh: Gütersloher Verlagshaus Gerd Mohn, 1963) 222. Also see the literature cited by B. S. Childs, *Introduction to the Old Testament as Scripture* (Philadelphia: Fortress, 1979) 580–81, 589.

[3]This was especially true when the concept of "God's mighty acts" was viewed as the main element in biblical theology, as was the case in America during the so-called "biblical theology movement." See G. E. Wright, *God Who Acts: Biblical Theology as Recital* (SBT 1/8; London: SCM, 1952); B. S. Childs, *Biblical Theology in Crisis* (Philadelphia: Westminster, 1970) 39–44.

thinking, *a fortiori* the task of making Qoheleth integral is next to impossible since it is peculiar even *within* that tradition.

However, since the work of von Rad and perhaps the attenuation of the concept of "revelation in history" as the dominant category for biblical theology there has been a much more positive valuation of the role of wisdom in biblical thought.[4] It is not an overstatement to say that there has been almost a complete reversal, so that wisdom recently has been counted as one of the richest motifs in the Bible. What was previously regarded as a negative factor, namely, a secular or humanistic thrust, has been made into a virtue. With its stress on the world "as it is" and its affirmation of human activity and freedom in the secular realm, wisdom is seen as giving meaning to life in radically humanistic and non-traditional terms.[5] Accordingly, wisdom is viewed by some as quite amenable to modern thought forms and perhaps even more palatable to contemporary human beings than other more standard biblical themes.[6] This development leads in turn to the possibility of interpreting Qoheleth in a more constructive manner. While it would undoubtedly be strained to attempt to soften the negative tone of the book, this too can be transformed into a virtue. Qoheleth may be understood as a radical form of human honesty and a courageous acceptance of the world as one confronts it. It is therefore not surprising that recent interpretations have offered a more positive estimation of Qoheleth's theological value.[7]

It seems to me that this present state of affairs can only be considered an improvement. The wisdom tradition need not be regarded as a peripheral part of the biblical tradition or as antithetical to "orthodox" biblical thought. Even the suggestion that wisdom's value for modern reflection lies in its affirmation of the tension, ambiguity and stark realism of secular or humanistic thinking has merit. Of course, if such themes are seen as having positive value for understanding human existence, then the appreciation of Qoheleth rises considerably. Nevertheless, while granting the validity of this emphasis, it may still be asked whether in the final analysis this is the best way to approach wisdom in

[4]See G. von Rad, *Wisdom in Israel* (Nashville and New York: Abingdon, 1972). Also, cf. James Barr, "Revelation through History in the Old Testament and Modern Theology," *Princeton Seminary Bulletin* 56 (1963) 4–14; Childs, *Biblical Theology*, 62–66.

[5]E.g. W. Brueggemann, *In Man We Trust: The Neglected Side of Biblical Faith* (Richmond: John Knox, 1972) 1-28.

[6]See W. Brueggemann, "Scripture and an Ecumenical Life-Style," *Int* 24 (1970) 3–19.

[7]E.g. James Crenshaw, "The Eternal Gospel (Eccl. 3:11)," in *Essays in Old Testament Ethics* (Festschrift for J. P. Hyatt; ed. J. Crenshaw and J. Willis; New York: KTAV, 1974) 29–30, 46, 48; R. K. Johnston, "'Confessions of a Workaholic': A Reappraisal of Qoheleth," *CBQ* 38 (1976) 14–28; Childs, *Introduction*, 580ff.

general or Qoheleth in particular. For one thing, this tends to regard a little too highly the positive value of the so-called secularism or humanism within the Bible or, for that matter, within the wisdom tradition itself. At the very least, the precise nature of this element needs to be more carefully spelled out. For another thing, such an approach also seems to make too little of wisdom's relationship to some of the more central motifs of biblical thought. It is evident that there are strains within the wisdom tradition that unquestionably are largely unrelated to the Bible's epic traditions, but to assert that this is the case for the wisdom tradition in its entirety is problematic. In fact, I believe a case can be made that much in the Bible's wisdom corpus is fairly closely related to classical biblical faith. This holds true for the major wisdom books, including Qoheleth. More precisely, in my opinion a more nuanced understanding of the varieties of wisdom material in the Bible leads to two important conclusions about Qoheleth. One, Qoheleth is indeed cynical, but that cynicism is of a very special kind. The issue is not whether Qoheleth is cynical, but rather what he is cynical about. It is highly questionable in my judgment whether his profound cynicism should be placed in the context of a secular or humanistic stance. Two, Qoheleth is closely related to "mainstream" biblical thought and as a matter of fact actually reflects one of the great epic traditions, namely, that of the Mosaic covenant.[8]

The first item that needs to be dealt with to make our case is the extent of wisdom literature in the Bible. It is not inaccurate to point out that the approach which has been followed in recent years is almost "pan-wisdom" in that scholars have been discovering wisdom characteristics and influence in places where previously neither were ascertained. For example, in addition to the customary hagiographic sources, the following have been adjudged to be wisdom in outlook: Genesis 1–11; 37; 39–50; Exodus 34:6ff.; Deuteronomy; 2 Samuel 9–1 Kings 2; Amos; Habakkuk; Isaiah; Jonah; Esther.[9] Perhaps the first observation to be made in the light of these identifications is that if all of these materials really constitute wisdom then wisdom can by no means be considered a relatively small portion of the biblical corpus. Another observation is that wisdom's place in the larger biblical framework is much less difficult to secure since many of these materials are intimately related to the great epic traditions. Thus, in the light of work done in

[8]See G. E. Mendenhall, "Ancient Oriental and Biblical Law," *BA* 17 (1954) 26–46; "Covenant Forms in Israelite Tradition," *BA* 17 (1954) 50–76; *The Tenth Generation: The Origins of the Biblical Tradition* (Baltimore: Johns Hopkins University, 1973) 1–31.

[9]See J. Crenshaw, "Method in Determining Wisdom Influence upon 'Historical' Literature," *JBL* 88 (1969) 129, nn. 1–3.

recent years, wisdom is more extensive and more related to the central themes of the Bible.

Of course, whether all these materials should be classified as wisdom may be debated. Crenshaw, for example, has asserted that scholars have been far too adventuresome in their willingness to assign all sorts of diverse material to a wisdom provenance. According to him, even though by definition wisdom has to do with the natural world, common people, ordinary events, and employs everyday language, images and metaphors, it does not automatically follow that any piece of literature which has these things should be categorized as wisdom. Other genres may make use of similar language and subjects. So Crenshaw calls for stricter formal criteria to be applied before a wisdom setting is posited, otherwise the definition is so broad as to lose meaning. He is of the opinion that if more exacting criteria were used many of the arguments advanced for wisdom origins could not be sustained.[10]

Even if one did not go along with Crenshaw completely it has to be granted that application of stricter criteria may in fact result in a smaller corpus of wisdom material. Be that as it may, this issue is secondary to that of the precise variety of wisdom being identified. Some of the significant distinctions among the various types of wisdom have tended to be blurred by referring to so many different materials simply as "wisdom." It needs to be stressed that identifying several different kinds of literature as wisdom is legitimate only when the specific variety is carefully described. Unless this is done either the richness of the wisdom tradition is downplayed or it becomes increasingly more difficult to speak of wisdom as a special genre.

In order to counter both of these extremes, Crenshaw has proposed the following. First is the matter of definition. At the outset it is important to distinguish between wisdom as literature, as a tradition and as a way of thinking. These categories may be further subdivided, so that one must be aware of whether the wisdom in question is juridical, natural, practical or theological. Second, it is imperative to note the presence of stylistic or ideological peculiarities found in wisdom literature about which there is no dispute. This guideline is intended to avoid the confusion between "general wisdom," which is about common sense and ordinary language, and "special wisdom," which is a genuine distinguishable entity. Third, care must be taken to observe differences of nuance. A wisdom word or motif may take on a different meaning in a non-wisdom context. For example, it is one thing to conclude that wisdom sayings are to be found in Amos but it is quite another to conclude therefore that Amos is a wisdom "book." Fourth, it should not be forgotten that much of the Hebrew Bible is actually negative toward

[10]Ibid., 135–42.

wisdom. Finally, the development of wisdom has to be taken into account—wisdom did not mean the same thing or function the same way in every era or social setting.[11]

Because Crenshaw applies much stricter criteria to the problem of identifying wisdom he ends up with a smaller corpus of genuinely wisdom materials and one which is fundamentally negative in outlook. By "negative" Crenshaw refers to the fact that in historical and prophetic sources the use of wisdom often leads to destruction and misfortune. As examples he cites the wise men of Egypt (Exod 7:8–13), the rape of Tamar (2 Sam 13:3–5), Joab and the Tekoan wise woman (2 Samuel 20), David's death-bed instructions to Solomon (1 Kgs 2:5–9), the deceitful counsel of Hushai (2 Sam 16:20–17:23), the clever serpent and Eve's desire to be wise (Genesis 3) and numerous prophetic denunciations of the wise counselors of the kings.[12] But it is not necessary to accept Crenshaw's argument that there are in reality fewer wisdom materials in the Bible than has been thought, though I am inclined to agree with him. More important is to realize that even if most that has been identified as wisdom *is* wisdom, that in no way diminishes the fact that wisdom is frequently depicted in a negative light in the Bible. When taken as a whole, it is not nearly as upbeat or nobly humanistic as has sometimes been claimed. In addition, when one considers that Job and Qoheleth are also negative in the sense that both reject the possibility of securing one's existence and guaranteeing one's future by means of wisdom, then the amount of positive wisdom is reduced even further. Some scholars have even questioned whether Solomon's association with wisdom is to be viewed positively or negatively, though for the most part the canonical form of the text seems to indicate a positive connection.[13]

The precise nature of the negative cast being attributed to part of the wisdom tradition here is more clearly seen in an analysis of the various kinds of wisdom. It is fairly customary to distinguish between

[11]Ibid., 130 35.

[12]Ibid., 134. See also G. E. Mendenhall, "The Shady Side of Wisdom: The Date and Purpose of Genesis 3," in *A Light Unto My Path: Old Testament Studies in Honor of Jacob M. Myers* (ed. H. N. Bream, R. D. Heim and C. A. Moore; Philadelphia: Temple University, 1974) 323–24. On the matter of the prophetic denuciation of the wise, see W. McKane, *Prophets and Wise Men* (SBT 1/44; London: SCM, 1965); J. Jensen, *The Use of* tôrâ *by Isaiah: His Debate With the Wisdom Tradition* (CBQ Monograph Series 3; Washington, D.C.: Catholic Biblical Association of America, 1973).

[13]See Mendenhall, "The Shady Side of Wisdom," 324–25; Brueggemann, *In Man We Trust*, 68-71. Cf. M. Noth, "Die Bewährung von Salomos 'Göttlicher Weisheit'," and R. B. Y. Scott, "Solomon and the Beginnings of Wisdom in Israel," in *Wisdom in Israel and the Ancient Near East* (ed. M. Noth and D. W. Thomas; VTSup 3; Leiden: Brill, 1955) 225–37; 262–79.

family/clan wisdom, court wisdom and educational wisdom. Crenshaw's listing is even a little finer than that, for he cites four separate kinds: 1) juridical; 2) nature; 3) practical; and 4) theological. These categories are then further explicated by the following:

> . . . one must distinguish between family/clan wisdom, the goal of which is the mastering of life, the stance hortatory and style proverbial; court wisdom, with the goal of education for a select group, the stance secular, and method didactic; and scribal wisdom, the goal being education for all, the stance dogmatic-religious, and the method dialogico-admonitory.[14]

Though I quite agree with the basic soundness of this description, I would suggest a somewhat more ideological framework. Certainly each of the categories to be suggested requires more evidence and detailed substantiation than is possible to provide in this essay, but their heuristic value for comprehending wisdom in general and Qoheleth in particular will I hope be evident.

There would probably be very little debate as to the presence of what might be called folk or village wisdom in the biblical tradition. This would for the most part correspond to Crenshaw's designation of family/clan wisdom. Such wisdom is based on ordinary peoples' rudimentary observations of all that is around them and is expressed primarily in proverbial form. Its social function has to do with living life well and appropriately. However, while folk/village wisdom is truly a part of general wisdom, it is crucial to recognize that there is a substantial difference between it, its social milieu and function, and the highly sophisticated literary productions referred to when one speaks of "wisdom literature."[15] Thus, if one is going to use the presence of folk/village wisdom elements in a piece of literature as an argument for wisdom provenance, it is imperative to keep in mind that a particular kind of wisdom is being dealt with, for what kind of wisdom one is discussing makes a great deal of difference in what can be said about it. It cannot be too strongly emphasized that different kinds of wisdom have

[14]See Crenshaw, "Method in Determining Wisdom Influence," 130. Others have acknowledged the existence of these different types of wisdom, but have tended to blur the distinctions when discussing their theological import. Cf. R. E. Murphy, "Wisdom and Yahwism," in *No Famine in the Land: Studies in Honor of John L. McKenzie* (ed. J. W. Flanagan and A. W. Robinson; Claremont: The Institute for Antiquity and Christianity, 1975) 117–26. I quite agree with Murphy that wisdom need not be approached from the standpoint of "canon within the canon." But even in its canonical context wisdom is fundamentally negative—it pits itself against something. However, the view that wisdom is to be understood as against normative Yahwism must in my view be thoroughly revised.

[15]Mendenhall, "The Shady Side of Wisdom," 319, 334 n. 2.

different ideological and social functions in the society, sometimes having little or nothing to do with each other and sometimes being clearly antithetical. Another issue in this regard is whether the presence of folk/village wisdom in a piece of literature, even if there is a considerable amount, of necessity means that the work in which it is found should be categorized as a wisdom genre per se. It appears that there are many folk/village elements scattered throughout the Bible and that by no means should all the books in which they are embedded be thought of as wisdom in the technical sense.[16] Of course, there are examples of folk/village wisdom in wisdom books, including Qoheleth, Job and especially Proverbs,[17] but that does not make them in terms of their literary essence an example of folk/village wisdom.

I designate the second major category of wisdom "royal wisdom," the context of which is the court and the primary function of which is training in the art of political administration. An illustration of this kind is found when Solomon requests wisdom so that he will be able to "administer" (לשפט) Israel (1 Kgs 3:9). Though he does not use the terminology adopted here, Mendenhall seems to have a similar category in mind when he refers to the ". . . educational system by which the children of the elite class of society were trained in the necessary skills that enabled them to compete in the ancient pecking order determined by the ancient states and empires."[18] Seen in this way, royal wisdom is more than a genre of literature though it could certainly have a literary component. It is rather principally a way of thinking and doing, and perhaps even a certain way of ordering reality. Just as virtually all levels of wisdom involve to one degree or another social function, that is, the art of doing something, royal wisdom too shares this aspect. But it is likely that royal wisdom heightens the aspect of social function in that it is intimately and inextricably bound to institutional and political structures the very purpose of which is to make sure that certain desired results are brought about. Royal wisdom ultimately then has to do with what might be legitimately called "political technique" or the "art of political administration."

[16]E.g., even if the argument about Amos' connection with the traditions of clan wisdom is correct, it is another matter whether that warrants designating Amos *the book* as wisdom literature. Cf. H. W. Wolff, *Amos the Prophet: The Man and His Background* (Philadelphia: Fortress, 1973). Also see C. Isbell, "A Note on Amos 1:1," *JNES* 36 (1977) 213–14.

[17]The same can be said of Ecclesiasticus and Wisdom.

[18]Mendenhall, "The Shady Side of Wisdom," 321. I have refrained from referring to "educational wisdom" as a special type because it seems to me that all the various kinds of wisdom could be fostered in an educational context of one sort or another.

In the positive sense, royal wisdom may be described as the art of administering a social or political institution so that the purposes of the institution are accomplished and its goals achieved efficiently and effectively. It was almost certainly the case in ancient Israel that this aspect of the royal wisdom tradition was regarded as legitimate and doubtless in some circles was seen as a divine gift.[19] From the very beginning of its existence Israel had all sorts of social and political institutions which in the main were seen as beneficial to the society. To the extent that royal wisdom was perceived as enabling such institutions to operate for the "common good" it would have been seen as a blessing and for the most part as a divine blessing.[20]

But royal wisdom was not an unmixed blessing. If in the positive sense it was viewed as the art of getting things done efficiently and effectively in the socio-political arena, negatively it was regarded as an attempt to manipulate and control people or events for political ends that were at best questionable and at worst downright inimical to Israel's ancient religious traditions.[21] Unless royal wisdom was cautiously appropriated and in addition tempered by the realization that socio-political institutions have a tendency to become autonomous and autocratic it could easily degenerate into an ideological foundation for just such institutions. Taken to its logical extreme, royal wisdom could be translated into a form of idolatry to the extent that it was used to legitimate and fortify an institution's claim for ultimate authority and power. It should not be denied that any socio-political institution in Israel's history would have been susceptible to the negative aspects of royal wisdom, though perhaps a case might be made that not all institutions would have been equally susceptible. But it seems to be fairly clear in the biblical materials that the negative features of royal wisdom are most often associated with the monarchy. It certainly overstates the case to suggest that the monarchy was viewed by all "true" Israelites as an unmitigated evil, but there seems to be little question that initial and subsequent objections to its establishment were at least in part due to the conviction that the monarchical institutions were by

[19]This is described in an impressionistic fashion by Brueggemann, *In Man We Trust*, 48–63.

[20]In the present form of the canon this beneficial aspect of royal wisdom is illustrated in 1 Kgs 3:3–28. Compare 1 Kgs 5:9–14 and see Noth, "Die Bewährung von Salomos 'Göttlicher Weisheit'," 225–26.

[21]The following passages may in one way or another reflect the use of wisdom as "political technique": 2 Sam 14:1–21; 16:20–17:23; 20:14–22; 1 Kgs 2:1–9; Genesis 3. Especially intriguing is the statement in 2 Sam 14:20: "In order *to change the course of affairs*, your servant Joab has done this" [emphasis mine].

their nature somehow more susceptible to the equation of divine and human sovereignty.[22]

If this brief explanation of the negative side of royal wisdom is essentially correct, it means also that this tradition is tied to the ideological tradition on which the Israelite monarchy was based, possibly by the time of David and certainly by the time of Solomon. This is of course the tradition of the Davidic covenant (see 2 Samuel 7). Mendenhall has characterized this tradition as "paganism,"[23] but whether that is an apt designation is less crucial at this point than the fact that the Davidic ideology/theology in its original historical context was regarded by at least a minority of Israelites as a departure from the tradition on which Israel had originally been founded, namely, that of the Mosaic covenant.[24] From the vantage point of the Mosaic tradition, Israel's transition to a monarchy could not be regarded as a simple change of social and political structure—the fundamental explanation of divine reality was at stake. Whether they were correct or not, Israelites steeped in the old Mosaic tradtion could not help but see in the monarchy a departure from Yahweh's rule as manifested in non-centralized, non-hierarchical and egalitarian socio-political forms.[25] If "paganism," to use Mendenhall's term, refers to the belief that the royal institutions were ordained by the divine world and the corresponding failure to comprehend the prophetic critique that Yahweh was not ultimately reducible to *any* of Israel's institutions then it may indeed be admitted that paganism was indeed latent in the Davidic ideology. As a corollary, the negative aspect of royal wisdom would also have been perceived as a pagan tradition and not merely a misuse of an otherwise acceptable administrative technique. Thus, to the extent that royal wisdom and the Davidic tradition were regarded as interrelated or even complementary they would both have been subject to repudiation from a Mosaic perspective.

The third wisdom category to be mentioned should be thought of in terms of a reaction to royal wisdom as described above. In the absence of a better nomenclature I call this level of wisdom thought "reformed

[22]See G. E. Mendenhall, "The Monarchy," *Int* 29 (1975) 155-70. 1 Sam 8:7 is of course the *locus classicus* for indicating that the monarchy was a rejection of divine rule. Others have suggested less ideological or theological factors in the resistance to the monarchy. See e.g. M. C. Astour, "The Amarna Age Forerunners of Biblical Anti-Royalism," in *For Max Weinreich on His Seventieth Birthday* (London: Mouton, 1964) 6–17.

[23]Cf. Mendenhall, "The Monarchy," 160–70.

[24]For an important description of the characteristics of the Mosaic and Davidic traditions, see W. Brueggemann, "Trajectories in OT Literature and the Sociology of Ancient Israel," *JBL* 98 (1979) 161–85. Also see n. 8.

[25]See N. K. Gottwald, *The Tribes of Yahweh: A Sociology of the Religion of Liberated Israel, 1250–1050 B.C.E.* (Maryknoll, NY: Orbis, 1979) 586–87.

wisdom." However, since it is a reaction to the use of royal wisdom as an ideological underpinning for the state it should not be considered a separate category in formal terms. It is the historical and ideological context which makes reformed wisdom identifiable, not any special use of wisdom forms. Reformed wisdom represents the thinking of those wisdom specialists in ancient Israel who had been taken aback and doubtless demoralized by royal wisdom's failure to uphold the Israelite state. Historically, this kind of thinking would have surfaced in the context of the exile when Jerusalem's ashes and the people's deportation provided sad illustration that royal wisdom not only could not guarantee the existence of the state but was in the final analysis an inadequate ideology on which to base Israel's sociopolitical structures.[26] Royal wisdom was designed to eventuate in "control over one's environment" but in the midst of social and political destruction that no longer made any sense. If wisdom was to have a meaningful place in Israel's traditions, it would have to be changed to cope with this new situation.

But the response of the wise men was not to discard wisdom forms. Instead, wisdom forms were retained but the theological outlook of wisdom was modified. The theological tradition which provided the impetus and content for this alteration was in my view the Mosaic tradition. When Mosaic theology, with its emphasis on Yahweh's sovereignty and its de-emphasis on centralized and hierarchical political forms, was combined with a thoroughly wisdom outlook the result was a kind of wisdom in which no ultimate human sovereignty could be claimed. Reformed wisdom proclaims the virtues of wisdom thinking, to be sure, but at the same time it never tires of warning of the dangers of unchecked or unqualified wisdom thinking. Reformed wisdom says above all that all human activity must be chastened by the belief that Yahweh is in control, not man, and that no matter how skillfully wisdom is used the future of Israel and its institutions are in the hands of a sovereign God.

It is my contention that reformed wisdom is the overarching theme of a considerable amount of wisdom writing in the Hebrew Bible, including Genesis 3, Job, Proverbs and, of course, Qoheleth. Each of these writings affirms in one way or another that wisdom cannot be used to maintain one's sovereignty over his own or someone else's existence. Genesis 3 points out that the primal offense is to "be wise" (להשכיל), that is, to be "like God" and therefore master life. The issue is whether God or humankind is sovereign.[27] Job's author argues forcefully and

[26]Mendenhall, "The Shady Side of Wisdom," 329.

[27]In my view it is not necessary to adopt Mendenhall's late dating of Genesis 3 to accept his argument that this passage is anti-wisdom. Almost surely

poignantly that only God is sovereign, therefore there are no absolute guarantees—not even the most devout can be sure about the outcome of life. No amount of the correct use of wisdom would have insured Job's "success," which was ultimately the gift of God. Even Proverbs, which surely contains in terms of individual sayings many royal wisdom elements, is a somewhat chastened tradition. No matter how much the value of wisdom is underlined, fearing God (=recognition of Yahweh's sovereignty) is where all wisdom must begin.[28] In these examples the writings are formally wisdom, but their function is to repudiate or at least modify another kind of wisdom thinking and the ideology and value system which it represents.

This leads us finally to Qoheleth itself. At the outset of this essay we noted that Qoheleth has been traditionally regarded as heterodox or aberrant on account of its cynical and nihilistic outlook.[29] Who can argue that its author fails to find meaning in human existence? For Qoheleth life is without direction, history makes no intrinsic sense and has no teleological goal. Indeed, time is cyclical, fate and determinism are the key concepts. Work, wealth, status and power all add up to zero. It is hardly surprising that such sentiments have been interpreted as running directly counter to normative biblical religion. But the issue is not whether Qoheleth is negative or cynical, but rather about what is he cynical.

As part of reformed wisdom, Qoheleth is pitted against royal wisdom. His cynicism is not a function of the author's radical humanistic or secular stance; to the contrary, Qoheleth may actually be thought of as a thoroughgoing "conservative." Qoheleth reaches back to the tradition and value system of the early covenant theology and uses that as a basis for rejecting the ideology and value system of a later day. His conviction is that Israel had deviated tragically from Mosaic religion and had sanctioned uncritically the policies of the Israelite state in the name of Moses' God. According to an unchecked royal wisdom outlook it was asserted that the worth of an individual or the society was directly proportionate to the accumulation of wealth, whereas Qoheleth observed that rich and poor alike share similar fates—wealth guarantees nothing (see Qoh 2:1–11; 4:7–8; 5:9–17; 6:1–6). According to an unchecked royal wisdom outlook high social and political status were considered goals worth coveting and striving after, whereas Qoheleth pointed out that

---

there was anti-wisdom thinking in seminal form going on before the Exile when such thinking would have matured and become far more widespread. Ibid., 327–29.

[28]See Prov 1:7, 29; 9:10.

[29]See Svend Holm-Nielsen, "On the Interpretation of Qoheleth in Early Christianity," *VT* 24 (1974) 1.

sorrow comes to all, the prince and the beggar. Status gives no assurance to the powerful, the wise or the rich (see e.g. Qoh 2:1–11; 9:11–12). According to an unchecked royal wisdom outlook the Israelite state, ordained by the deity and symbolized in the person of the king, was to be counted on for present and future welfare, whereas Qoheleth insisted that no amount of human power gives one ultimate control over his own or anyone else's destiny. The course of history is beyond human control (see Qoh 3:1–8). There is little question that Qoheleth is cynical or that in relation to other emphases in biblical thought he overstates his case. But that is due to his unalterable conviction that he was taking on nothing short of a semi-pagan ideology and value system. Qoheleth is cynical about any who have adopted the belief that wealth, status and power are to be sought after, retained and controlled at all costs (see 2 Kgs 12:1–11; 21:1–24).[30] Thus, in his repudiation Qoheleth attempts to reflect what he regards as an ethic and life-style in which human activity need not be frenzied or manipulative and characterized by an incessant attempt to achieve power or wealth:

> This, then, is my conclusion: the right happiness for men is to eat and drink and be content with all the work he has to do under the sun, during the few days God has given him to live, since this is the lot assigned him. And whenever God gives a man riches and property, with the ability to enjoy them and to find contentment in his work, this is a gift from God. He will not need to brood, at least, over the duration of his life so long as God keeps his heart occupied with joy (5:17–19; JB).
>
> Joy, then, is the object of my praise, since under the sun there is no happiness for man except in eating, drinking and pleasure. This is his standby in his toil through the days of life God has given him under the sun (8:15; JB).

In sum, Qoheleth is unorthodox only from the point of view of those who translated Mosaic religion into primarily ritualistic forms and transformed with the addition of their traditions the idea of the kingdom of Yahweh into the idea that the Israelite state was that kingdom.[31] When this "orthodoxy" failed, Qoheleth and other sages combined their chastened understanding of wisdom with Mosaic theology which had been forced "underground" for much of the time during the monarchy. In doing this they stood with those classical prophets who also used the vantage point of the Mosaic tradition to pronounce judgment against

[30]See von Rad, *Wisdom*, 232–33.

[31]See G. E. Mendenhall, "The Conflict Between Value Systems and Social Control," in *Unity and Diversity: Essays in the History, Literature, and Religion of the Ancient Near East* (ed. H. Goedicke and J. J. M. Roberts; Baltimore: Johns Hopkins University, 1975) 169–80.

the northern and southern states. The difference was that the two groups used different intellectual traditions. And, of course, the prophets predicted a destruction to which the reformed sages only reacted. Perhaps the supreme irony about Qoheleth is the allusion to royal and indeed Solomonic authorship, for the theology and ethic of Qoheleth is virtually opposite to that of Solomon, the king who made paganism fashionable, normative and even enviable, paving the way for all those "wise" fools who followed in his footsteps and instituted policies that resulted in the ashes in the midst of which Qoheleth composed his eloquent rebuttal.

From Holy War to Holy Martyrdom*

WILLIAM H. BROWNLEE†
CLAREMONT GRADUATE SCHOOL

MANY different themes serve to unite the Old and New Testaments and biblical theologies have been organized around a few of these. Only recently have scholars begun to realize how persistent the concept of holy warfare is in the Scriptures[1] and the importance of the intertestamental literature in the development of this theme as a background for the NT.[2] In fact, Jesus' own counsels of love for one's enemies and of turning the other cheek in the face of human foes is so adverse to human combat that it is manifest on the surface that there should be no continuity between the Testaments at all on this particular subject. That this appears to be so is emphasized by the frequent (if not constant) embarrassment the holy wars in the OT have brought to Christian students of the Bible. As P. D. Miller, Jr., has noted, it is the "Primitive language and imagery" of God as warrior in the OT which "was one of the principal factors in the Marcionite effort at destruction of the unity of the Bible and rejection of the OT as Christian Scripture."[3] One must approach this subject, therefore, by recognition of a radical discontinuity between the two testaments on this particular subject; but as we proceed we hope to show that there is a continuity which consists in tracing out

*An earlier draft of this paper was presented at the national SBL meeting in 1966.

[1]See G. von Rad, *Studies in Deuteronomy* (SBT 1/9; Chicago: Regnery, 1953) 45–69; *Der Heilige Krieg im alten Israel* (ATANT 20; Zürich: Zwingli-Verlag, 1951); R. de Vaux, *Ancient Israel, its Life and Institutions* (New York: McGraw-Hill, 1961) 258–67; F. M. Cross, Jr., "The Divine Warrior in Israel's Early Cult, *Biblical Motifs, Origins and Transformations* (ed. A. Altmann; Cambridge: Harvard University, 1966) 11–30; F. Stolz, *Jahwes und Israels Kriege, Kriegstheorien und Kriegserfahrungen im Glauben des alten Israel* (ATANT, 60; Zurich: Theologischer Verlag, 1972); P. D. Miller, Jr., *The Divine Warrior in Early Israel* (HSM 5; Cambridge: Harvard University, 1973).

[2]Cross, "Divine Warrior," stresses the significance of Holy War in late apocalyptic and in 1QM. Miller, *The Divine Warrior in Early Israel* 141–44, touches briefly on Enoch, 2 Maccabees, and 1QM. Only O. Betz, "Jesu Heiliger Krieg," NovT 2 (1957) 116–37, utilizes the intertestamental background for interpreting Jesus.

[3]"God the Warrior," *Int* 19 (1965) 39–46, with citation from n. 5, p. 41.

different motifs or strands associated with Holy War and in seeing how these undergo modification and transformation as one moves from the OT to the NT.

The origins of Holy War are associated by Gerhard von Rad with the amphictyonic league formed in Canaan. Its golden age would be the premonarchical period of Hebrew history, after which war became largely secularized until the revival of the Holy War concepts in the proclamation of the Deuteronomic Code. This code and other material in the Pentateuch are at variance with what von Rad believes to have been the originally defensive character of the Holy War.[4] It is also at variance with other presentations in the Pentateuch and in Joshua, where the necessary war is presented as offensive, being God's means of achieving the Exodus and His method of making real the promised gift of the land. Archaeological evidence of the widespread destruction of many Canaanite cities attributed to the Hebrews in the last third of the thirteenth century B.C. does not prove that Holy War was an institution, but at least it is consistent with such a view. Such evidence tends to favor the tracing of this institution (or the ideas connected with it) back into the wilderness sojourn.

The Pentateuch as we have it with its various traditional and literary strata justify considering the Pentateuch in its present form to be a description of the Lord's army in training. When the people of Israel were led up from Egypt they came out armed, but not prepared for an immediate conquest of Canaan (Exod 13:17–18). In the crossing of the Reed Sea, the Lord fought for them against the Egyptians. At Sinai there is the promised dispatch of the Angel of the Lord to go before them into Canaan and to give them victory there. The ark of the covenant is presented as a palladium for war as well as a center for the cult. The climax in this history is the sending out of the spies in which the requisite faith in the Lord, a prime essential for Holy War, was seen to be lacking and this doomed the Hebrews to thirty-eight more years of wilderness wandering. Finally, after Moses has disowned them, many in Israel attempted the conquest without the presence of Moses or the ark and the result was disaster.[5] In the Deuteronomic Code there are speeches by Moses outlining the rules and procedures for Holy War.[6] All this becomes further enhanced in the priestly code when in the Book of

[4]Von Rad, *Studies in Deuteronomy*, 60–69; *Old Testament Theology* (2 vols.; New York: Harper & Brothers, 1962–65), 1. 327–29.

[5]Num 13–14; Deut 1:19–46

[6]Deut 20:1–20; 21:10–14; 23:9–14; 24:5; 25:17–19. In his *Studies in Deuteronomy*, p. 57, von Rad states: "Deuteronomy's atmosphere of war . . . permeates the whole *corpus* as an unmistakable adjunct and gives it a very specific impress."

Numbers we have instructions for a military census and instructions for the use of military banners by the different tribes, whose encampment around the Tabernacle and Ark is fully prescribed.

Thus, the further one comes down in the tradition concerning the Hebrew sojourn in the Wilderness, the more Israel appears in the Wilderness period to be a cultic organization preparing for Holy War. Moreover, something of this, at least the concept of Yahweh as a God of war, belongs to the earliest traditions, as exemplified by the Song of Moses in Exodus 15:

> Yahweh is a man of war,
> Yahweh, His name;
> Pharaoh's chariots and army
> has he hurled into the sea.

In this same song there may be overtones of the creation myth in which Yahweh slays the sea monster.[7] Certain features of this myth may have been borrowed from the Canaanites, particularly the name Leviathan. In any case, very soon after the conquest, if not before, Yahweh figured as the slayer of the chaos monster when He created the world, and His warlike role was also celebrated in connection with the Exodus. Joshua 3–6 comprise an account of the Hebrew conquest of Canaan, which seems to be enriched with liturgical materials relating to an annual festival of the conquest held at the Jordan River, Gilgal, and Jericho.[8] The battles of the Judges portray Yahweh as a warrior in each new saving act. We are even told that "the spirit of Yahweh armed itself with Gideon," using him as a weapon.[9]

Yahweh, the Redeemer, like the kinsman redeemer, was often called upon to fight. His intervention to save His people involved the notion of theophany, His coming from Sinai, as in the song of Deborah (Judg

[7]See F. M. Cross, "Divine Warrior"; Miller, *The Divine Warrior in Early Israel*, 113–17.

[8]This view was first proposed by H. J. Kraus, "Gilgal. Ein Beitrag zur Kultusgeschichte Israels," *VT* 1 (1951) 181–98. It has been developed most fully by Eckart Otto, *Das Mazzotfest in Gilgal* (Stuttgart: W. Kohlhammer, 1975). F. M. Cross, Jr., in his "The Song of the Sea and Canaanite Myth," *JTC* 5 (1968) 1–25, presents a profound study of Exodus 15 in relation to mythology and cult and locates this cultic celebration at Gilgal, at the time of the spring New Year; see esp. 21–24. See my articles: "Gilgal," *The International Standard Bible Encyclopedia* (Fully Rev. Ed., Vol. 2, 1982); "The Ceremony of Crossing the Jordan in the Annual Covenanting at Qumran," in *Von Kanaan bis Kerala* (ed. W. C. Delsman, et al.; Neukirchen-Vluyn, Neukirchener Verlag, in press).

[9]Judg 6:34: "The spirit of Yahweh clothed [i.e., armed] itself with Gideon." For this use of *lbš*, see 1 Sam 17:5, 38; Isa 59:17. For God's use of men as weapons, see Zech 9:13.

5:4–5), or His descent from heaven. Whenever he appeared, it was in the role of *Yhwh ṣĕbā*ᵓ*ôt*, the commander of heavenly legions or of earthly armies, or both.[10] Also in the celebration of the New Year's festival, if one understands aright the enthronement Psalms, Yahweh the Warrior appeared in theophany to defeat the human forces of chaos which threatened the life of His people.[11]

In the prophets, Yahweh of Hosts appears as the Judge of His own people and He marshals the forces of enemy nations to scourge Israel and Judah. The development of the concept of the Day of Yahweh by the prophets is traced by Mowinckel to the New Year's Festival,[12] but by von Rad to the ancient institution of Holy War.[13] According to either alternative there would be a direct connection with the idea of Yahweh the warrior, and it is natural that these two generally parallel streams of thought should flow together in depictions of the Day of Yahweh.[14]

Prominent in the concepts of Holy War was the belief that numbers were less important in battle than the will of Yahweh.[15] In fact, upon occasion, the Lord might act alone. This happened in the classical example of the Crossing of the Reed Sea,[16] and it happened again in the deliverance of Jerusalem from Sennacherib through the instrumentality of His angel.[17] These occasions were exceptional, however. Normally there were the human warriors consecrated for war. Special laws of cultic purity were required by the Hebrews;[18] and, interestingly, in Isaiah 13, where Yahweh of Hosts commands foreign armies, He speaks of them in v 3 as "My consecrated ones."

When in post-exilic literature apocalypticism makes it appearance, more and more the element of theophany is played up; and frequently God is thought of as a lone Warrior. In contrast with Deutero-Isaiah

[10]See W. F. Albright's review of B. N. Wambacq, "L'epithète divine Jahve ṣĕḇāᵓôṯ," *JBL* 67 (1948) 377–81; Miller, *The Divine Warrior in Early Israel*, 151–55.

[11]T. H. Gaster, *Thespis—Ritual, Myth and Drama in the Ancient Near East* (New York: Henry Schuman, 1950) 73–108; S. Mowinckel, *The Psalms in Israel's Worship* (2 vols.; New York: Abingdon, 1962) 1. 181–82.

[12]*The Psalms*, 2. 116, n. 35.

[13]*Old Testament Theology*, 2. 119–25.

[14]Cross, "Divine Warrior," 30, finds the nexus between the two views for the origin of the Day of Yahweh in the ritual conquest celebrated in the cultus at Gilgal. For other literature, consult A. J. Everson, "The Days of Yahweh," *JBL* 93 (1974) 329–37.

[15]This is set forth dramatically in the story of Gideon: Judg 7:2–8. Cf. Gen 14:14–15; 1 Sam 14:6.

[16]Exod 14, esp. vv 13–14.

[17]2 Kgs 19:32–35 and Isa 37:33–36.

[18]Deut 23:9–14; 1 Sam 21:3–5

where Yahweh the Warrior makes use of Cyrus and His servant to accomplish His will in world affairs, the so-called Trito-Isaiah materials picture Yahweh as acting alone. He has looked for a man to accomplish His will; then not finding one, He himself has decided to trample alone the winepress of Edom (59:16–18; 63:1–6). As a prayer of great urgency one cries out (64:1): "O that Thou wouldst rend the heavens and come down." In Joel 3:9–12, the nations are summoned to come prepared for war to the Valley of Jehosphaphat and Yahweh is summoned to bring down His own heavenly warriors for a universal judgment. In other cases, as in Zechariah 14, God's people fight but are defeated; and then Yahweh comes with His heavenly army and simultaneously destroys the foe and delivers His people.

The role of the heavenly army in Holy War appeared at least as early as the Song of Deborah (Judg 5:21):

> From heaven fought the stars
> from their courses they fought against Sisera.

In the Pentateuch, also, the Angel of Yahweh was featured as a warrior.[19] Especially in apocalyptic literature are warrior angels prominent;[20] but angelic intervention is featured even in the historical narration, as in 2 Maccabees, in which Judah prays more than once for the coming of a good angel (11:6; 15:23). In the portents seen over Jerusalem, with opposing armies clashing in the sky (5:2–3), one is probably to see a new feature, the conflict of opposing heavenly armies—good angels warring with evil angels. 1QM lays down the regulations for the conduct of the eschatological war between the children of light and the children of darkness; and, while the human forces contend with one another on the earthly plane, the heavenly armies of the Lord and of Belial are also thought of as battling with each other. Victory achieved in the transcendent realm makes possible the intervention of Michael against the human foes on earth; and, before the drama of victory is fully achieved, there is also a manifestation of God Himself.

In the intertestamental literature men may become possessed with demons, and the Devil (or Spirit of error) may tempt men to sin. In withstanding temptation, one may be thought of as fighting against these transcendent powers; yet, in the eschatological war, the righteous are called upon to fight only the human wicked, not to rout Satanic

[19]Exod 14:19–20; 23:20, 23; 33:2; Num 20:16. Cf. Josh 5:13–14; 2 Kgs 19:35; Isa 63:9. On this angel, see Mendenhall, *The Tenth Generation, the Origins of the Biblical Tradition* (Baltimore: Johns Hopkins, 1973), esp. 59–61.

[20]Joel 4:11b (Eng. 3:11b); Zech 14:3–5.

armies.[21] This last is solely the work of God and His angels. In the Gospels, however, Jesus gives battle to demonic forces. His exorcisms are the inauguration of a holy war which reaches its climax in His death and resurrection wherein He decisively defeated the Devil and his hordes.[22] In this capacity He is acting as the divine warrior. The demons cringe before Him, confessing him to be the Holy One of God.[23] This title may be compared with the "holy ones" in the plural who appear as warriors in theophanies.[24] Here we see Jesus as the divine warrior. Aulén's *Christus Victor* rightly lays emphasis upon this aspect of the Christ's redemption in NT theology;[25] and Otto Betz rightly perceives Jesus' exorcisms as the beginning of the battle.[26] He also brings into consideration the spiritual warfare between the author of the Qumran Hymns and his earthly foes as an initial phase of, or prelude to, the eschatological war.[27] The Hymns, therefore, show the possibilities of a human warrior being engaged in spiritual as well as physical warfare.

The NT presents Jesus not only as the divine warrior but also as the human martyr. It is our intention now to show that in this capacity, also, Jesus was a holy warrior. This is perceived most clearly against the background of 1, 2, and 4 Maccabees. According to these books, the Syrian persecution of the Jews was brought by God to punish widespread apostasy on the part of the Palestinian Jews who were under social pressure not simply to Hellenize but to paganize. This is brought out most strongly in 2 Maccabees (whose account is summarized in 4 Maccabees), but it is also indicated by 1 Maccabees. The Maccabean deliverance, therefore, involved more than the necessity of military defeat

[21]In 1QM, opposing heavenly armies fight each other and presumably assist the forces of the opposing human armies (the sons of light versus the sons of darkness); but the sons of light fight directly only the sons of darkness. In 1QMelch, Melchizedek defeats the forces of Belial, which makes possible the announcement of coming salvation by the human herald on earth. See Brownlee, "Jesus and Qumran," in *Jesus and the Historian* (ed. F. T. Trotter; Philadelphia: Westminster, 1968) 52–81, esp. 64–69.

[22]See Matt 12:29; Mark 3:27; Luke 10:18; 22:3; John 12:31; 13:27; 14:30; 16:11; 18:3. Cf. 1 Cor. 2:8; Heb 2:14–15; 1 John 3:8; Rev 12:1–11.

[23]Mark 1:24; Luke 4:34. They also call Him "Son of God": (Matt 8:29; Mark 3:11; Luke 8:28).

[24]Deut 33:2; Zech 14:5; Enoch 1:9. Cf. Ps 89:6–8. Only in Ps 106:16 is "holy one" in the singular used of a man (Aaron).

[25]G. Aulén, *Christus Victor, An Historical Study of the Three Main Types of the Idea of Atonement* (New York: Macmillan, 1956).

[26]Betz, "Jesu Heiliger Krieg," 125–29. This is also the view of J. M. Robinson, *The Problem of History in Mark* (SBT 1/20; Naperville: Allenson, 1957) 34, 38, 42.

[27]Betz, "Jesu Heiliger Krieg," 118–24.

of the Syrian armies; it required the propitiation of God. This is accomplished in 1 Maccabees by attacks upon the apostate Jews and this is presented as phase one of the war of liberation. Mattathias slew a Jew about to offer pagan sacrifice at the altar erected in Modein. In this he is said to have emulated the zeal of Phinehas (2:23–26), who made atonement for Israel and turned away the wrath of the Lord by slaying Zimri for taking into his tent a Midianite woman associated with the fertility cult.[28] Mattathias issued an alarm for others to follow him in his zeal (2:27). Foremost was his own son, Judas:

> He went through the cities of Judah:
> he destroyed the ungodly out of the land;
> thus he turned away wrath from Israel. (3:8)

Here also the role of Phinehas is still in view, as may be noted by comparing Num 25:11–13, where the Lord tells Moses:

> Phinehas . . . has turned back my wrath from the people of Israel in that he was zealous with my zeal among them, so that I did not consume the people Israel in my zeal. . . . He was zealous for his God and made atonement for the people Israel.

In the ensuing Maccabean struggle, the role of Phinehas was united with that of the national liberator; but the theological significance of this was presented already in the poetic eulogy of Judas at 1 Macc 3:8.[29] This theological perspective is similar to that of Josh 7:1–8:29, whereby the defeat of Ai by Israel was impossible until Achan's violation of the ban (*ḥērem*) against Jericho was expiated.

When we come to 2 Maccabees we meet a different theology of atonement. Instead of being based upon the punishment of the apostates, it is grounded upon the suffering of the innocent martyrs. Intercession to God for mercy and deliverance is based upon this. The last of the seven sons of the widow about to be martyred declared:

> I like my brothers give up body and life for the laws of our fathers, appealing to God to show mercy upon our nation and by afflictions and plagues to make you confess that He alone is God. (7:37)

Judas then gathered about him those prepared to launch the war of liberation; but, first of all, they assembled in prayer, petitioning the Lord (8:2–4): "to look upon the people who were oppressed . . . to have pity on the temple . . . to have mercy on the city which was being

[28]Numbers 25, on which see Mendenhall, *Tenth Generation*, 105–21.

[29]This theological point has already been noted by Elias Bickerman, *The God of the Maccabees* (Leiden: Brill, 1979) 20.

destroyed . . . and to hearken to the blood that cried out to him . . ." This blood of the martyrs, like that of Abel, cried out for divine vengeance. So here, Judas and his men are asking God to accept the present national suffering as sufficient, not only to atone for the nation's sins, but as sufficient to invoke His wrath upon the Syrian armies. Following this assembly for prayer, "Maccabeus got his army organized, and the Gentiles could not withstand him, for the wrath of the Lord had turned to mercy" (8:5). It was the heroism and zeal of the martyrs in 2 Maccabees which as an overplus of national suffering made expiation and thereby made possible the military victories of Judas.[30] In 2 Maccabees the zeal of Phinehas is replaced by the zeal of the martyr as the ground of God's deliverance in the Jewish revolt. Implicitly, to suffer martyrdom is to engage in Holy War.

This implicit theology becomes explicit in 4 Maccabees where no battles are recorded at all—only the martyrdoms. The martyrs are portrayed as holy warriors who die vicariously for the redemption of the nation and who defeat tyranny, not simply by displaying the powerlessness of the tyrant over holy and resolute souls who are endowed with godly prudence and reason, but also by propitiating the Deity and by calling down His wrath upon the persecutors. Implicitly this deliverance was realized in the Maccabean war of liberation; but the military struggle is never mentioned—the martyrs receiving all the credit for the defeat of tyranny and the purification of the land. The book concludes (17:20–22):[31]

> These, then, having been sanctified by God, are honored not only with this distinction [of standing before the throne of God in heaven], but also by the fact that because of them our enemies did not prevail over our nation; and the tyrant was chastised, and our land purified—they having become as it were a ransom (ἀντίψυχον) for the sin of the nation. It was through the blood of these righteous ones, and through the expiation (διὰ . . . ἱλαστηρίου) of their death, that divine Providence preserved (διέσωσεν) Israel which had been ill used. (Cf. 6:28–29; 18:4)

Disillusionment with the Hasmonean dynasty, whose establishment is described in 1 Maccabees, may be responsible for 2 Maccabees limiting its history to the career of Judas. It seems irresistible to view this same disillusionment as carried further in 4 Maccabees, where the battles of Judas himself are not even referred to. The absence of any reference to

[30]This has been noted also by Bickerman, *The God of the Maccabees*, 22.

[31]The translation given here is that of Moses Hadas, *The Third and Fourth Books of Maccabees* (New York: Harper, 1958) 237. This is a rather prevailing theme, for which one may see my discussion in "Books of Maccabees," *IDB* (1962), Vol. K–Q, par. E, p. 213a.

the Jewish revolt could be explained in another way; for the book's announced theme of trying to prove that prudence, or reason, is sovereign over the emotions (chaps. 1–3) may have been thought of as best and sufficiently treated in the stories of the martyrs. However, the book's references to national deliverance take us beyond this philosophical proposition; and it is striking that in this material where a reference to Maccabeus would seem natural, even inevitable, neither his name nor the war itself is mentioned even once.

Now what is the significance of all this Maccabean literature for Christ's atonement in the NT? Both 2 and 4 Maccabees were written in the Diaspora, 2 Maccabees (I believe) in Alexandria and 4 Maccabees perhaps at Antioch.[32] What has this to do with the Palestinian Jew Jesus or with the interpretation of Him given in the NT? Some even date 4 Maccabees in the early second century A.D.—too late for any influence upon Jesus or His Apostles. I have argued for an earlier dating of 4 Maccabees:[33]

> . . . IV Maccabees bemoans the suppression of the temple cult as a great tragedy (4:20) from which the faithful suffering of the martyrs has brought relief. Consequently, the temple is presumed still to stand, and the book was composed prior to 70. . . .
>
> The most precise criterion for dating is the alteration of the title of Appolonius from "governor of the Coelesyria and Phoenicia" (II Macc. 4:4) to "governor of Syria and Phoenicia and Cilicia" (IV Macc. 4:2); for Cilicia was connected administratively with Syria and Phoenicia only for the brief span of A.D. 18–55. The persecution by Caligula occurred in the middle of this period (38–39); but this time, as also the years following, is excluded, since the auditors of the panegyric find it difficult to believe their ears concerning the cruelty of Antiochus (14:9). So, then, IV Maccabees was written between 18 and 37.

I have no intention of arguing that the doctrine of the atonement of Christ is directly dependent upon these books of Maccabees, but rather that the theological developments found in them illustrate interpretations of suffering which were already held by many Palestinian Jews as well. Moses Hadas argues in connection with 4 Maccabees that these beliefs had their origin in apocalyptic circles.[34] Supposing him to be right, the

[32]So I have argued in *IDB*, Vol. K–Q, at pars. C 9 and E 8, pp. 209a–210a, 214.

[33]*IDB*, Vol. K–Q, 213b–214. (All the cross references on p. 213b should be to par. E, not par. D.)

[34]Hadas, *Maccabees*, 121f. R. de Vaux, *Ancient Israel*, 265–66, considers the Maccabean war as "religious war" not "holy war," but he is thinking of the military aspect, not of the martyrdom.

eschatological aspect of Christ's suffering, which owes nothing to the presentations of 2 and 4 Maccabees, would most naturally derive from apocalyptic Judaism of Palestine.

The suffering of the martyrs refines and purifies in the eschatological setting in Daniel;[35] and when we come down to the eighth column of 1QS we find not only this, but also a redemptive element; for it falls to the special (or founding) group of fifteen men "to expiate iniquity through doing the right and through the anguish of the refining furnace" (viii 3–4). A bit later (at viii 6–7), they are described as being: "the chosen of divine acceptance to atone for the land, and to render to the wicked their dessert." This idea is stressed again at viii 9½: "These will be acceptable to make atonement for the land and to decree the condemnation of wickedness that there may be no more perversity."[36] This "condemnation of wickedness" is not to be thought of as a wholly distinct function, separate from atoning suffering; for this very endurance of unjust suffering not only propitiates God, but it invokes His wrath upon the wicked.

The opponents of Jesus, according to Matt 28:25, declared: "His blood be upon us and on our children!" This awful self-imprecation was doubtless thought of by Matthew as being completely fulfilled during the first Jewish revolt against Rome; for following the Zealots rather than Jesus led inevitably to a clash with Roman imperialism.[37] In Rev 6:10 the souls of the martyrs cry out from beneath the altar: "O sovereign Lord, holy and true, how long before thou wilt judge and avenge our blood on those who dwell upon the earth?" These are exceptional passages in the NT, for the effects of Christ's atoning death are generally presented as wholly of grace. Never on His lips is there an invocation of vengeance; and Heb 12:24 addresses those who have come "to Jesus, the mediator of a new covenant, and to the sprinkled blood that speaks more graciously than the blood of Abel." Instead of pleading for vengeance like the blood of Abel or that of the Maccabean martyrs, His blood pleads only for forgiveness and redemption.

Here in Jesus we see the human martyr who by vicarious suffering, the just for the unjust, makes expiation for sin and thereby breaks its binding power. At the same time He destroys the power of Satan as an

[35]H. L. Ginsberg, "The Oldest Interpretation of the Suffering Servant," *VT* 3 (1953) 400–404; Brownlee, "The Servant of the Lord in the Qumran Scrolls, I," *BASOR* 132 (1953) 8–15, esp. 12–15; *The Meaning of the Qumran Scrolls for the Bible* (New York: Oxford University, 1964) 211–12.

[36]Brownlee, "The Servant of the Lord in the Qumran Scrolls, II," *BASOR* 135 (1954) 33–38, esp. 34–35.

[37]Cf. Matt 23:37–39; Luke 13:34–35; 19:41–43; 21:20; 23:28. John 11:45–50 gives this an ironical twist, for Caiaphas judges Jesus a zealot.

accuser.[38] At this point, Jesus as the human martyr-warrior joins the divine Warrior Who defeats demonic forces, as presaged by His exorcisms.[39] All the triumphs of the Christ are proleptic; for, though the war against evil has been won, the final battle has not yet been fought. Though forgiveness and grace are now available, salvation in its fullness is yet to be experienced. We are called upon to enter His holy war; but "our weapons are not carnal."[40] Still it falls upon us to "fill up that which is lacking of the afflictions of Christ" by entering joyfully ourselves into His sufferings on behalf of all mankind.[41]

In the area of biblical theology, we often see modifications and enrichments as we move from the earliest to the latest Scriptures; but in the present case we have the most dramatic development and transformation of all, as we move from the institution of Holy War, with its *ḥērem* of total destruction of the enemy, to the divine-human Warrior, Who gives His life for the salvation of the whole world, including His own enemies. Yet, between the *ḥērem* and the Cross there is not simply contrast, a radical break with the substitution of one for the other, but a theological continuity whereby in the history of Holy War the one led to the other.

This treatment of holy war does not deny the theological values inherent in the Hebrew concept of holy warfare as elucidated by Miller and others. Indeed, however difficult it is to ferret out those values, that is a worthy and important task.[42] Yet the serious moral and theological

[38]Rev 12:7–11, which portrays in apocalyptic imagery the idea of Rom 5:1–9.

[39]When He is viewed as a man, Christ's atonement is to be considered an expiation (Romans 5; Phil 2:5–11); and yet, because of His divinity, this expiation needs to be subsumed under the larger category of what G. Aulén calls "the classic idea of atonement." Viewed in this way, the atonement of Christ is God's self-propitiation, and no mere punishment of the just on behalf of the unjust. To a holy being, it is painful to forgive, and yet God does forgive. The Cross is the revelation of the pain that God endures in order to forgive (Isa 63:9; Eph 4:30). As the divine Warrior who gives His own life in defeating sin, death, and the Devil, He is utterly different from the vengeful Deity tramping out the winepress of Edom (Isa 63:1–6).

[40]2 Cor 10:4. Cf. Eph 6:10–17.

[41]Col 1:24 does not refer to an inadequacy in Christ's sufferings as an expiation or propitiation, but it does indicate that further suffering, that of persecuted evangelists and missionaries, is required before the Church realizes its full redemptive role in the world.

[42]A penetrating grappling with the problem is that of P. C. Craigie, *The Problem of War in the Old Testament* (Grand Rapids: Eerdmans, 1978). On pp. 99–100, he interprets Jesus as holy warrior in precisely the same way as advanced here, but without the benefits of the Books of Maccabees. Mendenhall's theory of "The Hebrew Conquest of Palestine," *BA* 25 (1962) 66–87, is very appealing in

difficulties cannot be fully overcome or transcended without a study of the Intertestamental literature; for by this alone can one perceive the connection between the Testaments in the concept of holy warfare, whereby the holy warrior became the holy martyr, who instead of killing lays down his life for others in obedience to God.

---

resolving God's historical involvement in the Conquest as one of inspiring a peasant's revolt whereby social justice was achieved. There still remain, however, the theological difficulties inherent in the sacred literature, which presents the Conquest differently.

George Emery Mendenhall, A Bibliography

A. Books and Monographs
B. Contributions to Reference Works
C. Papers and Reports
D. Book Reviews
E. Doctoral Dissertations Directed

A. BOOKS AND MONOGRAPHS

A1. *The Aramaic Origin of the Gospel of John*. Unpublished B.D. Thesis, Lutheran Theological Seminary, Gettysburg, 1938.

A2. *The Verb in Early Northwest Semitic Dialects*. Unpublished Ph.D. Thesis, Johns Hopkins University, 1946.

A3. *Law and Covenant in Israel and the Ancient Near East*. Pittsburgh: The Biblical Colloquium, 1955. Pp. 51. Reprinted from C10 and C11. Translated as A3a and C10/11a.

A3a. *Recht und Bund in Israel und dem Alten Vordern Orient*. Translated by F. Dumermuth. Theologische Studien 64. Zürich: EVZ-Verlag, 1961. Pp. 63.

A4. *The Tenth Generation: The Origins of the Biblical Tradition*. Baltimore: Johns Hopkins, 1973. Pp. xviii, 248.

B. CONTRIBUTIONS TO REFERENCE WORKS

B1. *Ancient Near Eastern Texts Relating to the Old Testament*. Edited by James B. Pritchard. Princeton: Princeton University Press, 1950, [2]1955, [3]1969.

Akkadian Letters (in collaboration with W. F. Albright), 482–90.

B2. *Twentieth Century Encyclopedia of Religious Knowledge: An Extension of the New Schaff-Herzog Encyclopedia of Religious Knowledge*. Edited by L. A. Loetscher. Grand Rapids: Baker, 1955.

Amarna Tablets, vol. 1, 27
Amorites, vol. 1, 34–35
Elohim, vol. 1, 376
Hammurabi, vol. 1, 490
Mari Letters, vol. 2, 704

B3. *The Interpreter's Dictionary of the Bible.* Edited by G. A. Buttrick et al. Nashville and New York: Abingdon, 1962.
Call, Calling, vol. 1, 490
Covenant, vol. 1, 714–23
Election, vol. 2, 76–82
Humility, vol. 2, 659–60
Jeshurun, vol. 2, 868
Missions, vol. 3, 404–6
Predestination, vol. 3, 869
Testament, vol. 4, 575

B4. *Encyclopaedia Britannica,* 14th ed., revised (1964).
Decalogue, vol. 7, 153–54
Hezekiah, vol. 11, 471
Kenites, vol. 13, 281

B5. *The New Encyclopaedia Britannica,* 15th ed., Macropaedia (1974).
Covenant, vol. 5, 226–30

B6. *The Interpreter's Dictionary of the Bible, Supplementary Volume.* Edited by Keith Crim et al. Nashville: Abingdon, 1976.
Government, Israelite, 373–75
Tribe, 919–20

C. PAPERS AND REPORTS

C1. "The Creation of the Composite Bow in Canaanite Mythology" (in collaboration with W. F. Albright). *JNES* 1 (1942) 227–29.

C2. "The Lutheran Church and Biblical Research." *The Wittenberg Bulletin* 44/11 (December 1947) 1–5.

C3. "The Message of Abdi-Ashirta to the Warriors, EA 74." *JNES* 6 (1947) 123–24.

C4. "Christian Law." *The Wittenberg Bulletin* 45/7 (July 1948) 56–62.

C5. "God of Vengeance, Shine Forth." *The Wittenberg Bulletin* 45/12 (December 1948) 37–42.

C6. "Mari." *BA* 11/1 (1948) 1–19. Reprinted in *BAR* 2, pp. 3–20. Edited by D. N. Freedman and E. F. Campbell, Jr. Garden City: Doubleday, 1964.

C7. "The Churches' Responsibility for Secularism." *The Wittenberg Bulletin* 46/12 (December 1949) 29–33.

C8. "Israelite Law in the Period of the Judges." *JBL* 71 (1952) vi (abstract).

C9. "Biblical Faith and Cultic Evolution." *Lutheran Quarterly* 5 (1953) 235–58.

C10. "Ancient Oriental and Biblical Law." *BA* 17/2 (1954) 26–46. Reprinted with corrections in *BAR* 3, pp. 3–24. Edited by E. F. Campbell, Jr., and D. N. Freedman. Garden City: Doubleday, 1970.

C11. "Covenant Forms in Israelite Tradition." *BA* 17/3 (1954) 50–74. Reprinted with corrections in *BAR* 3, pp. 25–53. Edited by E. F. Campbell, Jr., and D. N. Freedman. Garden City: Doubleday, 1970. Translated as C11a. Excerpted in *BA* 42/3 (1979) 189–90.

C11a. "La alianza en Israel y los pactos en el Antiguo Oriente." *Selecciónes de libros de teología* (Barcelona) 5/17 (1966) 34–44.

C10/11. Reprinted together as A3 and translated together as A3a and C10/11a.

C10/11a. "Le forme del patto nella tradizione israelita. L'antica legge orientale e biblica." D. J. McCarthy, G. E. Mendenhall, and R. Smend, *Per una teologia del patto nell'Antico Testamento*, pp. 75–119. Translated by M. Bracchi et al. Turin: Marietti, 1972.

C12. "Puppy and Lettuce in Northwest-Semitic Covenant Making." *BASOR* 133 (1954) 26–30.

C13 "Old Testament Literature, 1954." *Int* 9 (1955) 454–60.

C14. "The Census Lists of Numbers 1 and 26." *JBL* 77 (1958) 52–66.

C15. "Old Testament Literature, 1956–1957." *Int* 12 (1958) 61–70.

C16. "The Relation of the Individual to Political Society in Ancient Israel." *Biblical Studies in Memory of H. C. Alleman*, pp. 89–108. Edited by J. M. Myers, O. Reimherr, and H. N. Bream. Locust Valley, New York: J. J. Augustin, 1960.

C17. "Biblical History in Transition." *The Bible and the Ancient Near East: Essays in Honor of W. F. Albright*, pp. 32–53. Edited by G. Ernest Wright. Garden City: Doubleday, 1961.

C18. "It's Great To Be Human! The Old Testament View of Man." *Frontiers* (Chicago) 12/6 (February 1961) 13–19.

C19. "The Hebrew Conquest of Palestine." *BA* 25/3 (1962) 66–87. Reprinted in *BAR* 3, pp. 100–120. Edited by E. F. Campbell, Jr., and D. N. Freedman. Garden City: Doubleday, 1970.

C20. "The Day the Church Blew Up" (a satire) (I. Kausitoros—pseudonym). *Dialog* 4 (1965) 59–62.

C21. "Method in the Study of Early Hebrew History." *The Bible in Modern Scholarship: Papers Read at the 100th Meeting of the Society of Biblical Literature (1964)*, pp. 30–36. Edited by J. P. Hyatt. Nashville and New York: Abingdon, 1965.

C22. "Report of the Director of the School in Jerusalem." *BASOR* 186 (1967) 6–7.

C23. "An Announcement Published by The Department of Antiquities of Jordan and the Archaeologists Dr. William H.

Brownlee and Dr. George E. Mendenhall Regarding the Decipherment of Carian Leather Manuscripts found in 1966 in the Hebron area, the Hashemite Kingdom of Jordan." *ADAJ* 15 (1970) 39–40, with 3 plates (pp. 73–75).

C24. "A New Chapter in the History of the Alphabet." *Bulletin du Musée de Beyrouth* 24 (1971) 13–18.

C25. "Philistine Manuscripts from Palestine?" (with William H. Brownlee and Jacoub Oweis). *Kadmos: Zeitschrift für vor- und frühgriechische Epigraphik* 10 (1971) 102–4.

C26. "The 'Philistine' Documents from the Hebron Area: A Supplementary Note." *ADAJ* 16 (1971) 99–102.

C27. "On a Visit with a Druzi Witch." *ASOR Newsletter* 9 (1972–73) 1–4; 10 (1972–73) 1–2.

C28. "The First Half of Human History" [The Henry Russel Lecture at the University of Michigan in 1973]. *Michigan Quarterly Review* 13 (1974) 254–69.

C29. "The Shady Side of Wisdom: The Date and Purpose of Genesis 3." *A Light Unto My Path: Old Testament Studies in Honor of Jacob Myers* (Gettysburg Theological Studies 4), pp. 319–34. Edited by H. N. Bream, R. D. Heim and C. A. Moore. Philadelphia: Temple University, 1974.

C30. "The Conflict Between Value Systems and Social Control." *Unity and Diversity: Essays in the History, Literature, and Religion of the Ancient Near East,* pp. 169–80. Edited by Hans Goedicke and J. J. M. Roberts. Baltimore: Johns Hopkins University, 1975.

C31. "The Inscription from Çatal Hüyük in the Plain of Antakya." *Kadmos: Zeitschrift für vor- und frühgriechische Epigraphik* 14 (1975) 48–63.

C32. "The Monarchy." *Int* 29/2 [The History of Israel and Biblical Faith: In Honor of John Bright] (1975) 155–70.

C33. "Samuel's 'Broken Rîb': Deuteronomy 32." *No Famine in the Land: Studies in Honor of John L. McKenzie,* pp. 63–74. Edited by J. W. Flanagan and A. W. Robinson. Missoula: Scholars, 1975.

C34. [David Engle, "Conversations With George Mendenhall On The End Of The World As We Know It." *Detroit Free Press Detroit Magazine,* 26 January 1975, pp. 5–10.]

C35. "The Ancient in the Modern—and Vice Versa." *Michigan Oriental Studies in Honor of George G. Cameron,* pp. 227–53. Edited by L. L. Orlin et al. Ann Arbor: University of Michigan, Department of Near Eastern Studies, 1976.

C36. "'Change and Decay in All Around I See': Conquest, Covenant, and *The Tenth Generation.*" *BA* 39/4 (December 1976) 152–57.

C37. "Migration Theories vs. Culture Change as an Explanation for Early Israel." *SBL 1976 Seminar Papers,* pp. 135–43. Edited by G. MacRae. Missoula: Scholars, 1976.

C38. "Social Organization in Early Israel." *Magnalia Dei, the Mighty Acts of God: Essays on the Bible and Archaeology in Memory of G. Ernest Wright,* pp. 132–51. Edited by F. M. Cross, W. E. Lemke, and P. D. Miller, Jr. Garden City: Doubleday, 1976.

C39. "Covenant in the Ancient World." *Sunday School Lesson Illustrator* 3/4 (1977) 6–10.

C40. "Between Theology and Archaeology." *JSOT* 7 (1978) 28–34.

C41. "On the History of Writing." *BA* 41/4 (1978) 134–35.

C42. "The First International Symposium on the Antiquities of Palestine [Aleppo, September 1981]." *BA* 45/1 (1982) 59–60.

D. BOOK REVIEWS

D1. *The Bible in the Church,* R. M. Grant. *The Wittenberg Bulletin* 45/12 (December 1948) 44.

D2. *Lexicon in Veteris Testamenti Libros,* Lieferung 1, L. Koehler and W. Baumgartner. *The Wittenberg Bulletin* 45/12 (December 1948) 44.

D3. *The Religious Pilgrimage of Israel,* I. G. Matthews. *The Wittenberg Bulletin* 45/12 (December 1948) 45.

D4. *Studies in Biblical Law,* D. Daube. *The Wittenberg Bulletin* 45/12 (December 1948) 45.

D5. *Introduction to the Old Testament,* A. Bentzen. *The Wittenberg Bulletin* 46/12 (December 1949) 36.

D6. *The Geography of the Bible,* D. Baly. *JBL* 76 (1957) 333–35.

D7. *The Ancient Near East in Pictures Relating to the Old Testament,* J. B. Pritchard. *Ars Orientalia* 3 (1959) 213–15.

D8. *Die Landnahme der israelitischen Stämme in der neueren wissenschaftlichen Diskussion,* M. Weippert. *Bib* 50 (1969) 432–36.

D9. *Comparative Philology and the Text of the Old Testament,* J. Barr. *Int* 25 (1971) 358–62.

D10. *Old Testament Theology: Basic Issues in the Current Debate,* G. Hasel. *Michigan Academician* 6 (1973) 249–51.

D11. *The Israelite Conquest of Canaan,* S. Yeivin. *JBL* 93 (1974) 108–10.

D12. *Atlas of the Biblical World,* D. Baly and A. D. Tushingham. *The Muslim World* 65/3 (1975) 225–26.

D13. *Exodus and Sinai in History and Tradition,* E. W. Nicholson. *JAAR* 43 (1975) 803.

D14. *The Making of China: Main Themes in Premodern Chinese History,* ed. by Chun-shu Chang. *BASOR* 223 (1976) 69–70.

D15. *Israelite and Judaean History,* ed. by J. H. Hayes and J. M. Miller. *JBL* 99 (1980) 589–91.

D16. *Prophecy and Society in Ancient Israel,* R. Wilson. *BA* 44 (1981) 189–90.

E. DOCTORAL DISSERTATIONS DIRECTED

E1. S. Herbert Bess. 1963. *Systems of Land Tenure in Ancient Israel.* DA 25, 1188.

E2. Herbert B. Huffmon. 1963. *Amorite Personal Names in the Mari Texts: A Structural and Lexical Study.* Subsequently published under the same title, Baltimore: Johns Hopkins, 1965.

E3. J. Tracy Luke. 1965. *Pastoralism and Politics in the Mari Period: A Re-examination of the Character and Political Significance of the Major West Semitic Tribal Groups on the Middle Euphrates.* DA 26, 5988.

E4. Kenneth L. Vine. 1965. *The Establishment of Baal at Ugarit.* DA 26, 2702.

E5. S. Douglas Waterhouse. 1965. *Syria in the Amarna Age: A Borderland Between Conflicting Empires.* DA 27, 431-A.

E6. Albert E. Glock. 1968. *Warfare in Mari and Early Israel.* DA 29, 847-A. Published in part in *CTM* 41 (1970) 558–608.

E7. Herbert C. Spomer. 1972. *Some Concerns in the Semantics of Biblical Hebrew.* DA 33, 5158-A.

E8. Theodore P. Townsend. 1972. *Historiography and the Time of the Judges.* DA 33, 2271-A.

E9. Alberto R. W. Green. 1973. *The Role of Human Sacrifice in the Ancient Near East.* Subsequently published under the same title, as American Schools of Oriental Research Dissertation Series 1, Missoula: Scholars, 1975.

E10. John W. Ribar. 1973. *Death Cult Practices in Ancient Palestine.* DA 34, 1800-A.

E11. William H. Shea. 1976. *Famines in the Early History of Egypt and Syro-Palestine.* DA 37, 6664-A.

E12. Frank A. Spina. 1977. *The Concept of Social Rage in the Old Testament and the Ancient Near East.* DA 38, 6866-A.

E13. Andrew E. Hill, III. 1981. *The Book of Malachi: Its Place in Post-Exilic Chronology Linguistically Reconsidered.* DA 42/2, 683-A.

E14. Gary A. Herrion. 1982. *The Social Organization of Tradition in Monarchic Judah.*

M. O'Connor

AUTHOR INDEX

SCRIPTURE INDEX